THE LSWR AT NINE ELMS

The Curl Collection Volume 1

The Works and its Products

1830 - 1909

THE LSWR AT NINE ELMS

The Curl Collection Volume 1

The Works and its Products

1830 - 1909

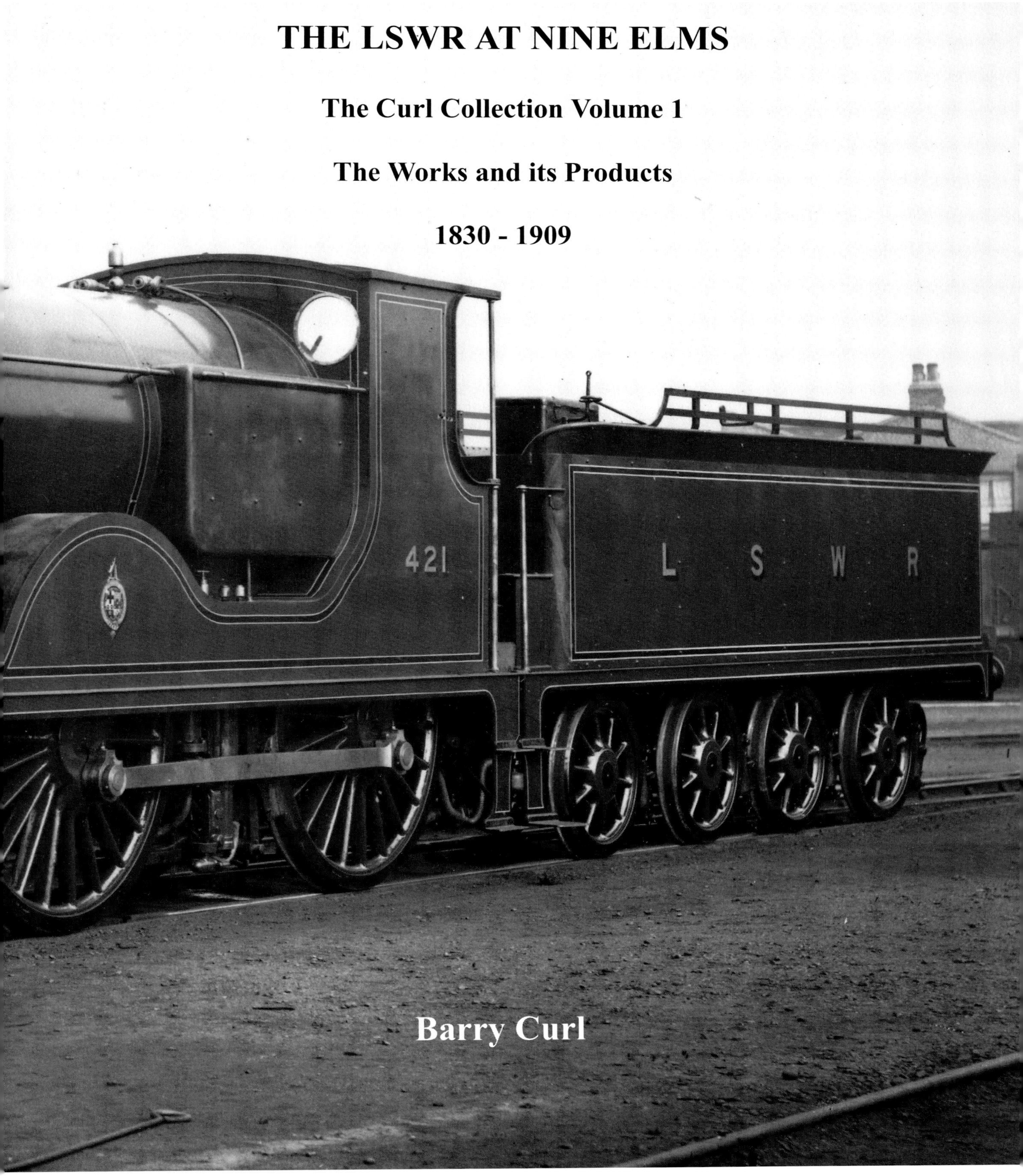

Barry Curl

©KRB Publications and Barry Curl 2004

KRB Publications
P.O. Box 269
Hedge End
SOUTHAMPTON
SO30 4XR

www.krbpublications.co.uk

Printed by the Amadeus Press

ISBN 0954203577

Front cover: *Adams T3 class locomotive No 561 in works grey livery at Nine Elms, February 1893.*

Frontispiece: *Drummond L12 class locomotive, number 421.*

Back cover, top: *Nine Elms erecting shop, 11th June 1902.*

Back cover, bottom: *A Dubs T9 passing Nine Elms Junction, circa 1900.*

Contents

Chapter 1	Introduction	vii
	Acknowledgements	viii
Chapter 2	The Objective of this Book	3
Chapter 3	In the Beginning (1830 – 1850)	
	Initial Development	5
	Joseph Woods (1838 – 1840)	12
	John Viret Gooch (1841 – 1850)	13
Chapter 4	Locomotive Procurement (1850 – 1871)	
	Joseph Beattie	25
Chapter 5	The Expansion of the Works (1865 – 1878)	
	Northern Workshop Performance	89
	New Locomotive Works	92
	1876 Changes	101
Chapter 6	Locomotive and Rolling Stock Procurement (1873 – 1878)	
	W.G. Beattie – Locomotives	107
	W.G. Beattie – Rolling Stock	108
Chapter 7	Environmental and Human Aspects	
	The Railway's Influence in its Environment	135
	Workers' Welfare	139
	Services to the Public	145
Chapter 8	Locomotive Procurement (1878 – 1895)	
	William Bridges Adams, Part 1 (1878 – 1890)	153
	Changes in the Works	215
	William Bridges Adams, Part 2 (1890 – 1895)	216
Chapter 9	Around the Works at the Turn of the Century	245
Chapter 10	Locomotive Procurement (1895 – 1908)	
	Dugald Drummond	261
Chapter 11	Conclusions	331
Appendix A	Chief Administrators and Officials	333
Appendix B	Mechanical Details	334
Appendix C	LSWR Locomotive Listing	335

Reg Curl in his works office in the late 1950s.

Reginald Lewis Curl

Born: 31 July 1901   Died: 16 March 1981

A Railwayman of Excellence for 53 years

1
INTRODUCTION

On the 12th October 1915, a young man walked the one and a half miles from his home, 7 Hardinge Road, Ashford, Kent to the works of the South Eastern and Chatham Railway, which was situated in that town.

In his own words:

At the age of 14 years, I left the Church of England elementary school, walked into the Ashford Works of the South Eastern & Chatham Railway, and asked for a job, my only support being a "Character" (as we called them in those days), from my Headmaster.

I was given a free pass to travel to London Bridge to undergo a medical examination. This, apparently, I passed and a letter came telling me to report 6.0 am Monday 12th October (1915). The job - I had no choice of course - was in the wagon paint shop writing S.E.& C.R. etc. on the painted wagons. Hours were 6.0 am until 5.0 pm with ½ hour for breakfast 8.30-9.0, and 12.0 till 1.0 for dinner. As I lived 1½ miles from the works - the other side of the town - I took my breakfast and dinner, going to and fro in the dark. No buses, no works canteen. It was a bitterly cold winter, and I remember I had to wrap cloth around my boots in order to stand up on the ice, let alone walk the 1½ miles, this at 5.30 in the morning.

A 54-hour week commencing at 4s (20p), the following week with a war bonus of 1s 6d, and the next week piece-work (27½%, no more) of 1s 2d made my wages for the first year 6s 8d per week. Bank Holidays at Christmas, etc, all resulted in loss of wages for lost time. Then I received through the post an "Exhibition" to evening classes value 3s. 6d. from my school Headmaster. This gentleman influenced my life more than any other one man. He used to send me to the building society office with his monthly investment. He once said "Reggie, I could trust you with untold gold." He died at the age of 56 years, before he could retire. And so, of course, I attended evening classes three evenings per week for Maths, Science, and Engineering Drawing. Rising at 5 o'clock - even on Saturdays - it was a long day up to 9 o'clock, home at 9.30, the first chance to sit by the fire, but I had to be up by 5 o'clock the next morning.

But I was happy on the job, and learnt much of the craft of paint mixing and grinding, and by keeping my eyes open learnt much of wagon building, which was to become useful later on. It was not heavy and exhausting work, but mostly out of doors on the working roads, and I remember the Chargehand using a blow-lamp to thaw the frost on wagons painted the previous day and booked away that morning for the War effort, so that we could write on them.

After describing life in the Paint Shop he continues:

My success at evening school was brought to Mr. Maunsell's notice 18 months later when an assistant was required in the chemical laboratory that he had installed in the works. I found this calling very interesting - indoors in the warm, and of course office hours of 9.0 to 5.0, and the ability to wear clean clothes. I was getting on very well with the testing of works materials.

Later on Mr. Maunsell gave this man an apprenticeship in view of his good results at evening classes and in the works, which eventually resulted in his entering the Drawing Office in 1922, and in 1924 he became an Associate Member of the Institute of Locomotive Engineers. In 1928 he was directed to the Drawing Office at Eastleigh Works and appointed to the staff, firstly in the Carriage Works, later in the Locomotive Works where he worked on the designs of Mr. Maunsell and, his most respected designer, Mr. Bulleid.

You may be wondering what all this has got to do with "The LSWR at Nine Elms"

In 1967, the gentleman, who was my father, was asked to stay on after his normal retirement date, to look after an office in the Carriage Works, where the remaining records, consisting of photographic negatives, prints, tracings, and drawings relating to obsolescent locomotives, rolling stock, etc, were kept. Much of the material had found its way there from Nine Elms. Part of the National Railway Museum, which at that time was at Clapham, had apparently visited and taken what they wanted. My father was told by his superior that everything that became obsolete had to be scrapped. When my father queried how it was to be scrapped he was told that he could do what he liked with it - throw it in the bin, burn it, or take it home! My father was naturally shocked and asked me what I thought should happen to it. We decided to bring as much as possible home.

My father was often asked to supply prints of drawings and photographs to members of the general public and one such person was the late Don Bradley, whose excellent books covering the details of most of the steam locomotives of Southern England are used as references in this book.

If it had not been for my father's foresight and effort in 1967/8, this archive material would have vanished and this book would not have been possible in the form presented.

This book is dedicated, therefore, to the memory of my father, Reginald Lewis Curl.

ACKNOWLEDGEMENTS

Rev Canon Brian Alman, Josephine Curl, Maurice Dart, the late Les Elsey, the late David Fereday-Glenn, Graham Hatton, the Historical Model Railway Society, Ian Allan Postcards, Kidderminster Railway Museum (in particular Audie Baker), Motco Enterprises Ltd (www.Motco.com), The Keeper and Staff of the Public Record Office at Kew, P.J. Loobey, John Scott Morgan, Steve Shrimpton for image scanning, Silver Link Publishing, John Spencer-Gilks, Peter Swift, Martin Tiller, Denis Tillman, Wandsworth Library Service (in particular Julie Gregson), Wandsworth Museum (in partiular Sue Barber), Webpraxis Consulting Ltd, Gordon Weddell, Len Wood.

Bibliography:

All about Battersea 1882 by Simmonds
An Illustrated History of Southern Wagons Vol. 1 LSWR by G. Bixley et.al.
Beattie/Adams/Drummond Locomotives by D.L. Bradley.
Booth's Poverty Map of London 1877
Change at Clapham Junction by Tim Sherwood
History of the Southern Railway by C.F. Dendy Marshall
LSWR Coaches Vol. 1 by G. Weddell
LSWR Carriages in the Twentieth Century by G. Weddel
Railway World 1980. Article by Peter Winding
The Engineer various issues
The Locomotives of the South Western by D.L. Bradley
The London & South Western Railway by O.S. Nock
The South Western Railway by C. Hamilton Ellis
Thomas Brassey - Railway Builder by Charles Walker

Note: Unless stated otherwise, all illustrations are from the Curl Collection.

Plate 1. Watercolour by an unknown artist of the Nine Elms Wharf area painted around 1845 showing one of the Goods Sheds, the wharf cranes, two steam ships used to ferry passengers to the City and numerous other local features. *(Wandsworth Museum)*

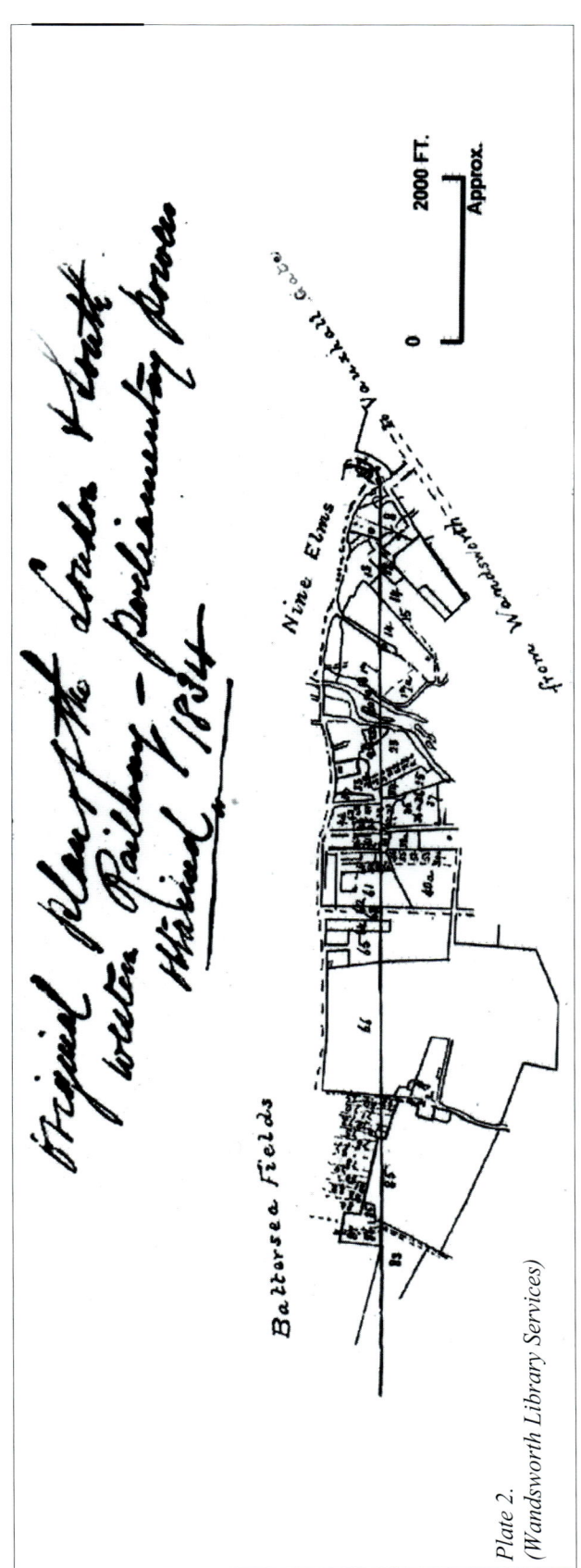

Plate 2.
(Wandsworth Library Services)

Fig. 1. Wagon No 1408, described in "An Illustrated History of Southern Wagons" as being new in February 1911, but which carries a Nine Elms worksplate.

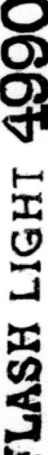

DEVELOPERS FOR IMPERIAL PLATES.

"IMPERIAL PYRO-SODA" DEVELOPER.

Stock Solution.

No. 1.	
Pyrogallic Acid	1 oz. - 111 grms.
Pot. Bromide	60 grs. - 13 ,,
Pot. Metabisulphite	50 grs. - 10 ,,
Water (boiled or distilled)	to 12 oz. - 1,000 c.c.

No. 1.

Stock Solution	3 oz. - 150 c.c.
Water (boiled or distilled)	to 20 oz. - 1,000 c.c.

No. 2.

Soda Sulphite	2 oz. - 100 grms.
Soda Carbonate	2 oz. - 100 ,,
(Washing Soda)	
Water (boiled or distilled)	to 20 oz. - 1,000 c.c.

For use take equal quantities of No. 1 and No. 2.
For under-exposure use more of No. 2; for over-exposure more of No. 1.

"IMPERIAL STANDARD" DEVELOPER.

No. 1.

Pyrogallic Acid	55 grains - 6 grms.
Metol	45 ,, - 5 ,,
Metabisulphite of Potash	120 ,, - 14 ,,
Bromide of Potassium	20 ,, - 2 ,,
Water (boiled or distilled)	to 20 oz.- 1,000 c.c.

No. 2.

Soda Carbonate	4 oz. - 200 grms.
(Washing Soda)	
Water (boiled or distilled)	to 20 oz. - 1,000 c.c.

For use take equal quantities of No. 1 and No. 2.

The "**Pyro-Soda**" developer should be used for comparatively long exposures; the "**Standard**" developer for short exposures.

Both developers keep indefinitely.

Fixing Solution.—Hypo, 1lb.; Water, 50 oz.

FLASH LIGHT 4990

The Imperial Dry Plate Co., Ltd., Cricklewood, London, N.W.

Fig. 2. Sample label from box containing glass negative plates setting forth the instructions for mixing suitable developing agents.

THE OBJECTIVE OF THIS BOOK

This book covers the period when the workshops of the London and South Western Railway were at the Nine Elms site, in association with the Motive Power department, Goods departments, and, in the early stages, its London terminus. The book includes some details of the whole site, as far as it has been possible to find relevant information, including several maps, and some photographs, particularly of the works' interior, taken around 1902. There are also some articles reproduced, two on the works themselves, and several relating to the area in general. The intention has been to include at least one illustration of each item produced at Nine Elms between 1839 and 1909, but this has proved difficult for the "Ballast Engines" and some of the earlier locomotives designed by Joseph Woods and John Gooch, other than line diagrams featured in the late D. L. Bradley's books.

With regard to the products of the works, thought was given to the justification for including the many locomotive types that were manufactured by outside contractors. The fact that probably all of them would have been modified, maintained, or repaired at Nine Elms at some time meant that they constituted a significant part of the premises' workload and inclusion was therefore right. The same attitude was adopted towards locomotives used at outposts such as the Engineer's department, Southampton Docks, etc. The question of carriages and wagons was not so clear. It is difficult to find definitive documentation on where these items were manufactured, and I found it impossible to find links which gave a direct correlation between vehicle number and place of manufacture for carriages and wagons such as exists for locomotives. As an illustration of the problem, Figure 1 (opposite) is a photograph of a wagon, number 1408, printed from the original glass negative, which is also depicted in the book *An Illustrated History of Southern Wagons* by Bixley, Blackburn, Chorley, King, and Newton. They describe it as having been photographed when new in February 1911 - 20 years after the carriage works moved to Eastleigh. However, as the enlargement in my photograph shows, it carries a Nine Elms Works plate. Was it just that they had a quantity of works plates left over from Nine Elms, or was it really built there? This typifies the problems that exist regarding the history of wagons and coaches which largely do not exist for locomotives.

From Minute Book No.5 of the LSWR, covering the period 2nd May 1872 to 7th October 1875, various minutes contain details of tenders from outside contractors for coaches, but no evidence that any items were made on-site. These minutes are shown in Chapter 6. Carriage and Wagon departments are indicated on the maps, but these may only be repair shops.

Although there may be the same logic for including repaired items as has been done for locomotives, there is also the problem that photographs and drawings of coaches and wagons that are known to have been manufactured before 1891, (when the Carriage and Wagon department moved to Eastleigh) are very rare. Preference was usually given to photographing locomotives, and usually main line types rather than goods or local service types, but there are some good images of coaches as part of trains taken in motion. There was a quantity of negatives of coaches and wagons acquired from Eastleigh, but they are believed to be largely of stock manufactured at Eastleigh after 1891.

With regard to the photographic aspect, a few facts about its history are relevant. Early attempts at photography only resulted in "one off" images, and copies were not possible. In 1835 William Henry Fox-Talbot produced the first paper "negative" from which copies could be made, but it was of poor quality and it was 1844 before he produced a photographically illustrated book. In 1848 a method of applying a photographically sensitive film to a glass negative was developed by Abel Niepce de Saint-Victor, but it was a "wet" process and was very slow to respond. In 1851, Frederick Scott Archer introduced the "Collodion" process, also a "wet" process, involving a mobile darkroom to process it, but the exposure times were reduced to a few seconds. It was not until 1871 that Dr. Richard Maddox invented a dry plate process which simplified development requirements, and produced much shorter exposure times. However, it was 1878 before dry plate negatives were manufactured commercially. In Figure 2, a label from boxes that contained the negative plates from which many of the Eastleigh photos were made is shown. It indicates that even around the turn of the century, the developing of photographic negatives was not a simple business. It is amazing that so many negatives have survived for over 100 years considering the care that one had to take in developing the plates, as the labels indicate. In comparison I have experienced some modern day commercially processed photographs that have deteriorated in only a few years.

With these facts in mind, it should be realised that good quality photographs for any items that were scrapped before 1878 are unlikely, and drawings are the only resource from which we can get a good idea of their appearance. A quantity of original tracings of engine diagrams were acquired, and prints from these are included for locomotives from 1909 back to the 1860s. Whilst the majority of the better quality photographs used here (printed from glass negatives) originated from Eastleigh, a number of earlier items were obtained commercially in order to "fill the gaps". One of the problems that I have encountered concerns the dating of drawings and photographs. It is apparent that very few items were dated when produced, and most of the dates applied in this book are educated guesses. Where there was a definite date to an item, it has been applied as recorded, but where the word "circa" is applied, it is only a guess.

The overall objective of this book is not only to inform readers of the final products, but also to give some idea of the processes and working methods involved in their production, the conditions under which the employees worked, and the effects the works had on the local environment. I hope that some readers will feel that they have, to a certain extent, "experienced" part of the works' atmosphere during their reading of the book.

Plate 3. A portion of Greenwood's 1830 map of London showing the area to be occupied by the Nine Elms site between Nine Elms Lane, which borders the Thames, and the Wandsworth Road running vertically on the right hand side. *(Reproduction from Motco Enterprises Ltd. Ref:www.motco.com)*

IN THE BEGINNING
1830 - 1850

Initial Development

The area of Nine Elms, which is largely situated in the Borough of Wandsworth, and which borders the Thames, is shown on the 1830 map in Plate 3. This was a farmland area which was later to become filled with the railway industry. Plate 2 on page 1 is a copy of an original map shown on the Parliamentary application for the approach to London of a railway between London and Southampton. The completion of the initial land purchase required for the building of The London and Southampton Railway from Nine Elms to its Southampton terminus was completed on 31st January 1835, and services were opened to Woking Common by 21st May 1838. During the initial stages, Francis Giles was employed as Engineer, but his performance was of dubious merit, and he was soon replaced by Joseph Locke on 13th January 1837 whose portrait is shown in Figure 3. Figure 4 shows Thomas Brassey, the civil engineer responsible for many contracts at home and abroad, who was employed to build the first 15 miles out of London, and who was also awarded a 10-year contract to maintain the completed line to Southampton.

The early development at Nine Elms is described in the following extract from an article by Tim Sherwood, in his book "Change at Clapham Junction":

The London and Southampton Railway was not only the first main line south of the Thames, but was the mainspring of the railway system in Battersea. With the general demand for fast low-cost transport, some sort of railway from Southampton to London had been under consideration since 1820. The solution to this problem (or technological breakthrough) came in 1830 with the opening of the Liverpool and Manchester steam locomotive railway, which had reliable equipment and paid a dividend of 10%. From Southampton, various approaches to London were investigated by an embryo railway company, who then engaged a professional Engineer, Francis Giles, his report stated:

"....nearly from the commencement I decided upon recommending the entrance (to London) to take place at Nine Elms, Battersea."

On the Indenture of Agreement for share subscriptions, there appears Giles' estimate of £1 million for the cost of construction of the railway, with three years for completion. Then, as now, civil engineering projects were under-estimated and this was no exception: the London and Southampton cost £2½ million and took six years to complete.

The terminus at Nine Elms was to be between the Wandsworth Road and Windmill pier, at the edge of the built-up area on the "suburban frontier of Lambeth", thus minimising the destruction of property.

The necessary Act of Parliament was obtained on 25th July 1834 for:

"....making a railway commencing at the River Thames, at or near Nine Elms in the parish of Battersea in the County of Surrey, to the shore or beach at or near a place called the Marsh in the parish of Saint Mary in the town and county of Southampton."

The Act contained environmentally protective clauses: one prohibited steam locomotives from crossing Nine Elms Lane to the river wharf – horses were to pull trucks across the road. Section 14 of the Act attempted to protect the water supply which the railway would disrupt in the cutting through Wandsworth Common; measures subsequently taken by the Company proved inadequate and residents succeeded in getting further legislation in 1841 to enforce their

Fig. 3. Joseph Locke, born 1805. Engineer on the LSWR from 1837. Died 1860.
Reproduced from 'A History of the Southern Railway'.

THE LSWR AT NINE ELMS

rights against the railway. Three years later they received £4,693 18s 6d in compensation for the loss of spring water.

Work began on the line in October 1834, but it is unlikely that it afforded much employment in Battersea and Wandsworth; contractors normally imported their own navvies as the work was exceptionally arduous and specialised. After many tribulations, the line was completed as far as Woking by May 1838, and on the 12th of that month, the Directors, accompanied by "several Noblemen and Members of Parliament" made a successful trip to Woking and back. A similar ceremonial run was made a week later, and the line was opened to the public on 21st May. It was not opened in is entirety until 11th May 1840, and in that month, the Morning Chronicle enthusiastically reported:

"(The line)....affords another, and beyond all doubt, a finer and more delightful outlet from the Metropolis, than any that modern ingenuity and enterprise have yet afforded."

The daily service then consisted of two fast trains in each direction, which took three hours to Southampton (the fastest mail coach had taken nine and a half hours), and two mixed passenger and goods trains, which took six hours – an improvement on road carriers which had taken 36 hours.

The early primitive locomotives often had difficulty getting their trains up the incline from Nine Elms and had to be assisted by horses. Trains could not attain more than 10 mph by the first mile out of the terminus, and then settled down to a steady 30 mph. The first station was on the north side of Battersea Rise Bridge and was called Wandsworth.

Figure 5 - opposite, shows a copy of the *Illustrated London News* and the opening timetable, obtained from the Public Records Office, Kew. The omnibuses referred to would, of course, be horse drawn. The lack of use of minutes in the main timetable is amusing.

This was not, however, the first railway development to ultimately become part of the London and South Western Railway Company. We have to travel about 250 miles approximately south-west from Nine Elms to Cornwall, in which county the Bodmin and Wadebridge Railway had been built. This railway was sanctioned in 1832, and the main line opened on 4th July 1834. The Bodmin and Wadebridge was never financially successful and in 1847 the LSWR acquired the property, to protect it from the advances of the GWR. The line was legally absorbed into the LSWR in 1886, but it had to wait until 1895 until the LSWR built its line to Padstow before it was physically linked to the rest of its owners system. Nine Elms (later Waterloo) the Bodmin and Wadebridge Railway, and Padstow comprised the eastern and western extremities of the LSWR system for most of its years. The Bodmin and Wadebridge has a specific interest because during the period from 1852 to 1895, Nine Elms Works was involved in supplying locos to the line, and because of the lack of a physical link between them, they had to be transported by sea, from Rotherhithe to Wadebridge Dock. Some coaches were also despatched in the same way. This railway is described in Volume 2.

Returning to Nine Elms, the station building was designed by William Tite, and a photograph is shown in Figure 7 on page 10, the date is unknown. The number of people and the sack barrows in the picture would tend to suggest a date in its passenger usage period, but the "Goods Offices" notice and the quality of the photograph would suggest a later date. However "Goods Offices" may mean what it says – an office for handling goods at the station rather than the Goods Depot itself, which the station eventually became.

Plate 1 on page 1, shows a copy of a watercolour painting of the Nine Elms Wharves area painted around 1845 from the direction of the river. The large building to the left of the windmill is one of the railway goods depots, the cranes in front of it being on

Fig. 4. Thomas Brassey, born 1805. Civil Engineer on the LSWR from 1837 to 1850. Died 1870. Reproduced from 'Thomas Brassey Railway Builder'.

IN THE BEGINNING

LONDON & SOUTHAMPTON RAILWAY.

The London and Southampton Railway is NOW OPEN for the conveyance of Passengers and Parcels from London to Woking Common (near Guildford), and the intermediate places.

The times at which the Trains will start are as follow:

FROM LONDON.		FROM WOKING COMMON.	
Morning	8	Morning	half-past 7
Ditto	10	Ditto	10
Afternoon	1	Afternoon	1
Ditto	half-past 3	Ditto	half-past 3
Ditto	6	Ditto	7

EXCEPT ON SUNDAYS,
When the Trains will start

FROM LONDON.		FROM WOKING COMMON.	
Morning	7	Morning	7
Ditto	9	Ditto	9
Afternoon	5	Afternoon	5
Ditto	7	Ditto	7

The Fares will be charged as under, viz.

From the Terminus at Nine Elms, NEAR VAUXHALL.

	FIRST CLASS			SECOND CLASS		
	£	s.	d.	£	s.	d.
To WOKING COMMON	0	5	0	0	3	6
To WEYBRIDGE	0	4	0	0	2	6
To WALTON	0	3	6	0	2	3
To DITTON MARSH	0	3	0	0	2	0
To KINGSTON	0	2	6	0	1	6
To WIMBLEDON	0	1	6	0	1	0
To WANDSWORTH	0	1	0	0	1	0

No Fee or Gratuity will be allowed to be received by any Servant of the Company.

Times at which the Trains are appointed to arrive at the undermentioned Stations, until further notice:

DOWN.

FROM Nine Elms		8 A.M.	10 A.M.	1 P.M.	3½ P.M.	6 P.M.
ARRIVE AT	Miles	h. m.	h. m.	h. m.	h. m.	h. m.
Wandsworth	2¼	8 7	10 7	1 7	3 37	6 7
Wimbledon	5¾	8 18	10 18	1 18	3 48	6 18
Kingston	10	8 31	10 31	1 31	4 1	6 31
Ditton Marsh	12¾	8 41	10 41	1 41	4 11	6 41
Walton	15½	8 51	10 51	1 51	4 21	6 51
Weybridge	17	8 59	10 59	1 59	4 29	6 59
Woking Comm.	23	9 15	11 15	2 15	4 45	7 15

UP.

FROM Woking Comm.		7¼ A.M.	10 A.M.	1 P.M.	3½ P.M.	7 P.M.
ARRIVE AT	Miles	h. m.	h. m.	h. m.	h. m.	h. m.
Weybridge	5¾	7 44	10 14	1 14	3 44	7 14
Walton	7½	7 51	10 21	1 21	3 51	7 21
Ditton Marsh	10	8 1	10 31	1 31	4 1	7 31
Kingston		8 10	10 40	1 40	4 10	7 40
Wimbledon		8 25	10 58	1 58	4 20	7 50
Wandsworth	20	8 35	11 5	2 5	4 35	8 5
Nine Elms	22¾	8 45	11 15	2 15	4 45	8 15

By Order of the Directors,

WM. REED, Secretary.

N.B. Omnibuses will convey Passengers to and from the Company's Station at NINE ELMS, near Vauxhall, from the following places, viz.

Spread Eagle, Gracechurch-street; Swan with Two Necks, Lad-lane; Cross Keys, Wood-street; White Horse, Fetter-lane; George and Blue Boar, Holborn; Golden Cross, Charing-cross; Universal Office, Regent-circus, Piccadilly.

Arrangements have been made with the London and Westminster Steam Boat Company, in consequence of which Steam Boats will be provided for conveying Passengers to and from the Station at Nine Elms, from and to the under-mentioned places, viz.

DYER'S HALL WHARF, Upper Thames-street; and HUNGERFORD MARKET.

Fig. 6. Plan of Nine Elms site, 1847.

The copy of the original plan received from the Public Record Office was of poor quality. It has been redrawn as accurately as possible.

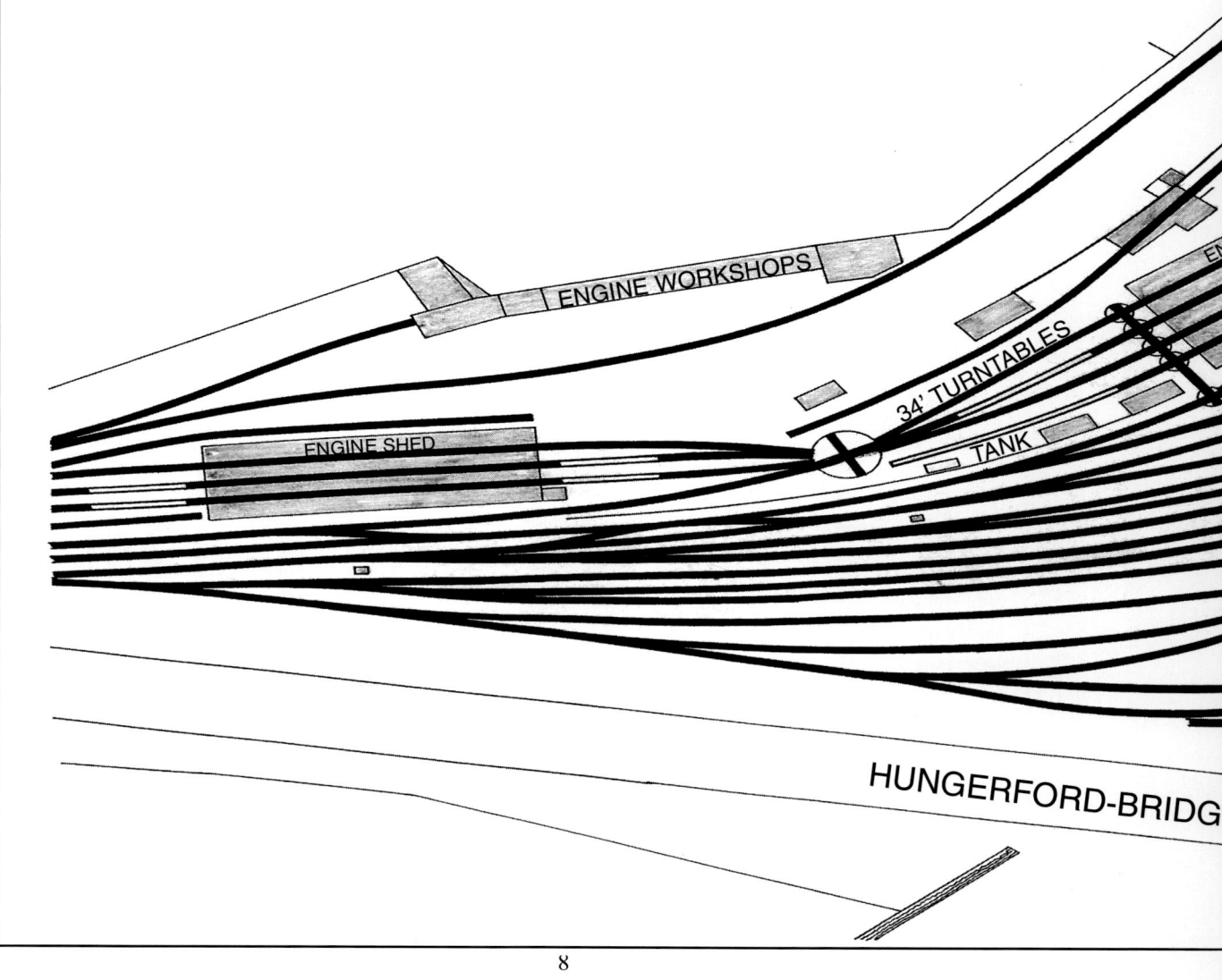

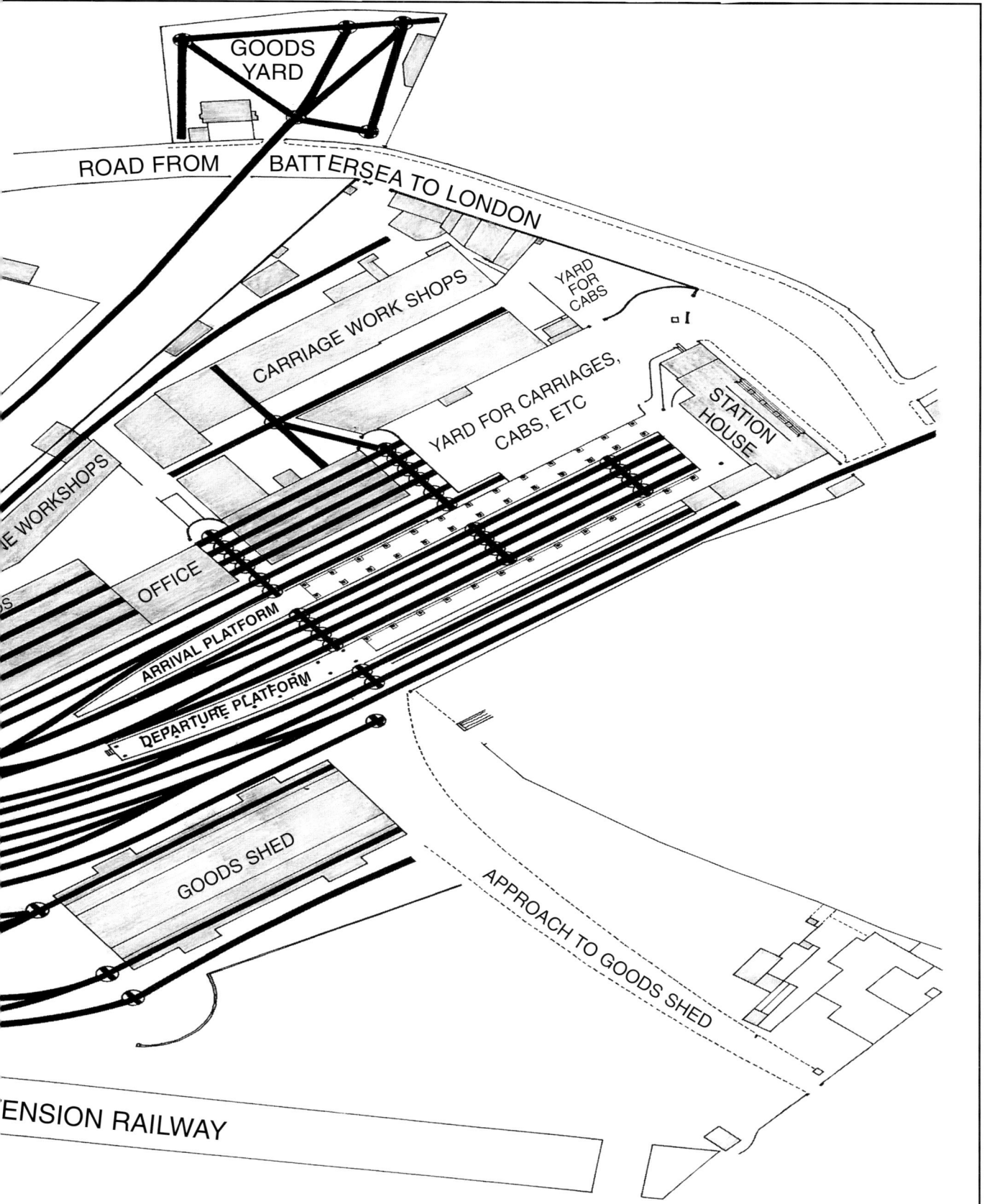

THE LSWR AT NINE ELMS

what was known as the Railway Wharf. Access to this goods shed was across Nine Elms Lane, and the only motive power permitted was horse power, as specified in the original act. Two paddle steamers are shown, which were probably those used to transport passengers to the City. A tramway operated along Nine Elms lane at a later date, but the only means of making the journey from the terminus to the city up to 1848, when the extension to Waterloo was opened, was by boat or horse and carriage. A photo of a tram in Nine Elms Lane is shown opposite. Recorded in the 1930s, (suggested by the vehicles), it has been taken near to the gasworks; the devices across the road were probably used to transport coal and coke across to, or from, the river wharves. The three workmen could be engaged in re-laying the granite setts within the tracks, a pile of which lay by the feet of the right-hand man.

Figure 6, on pages 8 and 9 shows a drawing of the Nine Elms site made in 1847. It is a very interesting drawing.

The universal use of turntables, in the station and for the only access to the carriage shed is noted. It would appear, by comparing the length of track on the turntable to the distance between the rails, that the maximum allowable wheelbase would have been about seven feet. The coaches would have been four-wheelers, but this restriction on wheelbase seems severe. There are two carriage workshops and one engine workshop with little or no rail access, and one engine workshop, with one track entry at one end. It can only be assumed that, as locomotives started to be built here in 1843 (although the boilers were bought from outside), those two buildings marked "engine shed" on the drawing were possibly used as workshops and erecting shops.

The workshops began operating in December 1839, but a fire in March 1841 had disastrous results, and most of the records were lost. This site, although very restricted in size, remained the Company's works until 1865, when new premises were built on the South side of the main line to Waterloo.

A book *All about Battersea, 1882* by Simmonds, provides some interesting insights into the background against which Nine Elms was developed. Here is one extract:

On the north side of Nine Elms Lane, nearly opposite the place where the "Southampton Arms" Tavern is situated was a windmill. On the site now occupied by Thornes' Brewery there used to be a Tan Yard and Fellmonger' Establishment. When the ground was opened for the purpose of drainage some old tanks were discovered in which the hides were soaked containing remains of lime and hair. In the rear of the Brewery there was a Hop Garden where

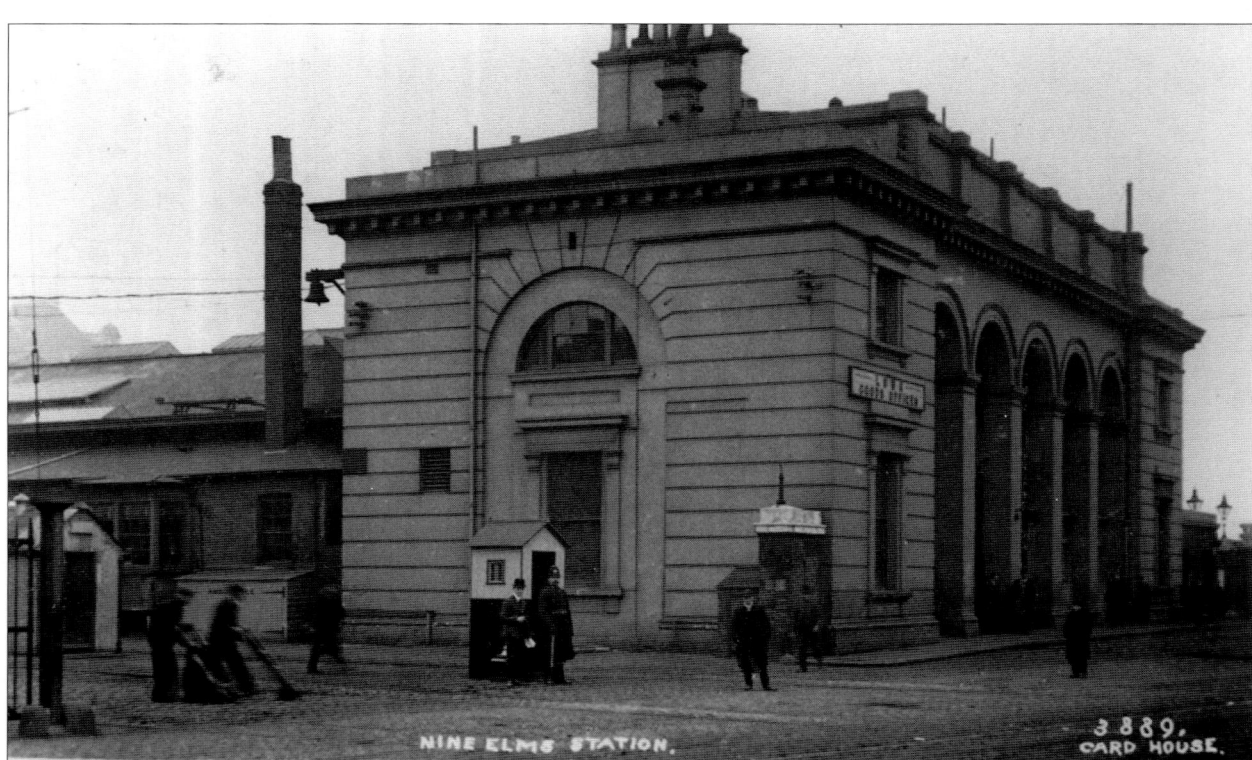

Fig. 7. Nine Elms station building, date uncertain. (Pat Loobey Collection)

IN THE BEGINNING

Fig. 8. A tram in Nine Elms Lane, near to the Gasworks in the 1930s. (Pat Loobey Collection)

that bitter plant much used for brewing was cultivated. The only regular vehicle that passed through Nine Elms Lane was the carrier's cart – the few inhabitants of the place used to "turn out" to see it pass – a marked contrast to the present hurried and incessant traffic! (A nineteenth century comment from 1882!- Ed.) Facing the Railway Terminus were two Steamboat Piers for landing and taking up passengers. At race times the excitement between the rival steamboat companies was intense – "touters," men hired expressly by each of these companies to induce passengers to go down their respective piers, became at times so exasperated with each other that they fell to blows, a sight which the baser sort of the crowds assembled on such occasions enjoyed to their hearts content.

 Many things have been said by way of disparagement of Battersea and not at all reflecting credit on certain localities within the parish. Battersea has been called the "the sink hole of Surrey." Europa Place, Bridge Road, has been designated "Little Hell," and the spot where Trinity Hall has been erected, at the end of Stewart's Lane received the epithet of "Hell Corner." Persons in the habit of receiving stolen property were said to reside in the neighbourhood; moreover, there was a gang called "Battersea Forty Thieves!" "Sharpers" are said to have abounded in every direction, so that strangers going to Battersea would be "cut for the simples." But we who know something of London life know that other Metropolitan parishes have their "dens of infamy" and localities of "Blue Skin," "Jack Sheppard," and "Jonathan Wild" notoriety, that beneath the shadow of St. Paul's Cathedral and Westminster Abbey, our Houses of Parliament and Mansions of the Nobility and Aristocracy, squalor and crime, vice and grandeur walk side by side, and often times hand in hand.

 Adjoining Thornes' premises and Swonnell's Malt houses, is the London and South Western Railway Company's Goods Station which, before the extension of that company's line in 1848 to Waterloo Road, was the Metropolitan terminus. Though this part of the line crosses the most grimy portion of Lambeth, a distance of two miles and fifty yards, yet it cost the Railway Company £800,000. The London and Southampton Railway (as it was first called) was opened on the 11th of May, 1840, which, in connection with the opposite wharf and warehouses on the banks of the river, at that time occupied an extent of between seven and eight acres. The entrance front of the (then) Metropolitan Terminus at Nine Elms, erected from designs by William Tite, Esq., Architect to the Company, was not unhandsome, though at present it has rather a dingy appearance for want of renovation, and has a central arcade which originally led to the booking of-

fice and waiting rooms now used for the manager's and clerks' offices for the goods traffic department."

Later he continues:

"Soon after the opening of the London and Southampton Railway a collision between two passenger trains occurred at the Nine Elms terminus resulting in the death of a young woman, a domestic servant, who, with a fellow servant, had been spending the day at Hampton Court. The Coroner's Jury returned a verdict of accidental death (and) a 'deodand' of £300 was levied on the 'Eclipse' locomotive engine, the moving cause of death. The Railway Company paid the £300 to Earl Spencer as Lord of the Manor, who most generously divided it amongst the deceased's relatives.

'Omnia quae movent ad mortem sunt deodanda':

What moves to death, or kills him dead,

Is deodand, and forfeited.

On the South Western Railway Stone Wharf are the agents' offices of the several depots for the sale of Portland stone, Bath freestone, etc. Huge blocks of stone direct from the quarries are here deposited and piled block upon block. A single block in some instances weighing ten tons elevated and removed by means of a steam traveller moving on a gantry.

Joseph Woods   1838-1840

Joseph Locke appointed Joseph Woods to be in charge of locomotive management on the 28th April 1838. Previous to this date, Locke had been in charge of purchasing and operating a number of locomotives, which were used to transport materials, and presumably men, to and from the various sites. They were known as "Ballast Engines", some being owned by the LSWR, and some by Thomas Brassey the Civil Engineer. Ownership of individual engines at any time is not entirely clear, and this is further confused by the fact that the railway sold a number of them to Thomas Brassey at various times during the construction period. Woods took over the responsibility for Ballast Engines when he was appointed, and also organised the purchase of locomotives for maintaining the passenger and freight services when the line was opened until he resigned on 23rd December 1840 to return to private practice. No locomotives were built at Nine Elms during Joseph Woods' period in charge of the department.

I have not been able to locate any drawings of the ballast engines, and it is unlikely that any survived until the era of photography.

Regarding those believed to have been purchased by the LSWR, Table 1 gives details of some of them upon which a varying amount of reliance should be made.

Thomas Brassey also purchased his own locomotives, and some of their names are possibly as follows: *Good Hope, Taurus, Shamrock, Mudlark, Defiant, Hercules, Vulture, Sam Slick.*

Vulture is also reported to have been an 0-4-2, and whether it is the same locomotive is not known.

*   Note, these three locomotives are alternatively referred to as being named *London, Southamp-*

TABLE 1

Date	Supplier	Wheel Arrangement	Name	Cost	Disposal
July 1835	Thomas Banks & Co.	0-4-0	*Alpha*	£800	Stationary Boiler 1839
July 1835	C. Tayleur & Co.	0-4-0	*St. George*	£890	McIntosh, Contractor, 1837
March 1836	Murdoch, Aitken, & Co.	0-4-0	*Vulture*	£657	Scrapped 1848
October 1836	Edward Bury	2-2-0	*Tramp*	£970	Brassey 1840
May 1837	John Jones	0-4-2	*Southampton* *	£1032	Brassey 1839
October 1837	John Jones	0-4-2	*Perseverance* *	£1045	Birmingham and Gloucester Railway 1839
January 1838	John Jones	0-4-2	*Trio* *	£1074	Brassey 1839

IN THE BEGINNING

ton, and *Reed* in that order downwards. Throughout this book readers are recommended to refer to the various excellent books by the late D.L. Bradley for further information on the details of the locomotives of southern England.

When Brassey completed his 10-year maintenance contract in December 1853, the responsibility for maintenance was given to Chief Engineer J. Strapp, who retained the policy of having a separate locomotive stock for his department. Initially the locomotives were those that were unwanted by the Locomotive Department, but after 1858 the department purchased its own locomotives, which were maintained and repaired by the Engineer's Department. These locomotives will be described in Volume 2.

The locomotives purchased by Joseph Woods for use on the passenger and goods services are listed in Table 2. Only brief details are given; for more details reference can be made to the full list of locomotives in the Appendix, or to the book by D. L. Bradley *L&SWR locomotives....The Beattie Classes* from where some of the illustrations came.

John Viret Gooch   1841 - 1850

Born in Northumberland on the 29th June 1812, Gooch was appointed Locomotive Superintendent at a salary of £300 per annum on the 1st January 1841. He was responsible for purchasing 59 locomotives of 6 different types, but he also started the design and construction of locomotives on the Nine Elms site. This began in 1843, and he designed 4 types resulting

Fig. 9. John Viret Gooch. Born 1812. Locomotive Superintendent on the LSWR from 1841 to 1850.

in 33 locomotives being built in 10 years. He resigned on 16th May 1850 to join the Eastern Counties Railway as locomotive superintendent just after construction of his last locomotive type, the 'Etna' class singles began.

During his time at Nine Elms, it was decided

TABLE 2

Build Period	Number purchased	Builder	Wheel Arrangement	Withdrawal Period	Figure Nos.
6/1838 - 11/1838	5	G. & J. Rennie	2-2-2	8/1854 - 11/1871	10,12 & 15
6/1838 - 12/1838	9	Sharp Roberts	2-2-2	2/1852 - 8/1873	11 & 16
6/1838 - 10/1839	12	C. Tayleur & Co.	2-2-2	4/1842 - 10/1872	
10/1838 - 8/1839	3	Nasmyth, Gaskell & Co.	2-2-0	1/1843 - 6/1844	
2/1839	1	Edward Bury	2-2-0	3/1841	13
6/1839 - 8/1839	2	Summers, Groves & Day	2-2-0	2/1851 - 10/1869	
7/1839 - 8/1840	4	Fenton, Murray & Jackson	2-2-2	9/1851 - 3/1856	
7/1839 - 11/1839	5	Rothwell & Co.	2-2-2	7/1851 - 4/1855	14

THE LSWR AT NINE ELMS

(Diagrams and photographs are included of some of the locomotives listed above, otherwise no other illustrations have been found.)

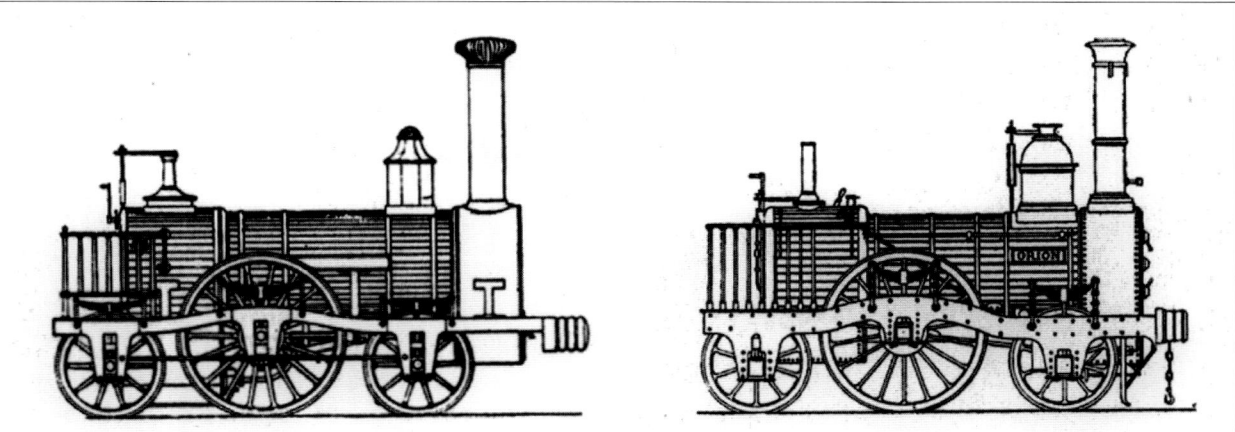

Fig. 10. *A 2-2-2 locomotive by G. & J. Rennie.* Fig. 11. *A 2-2-2 locomotive by Sharp Roberts.*

Fig. 12. *A 2-2-2 locomotive by G. & J. Rennie after rebuilding in 1856.*

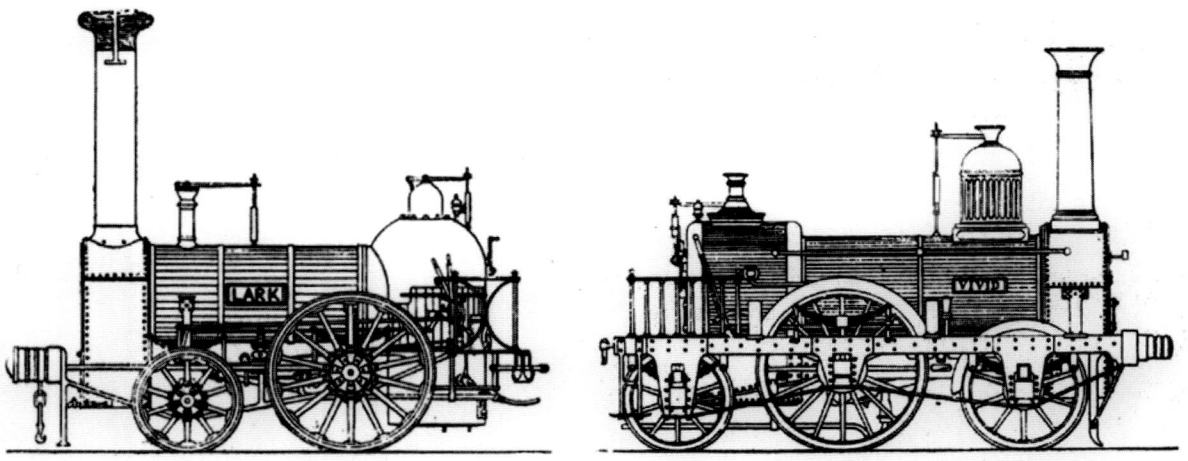

Fig. 13. *A 2-2-0 locomotive by Edward Bury.* Fig. 14. *A 2-2-2 locomotive by Rothwell & Co.*

Fig. 15. 2-2-2 locomotive by G.J. Rennie, No 24 "Elk". Built in 1838, it is shown at Romsey after being rebuilt in 1856.

Fig. 16. 2-2-2 locomotive by Sharp Roberts, No 8 "Vesta". Built in 1838, it is depicted at Dorchester in 1860 after being substantially rebuilt in 1854.

THE LSWR AT NINE ELMS

to build the extension to Waterloo Bridge, through Vauxhall. The original terminus became initially a carriage shed, and an extra engine shed was built in front of it, as shown on the map of 1855 in Figure 29 on page 24. Note that turntables still seem to form the main access to the carriage storage sheds. The extra engine accommodation allowed the larger of the older engine sheds to be converted into an erecting shop as shown on this map, facilitating more on-site locomotive building, although the site was already becoming crowded.

Table 3 summarises the locomotive production for which John Gooch was responsible. In all 92 locomotives were completed or delivered in a period of 12 years.

An article on the development at Nine Elms from 1838 to 1967 was written by Peter F. Winding and published in the November 1980 issue of the magazine *Railway World*, together with the map in Figure 29. The map shows the course of the extension to Waterloo Bridge, opened in 1848. The following is an extract which refers to the early days at the site:

"NINE ELMS was the last main line steam shed in the London area, and its closure to all traffic in July 1967 marked the end of an era which originated in 1838 when the London & Southampton Railway opened its metropolitan terminus just south of the Thames, near the junction of Nine Elms Lane and Wandsworth Road. At that time the surrounding district was described as a low, marshy area studded with windmills and pollard trees, consisting mainly of market gardens and a few houses. But with the coming of the railway this rural image, barely a mile from Westminster, was soon transformed into a typical Victorian slum comprising a fascinating hotchpotch of wharves, gasworks, breweries and railway yards linked together by mean streets of back to back terraced houses.

From one generation to another this image did not change much until the 1960s when the area was earmarked for redevelopment. Since then the old way of life has vanished beneath a vast complex of council housing estates, while what was once railway property; the great engine sheds, goods yards and the remains of Nine Elms Works, has been levelled, much of it to provide a foundation for the sprawling acres of the new Covent Garden Market. All that remains is the main line viaduct to Waterloo, and the faint hope that some day we may see a new depot giving rail access to the market.

Like many of the earliest railway establishments Nine Elms suffered the penalty of inadequate planning and inexperience. Shortage of space and

TABLE 3

Build Period	Number Ordered	Builder	Wheel Arrangement	Class	Withdrawal Period	Figure Numbers
10/1841 - 2/1842	5	William Fairburn & Sons.	2-2-2		12/1851 - 12/1852	
9/1840 - 2/1841	3	Jones, Turner & Evans	0-4-2	(Goods)	2/1851 - 10/1855	
11/1841 - 2/1842	4	Sharp Roberts	0-4-2	(Goods)	1851 - 10/1855	17 & 18
10/1843 - 7/1844	4	Nine Elms	2-2-2	Eagle	1862 - 5/1863	
12/1845 - 11/1848	10	Nine Elms	0-6-0	Bison	10/1863 - 8/1871	20 & 22
12/1846 - 9/1848	28	Rothwell & Co.	2-2-2		11/1862 - 4/1869	
12/1846 - 1/1848	11	William Fairburn & Sons.	2-2-2		7/1863 - 4/1872	
3/1847 - 12/1847	10	Nine Elms	2-2-2	Mazeppa	7/1862 - 3/1870	19, 21, 23 & 24
12/1847	2	Stothert & Slaughter	2-2-2		5/1862 - 12/1864	
10/1848 - 12/1849	6	Christie, Adams & Hill	2-2-2		11/1866 - 3/1870	25 & 27
3/1850 - 10/1853	9	Nine Elms	2-2-2	Etna	3/1870 - 5/1880	26 & 28

IN THE BEGINNING

Fig. 17. An 0-4-2 locomotive "Pluto" by Sharp Roberts, in original condition.

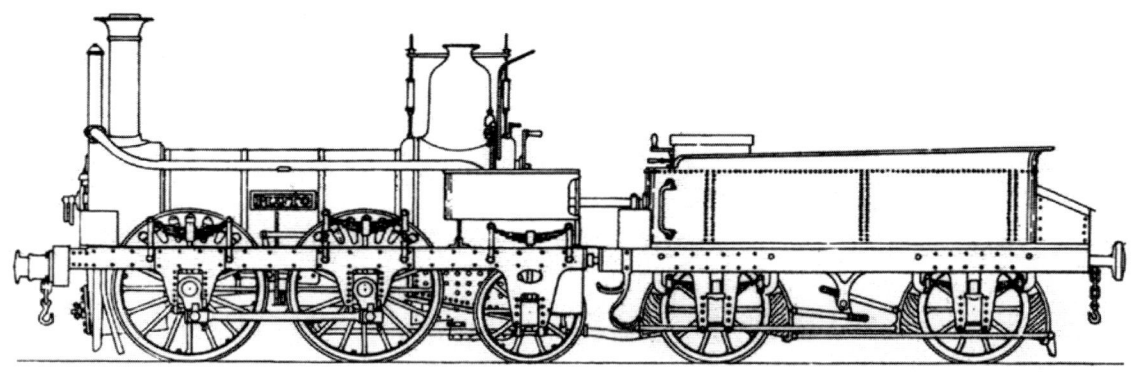

Fig. 18. An 0-4-2 locomotive "Pluto" by Sharp Roberts, as rebuilt by Joseph Beattie at Nine Elms in 1854, just before being despatched for service on the Bodmin & Wadebridge Railway.

Fig. 19. A 2-2-2 Mazeppa class locomotive "Serpent", built at Nine Elms in December 1847.

Fig. 20. Bison class 0-6-0 locomotive built at Nine Elms in 1846, "Elephant", as rebuilt in 1863.

Fig. 21. Mazeppa class 2-2-2 locomotive built at Nine Elms in 1847, No 57 "Meteor" in original form.

IN THE BEGINNING

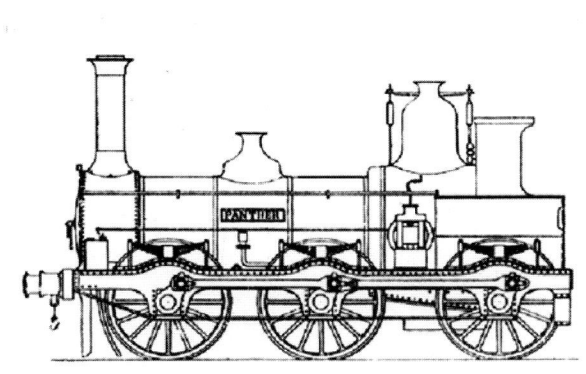

Fig. 22. Bison class locomotive, "Panther".

Fig. 23. Mazeppa class locomotive, "Snake".

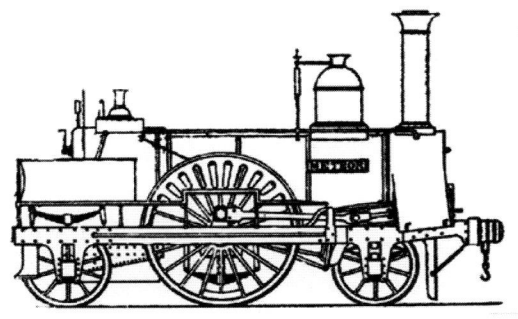

Fig. 24. Mazeppa class locomotive, "Meteor".

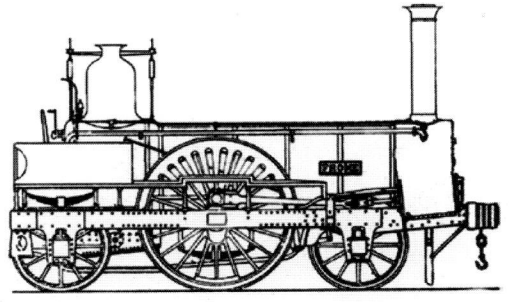

Fig. 25. Christie, Adams & Hill locomotive, "Frome".

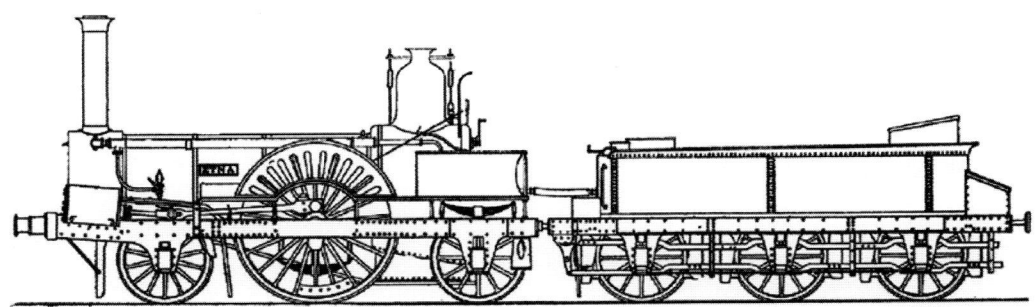

Fig. 26. Etna class locomotive, "Etna".

Note regarding Figures 14, 15, 20, 21, 27 and 28. These photographs were taken long before dry plate negatives were in general use, and it is remarkable that such good results were achieved and have survived.

Fig. 27. 2-2-2 locomotive built by Christie, Adams & Hill, in 1849, No 114 "Frome", shown at Yeovil in 1862.

Fig. 28. Etna class 2-2-2 locomotive built at Nine Elms in 1850, No 118, "Etna".

cramped facilities dogged the depot throughout its history, while the Waterloo extension with its subsequent realignment and later widenings caused difficulties that were never properly resolved. Much of this unfortunate legacy was inherited from the London & Southampton, whose original development prevented further enlargement of the passenger terminus by crowding it between the locomotive, carriage and wagon workshops to the north, and a goods depot to the south. The best that could he done in this respect was to extend the length of the train shed and add another track at each side.

A further drawback was the inconvenience caused to passengers, the majority of whom were obliged to use the steam ferryboat or omnibus service which linked the terminus with Westminster and the City. Obviously this arrangement did not suit City businessmen, and it was probably with this lucrative source of revenue in mind that in 1844 the railway management decided to extend the line nearer the City. Authorization for this scheme was obtained the following year, and the work of extending the line from Nine Elms Junction to a point just south of Waterloo Bridge was completed with the opening of the new terminus on 11 July 1848, when the old terminus was closed to passenger traffic. One of the plans reproduced in this article is based on a survey of 1855 and depicts the main line extension between Nine Elms Junction and Wandsworth Road in relation to the original site, and has considerable interest in that it shows much of the layout dating from 1838, including the small three road engine shed with its 34ft turntable, and the layout of the first locomotive, carriage and wagon works.

The works was brought into use in 1839 and began the construction of new engines in 1843. Following the closure of the passenger terminus the earlier part of the train shed was used as an extension of the carriage works, while the later part at the western end was adapted as an additional six road engine shed. The same period also saw a further development of the goods depot, including in August 1855 the acquisition of the remaining land bounded by Nine Elms Lane, Wandsworth Road and the Thames. As may be seen from the plan, the layout is typical of the period in its prolific use of wagon tables; a practice that gradually declined as the size and weight of vehicles increased. Traffic figures show that in its final year the old terminus handled no less than 1,250,000 passengers, while in 1849 goods traffic amounted to 125,000 tons.

After the closure of the passenger terminus a rather odd situation prevailed, whereby certain facilities were retained so that the Royal Family could continue to use the station as they had done since 1843. No doubt this was in deference to the wishes of Queen Victoria, who greatly appreciated the privacy and informality afforded by premises from which the public were excluded. On the other hand, from the Company's point of view this makeshift arrangement set in the middle of a workshops area was highly inconvenient, and in 1854 a compromise was reached by providing a new Royal station just south of the bridge which carries the main line over Wandsworth Road. To judge from the site plan it was quite a simple affair, and in later years when the Queen was more often at Windsor it was seldom used. However, the spur which served the station also functioned as a shunting neck for the carriage works, and was retained after the station buildings were demolished towards the end of the century."

The Minute Books of the LSWR afford a wonderful insight into the practices, working conditions and often the behaviour of the staff. Several examples specific or otherwise are included within the text:

August 12 1872   4024
'Tillman' Engine Driver.
Read report from Mr. White, Supt. At Portsmouth of 3 inst. complaining of the conduct of the above man when remonstrated with by him for leaving his Engine and allowing the Fireman to move the train in his absence.
'Tillman' to be fined £1 and informed that in the event of another complaint of a similar nature being made against him he will be dismissed from the Company's service.

September 30 1872   4070
'W. Box' Driver.
Read reports from Mr. Anwell dated 26 inst. Against the above man for loosing time with his Train and refusing to shunt Wagons at Guildford when requested by the Yard Foreman to do so.
'Box' to be dismissed from the Company's service.

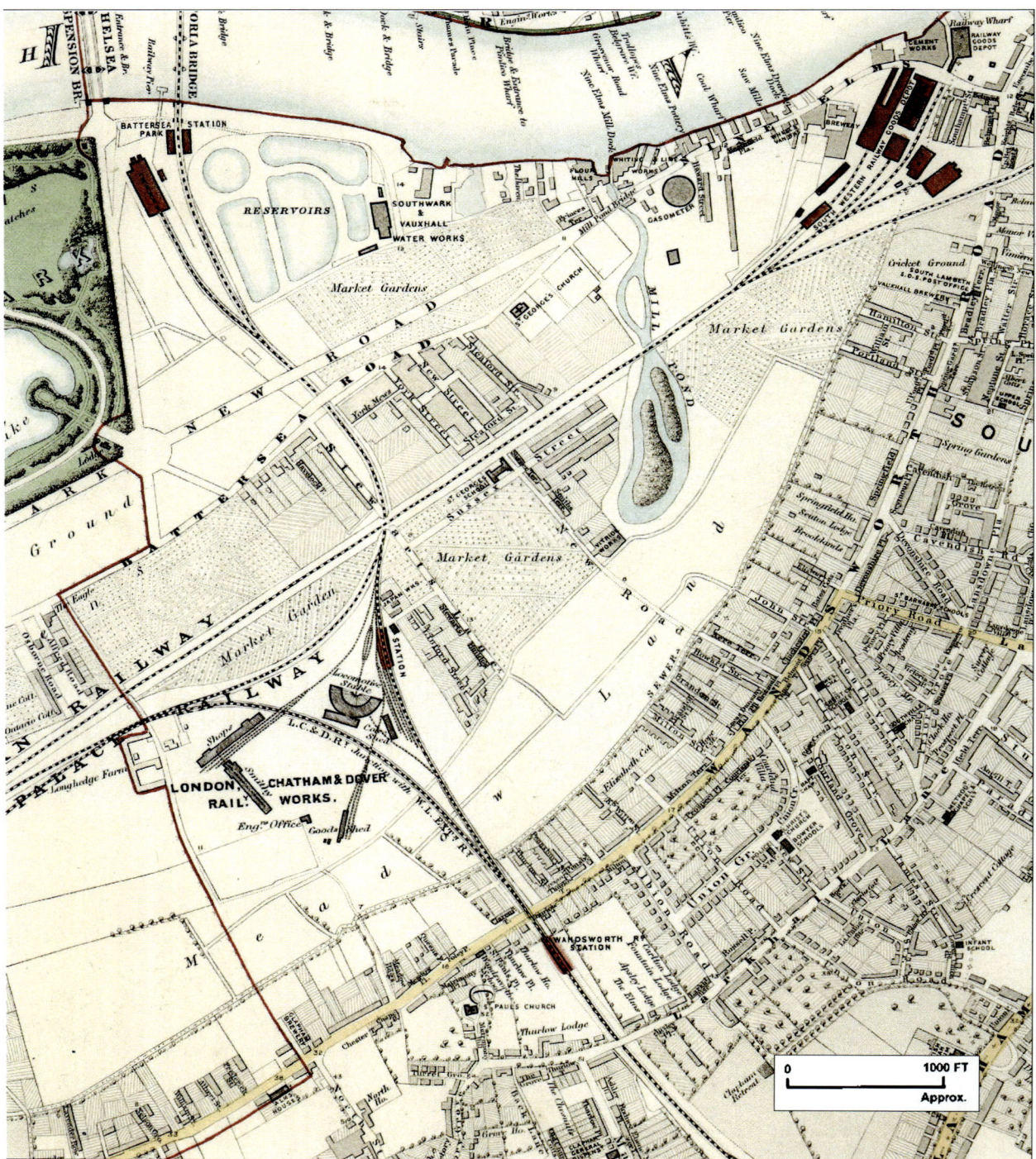

Plate 4. A section of Stanhope's map of 1862, showing the London & South Western Railway running from the South West to the goods depot, locomotive depot and works in the top right hand corner, where also, until 11 July 1848, the passenger terminus was situated. After that date, passenger traffic took the newly-constructed branch to the right just before the depot and ran through Vauxhall to the new terminus 1¾ miles away, then named Waterloo Bridge. The former station (train shed) appears to be labelled "Government Emigration Depot" on this map. Stewarts Lane depot of the London and Chatham Railway is within the triange of lines labelled "Locomotive Stable". (Reproduction from Motco Enterprises Ltd. Ref:www.motco.com)

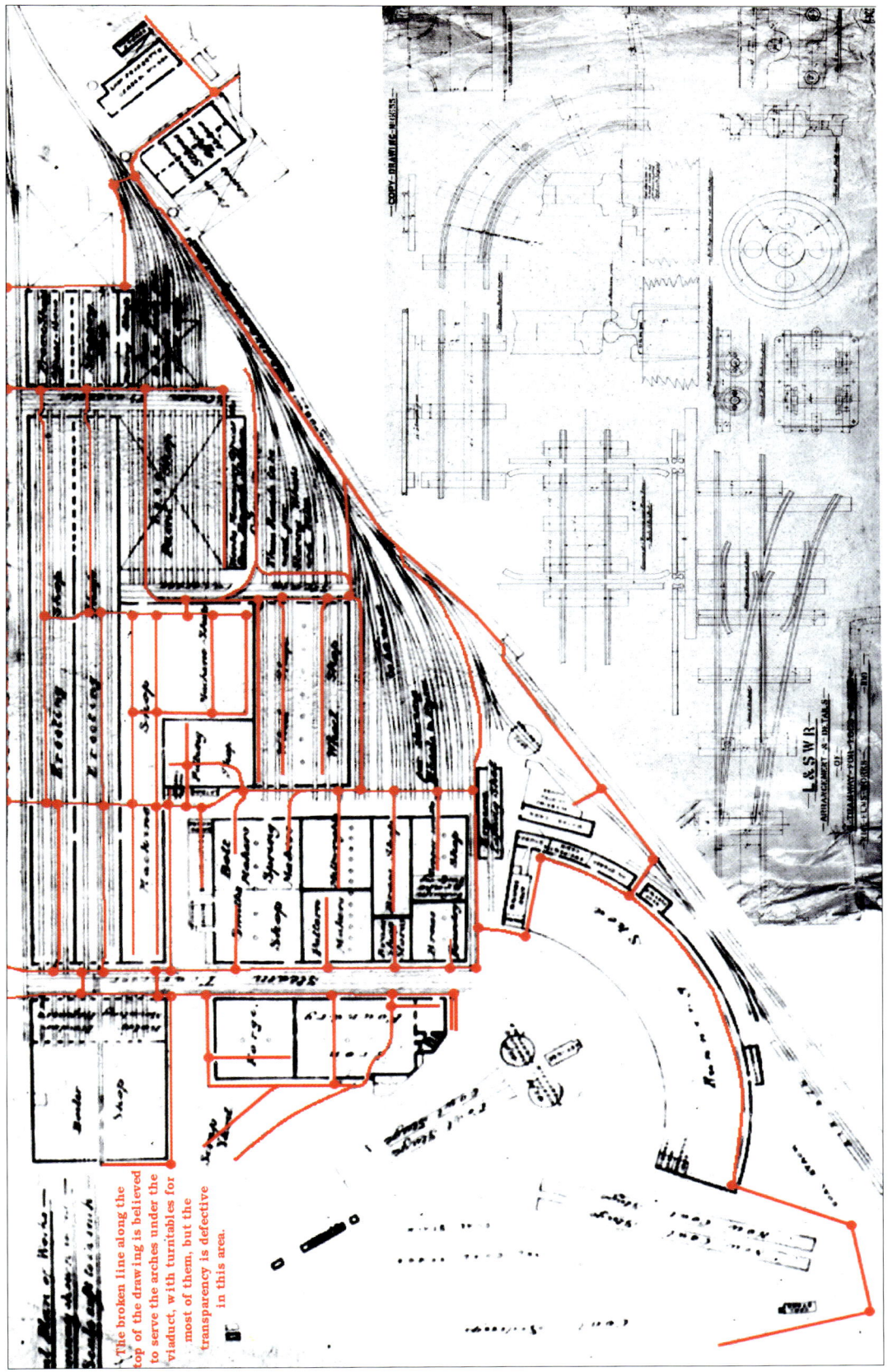

Plate 5. An extensive internal tramway network, highlighted in red, served the Nine Elms Works site.

THE LSWR AT NINE ELMS

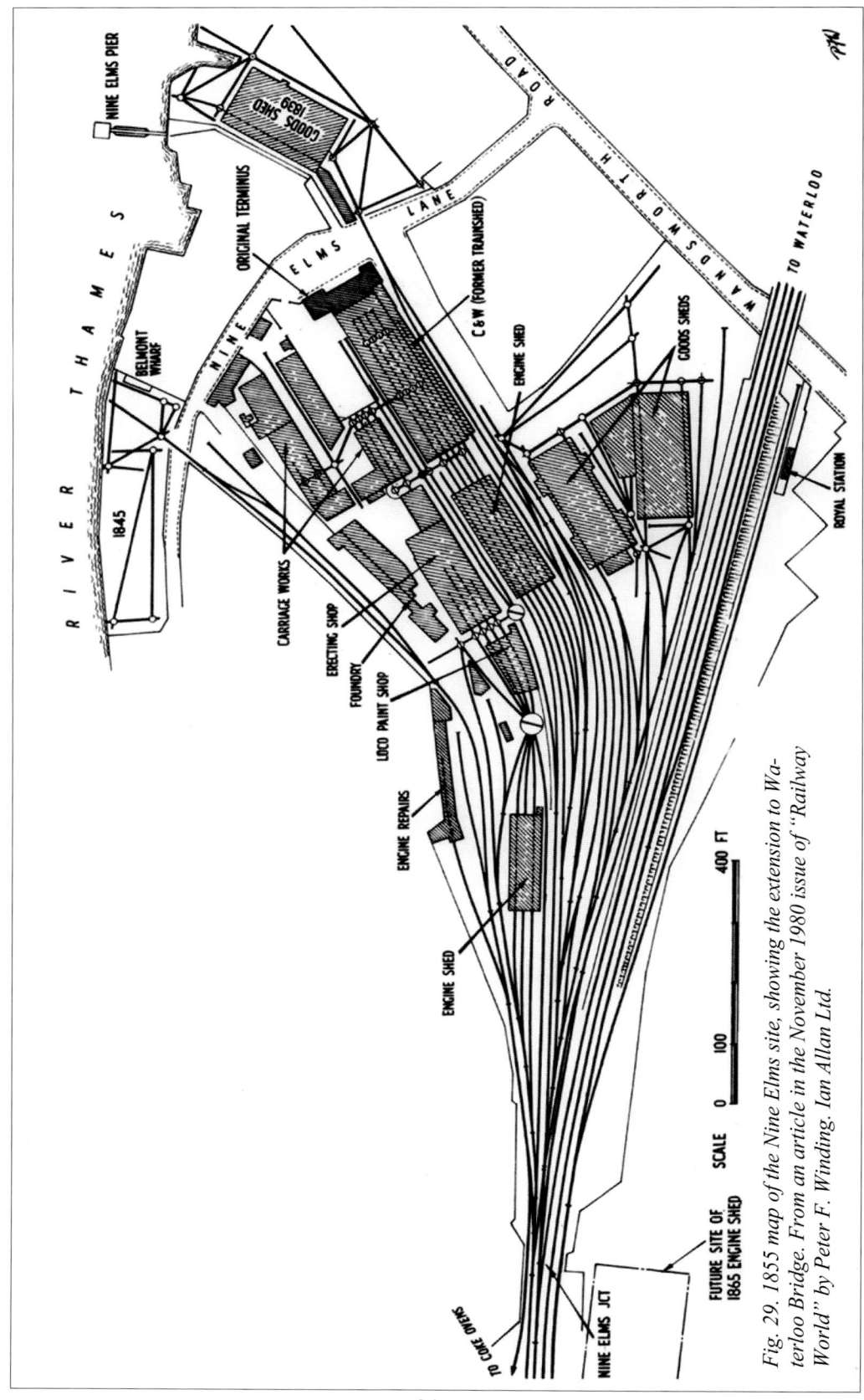

Fig. 29. 1855 map of the Nine Elms site, showing the extension to Waterloo Bridge. From an article in the November 1980 issue of "Railway World" by Peter F. Winding. Ian Allan Ltd.

4
LOCOMOTIVE PROCUREMENT
1850 - 1871

Joseph Beattie

Joseph Beattie joined the London and South Western Railway Company in March 1837, as an assistant engineer, and was appointed as Locomotive Superintendent on 1st July 1850 when John Gooch left the Company; he is depicted in Figure 30. He was born in Ireland on the 12th May 1808, and died in service on the 18th October 1871. During his period in office he was responsible for the procurement of 338 locomotives of 25 classes, 220 of them being built on the Nine Elms site. This is a remarkable achievement considering how cramped the workshops were, restricted to the area north of the main line until 1866. This performance was aided by the policy of buying many of the component parts, such as boilers, wheels, and cylinders from outside. Apart from the six 2-2-2WT "Tartar" class, built by Sharp Brothers, all the other locomotives from outside contractors were built by Beyer Peacock & Company, and were generally very handsome designs. The locomotive production is summarised in Table 5 overleaf.

It should be noted that the detailing of new locomotive building is sometimes more complicated than it appears, as such building can vary from being the manufacture of all new components, through the usage of a combination of new and second-hand components, to the complete rebuild of an earlier locomotive. The policy mentioned earlier of buying some new components from outside contractors further complicates the issue.

As an example of this, shown in Table 5, the first "Minerva" Class, built from 9/1850 to 10/1854, consisted of the rebuild of the following four engines all listed previously in Table 1:
1. Sharp Roberts 2-2-2, No. 11 "Minerva", built 6/1838, rebuilt 9/1850 as 2-2-2WT.
2. Rothwell 2-2-2, No. 38 "Vizier", built 9/1839, parts used in build of 2-2-2WT, 3/1852.
3. Fenton, Murray & Jackson 2-2-2, No. 34 "Crescent", built 8/1840, rebuilt 3/1852 as 2-2-2WT.
4. Taylor 2-2-2, No. 3, "Transit", built 10/1838, rebuilt 10/1854 as 2-2-2WT.

Most of the "Undine" 2-4-0 class were built from 7/1859 onwards, but "Ironsides" in this class was a 12/1855 rebuild of 'Canute' class 2-2-2 No. 134 of the same name.

The "Firefly" 2-2-2WT locomotive in Table 5 was a partial rebuild of the Rothwell & Co. "Firefly" 2-2-2, one of the batch of 24 locomotives built between 12/1846 and 9/1848 by that company and listed in Table 2. It utilised the boiler, leading wheels, and frames of the former locomotive, plus other material to hand.

D. L. Bradley details some buying from outside contractors, shown in Table 4. Doubtless there were more instances of subcontracted work.

Returning to details of the site, and expanding on the information given on pages 16 and 21 regarding the 1855 map shown in Figure 29, there appears to be just one building where locomotive construction can be assumed, labelled "erecting shop". If the tracks existed only as far as drawn, a maximum of about 14 engines, without tenders, could have been accommodated. This presumably would have had to provide for the more major repairs as well as new locomotive building, including tenders. The small shed labelled "Engine Repairs" would have taken about four engines, and was probably only for the more minor repairs. The two sheds labelled "Engine Shed" are assumed to be for the storage of engines "in service", and could have accommodated about 36 engines, equally distributed between tank and tender types. Locomotives did have their own paint shop. These fig-

TABLE 4

Class	Build Period	Items	Supplier
Sussex	1/1852-7/1852	Boilers, Cylinders, Wheels	The Vulcan Foundry
Canute	12/1855-6/1859	A significant proportion	Unspecified
Undine	12/1855-6/1860	Boilers, Cylinders, Wheels, Frames, Donkey pumps, Tenders	Beyer Peacock & Co.
Eagle	7/1862-11/1862	Boilers, Wheels, Frames, Tenders	Beyer Peacock & Co.
Falcon	12/1862-10/1867	A proportion	Beyer Peacock & Co.

THE LSWR AT NINE ELMS

TABLE 5

Build Period	Number Built	Builder	Wheel Arrangement	Class	Withdrawal Period	Figure Nos.
9/1850-10/1854	4	Nine Elms	2-2-2WT	Minerva	3/1856-10/1872	
6/1851-3/1855	15	Nine Elms	2-4-0	Hercules	3/1875-4/1885	35,36,47,48
1/1852-7/1852	8	Nine Elms	2-2-2WT	Sussex	10/1871-6/1877	38,39
5/1852-7/1852	6	Sharp Brothers	2-2-2WT	Tartar	7/1871-5/1874	37,49
4/1855-12/1857	12	Nine Elms	2-4-0	Saxon	11/1877-9/1885	50,51,55
12/1855-6/1859	12	Nine Elms	2-2-2	Canute	12/1875-1/1885	52,53,54,56,57
5/1856-7/1856	3	Nine Elms	2-4-0WT	Minerva	8/1877-9/1883	58
7/1856-8/1856	3	Nine Elms	2-2-2WT	Chaplin	1/1871-8/1877	
12/1856-6/1859	7	Nine Elms	2-4-0	Tweed	6/1877-7/1881	59
7/1858-8/1858	3	Nine Elms	2-4-0WT	Nelson	8/1882-4/1885	62
1/1859-7/1864	7	Nine Elms	2-4-0	Clyde	6/1883-5/1888	60,63,64,65,66
4/1859-6/1859	3	Nine Elms	2-4-0WT	Nile	7/1882-9/1882	67,70
12/1855-6/1860	13	Nine Elms	2-4-0	Undine	5/1884-12/1886	61,68,72
7/1862-11/1862	3	Nine Elms	2-4-0	Eagle	12/1886-3/1887	73
11/1862-2/1863	1	Nine Elms	2-2-2WT	Firefly	10/1871	69,70
12/1862-8/1863	6	Nine Elms	2-4-0	Gem	4/1884-11/1885	76
12/1862-10/1867	17	Nine Elms	2-4-0	Falcon	2/1885-5/1898	74,75,77,78,79,80
2/1863-11/1875	82	Beyer Peacock & Co.	2-4-0WT	Standard Well Tank	6/1886-12/1962	81,82,83,84,85,86,87,
10/1863-10/1873	44	Nine Elms	0-6-0	Lion	4/1882-5/1900	88,89,90,91,92
2/1866-1/1867	24	Beyer Peacock & Co.	0-6-0	Double framed	7/1891-5/1924	93,94,95,96,97,98,99,100
7/1866-8/1866	6	Beyer Peacock & Co.	2-4-0	"231"	9/1892-1/1899	101,102,103,104
12/1866-3/1873	18	Nine Elms	2-4-0	Volcano	5/1886-12/1897	105,106,107,108,109,110,111
8/1868-10/1868	6	Nine Elms	2-4-0	Centaur	10/1894-5/1899	112,113,114,115,116,117,118,119,120
12/1869-5/1875	32	Nine Elms	2-4-0	Vesuvius	12/1893-2/1899	121,122,123,124,125,126,127,128,129,130
11/1871-12/1871	3	Nine Elms	2-4-0WT	Standard Well Tank	10/1890-7/1899	131,132,133

Standard Well Tank numbers 314 (BR 30585) and 298 (BR 30587) are in preservation.

LOCOMOTIVE PROCUREMENT 1850 -1871

TABLE 6

Class	Number	Builder	Build Date	Fracture Date	Item	Illustration
Double Framed Goods	273	Beyer Peacock	8/1872	19/8/1890	RH Driving Crank	Plate 9
Double Framed Goods	274	Beyer Peacock	8/1872	29/5/1891	LH Driving Crank	Plate 6
Canute	153	Nine Elms	6/1859	18/8/1879	Driving Axle	Figure 42
Clyde	159	Nine Elms	3/1859	12/9/1879	Tyre	Figure 40
Undine	164	Nine Elms	9/1859	5/9/1879	Tyre	Figure 41
Undine	165	Nine Elms	10/1859	19/8/1878	LH Tyre	Figure 43
Standard Well Tank	245	Beyer Peacock	2/1867	11/6/1878	Tyre & Wheel	Figure 46
Lion	272	Beyer Peacock	6/1872	10/6/1879	Crank Axle	Figure 45
Standard Well Tank	202	Beyer Peacock	5/1874	11/6/1878	Trailing Axle	Figure 44

ures illustrate how difficult it must have been to attain the level of production shown in Table 5 up to the time the works was moved to the South side of the main line in 1866, and one of the reasons why outside contractors started to be used again in 1863.

Locomotives did suffer from broken axles and tyres occasionally, and a careful record was kept of their occurrence, often with elaborate coloured drawings being made of the fracture. From the "Broken Tyres and Axles" book covering 1878 to 1905, we include some selected items in Table 6 above since they concern some of the locomotives in Table 5.

Employees were frequently admonished for their wrongdoings whilst on duty, and footplate staff seemed to be particularly prone to this form of attack. The discussions in the "Officers" and "Locomotive & Traffic" Committee meetings were recorded in minute books kept by the secretary in "copperplate" handwriting, and these records included workers' errors and the action to be taken by the management amongst a variety of other items such as the ordering of engines, rolling stock, etc. One such minute book, for the years 1872 to 1875 has survived, and we have reproduced a number of the more interesting items exactly as written in a number of places in this book. One of them (No 5048 of 23rd August 1875) appears in Figure 31, as it involves the engine No 70, "Ariel", one of the Falcon class featured in Table 5.

Figures 32 to 34 depict some more excerpts from the minute book. Numbers 3939 and 4032 relate to the loan by Nine Elms of locomotive number 36 "Comet" to the Newport Junction Railway on the Isle of Wight. Number 4032 probably arose as a result of the opening of the line (from Sandown to Shide) being delayed because of the refusal of the Board of Trade to sanction it. It appears, however, that the locomotive was used for ballasting purposes until being returned to the mainland in 1875.

Number 4990 (17th June 1875), shown in Figure 34, refers to two engines, believed to be numbers 9

Fig. 30. Joseph Beattie. Locomotive Superintendent 1850-1871.

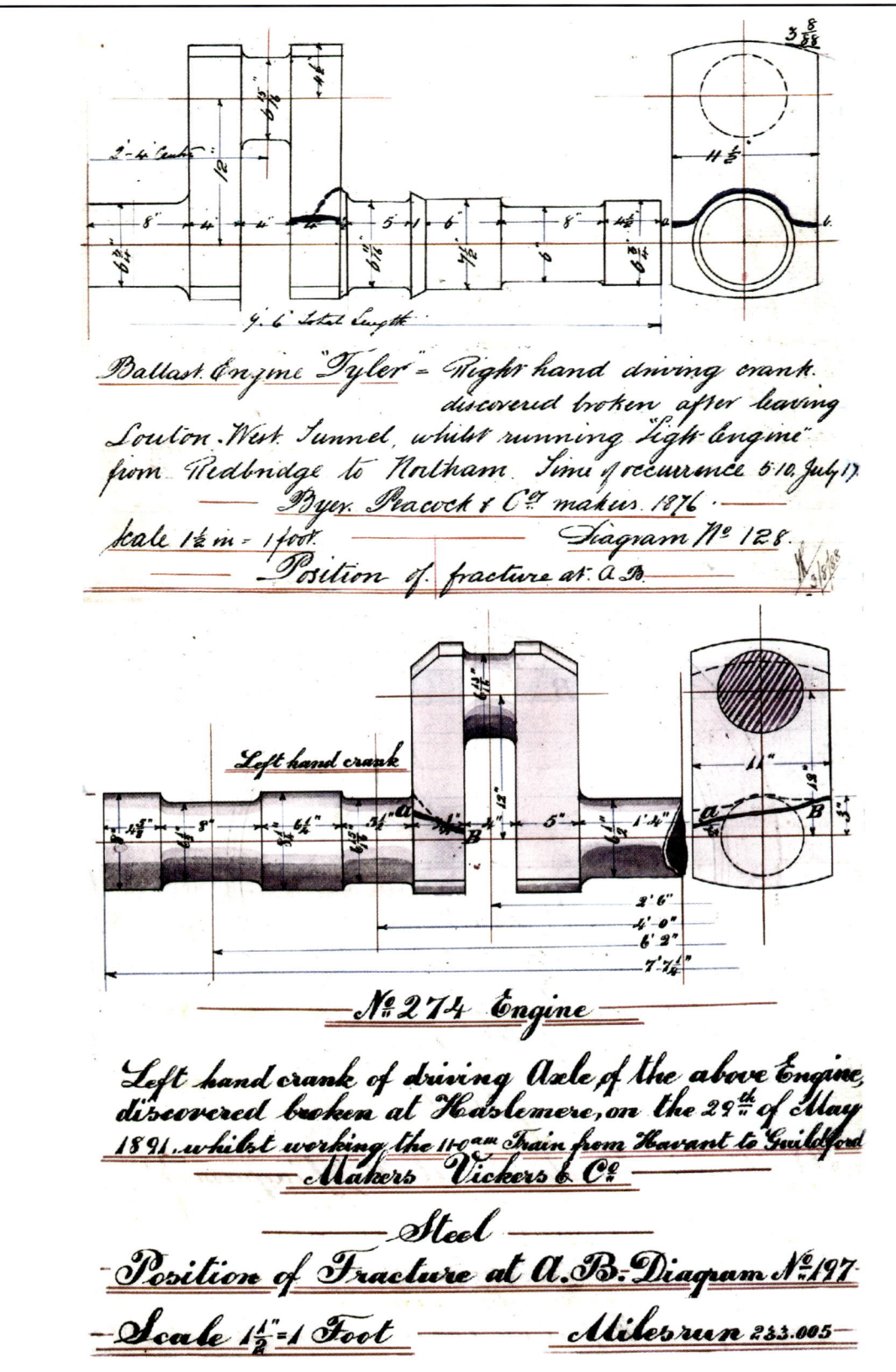

Plate 6. Two drawings of broken locomotive driving axles, from the "Broken Tyres and Axles" record book. The upper one is from an engine "Tyler" operated by the Engineer's Department and described in Chapter 9. The lower one is from the double framed engine No. 274 referred to in Table 6 on Page 27.

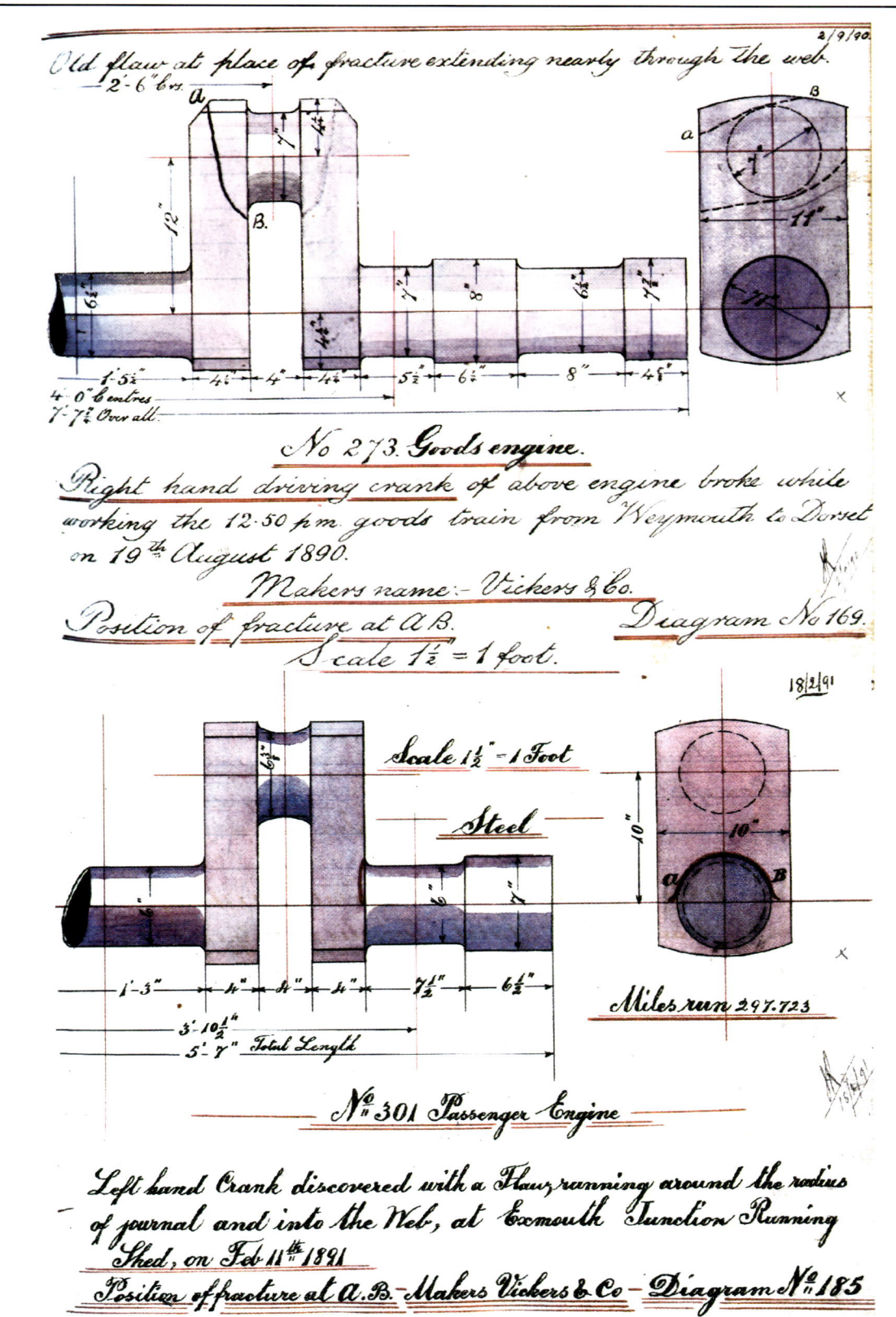

Plate 7. Two more drawings of broken locomotive driving axles. This time the top one is from a double framed goods engine No. 273, see Table 6 on page 27, and the lower one from an "Ilfracombe Goods" engine, No. 301, described in Chapter 7.

Fig. 31.   5048

August 23 1878
Engine "Ariel"
Read report from the Loco: Dept as to the above engine having stopped at Guildford Station with the 5 pm down train on the 4 inst through being short of steam.
Driver Hawkins to be fined 2/6.

Fig. 32.   3939

May 2 1872
Engine for Newport Junction Rly.
Referring to minute of 11th ulto read letter from Mr. Beattie of 13th ulto as to two of this Co's Tank Engines either of which might be hired to the above at the price of £2 per day including Engineman and Fireman, with an option of purchase at the sum of £1000.
Approved

Fig. 33.   4032

August 26 1872
Engine lent to Newport Junction Railway Co.
Referring to Locomotive Committee Minute of 2nd May 1872 upon the report of Mr. Scott that in all probability the Engine lent to the Newport Junction Company would not be required by them for some time, and was now standing in a position exposed to the weather: it was ordered that Mr. Beattie be requested to obtain its return from the Newport Junction Company.
A letter to be written by the Secretary to the Secretary of that Company to the above effect.

Fig. 34.   4990

June 17 1875
Engine for Ryde & Newport Rly.
Mr. Scott reported an application from Mr. Young for two of this Company's Locomotive Engines suitable for working the above new line, and it was agreed that 2 tank Engines may be sold at a price to be fixed by Mr. Beattie.

and 10, "Chaplin" and "Aurora" of the Chaplin class in Table 5. It had been proposed that these engines be used on the Ryde and Newport Railway (Isle of Wight). However, the information provided by the normally reliable D. L. Bradley appears to conflict in reports given in several documents. The two locomotives were never actually used on the Isle of Wight. In one report they reached the island, but the engineer there realised that owing to the provision of outside cylinders, they would foul the loading gauge, and they were therefore returned to the mainland. Another report said the railway's engineers inspected the engines (at Nine Elms?) and decided they were "obviously worn out and weak machines" and rejected them. Another cause of conflict is another report from the same source that Aurora's boiler was severely damaged as a result of the fire being lit with no water in it, and was condemned on the 17th January 1872. It is possible that the second locomotive was, in fact, the third in the class, referred to as number 34 "Osprey" which lasted until 1875, but we have no proof.

A mention of boiler feed arrangements would be appropriate here. Boiler feeds are of two types, solid and liquid. Dealing with the solids first, when steam engines began to be introduced complaints were raised regarding the smoke produced by their chimneys; as a result, a law was enacted which required that all steam engines must "consume their own smoke". This was achieved initially by the use of coke as the solid fuel. In the process of making "coal gas" (which was used throughout the country up until the time that it was replaced by North Sea gas), coal was roasted and mixed with water in such a manner that hydrogen and carbon monoxide were obtained, these constituents forming the main components in coal "town" gas. As a result of this process the coal is turned into coke, having had all of its volatile components driven off. Subsequently burning it in a steam engine boiler produced little smoke, and the law was obeyed.

The problems started to arise as the number of steam engines rose, but the supply of coke remained static, demand began to exceed supply and the price rose as a result. Coal was then a much cheaper fuel, as the supply was almost unlimited, and labour cheap. There were a number of schemes devised to solve the problem. Joseph Beattie designed a special "double" coal burning firebox, which was initially installed on one of John Gooch's Etna Class locomotives, No 122, "Brittania" in 1853. Details of the firebox are shown in the drawing of Beattie's locomotive No 43 "Milo" in Figure 128, and also in Figure 60 for an engine of the "Clyde" class. The firebox is divided into two sections by means of a sloping hollow *divisor* placed across the firebox through which water flows, in order both to

LOCOMOTIVE PROCUREMENT 1850-1871

Fig. 35.

Engine No. 41, "Ajax" of the Hercules class with triple feed-water heater tubes in front of the chimney.

(HMRS)

cool it and to enhance circulation. Although not shown in the drawing it would have to contain stays in order to prevent explosion by boiler pressure into the firebox. There is a shorter, similar, vertical divisor in the roof of the firebox. With this arrangement two fireholes are provided, a lower one to supply the lower, rear section of the firebox, another, upper one to supply the forward section which leads to the boiler tubes, sometimes via a combustion chamber. These fireboxes were employed from about 1850 to the time William Adams arrived on the scene, although there were various modifications to the design including combustion chambers with tubeplates at each end, and the use of firebricks to conserve heat in the forward box.

The idea behind the design of this firebox is that although coal is fired to both sections via their respective fireholes, the forward section quickly becomes much hotter as a result of the heat and fumes from the rear section, and behaves as a coke fire, burning both its own volatile products and those from the rear section. This is aided by the combustion chamber, where fitted, as the fumes have further time to burn before being cooled by the boiler tubes. The main problems with these arrangements resulted from maintenance difficulties. It is easy to see from the diagram how difficult stay replacement would be with the restricted space available within the firebox. J. Cudworth of the South Eastern Railway produced his own design of firebox to achieve similar smoke-reducing results, and comparative trials were organised in 1870 to determine whether either design was superior, but there appeared to be little difference between their performance.

As previously mentioned, William Adams removed these fireboxes over a period of time, Figure 129 shows the same locomotive with a standard pattern firebox, which was fitted sometime between 1879 and 1886. The reason why it became unnecessary to employ the complicated arrangement of Joseph Beattie is due to a number of reasons. Firstly, enthusiasm for applying the law had probably subsided. Secondly, the combined effect of using a brick arch in front of the tubeplate, and a firehole deflector plate to deflect "top" air from the firehole downwards onto the hot fire resulted in better combustion. Thirdly, there were better quality "steam" coals available that burnt at a higher temperature and produced less smoke anyway.

Turning to the subject of liquid feeds, or water, it was soon realised that the venting of exhaust steam to the atmosphere was wasteful both in terms of heat loss and water loss. A condensing type system was designed around 1850 whereby exhaust steam was fed via a jet into a chamber, or chambers, and mixed with water from the storage tank. Water from the tank was pumped by either a "donkey" pump, with its own steam cylinder, or pumps actuated by either the valve motion eccentrics or the piston cross-head, and the warmed supply water with condensed exhaust steam was forced into the boiler. (I do not know how the pressure conditions within the system were arranged, so I cannot describe how it operated in further detail.) There was a two-way valve mounted on the side of the boiler towards the front, apparently to permit direct pumping of cold water into the boiler without using the condensing facility.

There were versions of the system using 1, 2, or 3 chambers arranged across the smokebox in front of

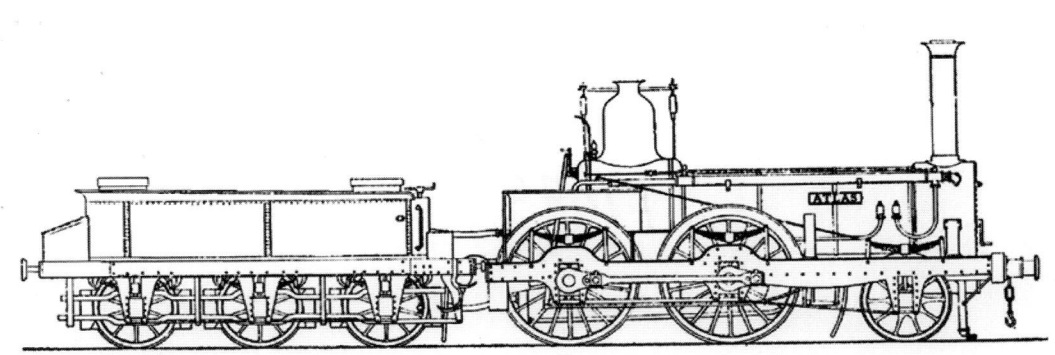

Fig. 36. Engine No 42 "Atlas" of the Hercules class.

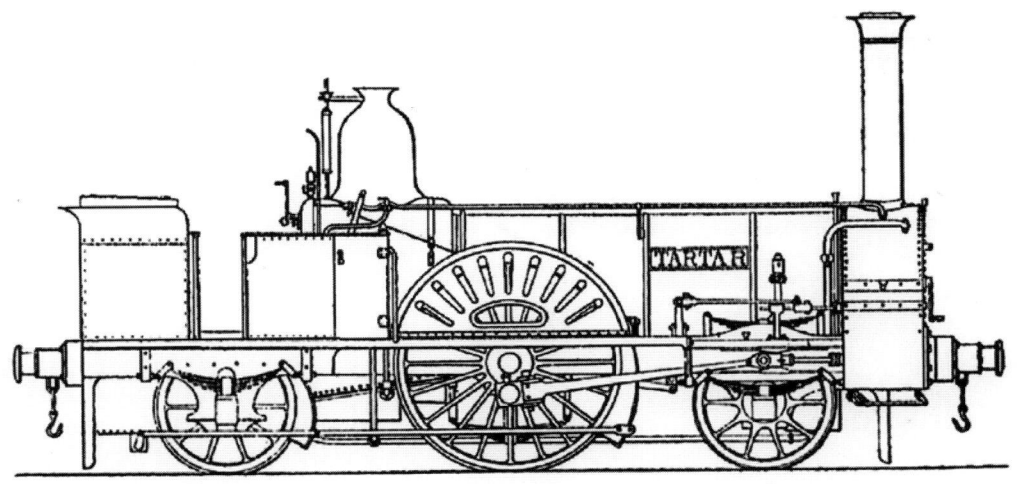

Fig. 37 - above. Engine No 2, "Tartar", of that class.
Fig. 38 - below. Diagram of Engine No 1, "Sussex", of that class.

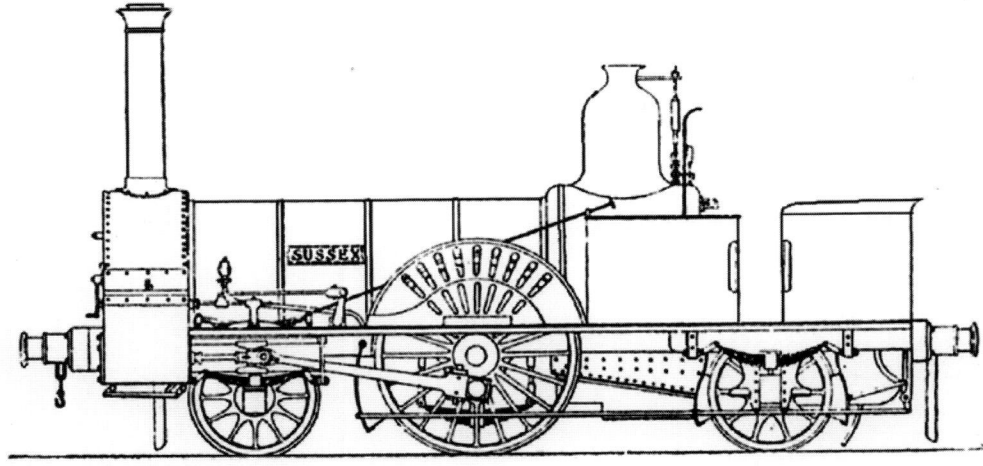

LOCOMOTIVE PROCUREMENT 1850 -1871

Fig. 39.

An early photograph of engine No 1, "Sussex", of that class taken at Gosport. Circa 1859.

the chimney. The single version in some applications gave the impression of a secondary, smaller chimney and was sometimes referred to as a "pup" chimney as shown in Figures 73 and 76. There are smaller versions in Figures 48, 56, and 57. A two-pipe version is shown in Figure 72, and a three-pipe version in Figure 35.

There was always a problem with this system. Oil was injected into the steam supply to the cylinders to lubricate them and the valves and associated parts. The system is known as "total loss lubrication" which means that unused oil remains in the steam all the way to the exhaust, where it becomes mixed with the supply water and enters the boiler. Oil is very harmful on the inside of a boiler as it can coat the waterside of the firebox. This can result in a thermal insulating layer being developed, which prevents the water from cooling the firebox plates, leading to cracking and eventually to failure. Also it is thought that the firebox temperature breaks down the oil and produces corrosive products further accelerating failure.

As a result the condensing type conservation systems were gradually removed and new tubular concentric heat exchangers substituted in old engines, and installed in some new ones. In these the exhaust steam merely warmed the feedwater, and was not allowed to mix with it. These devices can be seen running lengthwise along the boiler entering into the smokebox, just below the base of the chimney, in Figures 36, 50, 52, 53, 55, 59, 74, 89, and 105. These devices lasted until around 1880, and injectors began to be introduced around 1870. They could fill the boiler using live steam without the disadvantage of involving moving parts that used up energy, and required more maintenance. In addition the type of pump that was connected to the eccentrics, or to the piston crosshead, often caused trouble in cold weather, because they were always full of water, and if they froze, the engine could not be moved, even with another engine. Also if no "donkey" pump was provided, the engine's boiler could only be replenished by running it up and down the track. The disadvantage of injectors is that they become less efficient as the supply water temperature is raised, eventually, at a given temperature, stopping altogether. This was the death knell to feedwater heaters, and they were all removed by 1882. For a number of years from about 1870 to 1880, some locomotives were equipped with feedwater heaters, using mechanical pumps, and an injector which used unheated water. (W. G. Beattie's "348" class, produced by Sharp Stewart & Co. for example.)

THE LSWR AT NINE ELMS

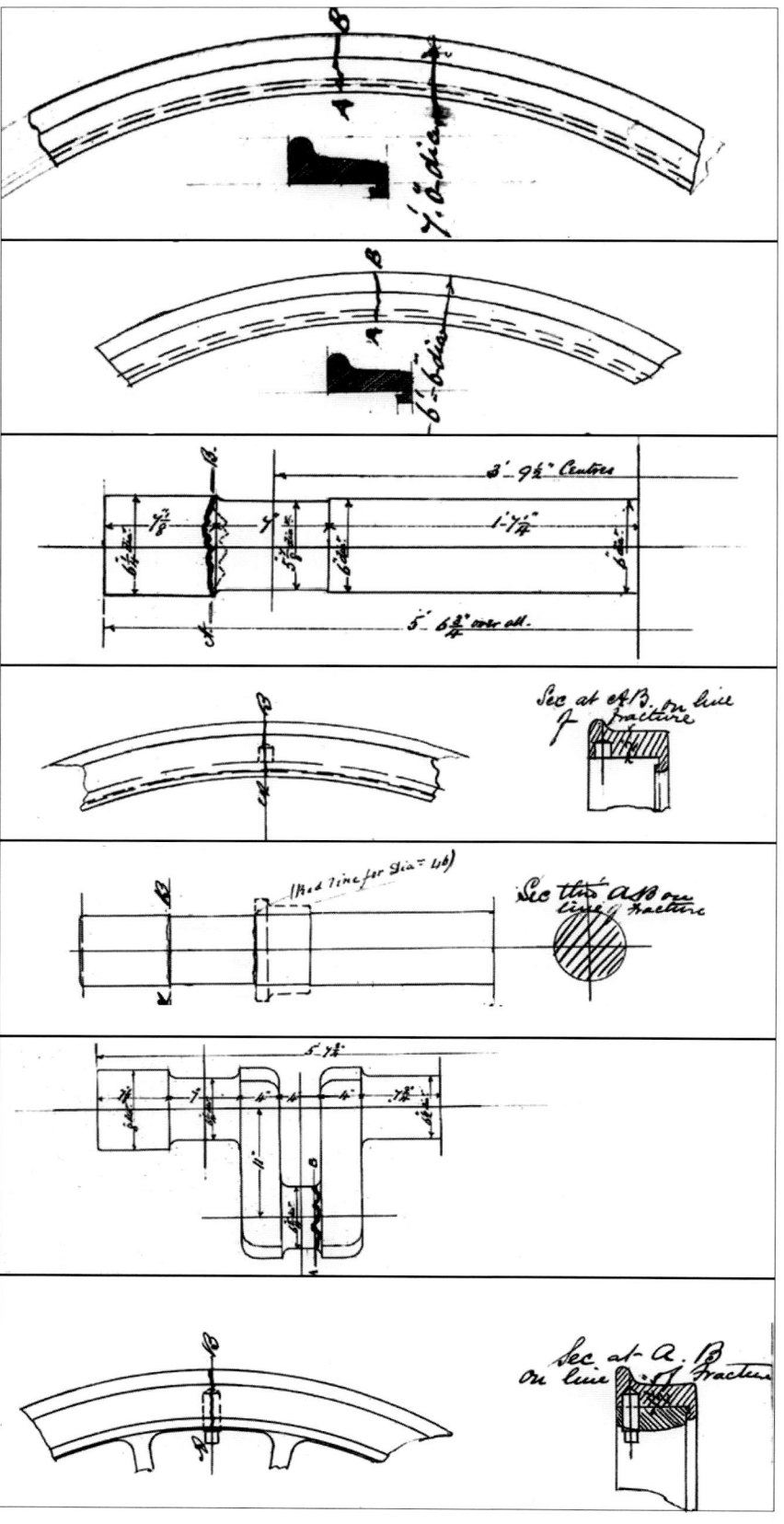

Note: In the following diagrams, the line 'A-B' indicated the position of the fracture.

Fig. 40. Steel tyre of Clyde class engine No 159, fractured at Downton whilst working 1.10 pm train from Weymouth to Salisbury, 12th September 1879.

Fig. 41. Steel tyre of Undine class engine No 164, discovered broken in shed at Dorchester, 5th September 1879.

Fig. 42. Iron driving axle of Canute class engine No 153 broken when starting from Southampton with the 9.30 pm train to Winchester, 18th August 1879.

Fig. 43. Left driving wheel of Undine class engine, No 165, found on arrival at Waterloo after having been empty stock from Nine Elms, 19th August 1878.

Fig. 44. Broken trailing axle of Standard Well Tank, No 202, failed 9th December 1878 whilst going from shed road to coal road (at Nine Elms?). Steel axle made by Beyer Peacock & Co. 'Not reported to Board of Trade'.

Fig. 45. Crank axle of Lion class engine No 272 broken whilst coming from Southampton with an up goods train, 10th June 1879.

Fig. 46. Left trailing wheel - tyre and rim, of Standard Well Tank, No 245 broken on arrival at Kingston with the 6.50 am train from Waterloo, 11th June 1878.

LOCOMOTIVE PROCUREMENT 1850 -1871

Fig. 47. Photograph of engine, No 31, "Leeds" of the Hercules class with larger than original dome and closed wheel splashers.

Fig. 48. Photograph of engine No 26, "Gazelle" of the Hercules class with feedwater heater, otherwise in original condition.

THE LSWR AT NINE ELMS

Fig. 49. Photograph of engine No 2, "Tartar" of that class in original condition.

LOCOMOTIVE PROCUREMENT 1850 -1871

Fig 50. Photograph of engine No 128, "Samson" of the Saxon class, with original weatherboard and feedwater heater.

Fig. 51. Photograph of engine No 129, "Albion" of the Saxon class, fitted with the luxury of a cab.

THE LSWR AT NINE ELMS

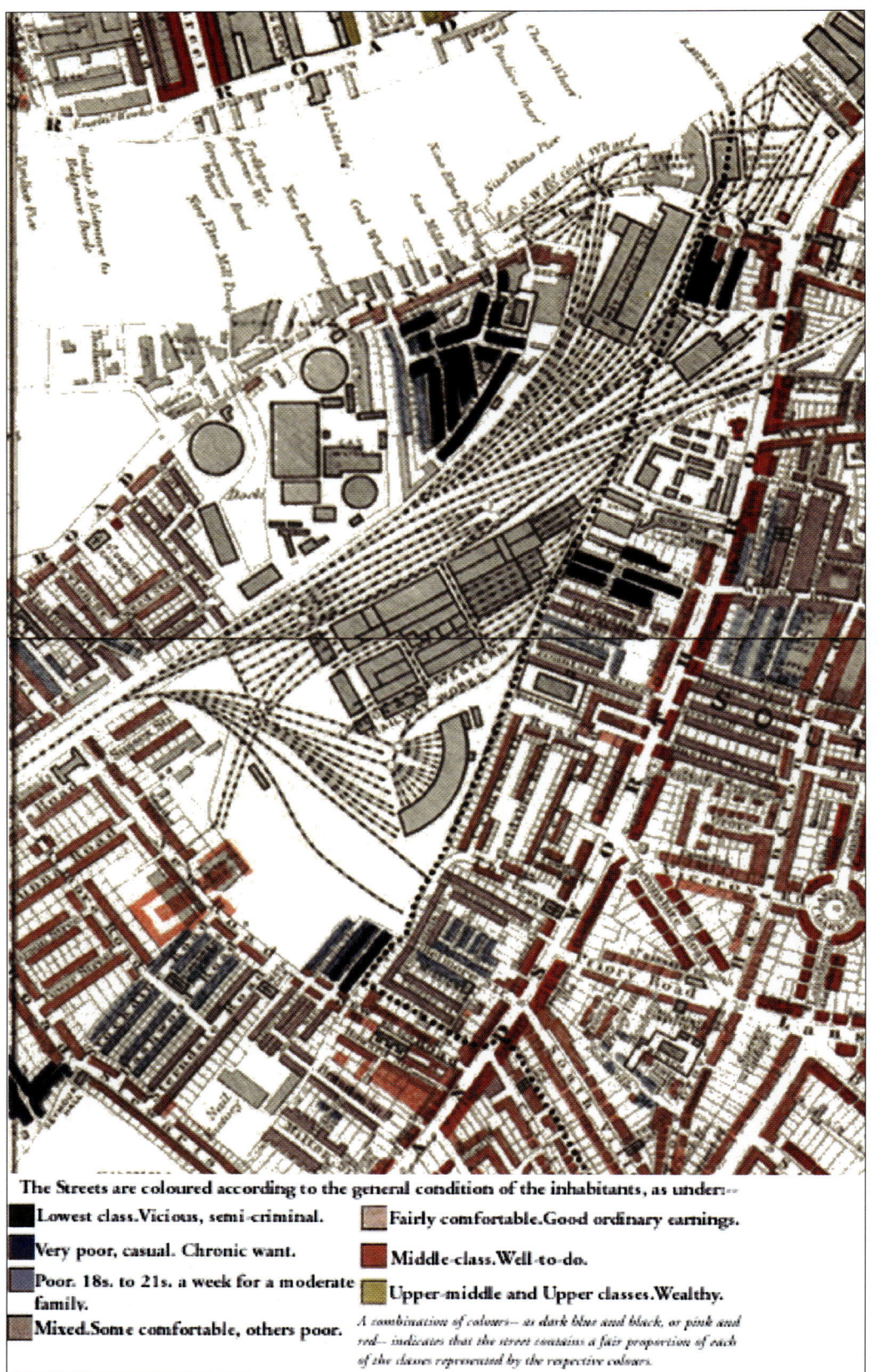

Plate 8. A section of "Booth's Poverty Map" of London, showing the Nine Elms site in 1876/7.

LOCOMOTIVE PROCUREMENT 1850-1871

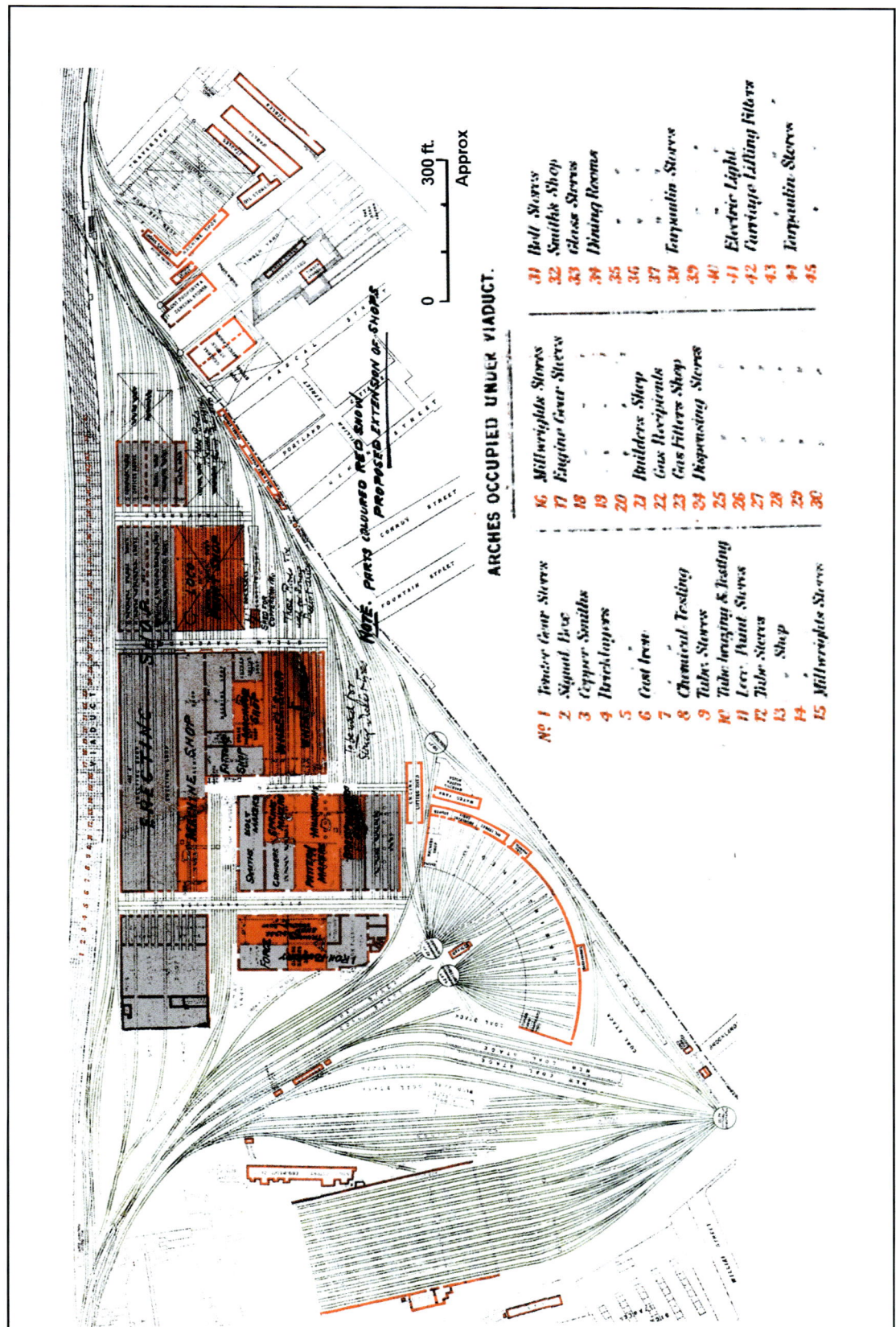

Plate 9. 1889 map of the Nine Elms Works showing, in red in-fill, the alterations proposed to be made consequent upon the move of the Carriage and Wagon Department to its new premises at Eastleigh. In addition, the proposed extension of the erecting shop into the next building on the right is depicted as a greyed-in area.

Fig. 52 - left. Photograph of engine No 151, "Montrose" of the Canute class with no lock-up safety valve, and tubular feedwater heater still in place.

Fig. 53 - centre. Photograph of engine No. 130 "Harold" of the Canute class, circa 1868, with lock-up safety valve on front boiler ring and tubular feedwater heater still in place.

Fig. 54 - bottom. Photograph of engine No 153, "Victoria" of the Canute class after reboilering with a lock-up safety valve on the centre ring and the addition of a cab, taken at Northam depot in the early 1880s. (HMRS)

LOCOMOTIVE PROCUREMENT 1850-1871

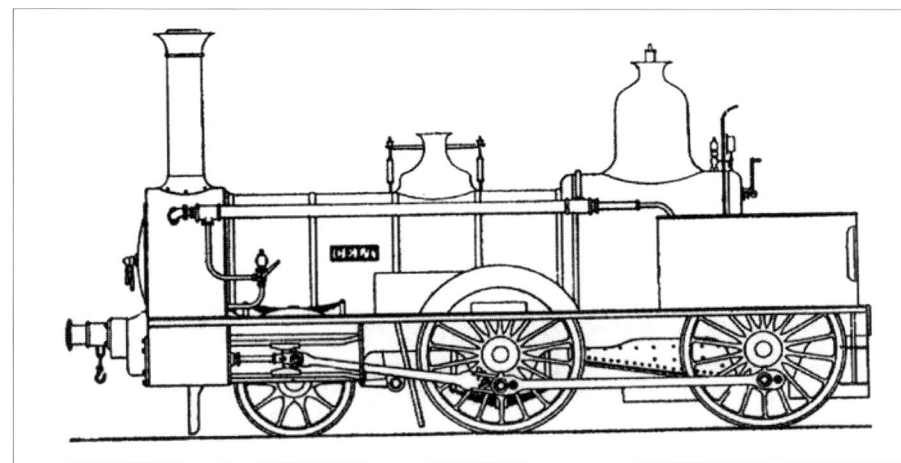

Fig 55. Diagram of engine No 141, "Celt" of the Saxon class.

Fig. 56. Diagram of engine No 135, "Canute" of that class.
(Dendy–Marshall)

Fig. 57. Drawing of engine No 135, "Canute". (Hamilton-Ellis, by permission of Tothill Press.)

THE LSWR AT NINE ELMS

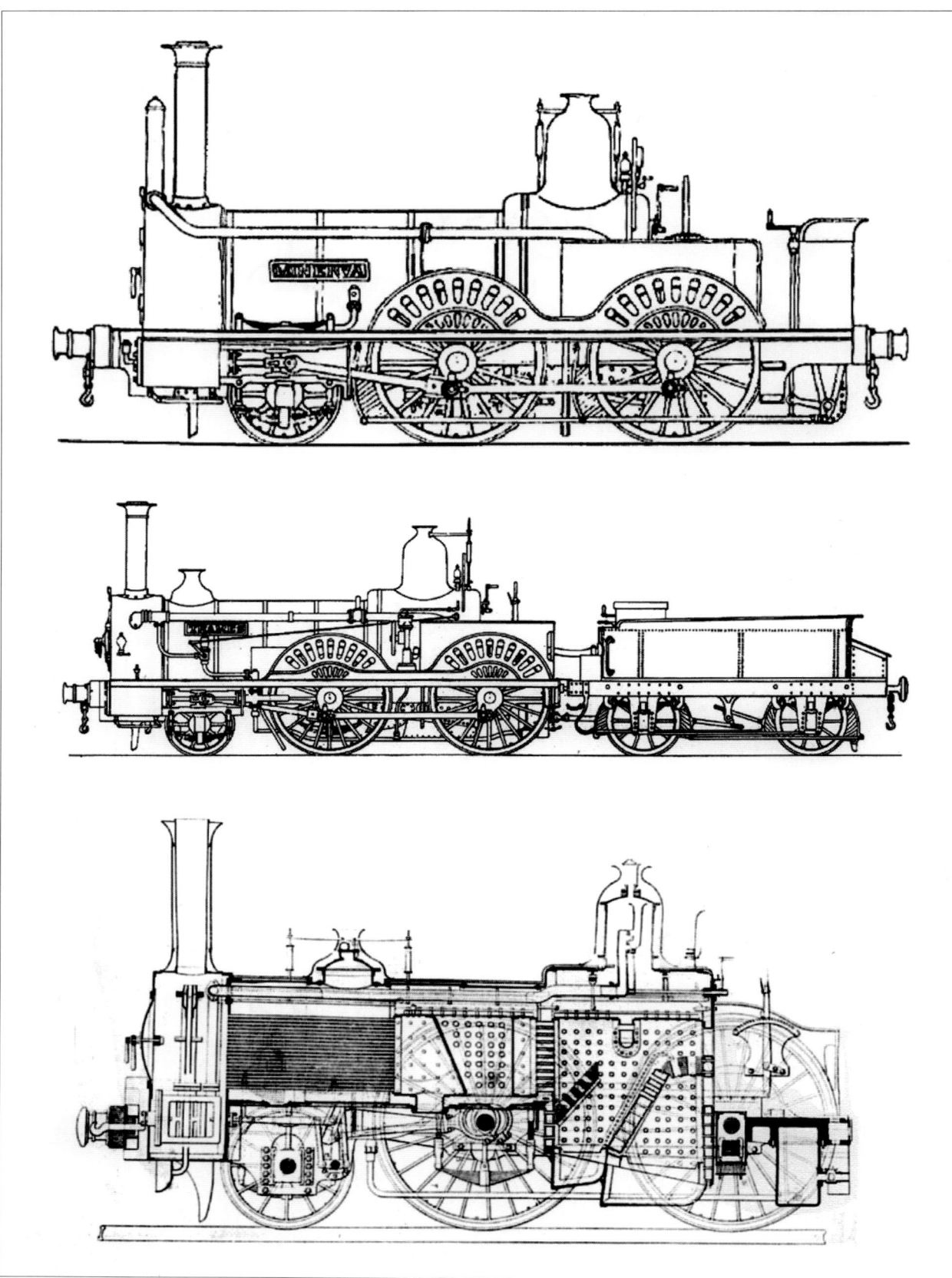

LOCOMOTIVE PROCUREMENT 1850 -1871

Fig. 61. Photograph of engine No 163, "Circe" of the Undine class, with replacement boiler and no feedwater heater. Fitted with Adams chimney, and recorded at Northam depot in the early 1880s.

Opposite page:

Fig. 58 - top. Diagram of engine No 11, "Minerva" of that class.
Fig. 59 - centre. Diagram of engine No 146, "Thames" of the Tweed class.
Fig. 60 - bottom. Cross sectional diagram of an engine of the Clyde class showing the special firebox arrangement designed by Joseph Beattie for burning coal instead of coke. (Dendy-Marshall)

June 4 1872.   3970
'J. Stanley' Driver.
Reports were submitted as to the above man having allowed Mr. Slade, Booking Clerk at Kew Gardens Station, to ride with him on the Engine of the 7.12pm Ludgate Hill train on the 16th ulto, without cause, upon which it was ordered that 'Stanley' and 'Slade' be fined 3/- each.

September 12 1872.   4058
Narrow escape from Collision at Micheldever, 20 August 1872.
Read Minute of Officers Committee of 9 inst, recommending that a reward of 10/- be given to Driver 'Chivers' for his praiseworthy conduct on the above occasion. (No other details appear elsewhere.)

October 27 1873.   4407
Nine Elms.
Read report from the Loco. Dept as to the Shunting Engine having come into collision with a Goods train when leaving the above Yard on the 10th inst.
'Laing' Driver of the Shunting Engine to be fined 2/6, and a new signal Post with two arms to be put up where the occurrence took place

THE LSWR AT NINE ELMS

Fig. 62. Photograph of Well Tank engine No 143, "Nelson" of that class, in original condition.

LOCOMOTIVE PROCUREMENT 1850-1871

Fig. 63. Photograph of engine No 157, "Clyde", one of the earliest members of that class, taken on the turntable in front of the office block and clock tower at Nine Elms. Circa 1882.

Fig. 64. Photograph of engine No 73, "Fireball", a later member of the Clyde class also taken by the office block. Circa 1882.

Fig. 65. Photograph of engine No. 158 "Lacy", an earlier member of the Clyde class in original condition. Taken in 1863 on the new steam driven traverser installed in the extension to Nine Elms Works, on the south side of the main line. *(Hamilton Ellis)*

Fig. 66. Photograph of the other side of "Lacy" and the traverser. *(HMRS)*

LOCOMOTIVE PROCUREMENT 1850 -1871

Fig. 67- below. Diagram of engine No 156, "Hogue" of the Nile class.

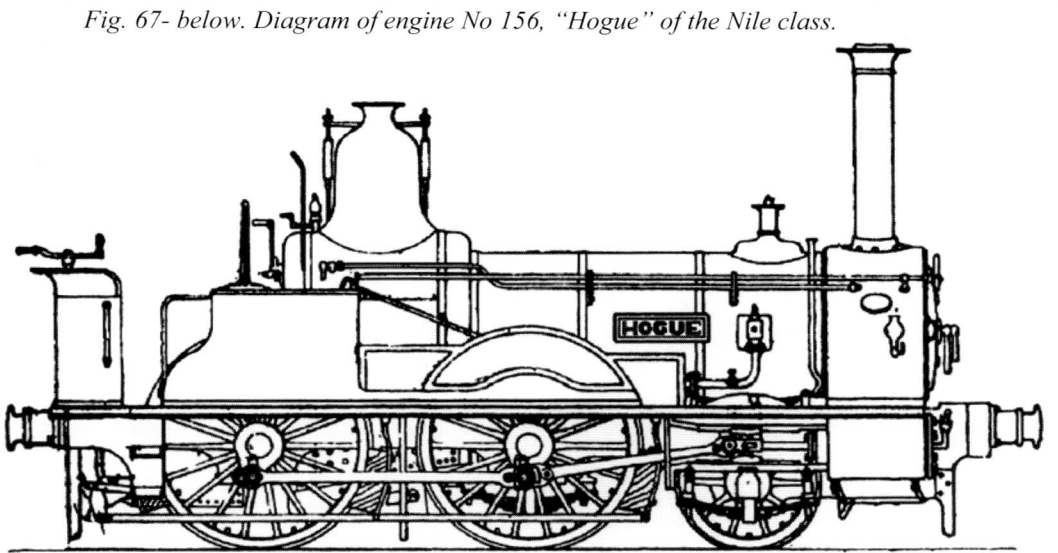

Fig. 68- below. Diagram of engine No 165, "Circe" of the Undine class.

Fig. 69- below. Diagram of engine No 76, "Firefly", the only one of its class.

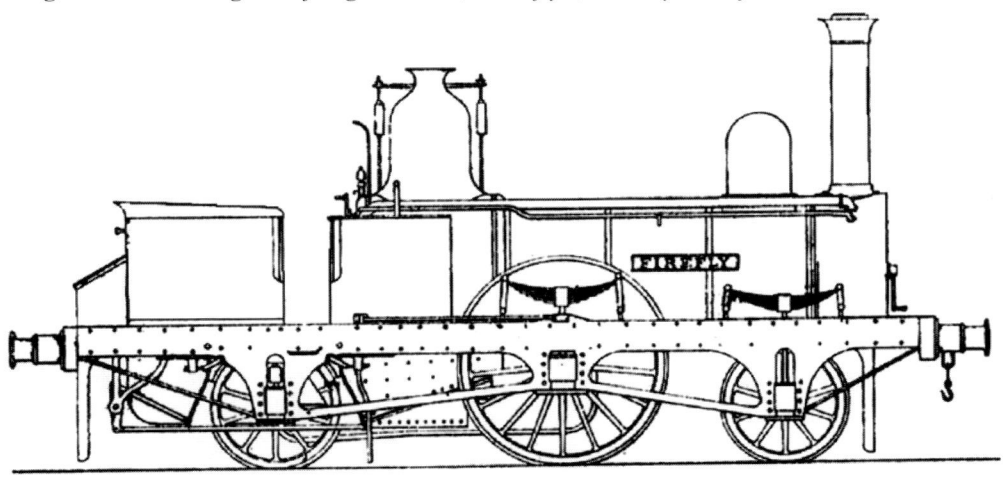

Fig. 70. Photograph of engine No 156, "Hogue", of the Nile class. (HMRS)

Fig. 71. Photograph of engine No 76, "Firefly", the only one in its class and in original condition.

LOCOMOTIVE PROCUREMENT 1850 -1871

Fig. 72. Print from a transparency of engine No 167, "Atlanta" of the Undine class, taken early in its life with double pipe exhaust condenser. Circa 1860.

Fig. 73. Photograph of engine No 30, "Vulture" of the Eagle class, with feedwater heater in front of the chimney. Shown at Exeter, circa 1865.

Fig. 74. Photograph of engine No 70, "Ariel" of the Falcon class, in original condition with concentric tubular feedwater heater.

LOCOMOTIVE PROCUREMENT 1850 -1871

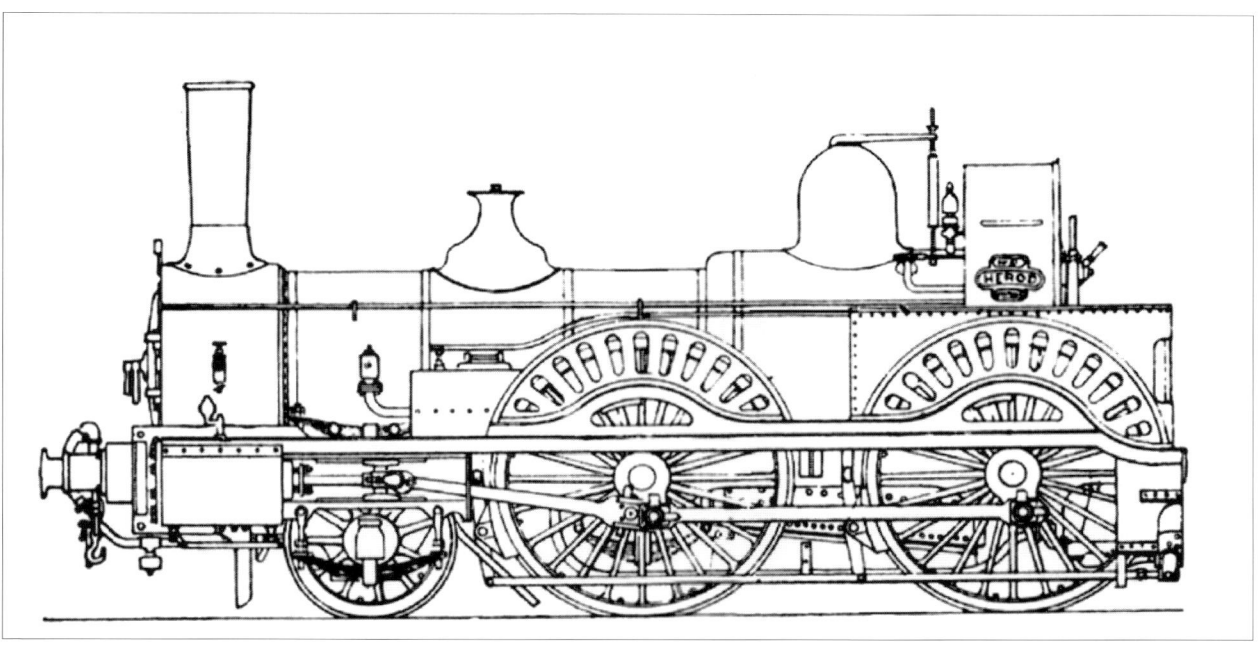

Fig. 75. Diagram of engine No 81, "Herod" of the Falcon class.

Fig. 76. Taken from a painting by Hamilton Ellis of engine No 55, "Medusa", of the Gem class and also other engines as they would have appeared circa 1865. Joseph Beattie is portrayed on the far right, standing next to the artist.

Fig. 77. Photograph of engine No 86, "Shark" of the Falcon class, with Adams stove-pipe chimney. Taken at Nine Elms, circa 1892.

LOCOMOTIVE PROCUREMENT 1850-1871

Fig. 78. Photograph of engine No 80, "Hornet" of the Falcon class with original chimney. Taken by the Nine Elms office block.

THE LSWR AT NINE ELMS

Fig. 79. Photograph of engine No 82, "Sultana" of the Falcon class with original chimney. Taken at Northam depot, circa 1880.

Fig. 80. Photograph of engine No. 83, "Siren" of the Falcon class with Adams stove pipe chimney.

Opposite page:

Fig. 81 top. Diagram of Standard Well Tank engine as originally built by Beyer Peacock & Co.
Fig. 82 bottom. Diagram of Standard Well Tank engine Nos 0298, 0314 and 0329, built by Beyer Peacock & Co, but rebuilt by Adams in the 1890s with new boiler and cab, and used until 1962 on the Bodmin and Wadebridge line in Cornwall.

LOCOMOTIVE PROCUREMENT 1850 -1871

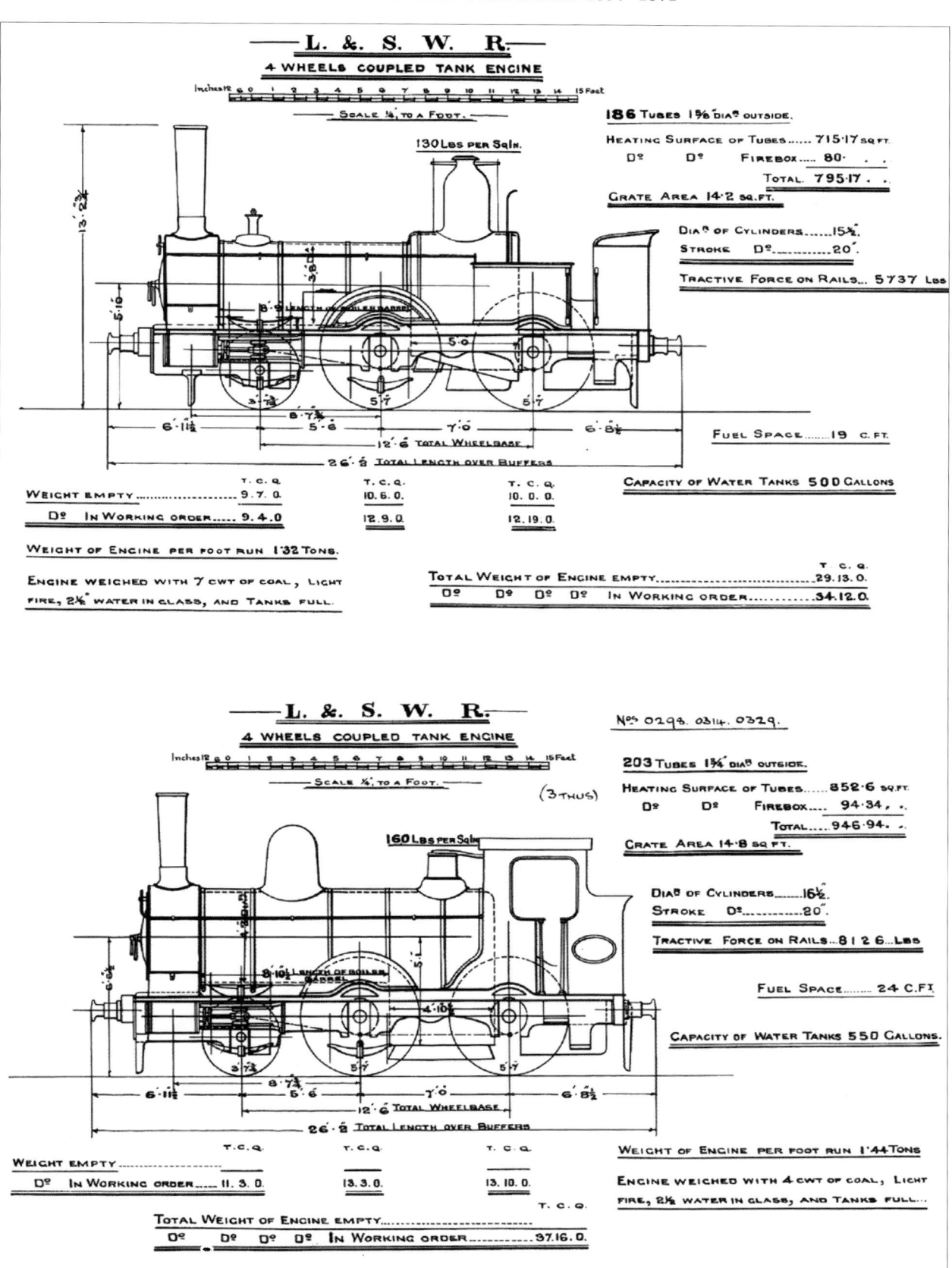

Fig. 83. Photograph of Standard Well Tank engine No 263, with Adams stove-pipe chimney, but retaining donkey and cross-head pumps. Circa 1880.

LOCOMOTIVE PROCUREMENT 1850 -1871

Fig. 84. Photograph of Standard Well Tank engine No 0208, with Adams stove-pipe chimney, but with original boiler and steam-driven donkey pump. Circa 1893.

Fig. 85. Photograph of Standard Well Tank engine No 190, on a train at Addison Road, Kensington.

10 October 1872.   4085
Goods Train fouling Main Line at Woking.
Read Minute of Officers Committee of 30th ulto recommending a fine of 10/- on the Breakman 'Nicholls' and rewards of 10/- to Goods Guard 'Elliott' and 5/- to the Signalman and 5/- to the Engine Driver 'Stockley' for their conduct on the above occasion.

9 December 1872.   4130
'Howe' Engine.
Upon the report of Mr. Beattie it was ordered that a fine of 10/- be inflicted on driver 'Tildsley' for acting contrary to instructions in attempting to repair the above Engine himself instead of obtaining the services of a Fitter.

6 January 1873.   4152
Driver 'Bartlett'
Various reports were submitted as to driver 'Bartlett' having arrived at Exeter Station with the 11.35 am down special train from London on the 24th ulto: 83 minutes late, upon consideration of which it was ordered that he be reduced to a Goods driver for 6 months.

27 October 1873.   4408
Various reports were submitted as to the Turntable in the Loco. Yard at Nine Elms having been damaged on the 17th inst. upon which it was advised that Inspector Hill be fined 10/- and Driver 'H. Compton' and his fireman 'N. Bennett' 5/- each for their carelessness.

LOCOMOTIVE PROCUREMENT 1850 -1871

Fig. 86. Photograph of Standard Well Tank engine No 298, with Adams boiler, cab and stove-pipe chimney. Circa 1898.

Fig. 87. Photograph of Standard Well Tank engine No 3298, with Drummond boiler and chimney. Post 1923.

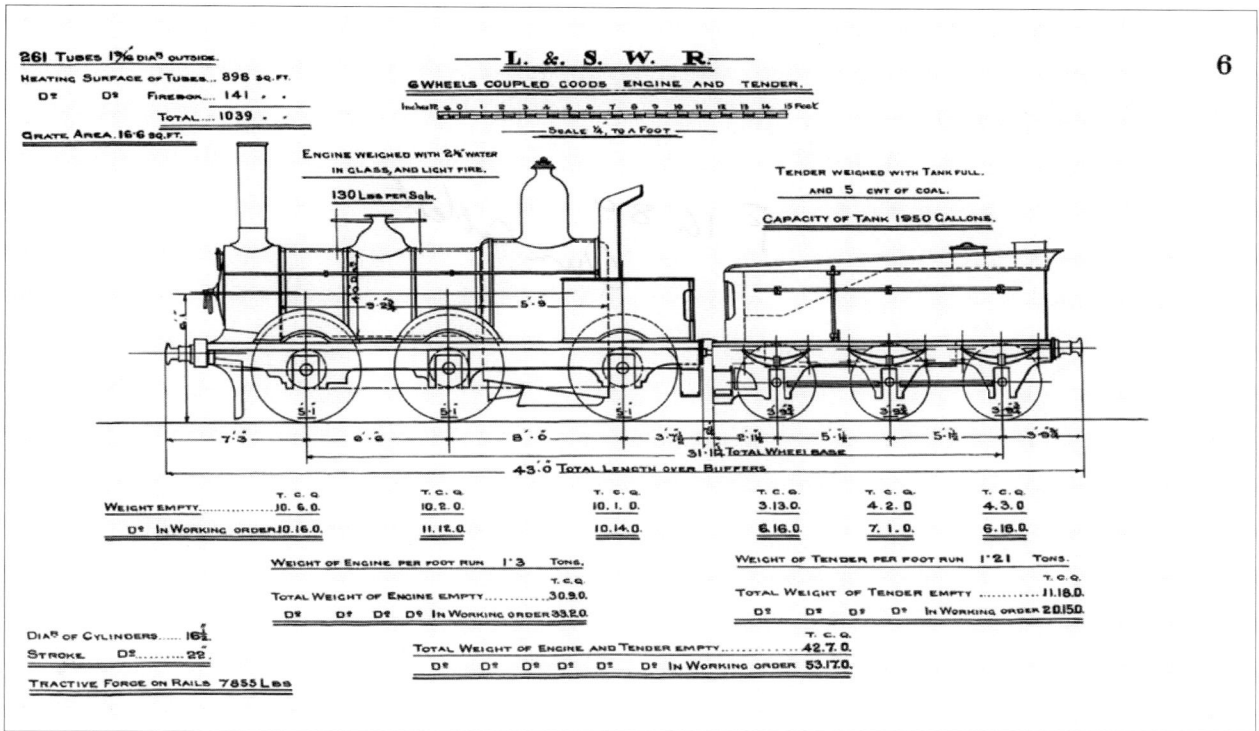

Fig. 88. Diagram of Lion class engine, as originally built.

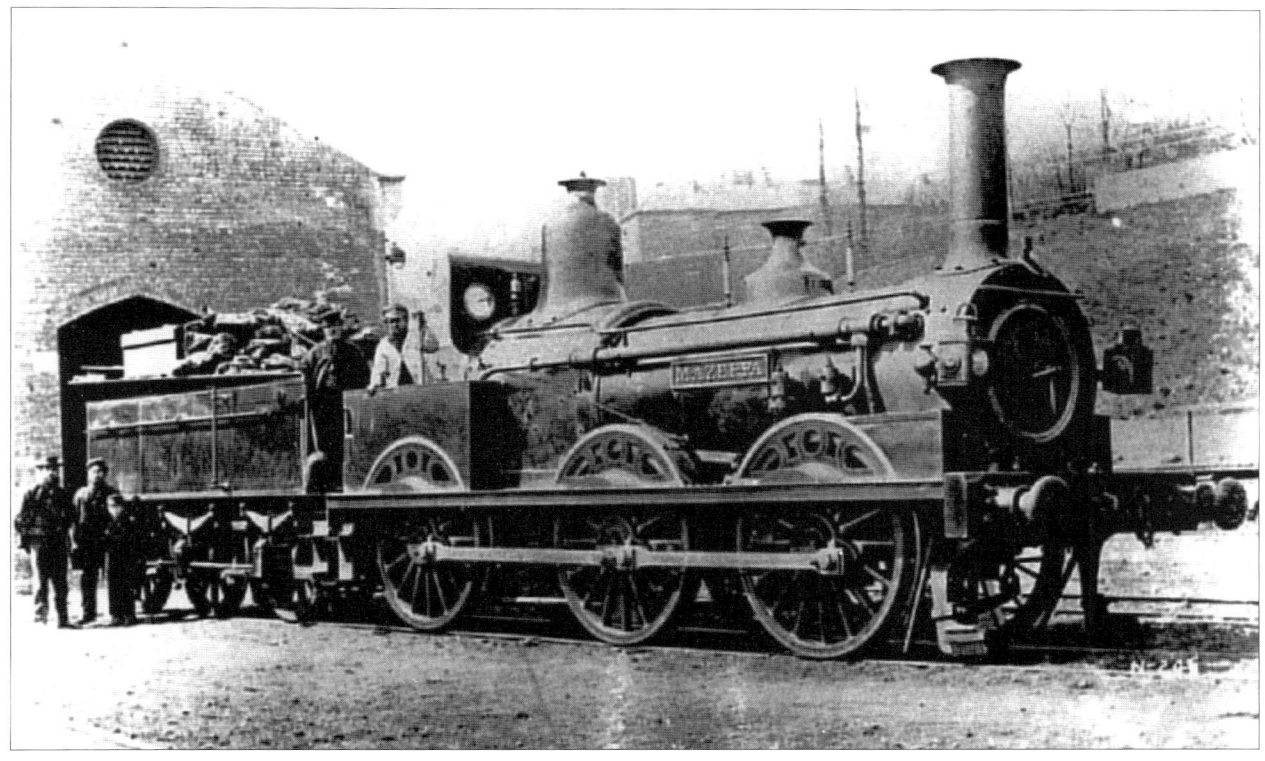

Fig. 89. Photograph of Lion class engine No 53, "Mazeppa", in original condition with snow clearing devices in front of leading wheels and concentric tubular feedwater heater. Taken at Exeter, circa 1870.

Fig. 90. Photograph of Lion class engine No 102, "Lioness" with improved weather board. Taken at Nine Elms.
(HMRS)

Fig. 91. Photograph of Lion class engine No 092, "Charon" with Adams cab, by the Nine Elms office block circa 1900.
(HMRS)

LOCOMOTIVE PROCUREMENT 1850 -1871

Fig. 92. Photograph of Lion class engine No 58, "Sultan" with improved weather board. Recorded at an unknown location, circa 1887.

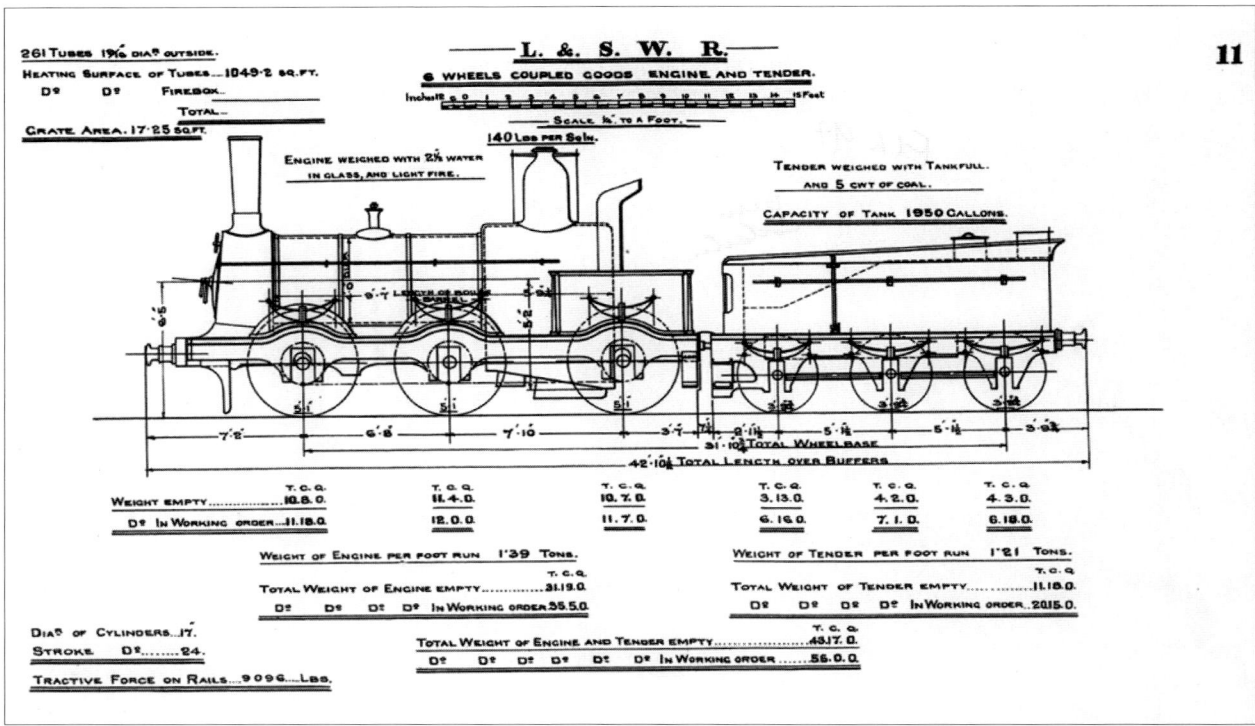

Fig. 93. Diagram of Double Framed Goods engine, applicable to the 1872/3 batch when in original condition.

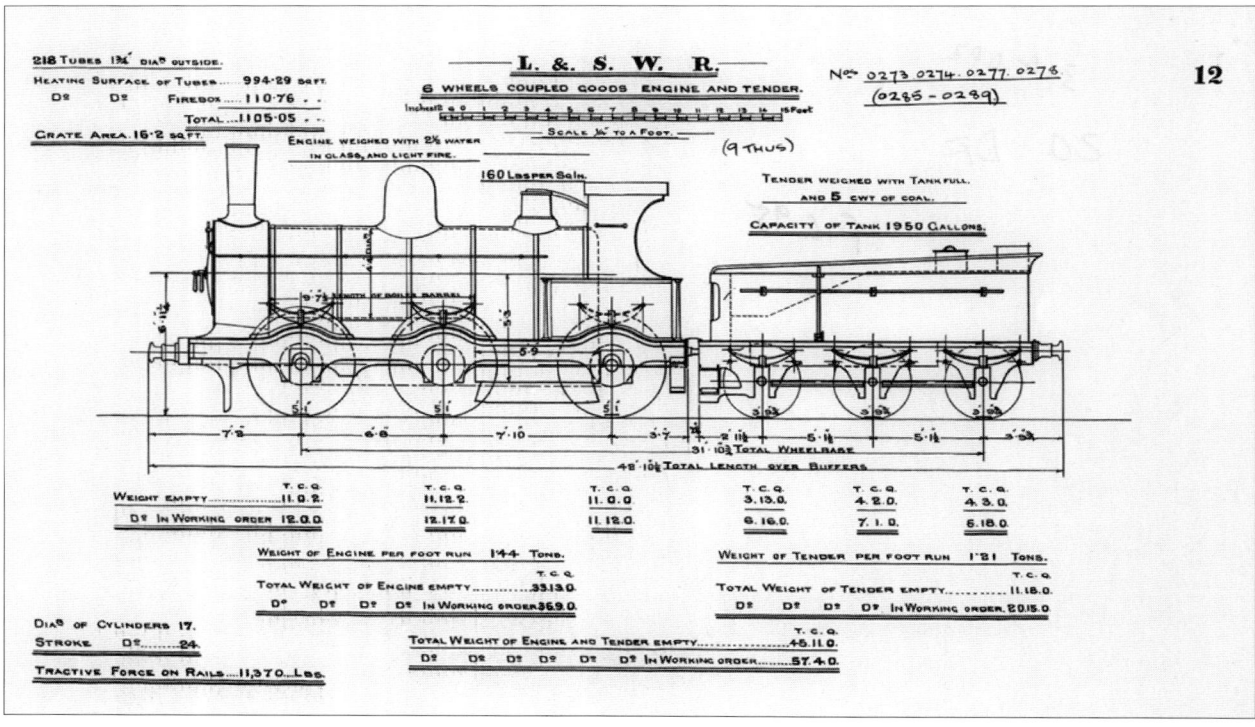

Fig. 94. Diagram of Double Framed Goods engine with Adams boiler and stove-pipe chimney.

LOCOMOTIVE PROCUREMENT 1850 -1871

Fig. 95 top. Beyer Peacock works photograph of Double Framed Goods engine of the 1866/7 batch as originally built with "Colonial" type cab.
Fig. 96 centre. Photograph of Double Framed Goods engine of the 1872 batch as originally built with sloping cab and changed arrangement of dome and safety valve.
Fig. 97 bottom. Photograph of Double Framed Goods engine No 239 with Adams stove-pipe chimney and modified "Colonial" type cab circa 1890.

Fig. 98. Photograph of Double Framed Goods engine No 0351 in Nine Elms Works, July 1906, after being involved in the Salisbury accident.

July 21 1873.   4333
'Perrin' Driver.
Various reports were submitted as to the above man having detached the Engine from his Train on the Crewkerne Incline whereby it ran back a considerable distance before being stopped.
This appears to have arisen in consequence of 'Perrin' having left Yeovil Junction short of water and upon consideration of the whole matter it was ordered that he be reduced to the lowest grade of Driver.

February 2 1874.   4506
'Potter' Engine Driver.
Upon the report of Mr. Beattie that a series of complaints had lately been made against this man for losing time in the working of trains on the Direct Portsmouth Line, he was instructed to find another place for 'Potter' on a branch line.

June 22 1874.   4642
'Sherwood' Driver.
Read report from Mr. Anwell of the 16th inst as to the above man having caused damage to his Engine through allowing the Fire Box to be short of water.
'Sherwood' to forfeit half his Security money. (£2.10.0) Fine equal to 20/1.

July 20 1874.   4673
'Barnett' Driver & 'Ballard' Fireman.
Various reports were submitted as to the above men fighting in the Yard at Nine Elms on the 15th inst upon which it was ordered that 'Barnett' be fined 20/- and 'Ballard' 10/-.

LOCOMOTIVE PROCUREMENT 1850 -1871

Fig. 99. Photograph of Double Framed Goods engine No 277, with Adams boiler and round-windowed cab, circa 1898.

THE LSWR AT NINE ELMS

Fig. 100. Photograph of Double Framed Goods engine No 286, with Adams boiler and square-windowed cab on Nine Elms turntable, circa 1898.

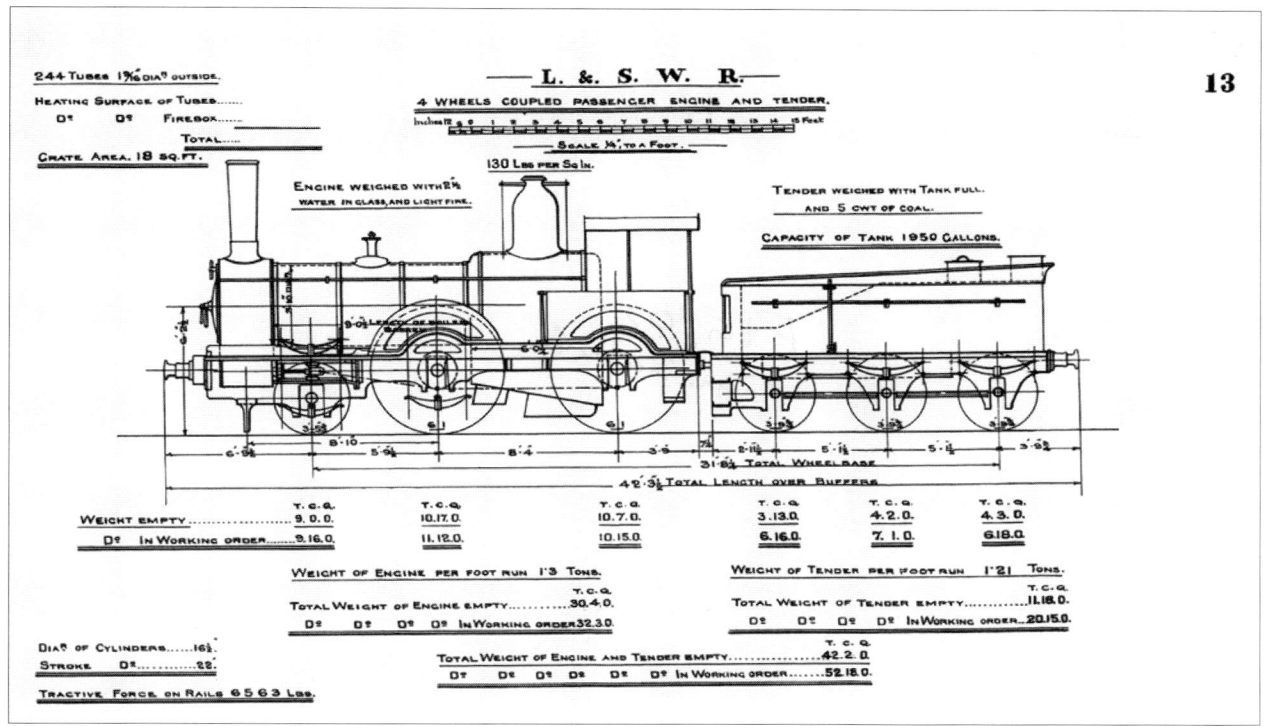

Fig. 101. Diagram of 231 class engine in original form with "Colonial" type cab.

Fig. 102. Photograph of engine No 231, of that class, in original form.

THE LSWR AT NINE ELMS

Fig. 103. Engine No 0236 of the 231 class at Northam on a Salisbury to Southampton Docks train via Eastleigh, circa 1897. The stock commences with a 30ft Third, then three four-wheeled Composites of the 1870s, a 30ft Third, 22ft Passenger Brake Van and a short Open Carriage Truck.

LOCOMOTIVE PROCUREMENT 1850 -1871

Fig. 104. Photograph of engine No 231 of that class with Adams chimney and replacement cab. Circa 1890.

THE LSWR AT NINE ELMS

Fig. 105. Photograph of engine No 90, "Sybil", of the Volcano class as originally built with concentric tubular feedwater heater.

Fig. 106. Photograph of engine No 23, "Reindeer" of the Volcano class as originally built, but showing the closed splashers and longer side-sheets of the 1867 batch. Circa 1880. (HMRS)

Fig. 107. Photograph of engine No 89, "Saturn" of the Volcano class by the Nine Elms office block. The view shows the engine in original condition, but depicts the open splashers and standard side-sheets of the 1867 batch. Circa 1880. (HMRS)

Fig. 108. Photograph of engine No 61, "Snake" of the Volcano class by the Nine Elms office block showing the open splashers and standard side-sheets of the 1867 batch but with Adams stove-pipe chimney. Circa 1885. (HMRS)

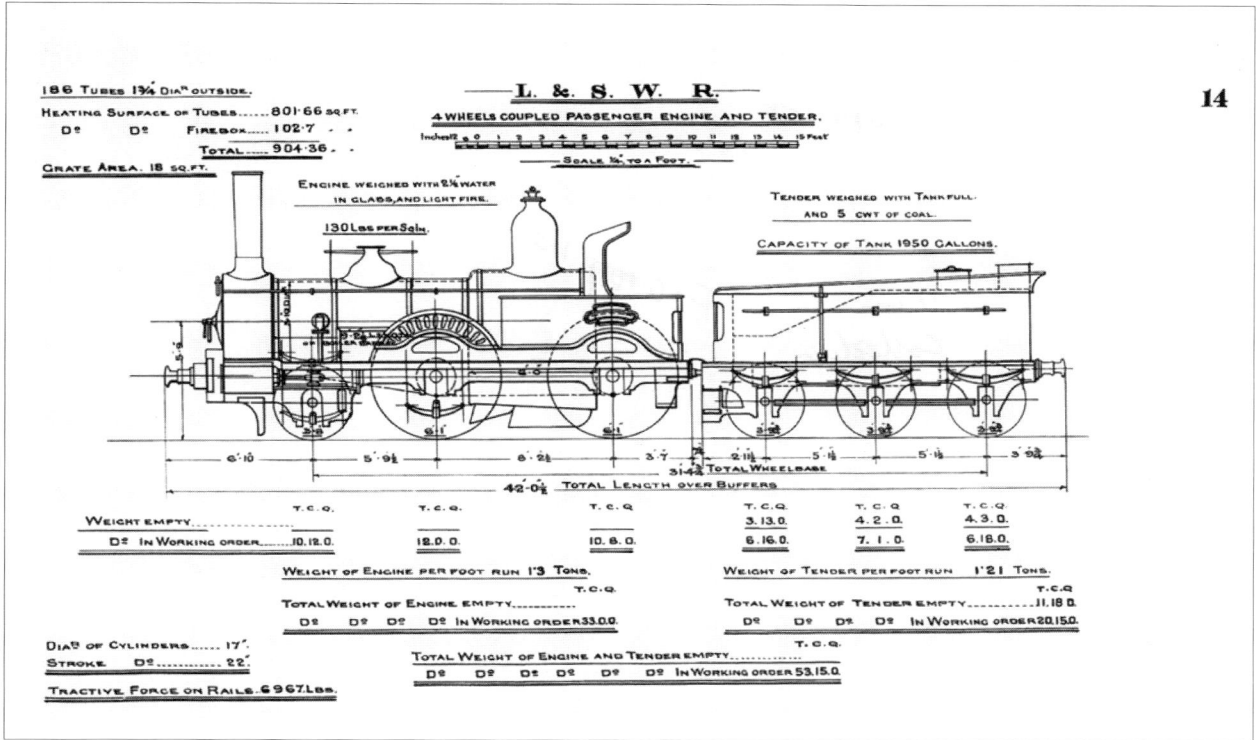

Fig. 109. Diagram of earlier version of the Volcano class with open splashers, as originally built.

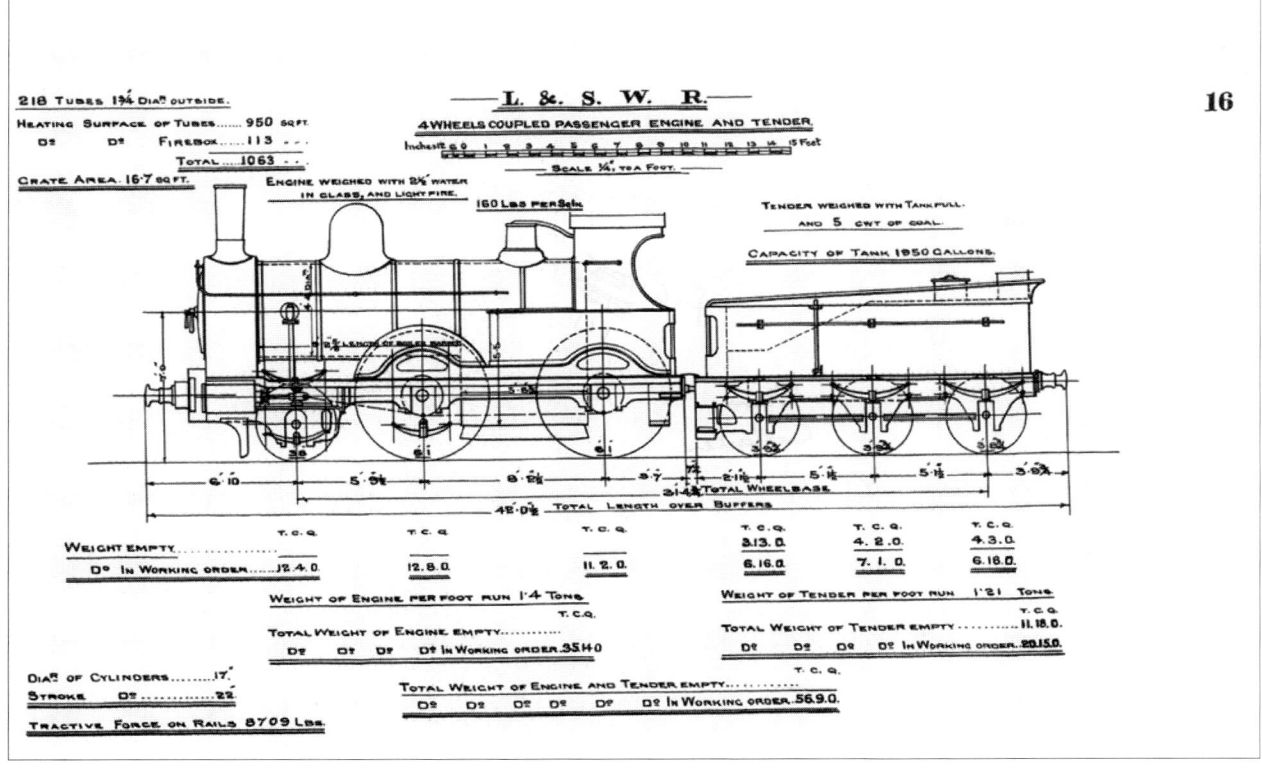

Fig. 110. Diagram of Volcano class engine with Adams boiler and cab.

THE LSWR AT NINE ELMS

Fig. 111. Photograph of engine No 116, "Stromboli" of the Volcano class, with Adams boiler, cab and stove-pipe chimney, circa 1888.

LOCOMOTIVE PROCUREMENT 1850 -1871

Fig. 112. Photograph of engine No 99, "Phlegon" of the Centaur class with original boiler but with Adams stove-pipe chimney, circa 1895.

THE LSWR AT NINE ELMS

Fig. 113. Photograph of engine No 99, "Phlegon" of the Centaur class with original boiler but with Adams stove-pipe chimney, circa 1895.

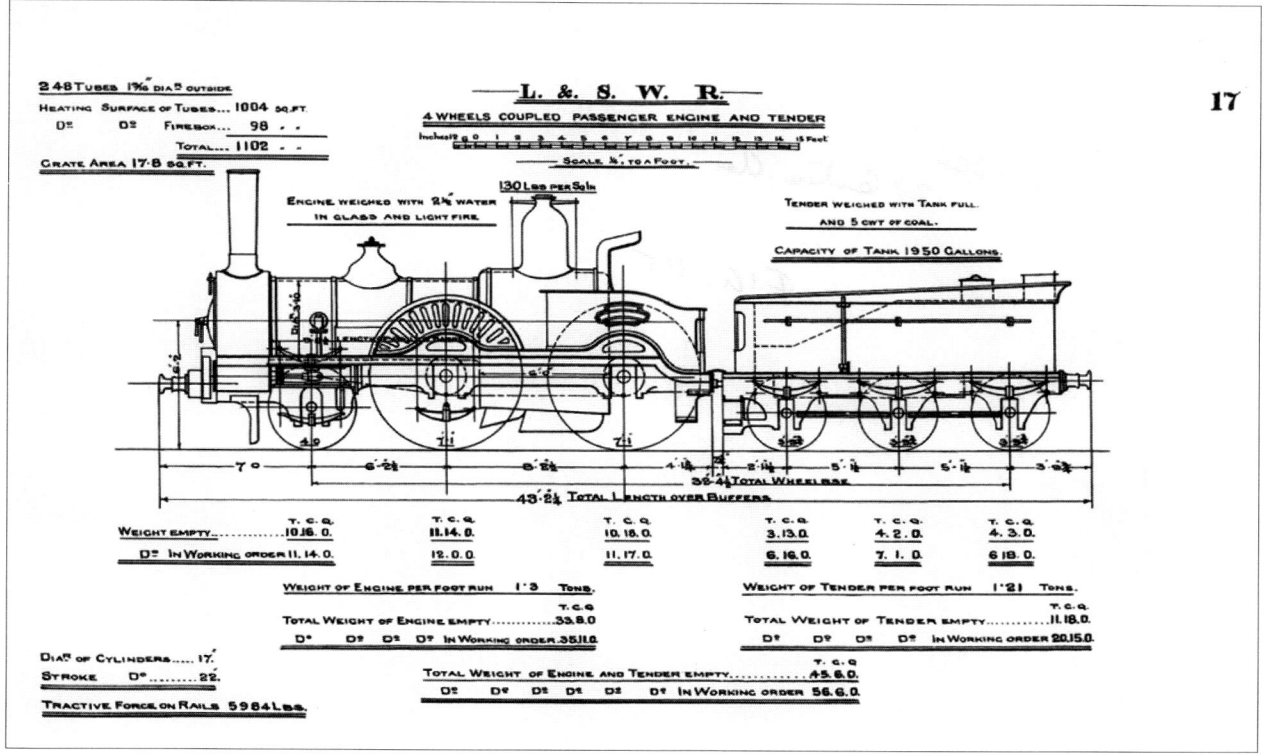

Fig. 114. Diagram of Centaur class engine in original condition except for a stove-pipe chimney.

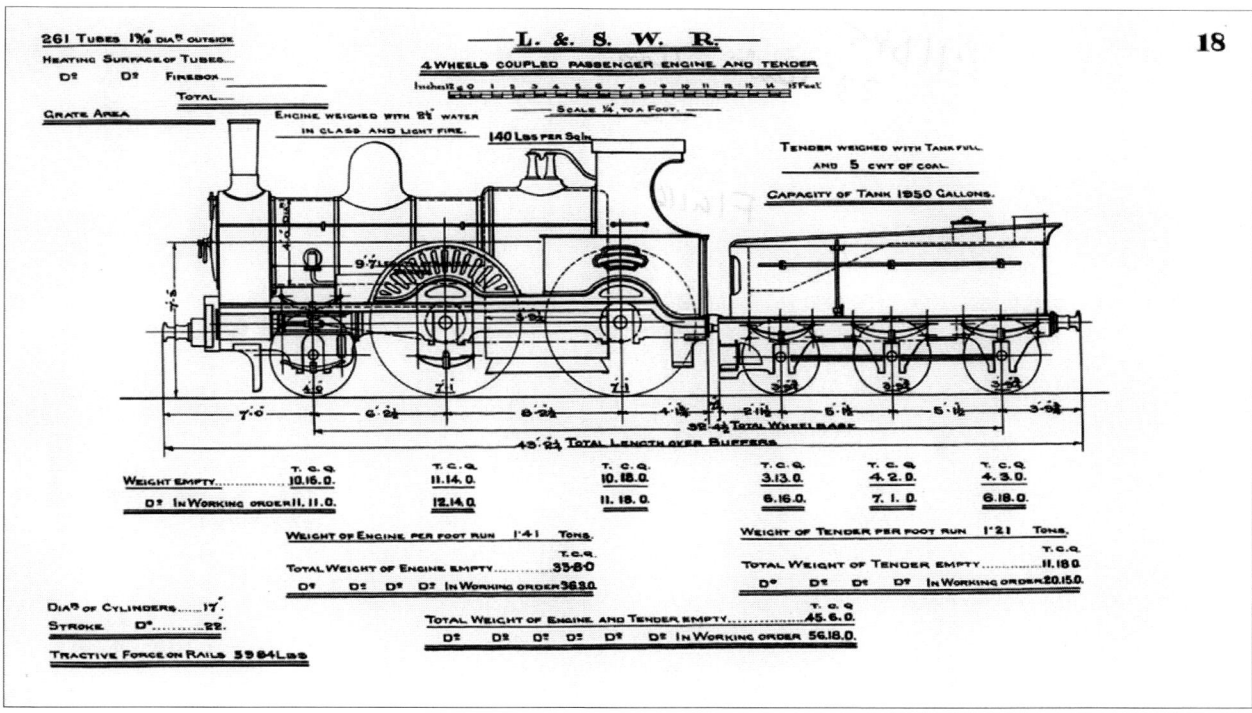

Fig. 115. Diagram of Centaur class engine with a boiler from a single frame goods engine, a stove-pipe chimney and an Adams cab.

THE LSWR AT NINE ELMS

LOCOMOTIVE PROCUREMENT 1850 -1871

This page, top. Fig. 119. Photograph of engine No 98, formerly "Plutus", of the Centaur class, but nameplates removed. Modifications as for "Castor" in Fig. 118, but with closed splashers. (HMRS)
This page, bottom. Fig. 120. Photograph of engine No 97, "Pegasus", of the Centuar class. Otherwise as for Fig. 118.

Opposite page, top. Fig. 116. Photograph of engine No 97, "Pegasus" of the Centaur class in original condition. Circa 1880.
Opposite page, centre. Fig. 117. Photograph of engine No 96, "Castor" of the Centaur class, with original boiler, but fitted with Ashton blow-back safety valve. Circa 1882.
Opposite page, bottom. Fig. 118. Photograph of engine No 96, "Castor" of the Centaur class, with a boiler from a single frame goods engine, a stove pipe chimney, and an Adams cab. Circa 1888.

THE LSWR AT NINE ELMS

LOCOMOTIVE PROCUREMENT 1850 -1871

This page, Fig. 123. Photograph of engine No 4, "Locke" of the Vesuvius class shown in original condition between 1873 when the nameplates were fitted and 1882 after which the chimney was replaced.

Opposite page, top. Fig 121. Photograph of engine No 119, "Vesuvius" of that class, with Adams stove-pipe chimney. Otherwise as originally built, post 1882.

Opposite page, bottom. Fig. 122. Photograph of engine No 41, "Ajax" of the Vesuvius class. This was an engine of the 1874-5 series and differed from the 1869 and 1873 series by having rounded cabs and separate closed driving wheel splashers. It was delivered in W.G. Beattie's control of the Locomotive Department and is shown with a replacement Adams chimney, but otherwsie as original. Post 1882.

Fig. 124. Photograph of engine No 37, previously "Arab", of the round-cabbed 1874-5 Vesuvius series with stove-pipe chimney. Circa 1888.

Fig. 125. Photograph of engine No 4, previously "Locke", of the Vesuvius class but with Adams boiler, cab, and stove-pipe chimney fitted 1888.

LOCOMOTIVE PROCUREMENT 1850 -1871

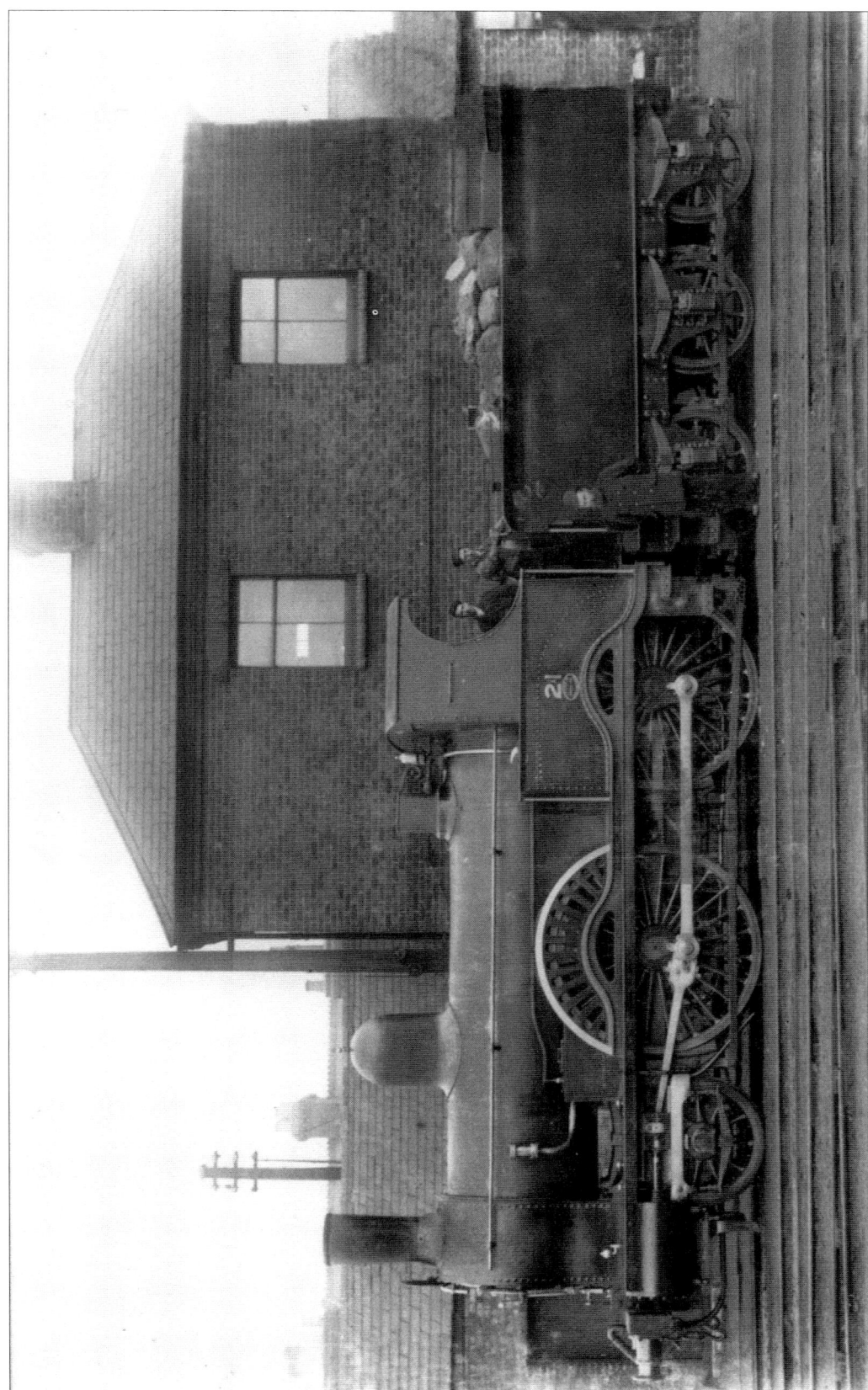

Fig. 126. Photograph of engine No 21, previously "Prince" of the Vesuvius class with Adams boiler, cab and stove-pipe chimney fitted in 1886. Seen at Northam depot.

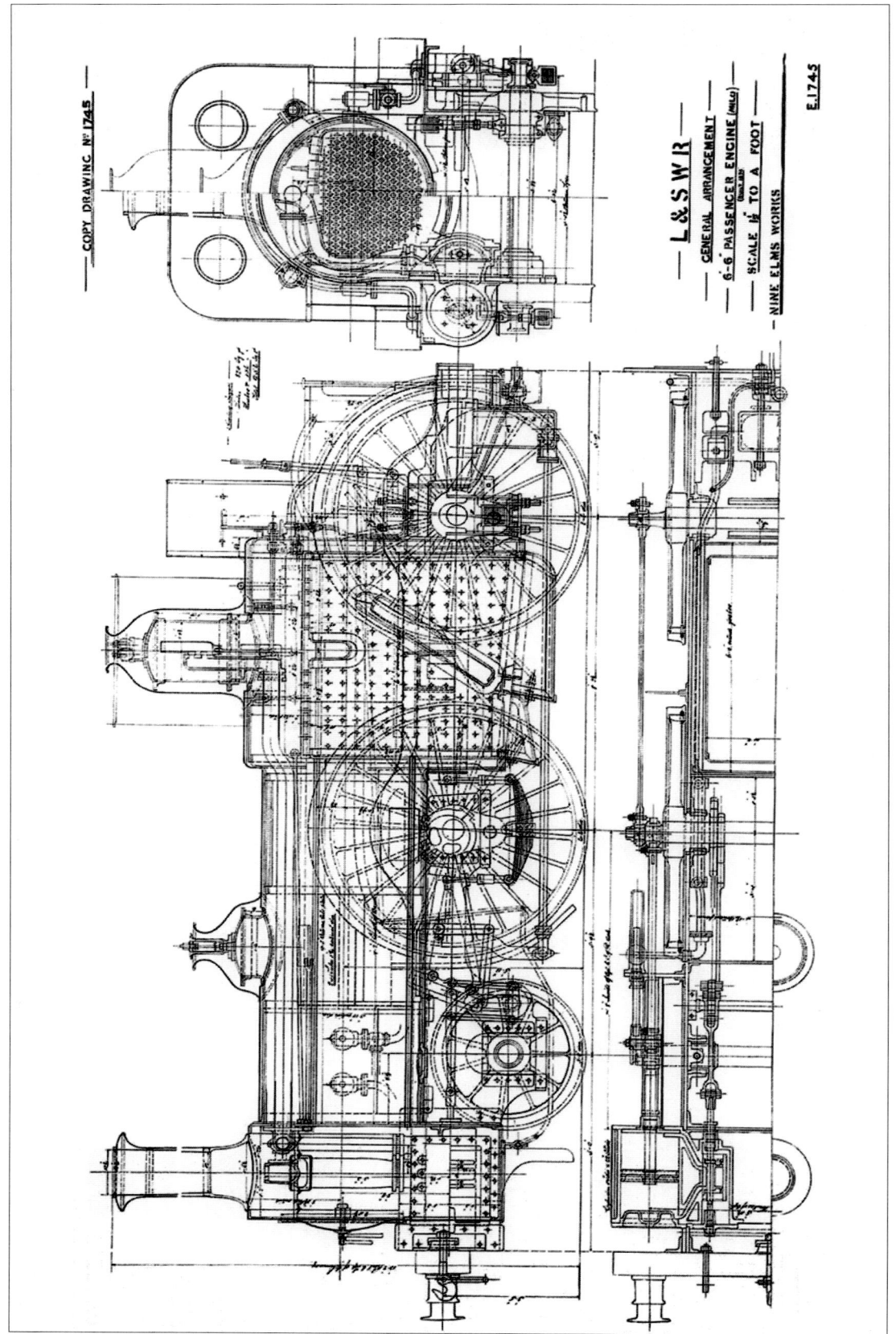

Fig. 127. General arrangement drawing of engine No 43, "Milo" of the Vesuvius class showing a cross section of the Beattie coal-burning firebox as fitted to this locomotive when new.

LOCOMOTIVE PROCUREMENT 1850-1871

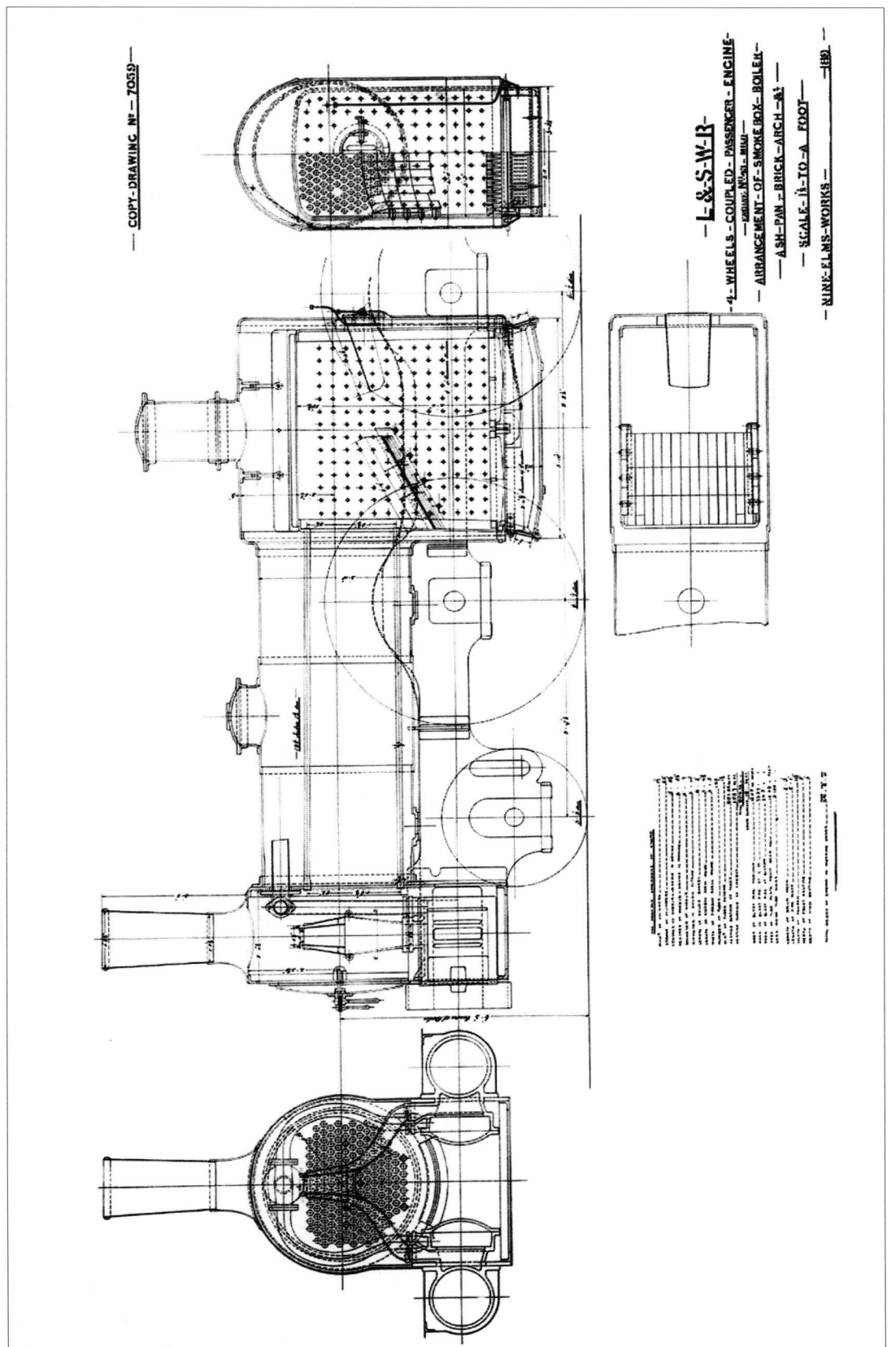

Fig. 128. Boiler and smokebox arrangement drawing of Vesuvius class No 43, "Milo", showing later 'normal' firebox arrangement with brick arch and fire-hole deflector plate as fitted to the original boiler sometime between 1879 and 1886.

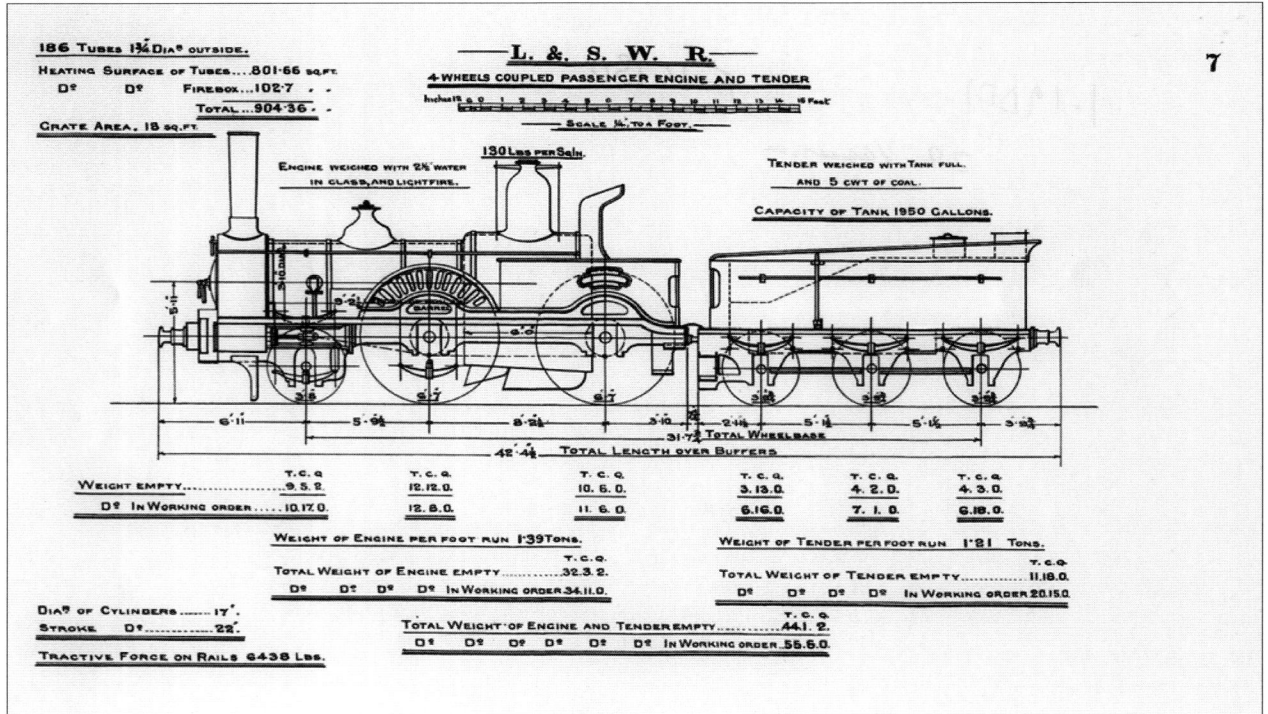

Fig. 129. Diagram of Vesuvius class engine in original condition apart from the stove-pipe chimney.

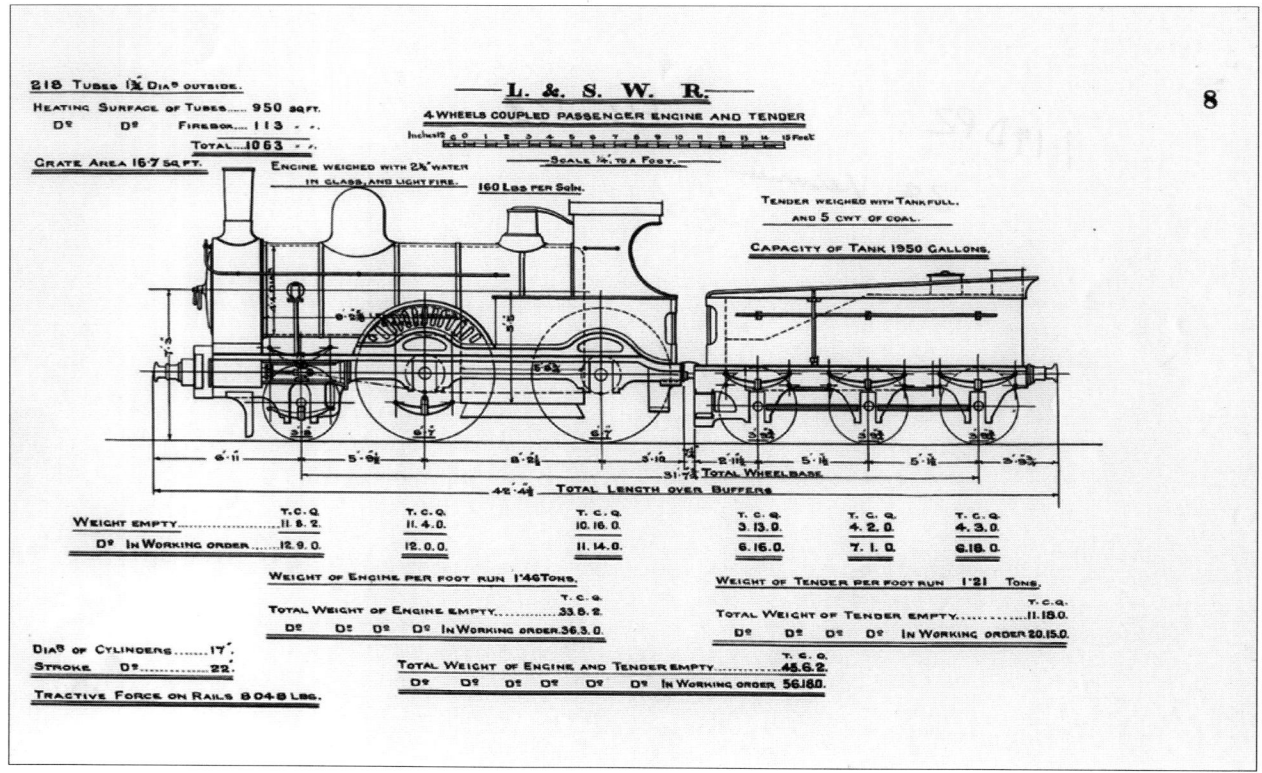

Fig. 130. Diagram of Vesuvius class engine with Adams boiler, cab and chimney.

LOCOMOTIVE PROCUREMENT 1850 -1871

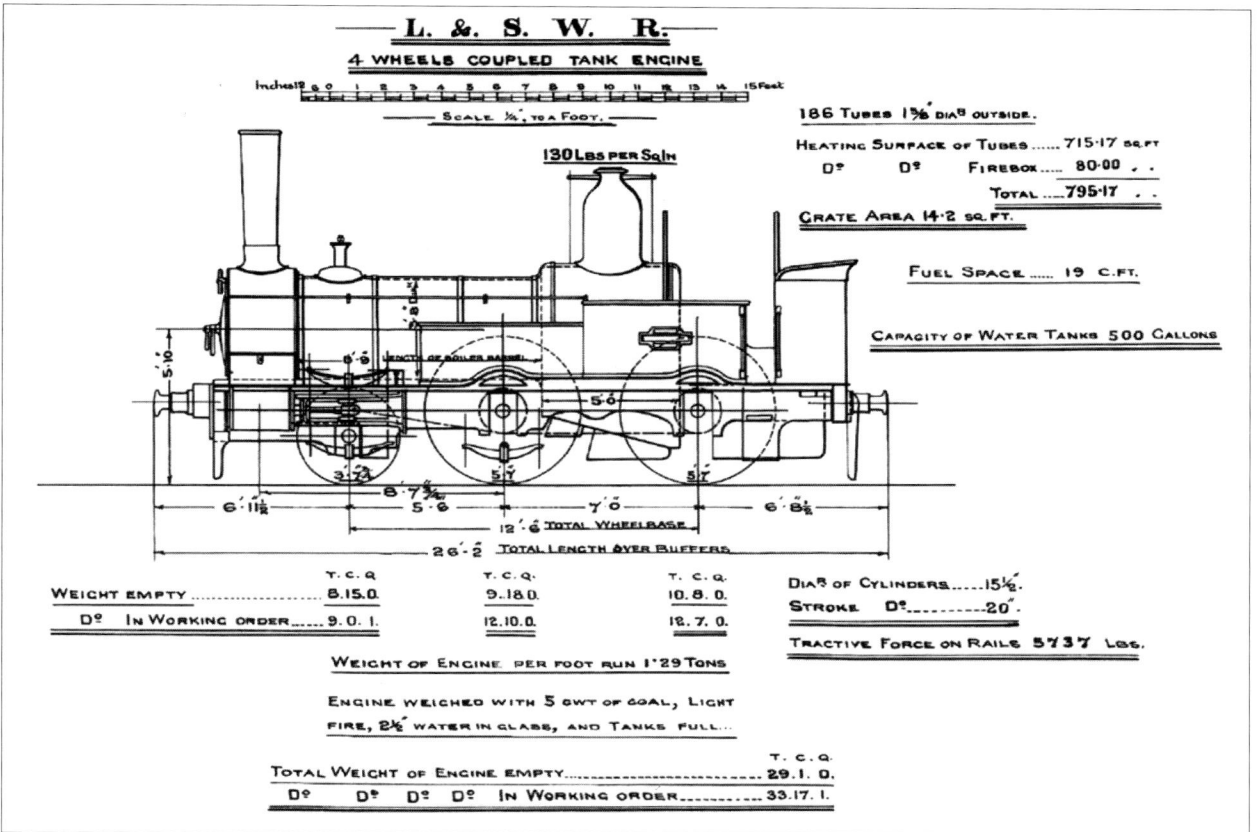

Fig. 131. Diagram of Standard Well Tank locomotive as built at Nine Elms in 1871, showing the rectangular splashers over the leading driving wheels.

Fig. 132. Unidentified photograph of Standard Well Tank engine as originally built. Believed to be one of the group built at Nine Elms (No 33, 36, or 37) with rectangular splashers over the leading driving wheels. (HMRS)

Fig. 133. Photograph of Standard Well Tank engine, No 33, "Phoenix", of the group built at Nine Elms, by the West Joint Signal Box, Wimbledon, in 1882.

5
THE EXPANSION
1865 - 1878

Northern Workshop Performance

Up to the time of the expansion all of the locomotive procurement was the result of either production from the restricted Nine Elms site north of the main line, or from subcontractors. Figure 134 is a bar chart illustrating the production, from both sources, from 1835 to 1877, when W. G. Beattie relinquished his post to William Adams. This period includes the years when the works were expanded. It can be seen that all procurement was from sub-contractors from 1835 up to the time when J. V. Gooch produced engine no 27, "Eagle", the forerunner of that class, at Nine Elms, in October 1843.

Nine Elms annual production varied from the year 1843 and reached a peak of 16 in 1859, consisting of three Nile, four Clyde, five Undine, three Tweed, and one Canute class locomotive, with a total value of about £44,000, produced from the original workshop area of around 15,000 square feet. However a significant proportion of the work, consisting of some tenders, boilers, frames cylinders and wheels was still obtained from sub-contractors. From information supplied by "Economic History Services" on the Internet, £1 in 1859 would be worth £51 in 2004, so that the cost of these 16 locomotives today would be £2.24m. I would imagine that even with modern technology today's price for constructing 16 medium sized locomotives (and tenders) of 5 different types would be considerably higher than this figure (£140,000 each). Making a wild assumption that half the total cost of £44,000 was incurred by sub-contract bills, we arrive at the figure of £75 as the equivalent figure in 2003 for the income achieved per square foot per annum from these old industrial premises. Modern rental charges for warehouses of this size vary from about £1 to £5 per square foot per annum so this income would appear to represent a good return on the facilities. It has been difficult to determine how many men were employed in the workshops at this time but it was probably no more than 50. Their wages would range from about £50 per year for a labourer to £120 per year for a engineer or skilled labourer. The minute displayed here for 6th March 1873, number 4213, indicates the larger size of salaries for two, probably supervisory positions; other minutes do give agreements

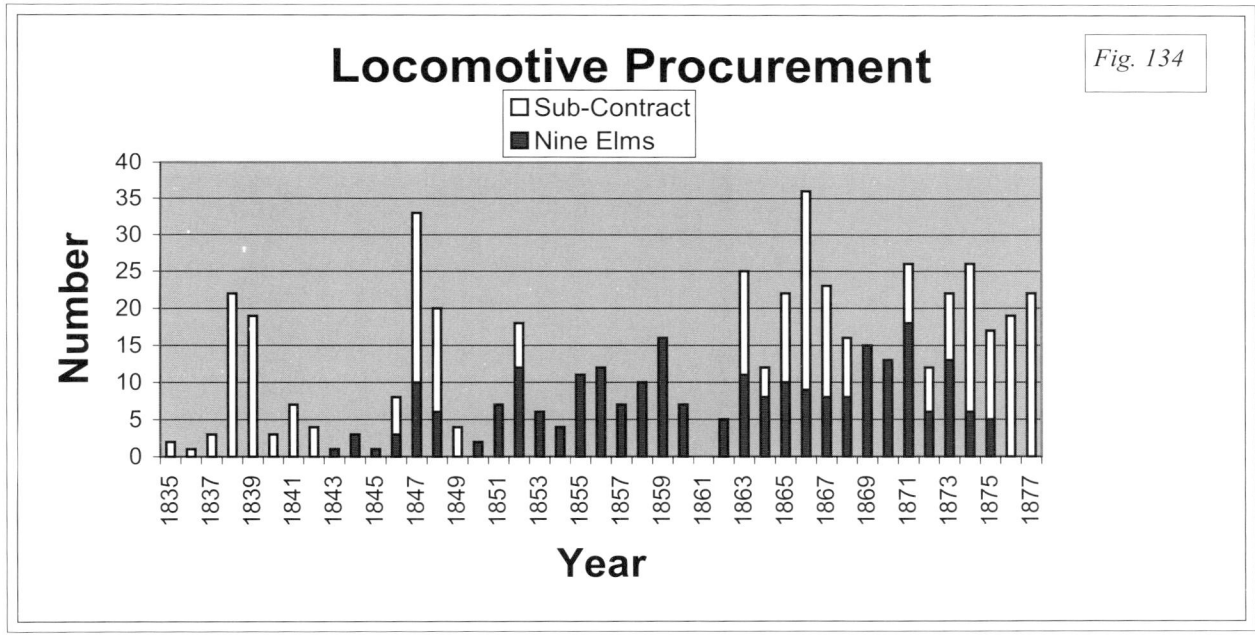

Fig. 134

4213 Court of Directors

March 6th 1873

Staff Alterations

Upon the recommendation of the Loco Committee of the 27th ulto: it was agreed as follows viz Mr. Ortton Loco: Dept. to be raised from £300 to £350 a year. Mr. Sedgwick Loco: & Carriage Depts. to be raised from £190 to £200 a year.

for increases to the "lower" workers but do not detail the amounts.

The following year, 1860, production dropped to 7 locomotives, all being of the Undine class, and in 1861 there was no locomotive production. It is difficult to understand, on these facts alone, why, in August 1861 it was decided that the site was not big enough, and a new works would be built on the South side of the main line. This anomalous situation may have arisen as a result of there being a large stock of locomotives at that time due to previous building efforts, but that a rise in future demand was forecast. The new works were opened on January 1865, and up to this time from 1862 locomotive building on the North side was resumed.

We do not know exactly when production on the North side ceased, but assuming a date of January 1865, a total of 152 engines were produced in the 30 years it was operating. Additionally, 143 locomotives were purchased from sub-contractors during this period. It was not until 1871 that the previous record of 16 locomotives in a year on the old site was exceeded by a figure of 18 being attained on the South side. In addition the purchase of complete locomotives from

4169 Locomotive & Traffic Committee
January 23 1873

Fig.135a

Half Yearly Accounts

The Statements of Accounts in the Loco and Carriage Departments for the half year ending 31 December 1872 were submitted.

The Locomotive Accounts show

	Dec. 1872	as against	Dec. 1871
Engine Mileage	3,816,151		3,631,915
Train Mileage	3,637,693		3,448,053
Expenditure	£131,714 10s 8d		£110,005 18s 9d
Rate per mile per Engine	8.28		7.27
do Train	8.69		7.66
Increase of Expenditure at December 1872			£21,708 11s 11d

The Carriage Accounts show

	Dec 1872	as against	Dec. 1871
Train Mileage	3,637,693		3,448,053
Expenditure	£37,064 17s 2d		£35,366 5s 2d
Rate per mile	2.44		2.46
Increase in expenditure at December 1872			£1698 12s 0d
Total Increase in both Depts at Dec 1872			£23,407 3s 11d

THE EXPANSION 1865 -1878

sub-contractors was resumed in 1863, after a break of 11 years. 88 were purchased between 1863 and 1871, when W. G. Beattie took over from Joseph Beattie. Another peculiarity was that although production of locomotives initiated by Joseph Beattie continued on-site until 1875, all those ordered by his son, were obtained from sub-contractors, in spite of the availability of brand new, well equipped workshops. However, these peculiarities may have been caused by a general increase in the amount of repair work as locomotive mileage increased. Figure 135 shows the half-yearly accounts for the years 1871 to 1874 detailed in the

---

4865 *Locomotive Committee*

January 21 1875

Fig.135b

Half Yearly Accounts

The Statements of Accounts of the Loco and Carriage Departments for the half year ending 31 December 1874 were submitted and examined and approved.

The Locomotive Accounts show

	Dec. 1874	as against	Dec. 1873
Expenditure	£147,114 15s 6d		£152,775 13s 3d
Train Mileage	3,909,530		3,724,640
Cost per train mile	9.03		9.84
Decrease of Expenditure at December 1874			£5,660 17s 9d

The Carriage Accounts show

	Dec 1874	as against	Dec. 1873
Expenditure	£45,451 12s 1d		£40,300 7s 2d
Cost per train mile	2.79		2.60
Increase in expenditure at December 1874			£5151 4s 11d

Net Decrease between the two Depts at Dec 1874. £509 12s 10d

4214 *Locomotive & Traffic Committee*

March 13 1873

Third Class Carriage No. 89

Read letter from Mr. Cooper of 11th inst as to the leaky state of the above Carriage and others of similar construction which are still running on the Line, and are much complained of by Passengers.
Mr. Beattie to see Mr. Cooper on the subject.

minute book, and these include details of the mileages run in each of these years. It can be seen that the average annual increase was about 4.3%. At this rate, train mileage would have doubled in 16 years.

New Locomotive Works

On page 16 was reproduced the first part of an article published by Peter F. Winding in the magazine *Railway World*. It is now appropriate to present the next part, which deals with the move of the works to the South side. Reference can be made to the Ordnance Survey map in Figure 136.

By 1860 it had become obvious that despite some improvements, Nine Elms was an anachronism based on a small, congested site that could no longer hope to meet the requirements of a rapidly expanding main line system. Already the South Eastern and Brighton companies had given a lead by building new workshops outside London, while the smaller London, Chatham & Dover had almost completed its superb Longhedge Works and running shed in nearby Battersea, on a site three times the size of the South Western's antiquated establishment, and on a scale that made the latter look ridiculous. It was a situation that called for immediate action, and in 1861 the Company decided to take the opportunity of purchasing some 30 acres of land on the south side of the main line for a new locomotive, carriage and wagon works and engine shed, so that the whole of the original site could be made available to the Goods Department.

Work on the new site commenced in 1862, and was carried out under the supervision of Joseph Beattie, who had succeeded Viret Gooch as Mechanical Engineer in 1850. The first building to be completed was the new running shed on a six-acre site alongside the main line at Nine Elms Junction. As may be seen from the accompanying plan, the unique layout with its four 40ft turntables and numerous coal stages bears the unmistakable stamp of Beattie's inventive genius, and appears to have been designed to deal with every possible contingency. Allowing for the size of locomotives at that time, and that at least 50% of the allocation were tank engines, the shed was evidently designed for about 100 locomotives. Access to the main line was from Loco Junction, situated just to the west of Nine Elms Junction. This awkward arrangement was dictated by the site, and required the reversal of all locomotives using Waterloo, but in the absence of any practical alternative it was retained until the closure of the depot in 1967.

The construction of the locomotive, carriage and wagon works was completed in 1865, but due to an explosion in the nearby gasworks, the shops were not fully operational until the following year. However, it may be assumed that the transition from the old works to the new was a gradual process that began in 1864, and on this assumption one can estimate that the old works built a total of about 130 new engines. Considering that in addition to this there was a prodigious amount of rebuilding, and ordinary routine repairs, and the extra work of coping with Beattie's inventive gadgetry, it is extraordinary how such a small establishment managed to accomplish so much. On the other hand, the records show that during this period, a great deal of work was contracted out to local firms, and this must be the explanation of how it was managed.

Unlike its neighbour at Longhedge, the South Western did not concern itself with architectural style, and the new workshops had an appearance that was plain to the point of austerity. All the main buildings were constructed on an alignment parallel with the engine shed, and perhaps the most interesting point to notice is the extensive use of outside traversers to save space and make the most of a site that was still far from adequate.

A survey by the Ordnance Survey of the area was completed in 1869. Figure 136 shows the result. Unfortunately the Nine Elms area falls on the join between two maps, necessitating careful juxtaposition of the two items, and this accounts for the horizontal line across the page. The map gives a very detailed picture of the whole site including the new works. Enlargement of the original map enables every track and point to be seen clearly; this feat is amazing when one realises that the collection of detail must have been done manually, with surveyors "on the ground", with only basic measuring instruments, there being no aeroplanes, satellites or photography to aid them.

The blank area to the south-west of the works later became the motive power depot. The running shed at this time was near to the main line as shown. The whole of the works area to the North had already been converted to a goods depot.

It will be useful to divert our attention away from the immediate vicinity of the works and view the environs around Battersea. Figure 137 is a smaller scale version of the previous map, and shows the considerable amount of development that has taken place, both as regards the railways and industry in the area, and in house building. Compare it with Plate 4, Stanhope's map of 1862, on page 22. In less than 7 years all of the market gardens have disappeared and the "Mill Pond" has been swallowed up by the sidings at the south-west end of Nine Elms Works and by the houses to the North of them. The long strip of orchards bordering the Wandsworth Road, amounting to ap-

THE EXPANSION 1865-1878

Fig. 136. Nine Elms as surveyed in 1869.
(The Ordnance Survey)

proximately 60 acres, has been converted into housing and the large area south east of the Wandsworth Road has had its density of housing considerably increased. The only area that has been fully retained as an open space is Battersea Park.

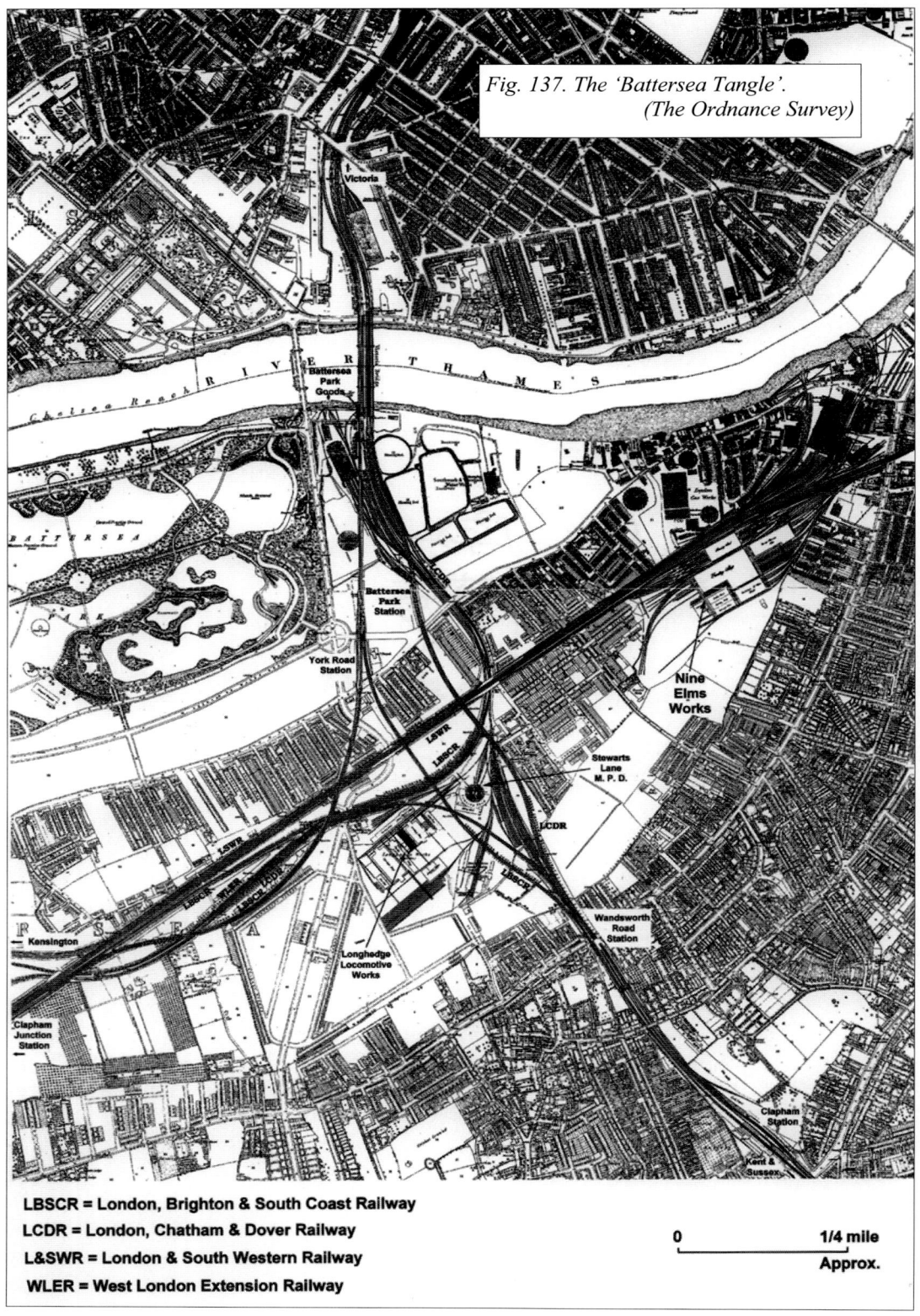

Fig. 137. The 'Battersea Tangle'. (The Ordnance Survey)

LBSCR = London, Brighton & South Coast Railway
LCDR = London, Chatham & Dover Railway
L&SWR = London & South Western Railway
WLER = West London Extension Railway

THE EXPANSION 1865 -1878

Most significant of all has been the railway development. The lines from Waterloo towards the south-west have become "entangled" with the lines from Victoria, spreading into the south-east. With each Company – four of them at this point – wishing to go in every possible direction, a number of loop lines have resulted, and this conglomeration of junctions has earned the name "The Battersea Tangle". Development of the Stewarts Lane motive power depot, the Longhedge locomotive works, the Battersea Park goods depot, and the London Gasworks has also taken place.

It can be seen that the expansion of the locomotive works is in line with the expansion of the whole area, and can be considered as following the general increase in traffic, goods and passenger, that was a result of the increase in industrialisation and associated housing development.

Amongst the photographic records that were saved from Eastleigh, we were lucky to find two items. One was a pair of 12in. x 10in. glass negatives which contained the images of an article from *The Engineer* dated 21st August 1868. It was a complete description of the Nine Elms works by a person, unfortunately nameless, who had visited the site and had recorded the facilities there in great detail. It also included a diagram, shown here in Figure 138. The article is reproduced here in its entirety.

The second item resulted from the policy adopted by the Southern Railway in the early years of World War II, to record on an early form of photostat, all the drawings in the Eastleigh office that were important and which referred to items that were current at that time. This was done in case of enemy action and they were presumably kept at a remote location. Luckily they were returned to Eastleigh. It is difficult to understand, but lucky for us, why they chose to record the tramway system that was built into the new works in 1865 onto a photostat. It was not in good condition when found but with some care and patience it has been resurrected and is shown in Plate 5. The drawing of the component parts in the southeast corner of the plate represents the size of the transparency, and the missing area in its northwest corner was the total area taken up by the map! Some re-highlighting of the tramway has had to be resorted to.

This 18-inch gauge hand-operated tramway system is referred to briefly in the article in *The Engineer* - and erroneously stated to have been 2' 6", but the photostat of it shows just how extensive it was. The date is not known, but the original drawing stems from a later time when the running sheds had been moved to their new position south west of the works, and the main line moved adjacent to the works. This had been done around 1876. As can be seen, the tramway had even been extended into the motive power department.

The full description of the new works published in the August 1868 issue of *The Engineer* now follows, it should be read in conjunction with Figures 136 and 138.

THE LONDON AND SOUTH-WESTERN ENGINE AND CARRIAGE WORKS AT NINE ELMS.

In the railway world Mr. J. H. Beattie, engineer-in-chief of the South-Western Railway, is favourably known for the important improvements he has effected in the locomotive engine. We have had an opportunity during the week of inspecting a number of engines in course of construction at the South Western Company's works at Nine Elms, by which we would have been impressed if we had not been aware of the fact previously, that Mr. William George Beattie is following worthily in his father's footsteps in the further important improvements he is effecting in the vital parts of the locomotive. In an early number we propose to give an illustrated description of the new modifications introduced in these engines, and meantime, as introductory, subjoin a few particulars concerning the reconstructed and enlarged works of the company, which claim attention as the most recently completed establishment for the prosecution of this important branch of industry - the manufacture and repair of railway rolling stock.

The workshops and yards, which comprise an area of above twenty-three acres, lie to the south-east of the main line. The goods yards and warehouses - which occupy a still larger area - are situated on the opposite side of the line, and extend down to the river, with which the company has direct connection by its own wharves, fitted with cranes for loading and unloading. The engine and carriage works in the numerous, compactly arranged blocks of building, have an aggregate of above seven acres of roofed-in space, viz., four and a half acres for the locomotive, and two and three-quarters acres for the carriage departments. The yard occupies an irregularly shaped plot of land, about 750 yards long by about 200 yards wide. Thirty-eight lines of rails cross abreast under the roofs of the principal shops, and in the spaces between them or past the sides, all of these lines having communication with each other, and with the main line by traversers or by turn-tables.

A first impression likely to be taken by a visitor on entering the yard is, that not a shilling has been expended upon the works with a view to architectural effect. The buildings, of brick with stone facings, are thoroughly substantial, plain in style, but far from being unsightly. The walls of the shops, where they are to the open, are for the greater part furnished with ranges of side lights by uniform tiers of windows with

THE LSWR AT NINE ELMS

flat segmental lintels. The whole of the shops have numerous large roof lights, the glass having an aggregate surface nearly equal to the slating. The cardinal merit of the design of the works is only to be discovered by making the tour, and noticing the successive processes and the arrangements and contrivances for minimizing time and labour in their prosecution, in the studied relation between the work to be done and the means and localities employed and appointed for doing it. There is communication between the main line and the works near the little erection in the Wandsworth-road dignified by the name of the "Royal Station", which is only put in requisition when royal personages use the line, but the principal connection is at the opposite end of the yard. From the junction with the main line at that end eleven lines diverge, of which two run one on each side of the two coal stages of 370ft long, close to the main line, from which the running engines receive their supplies of fuel. Water columns are conveniently placed at the ends of the coal stages from which the tenders are charged. Passing inwards from the coal stages, and appropriately nearest to the main line, are the first ranges of covered buildings - the three running sheds 300ft long by 140ft wide - which have seven lines of rails across, and are capable of containing fifty engines and tenders. The sheds are furnished with four travelling hoists, worked by hand, and have sufficient head room for lifting engines when necessary for repairs. Between the lines of rails are ranges of covered wells from which water is obtained for washing out the engines. At each end of the running shed there are two water tanks, each capable of containing 26,000 gallons. Under the water tanks, stores of oil, brake blocks, and other necessaries for daily working, are conveniently stowed in readiness for current wants. At each end of the sheds there are two 40ft turntables for reversing engines and tenders, into which all the lines converge. Two lines of rail between the steam shed and the main body of the building are used as shunting lines for all vehicles brought in for repairs. One of these lines communicates with the three traverser roads which run transversely to the shops and yard, and thus furnishes means of communication with the particular engine or carriage shop, or other locality desired to be reached. Two of the traversers roads have steam traversers by Messrs. Thos. Dunn and Co of Manchester. The locomotive department has fifteen lines of covered rails, and the carriage department twelve lines. Two lines of rails intervene between the running sheds and the principal block of building. This block contains a large number of shops and store rooms conveniently situated in relation to each other and to their respective uses. These include two erecting shops and a machine shop, each 300ft long by 57ft 3in wide. The erecting shops have six lines of rails and pits, and are equal to the accommodation of sixty engines for erection or repair. The average number of engines under repair at one time is about forty-five. Each erecting shop is furnished with two 25-ton overhead travelling cranes, by Messrs. Wren and Hopkinson of Manchester. They are worked by a cord motion, the speed of the cord being about 5000ft per minute. One of these erecting shops, in the centre of the building, is in line with the millwrights' shop, 40ft long, and the boiler repair shop 160ft long, and each of the same gauge in width as the erecting shop, 57ft. 3in. By the overhead cranes there is communication from one end to the other of this 500ft. range, and boilers, wheels, or other work, are transferred from one point to another with the greatest facility. The coppersmiths' shop, 40ft long, and the tender repair shop, 160ft long, are in line with the other erecting shops, and occupy together one of the outer sides of the main block of building. The coppersmiths' shop has fixed and movable fires with pits and furnaces for remelting white metal, and running the bearings. The tender shop has space, on three lines of rails, for the accommodation of twenty-one tenders. The spring repairing and testing is carried on at the end of this shop, where is situated the spring furnace and spring testing machine. The tender shop is also furnished with an overhead travelling crane, worked by the cord motion, and with drill and shearing machines. The millwrights' shop is supplied with two powerful hydraulic presses, each carried by a vertical hydraulic ram worked by the water service. By simple action upon the water supply the presses are raised or lowered with the utmost ease, so as to suit the various sizes of wheels. The presses are also served by two parallel cranes and two swing cranes worked by hand.

The boiler shop, which has space for ten boilers, has one plate furnace constructed to consume its own smoke, and along the side of the shop two sets of rolls, a plate-edge planing machine, three shearing and punching machines, a circular shearing machine for splasher plates, a radial drill, and a fired vertical drill, all worked from the same line of shafting that gives the driving motion to the overhead cranes. Parallel to the boiler shop is the wheel shop, where the tyres are fitted and fixed or removed. This shop has two tyre furnaces, in which the flues are so constructed as to secure nearly complete smoke combustion. The three fires, with pits, in the shop for welding tyres, are falling into disuse since the introduction by the makers of tyres of any size, rolled solid. The tyres are supplied somewhat smaller in diameter than required, and the exact dimensions are obtained by rolling them out upon a powerful rolling mill, from which they are taken of the size required for the lathe, and nearly perfectly circular. The rolling mill is a notable ma-

THE EXPANSION 1865 -1878

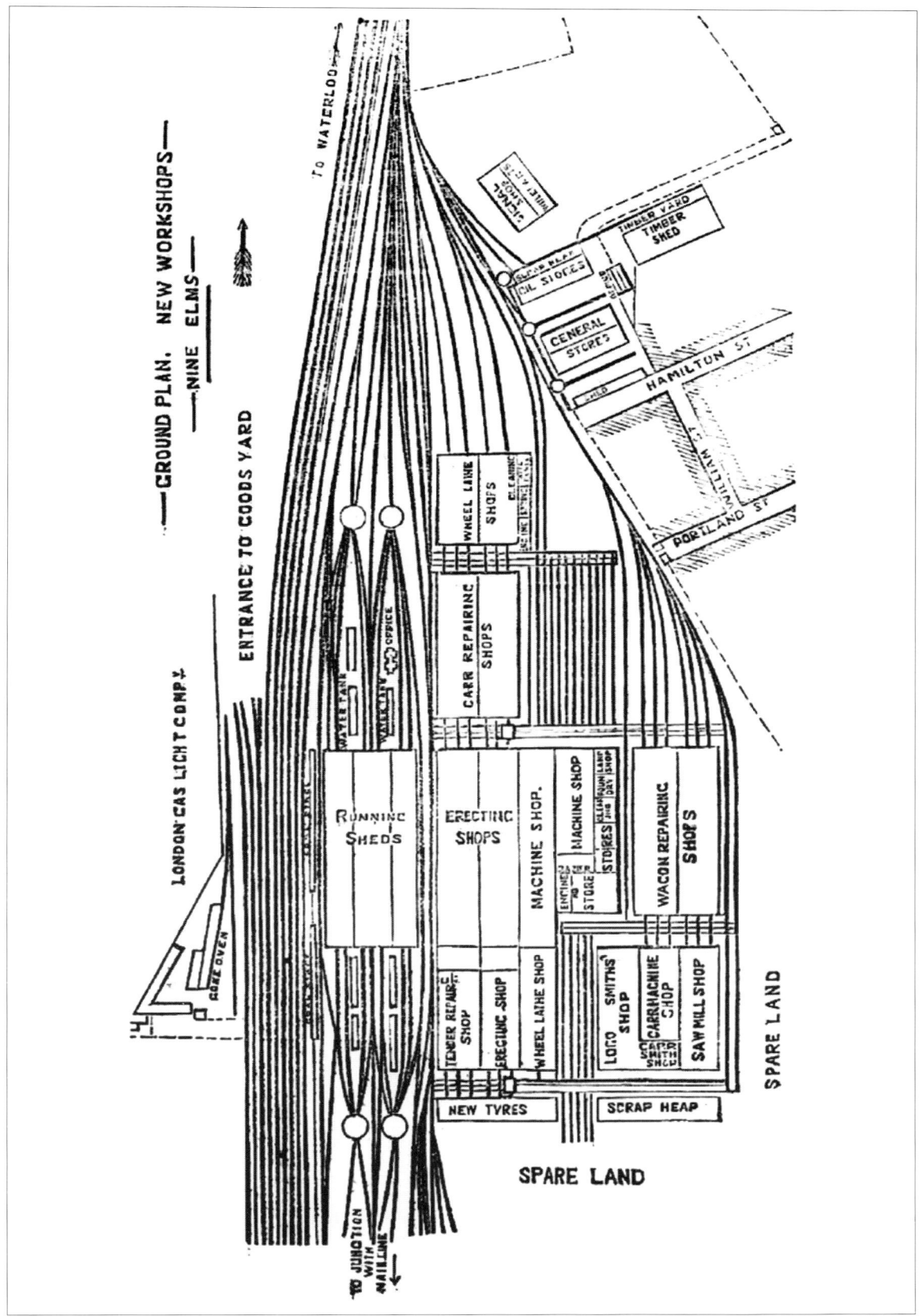

Fig. 138. The map of Nine Elms Works included in the article published in "The Engineer" for 21st August 1868.

chine, the great power and ingenious construction and principles of which cannot be adequately apprehended without examination of the contents of the spacious covered pit which contains the gearing of the machine. The pit is about 13ft to the foundations, below the floor of the bed-plate of the mill. The tyre furnaces and rolling mill are served by a swing crane worked by cord motion. The tyres are all secured by Mr. Beattie's tyre fastening, which is now so extensively used, and which, as is well known consists of a continuous projecting or dovetail lip round the wheel and tyre, which is attached by screws or dovetail clips. The wheel-turning occupies three 7ft lathes, two 6ft lathes, and four 4ft lathes, arranged round the shop, the shaft and countershafts being carried by light wrought-iron girders projecting out from the wall, and attached to cast-iron columns placed between the lathes. The driving power in the wheel, lathe, and boiler shops is communicated direct to the shafting by a vertical double-cylinder high pressure engine, in the manner introduced by Messrs. Beyer, Peacock, and Co., of Manchester, and the supply of steam conveyed from a boiler placed at a short distance from the engine. On both sides of the shop the wheel lathes are served by travelling cranes worked by the cord motion. They run on a single rail, and are guided at the top between two parallel walls. In addition to the lathes in the wheel shop, there are two auxiliaries, one 7ft, the other 6ft, placed at the end of the erecting shop, in convenient proximity to the running shed. These lathes are used for turning up the wheels of engines which may be undergoing slight repairs. In line with the wheel lathe shop is a machine shop 300ft long by 57ft 3in wide, furnished with fitters' benches and racks, for motion work under repair, arranged along the side nearest to the erecting shop; the shaping, drilling, and slotting machines extend along the opposite side wall, the slide lathes for iron and brass turning, and the screwing machines, are ranged along the centre of this shop. These tools are all driven by a central line of shafting, carried on a row of cast iron columns 15ft apart, and connected with a direct-acting vertical double cylinder engine, similar to that which supplies power to the wheel lathe shop. The counter shafting is carried on brackets attached to the cast-iron columns, and at the side walls on cast-iron brackets. Parallel to the machine shop last referred to there is a smaller shop 200ft long by 57ft 3in wide, containing additional slotting, planning and shaping machines. The machines for fitting up the cylinders are conveniently placed alongside of each other, or closely adjoining, with a view to the successive processes through which the work has to pass. From the lathe where the projecting faces are turned, the casting passes to the boring machine close at hand, where it is chucked by the turned surfaces and bored; thence it passes to the planing machine where it is fixed on coned centres and planed on the flanges and faces and has also the guide of the valve spindle bored out. It is then lifted to the radial drill, and passes afterwards to the fitting bench, where it is completed and passed on into the store, the successive processes having been conducted without crowding or confusion upon a very small area. All the movements are effected by a travelling crane, somewhat similar to those in the wheel lathe shop, which serves all the heavy machines of the shop.

The long machine shop before mentioned has also a crane of the same description, extending between the heavier machines; the fitting and machine shops are provided, in addition, with 2ft 6in gauge tramways, (*) which extend into the erecting shops, and to the stores, and greatly facilitate the removal of heavy articles, such as axles, axle-boxes, or cylinders. We noticed as favourable specimens of new machinery in these shops, the duplex key-way cutting and grooving machine, the double shaping machines with 16ft bed, the duplex axle turning lathe, the new radial drills, and. the slotting machines of the last make. At the curl of the shorter machine shop is the grindery, containing two 7ft grinding stones, two glaziers, and a machine for surfacing and polishing slide bars. In this last machine a reciprocating horizontal motion is given to the slide-bars, fixed on a carrier, and a transverse motion is given to the small revolving grindstone. The shafting in the machine shop and the adjoining grindery is carried on cast-iron pillars, in a similar manner to that in the long machine shop, and each of the planing machines have their driving fast and loose pulleys carried out to a position vertically below the line shaft, from which they are driven by twisted leather straps. The line shafting bearings are fitted throughout with lubricators, and each length of shafting, 15ft long has two bearings on each side of the couplings, which are bolted together, one end of each shaft projecting a short distance into the next coupling. The main shafting throughout the works is of Bessemer steel 3½ in diameter. By the arrangement of the shafting on the cast iron columns the roofs, which are of iron throughout, are saved from strain, and the shafting and roof kept quite independent of each other.

Next to the wheel lathe shop, and between it and the smiths' shop and forge, is a space occupied by five lines of wheel roads, which are served by one of the steam traversers at one end and by a hand traverser at the other. It is intended to provide an overhead traverser for these lines to facilitate the handling of wheels and tyres.

The smiths shop, 200ft long by 57ft 3in wide, contains thirty hearths, and has four small 13 cwt.

THE EXPANSION 1865-1878

steam hammers for the use of the smiths, with a 25 cwt hammer for the forge. Outside the forge and alongside the steam traverser there is a powerful steam shears served by a hand crane, and immediately adjoining it, a scrap cleaning machine, which makes capital work by churning the charges of the cylinder, delivering them perfectly clean and free from caked rust. From the cleaner, the scrap passes to the inside of the building, and is piled ready to be passed into one or other of the three air furnaces. As a rule, and as far as practicable, such forgings as crossheads, rods, knees, &c, are shaped in block dies and tools, and passed direct to the machines. The forge is served by three swing cranes on wrought-iron pillars. It is lofty, well ventilated, and well lighted, and is furnished with shearing and punching machines. The bolt making hearths occupy the north end of the smithery. A further range of shops, in line with the smiths' shop, includes the dispensing and, other store rooms, time keeper's office, brass foundry, and lamp repairing shops, which complete the accommodation provided for the locomotive department.

An object aimed at in designing the works, and which is attained in actual practice, appears to have been that the work should pass from the forge to the machines, next to the fitters, and from them to the erecting shops, or to the running sheds, with as little movement and handling as possible. The cord driven travelling and overhead cranes, fitted by Messrs. Wren, Hopkinson, and Co., the traversers, special features, and the small tramway, are all found most useful in diminishing labour and cost and increasing production.

We next proceed to the inspection of the carriage department works, which occupy two ranges of buildings parallel to the locomotive workshops, and on the side of the yard furthest from the main line. The carriage machine shop, 134 ft by 57ft 3in, is the central length of a block which has the locomotive smithery on one side and the saw mill on the other. The middle of the shop has a range of lathes, and along the side walls shaping tools, drills, and screwing machines. The line shaft is carried in a manner similar to that in the locomotive machine shop, on cast iron columns placed along the centre of the space. Part of the shop is occupied by a hydraulic wheel press, and fitters' benches are placed across one end for the repair of brake work. Alongside of the carriage machine shop is the saw mill shop, 194ft long by 57ft 3in wide. It consists of seven circular and vertical saws, planing and boring machines, and turning lathes, all driven from the line shafting of the machine shop. Two cross shafts, in underground pits, are driven from a heavy intermediate counter shaft by powerful twisted straps, and belting is led right and left of each cross shaft to the saws, by which arrangement overhead shafting is dispensed with. In line with the carriage machine and saw mill shops there are two wagon repairing shops, joined side to side. They are 253ft long by 57ft 3in wide and have each three lines of rails, and working room for sixty wagons; benches are arranged along the outer side of each shop, which has side lights in addition to the roof light. The four workshops last referred to are served by the two steam traversers and by a band traverser; this provision greatly facilitates the supply of timber to the saws and its removal after preparation, to the wagon shop, as also the supply of ironwork from the forge to the machine shop, and from the machine to the wagon-building shop. Break vans are repaired over two long pits provided for the purpose, outside and adjacent to the wagon shops. The principal yard space for the accommodation of vehicles laid up for a time, or undergoing slight repair, is bounded on one of its sides by the block of two carriage-repairing shops, the twelve lines of rails in the yard being served by a traverser at each end. These carriage shops, each 218ft 6in long by 57ft 3in wide, are in line with the locomotive erecting shops, and are two storey buildings. The ground floor, which has six lines of rails, is devoted to the repair of the under frames of carriages, to turning up the wheels, renewing axle boxes, springs. &c. The carriage bodies are lifted, by means of two hoists, to the upper floor, and are there repaired, trimmed, and painted. In line again with the carriage-repairing shops, and with a traverser passing between them but forming part of the same continuous block of building, are two wheel lathe shops, each 133ft long by 57ft. 3in. wide, with four lines of rails. These shops have eight four-wheel lathes ranged under the side windows of the shops, and driven from line shafts carried on cast-iron brackets suspended from the overhead girders of the upper floor; the countershafts are carried by cast iron brackets attached to the walls. The shafting is driven by a double-acting vertical double-cylinder engine. The boiler which supplies the engine is of the same pattern as the other three boilers in the locomotive and carriage department, and is a modification of the ordinary locomotive boiler. The barrel is 13ft long by 4ft 6in diameter and the firebox 7ft by 4ft 6in, flush with the barrel, and not very deep. Below the boilers, which are well protected with clothing, a water pit extends, and by a simple arrangement the fire-bars can be lowered and the fire dropped or cleaned. Two brick arches are thrown in the firebox constructed with a design to consume the smoke, which is very thoroughly accomplished. The upper floor of the carriage shops is carried on strong wrought-iron girders placed at 15ft between centres. A portion of the upper floor of this block is occupied as offices of the locomotive and car-

riage department, and by the pattern loft and trimmers benches.

Among the most useful tools in the carriage shop that we noticed was a triplex nut tapping machine with three vertical spindles. By this machine a stout lad can easily turn out eight gross of ¾in nuts per day, for which he is paid 3d. per gross, and earns a better wage than an adult Dorsetshire labourer. The machine will tap nuts up to 1¾ in diameter. It has a small pump worked from the top spindle, by which the oil is kept in circulation, returning to a round of duty only ended by its consumption. Next to the nut tapping machine is a screwing machine, used to screw 1¾ in draw bar ends, as well as ordinary-sized bolts. These machines are both by Messrs. Smith and Coventry of Manchester.

As a safeguard in case of fire, the carriage repairing and painting shops are fitted with Mr. Beattie's fire apparatus, by which water can be conveyed from the fire main through large pipes, and distributed through a series of 3in, gutter pipes, perforated with 1/8in. holes at about 9in apart. These pipes extend along the whole length of the building, and the discharge of water can be directed upon any part by means of valves placed within reach of the ground. The painting shop is effectively warmed in winter by hot-water pipes placed between the joists and protected by gratings. The waste heat of the engine boiler is used to heat the water, and a rapid circulation can be maintained by the employment of a steam pump. The benches for fitting axle-boxes are situated between the wheel lathe shops, which are also furnished with a hydraulic press on the principle before referred to, for fixing the wheels upon the axles or detaching them, as may be required. Alongside of the wheel lathe shops, and first within the outer wall of the block of buildings, are the engine-house, shops for repairs of light ironwork, of springs, and for cleaning axle-boxes, &c.

We reserve till the conclusion a few general and special notes made in the course of the tour, and will now only allude, more in the way of mere catalogue than more amply and worthily, to the further accommodation provided at Nine Elms for the wants of the company in relation to the daily working of its rolling stock. About l50f. from the main block of buildings, and near Wandsworth-road, are the store buildings for materials in constant requisition by the locomotive and carriage departments. The lower portion of the building is stored with bar iron, plate iron, cylinders, and other materials and articles required for the construction and repair of rolling stock. The upper part of the building contains brasswork, such as boiler mountings, lamps, and all the fittings in use in the carriage department. The general stores have an easy communication with all the workshops by rails and turntables laid down for the purpose. Opposite the general stores, and completely isolated are the oil and the old material stores, and behind these again the signal, and the wheelwrights' shops for the repair of the company's road vans used for the collection and delivery of goods. This shop is furnished with a smiths' hearth, a spring furnace, and a tyre furnace, suitable for the description of work required to be done. The timber shed, 170ft long by 150ft wide, is situated about 100ft from the stores, and is well covered in, and contains the timber supplied for the construction and repairs of the carriage, wagon, and trucks made or repaired at the works. The timber store has direct railway communication with the saw-mill shop. The coalyard is on the opposite side of the main line. It has ten coke ovens, of which three only are in constant use for the supply of the workshops. In the same detached corner there is a small range of shops, which include an engine brickmaking machine, and a pair of powerful edge rammers. The firebricks and slabs used in the locomotive engines and the furnaces of the works are maintained in this locality.

In conclusion we gather up and dispose very summarily of the stray notes not absorbed in the brief description we have attempted to give of these works. Concerning the admirably constructed boilers which supply power to the works, it might have been noted that they are well-stayed, and of nine-sixteenths plate. The fire-brick lining is so arranged as to give excellent advantages in getting steam up quickly. The governors of the vertical engine employed are also very effective. A notable feature in the arrangement of the Nine Elms Works is presented in the number, quality, capabilities, and situations of the cranes and grabs, fixed and travelling, for lifting and moving heavy weights. The duplex lathes employed in the wheel-turning shop differ little, if at all, from those introduced by Mr. Beattie about twenty years ago, and which are now in common use. All the wheels of the engines and brake-vans on the South-Western line are now furnished with steel tyres, and it is intended to apply them to carriage wheels as well. The tyres are now obtained solid without welding, which is found to be a great advantage, both in the saving of labour and in the superiority of the work. The sizes of engine wheels made at Nine Elms are of 5ft diameter for goods engines, 6ft the most for general work and 7ft for express, passenger, and mail engines. This great size is exceeded by the engines on the Caledonian line which are 7ft 6in, and by those on the Bristol and Exeter, which are 8ft 6in diameter. In those cases, however, the wheels are single, whereas they are coupled in the case of the South Western engines.

In the wagon shops, redolent of English oak, a number of coal trucks were in various stages of

THE EXPANSION 1865-1878

manufacture, that were novel in the particular of having spring buffers and spring draw bars. The extra cost of these fittings is more than saved, we believe, in the diminished wear and tear caused by the violent shocks to hooks and couplings. This mode of construction is also necessary in the case of a southern railway from the fact that the wagons may be occasionally put to other uses than the transport of minerals, crystal china and stoneware for instance. The coal traffic of the South Western, which is considerable, consists chiefly, as may be supposed, of transhipment for consumption in the districts traversed by the company. Its supplies are, for the greater part, from South Wales, from the north via the London and North Western to Willesden Junction and a small portion of sea-borne coal delivered from the river at the Company's wharf at Nine Elms. It need not be said that the coal is likely to sustain injury by carriage in wagons with spring buffers and draw bars. The wagons are in other respects, in the strength of their oak framing and of the ironwork, of excellent pattern, and likely to justify by their durability their extra first cost.

It will have been noticed that almost all the shops are on a gauge of 57ft 3in wide. This result was arrived at from a calculation of the working room necessary for a certain number of lines of rails four as a maximum and for uniformity and compactness in the other buildings. The shop walls throughout are 16ft high, from the floor to the tie rods, excepting the range which includes the boiler, coppersmiths and erecting shops, which are 26ft. high. The roofs, very light in appearance, are all of iron, and abundantly supplied with large surfaces of glass. The warming of the premises we have already referred to, and may here mention that, as we noticed, in this weather, when the idea of warming almost causes sickness, the apparatus employed is available, and is actually used for blowing cool air into the shops through numerous openings from which the plugs had been unscrewed.

It only remains to say the arrangement of the buildings, the power, the tools, the lines, the traversers, turntables, and points, or, in a word, the whole design was provided by Mr. Joseph Beattie, engineer in chief of the South Western Railway, and carried out under his personal superintendence, assisted in the design, as well as in the execution, by his son, Mr. William George Beattie.

(* Views of the tramways referred to can be seen in Chapter 9 and in many other photographs.)

1876 Changes

This amount of expansion was not sufficient for very long. The next exertion of pressure was on the Goods Depot to the North, which soon began to experience problems due to the ever-increasing volume of goods traffic and the proximity of the shunting yard to the main line. As a result, the changes described in the part of the *Railway World* article which now follows were initiated in 1876, resulting in a brand new Motive Power Depot, and further enlarged workshops by the end of 1878. The article should be read in conjunction with the 1885 map, shown in Figure 139, which accompanied it, and with the map shown in Figure 140.

Although it was not foreseen at the time, the expansion of the Goods Department following the removal of the locomotive, carriage and wagon works was to have far-reaching consequences in the next few years. This situation arose because of the proximity of the shunting neck of the goods yard to the main line, so that as traffic increased, so did the number of accidents, and after several derailments had fouled the running lines it was accepted that the layout would have to be altered to give a safe distance between the main line and shunting operations. The boundary to the north with the Gas Light & Coke Company prevented any development in that direction, so the only alternative was to move the main line further to the south. This was an enormous task that involved the removal of most of the main line embankment and the adjacent locomotive depot, the construction of a viaduct for the new alignment, and a new locomotive depot to replace the old one. Under powers taken on 11th August 1876 the work was carried out in stages, beginning with the new locomotive depot, which had to be ready before the old one could be knocked down to make way for the viaduct. The latter consisted of a series of brick arches with provision for skew lines underneath connecting the North and South Yards. It was brought into use between October 1877 and July 1878, so that it seems likely that the new running shed was in traffic by the end of 1876. The site was on waste ground at the western end of the locomotive works, and as the 1885 plan shows the layout was every bit as fascinating and unusual as its predecessor. To judge by the date, it must have been the work of William George Beattie who succeeded his father as Mechanical Engineer in November 1871. Certainly the style was very different to that employed by the father, and was if anything more ornate than was strictly necessary for an engine shed. The centrepiece was an elegant two-storey office block, surmounted at one end by an ornamental clocktower that might well have graced the local town hall. The shed itself was a semi-circular roundhouse with 26 roads off two adjacent 42ft turntables, each road having a length of roughly 200ft, half of which was inside the building. The frontage was made up of 26 arched entrances, each with its own ornamental lamp standard and a pair of heavy wooden doors, above which was a panelled facia with a roundel in the centre. Even the coaling stage received special treatment,

THE LSWR AT NINE ELMS

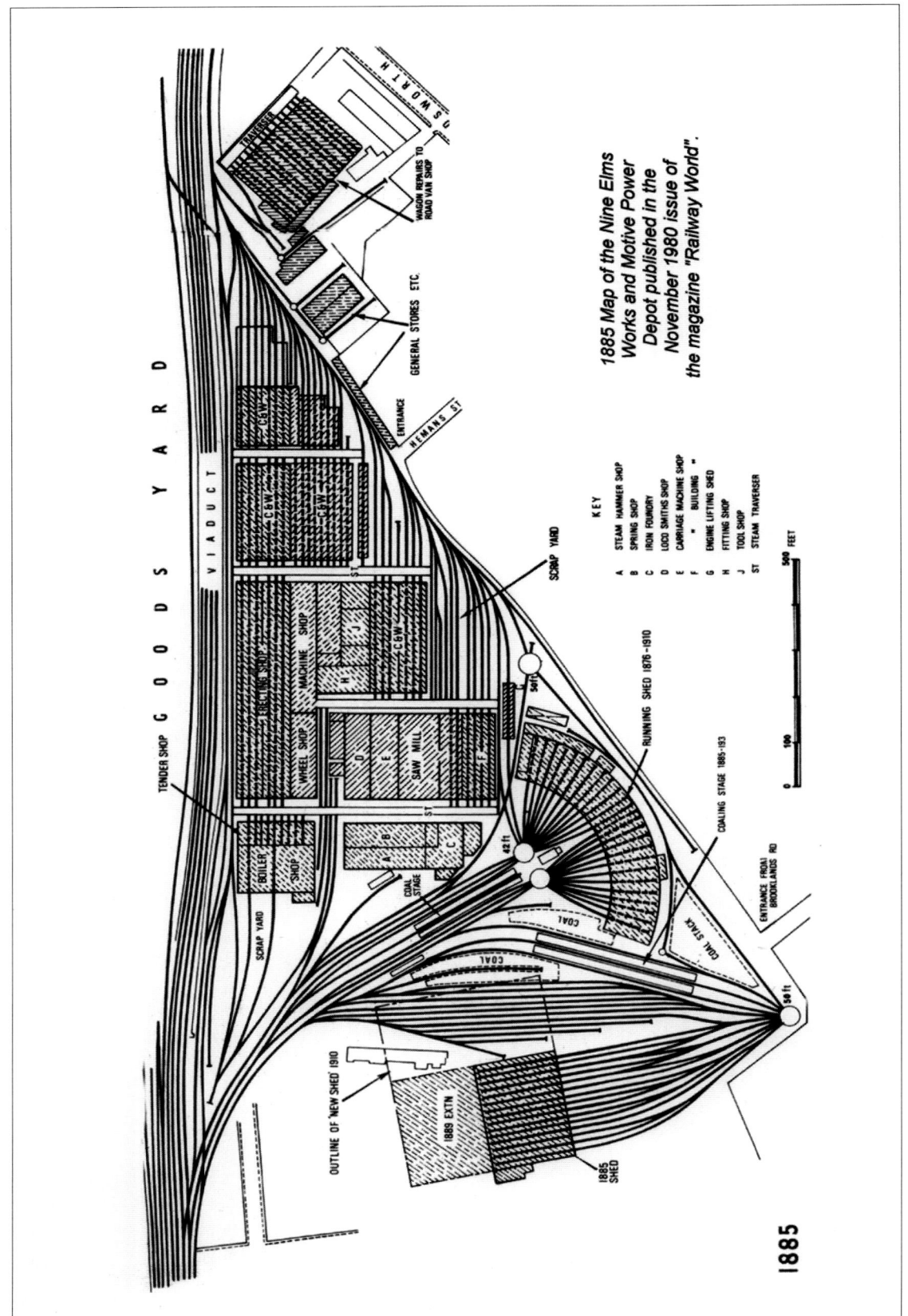

Fig. 139.

THE EXPANSION 1865 -1878

being largely enclosed by a wooden canopy decorated with strip mouldings and ornamental valances of the type used on platform awnings.

With its open aspect, ideal lighting and attractive buildings, the shed was much favoured by Victorian photographers, who have left a splendid record of the engines there - ranging from Joseph Beattie's fantastic 2-4-0s with 7ft driving wheels to such occasional visitors as the diminutive dock shunters that came up to Nine Elms for repairs.

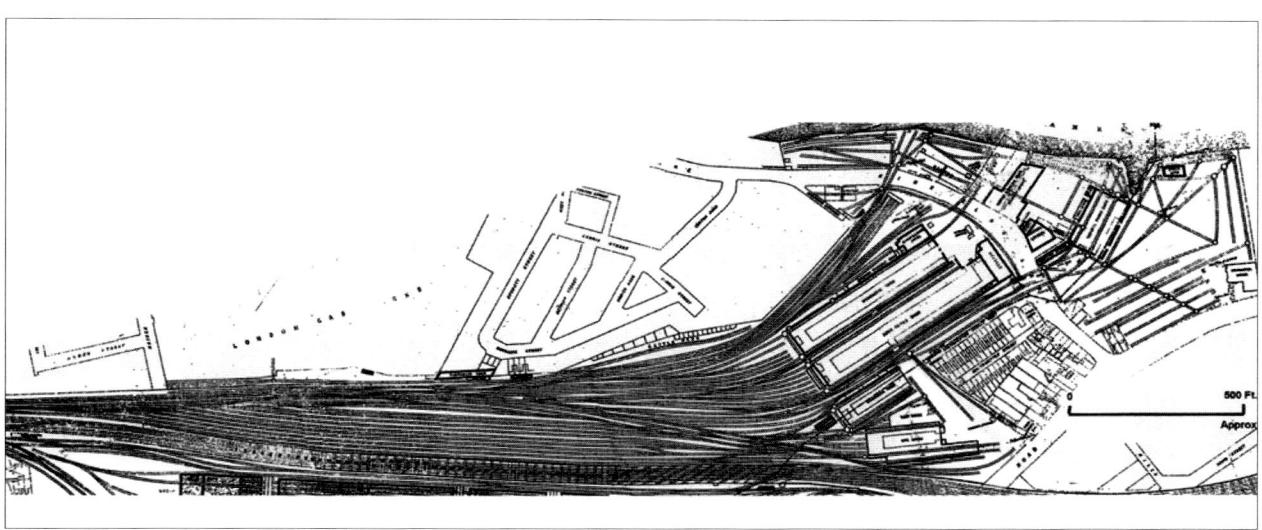

Fig. 140. As a comparison with Figure 139, this was the extent of the extended goods facility at Nine Elms on the north side of the site. It is taken from an 1889 map.

THE LSWR AT NINE ELMS

The map shown in Plate 8 (Page 38) is an interesting one. It is part of "Booth's Poverty Map" which surveyed most of London. Apart from designating housing areas according to the type of people who, presumably he thought, lived there, it shows the Nine Elms Works at an interesting stage of development. In order to expand the goods depot, it was necessary to firstly build a new motive power department (the roundhouse). Subsequently the old running shed was demolished; this is the stage that had been reached in this map. It is before the old turntables and associated tracks were removed, and therefore before the new viaduct could be built to carry the diverted main line next to the workshops. The goods depot is still in its old form. These facts date the map fairly accurately between 1876 and 1877.

Pages 104-5 feature nine more extracts from the minute book, all of which deal with the construction of the new roundhouse, office block, and ancillary services. Number 5081 reports subsidence affecting the water tower supports. It is possible that this was because the tower was being built near to the filled-in "Mill Pond" shown in Plate 4 on Page 22.

Figure 140 is a part of the 1889 map of Nine Elms and shows the extent to which the goods facilities expanded, after the works had moved to the south side, and after the main line had been moved onto the new viaduct. Now the whole of the site north of the main line was devoted to goods and included a large marshalling yard parallel to the viaduct. Figure 169 on page 134, is an 1885 map which shows all the developments described for the south side of the main line, plus the addition of a new linear-arranged running shed on the south-west border of the site. This facility was itself later extended towards the main line as shown on the 1889 map in Plate 9 on page 39.

This arrangement of the completed Nine Elms site lasted until 1890, when the Carriage and Wagon Works were moved to Eastleigh.

4220 *Way and Works Committee* *March 13 1873*

Loco Running Shed. Nine Elms

Read Minute of Board of 6th inst appertaining of the erection of the above new Shed at a cost of £15,500 on Capital Account and referring the plans to this Committee to carry out.

Upon the report of Mr. Jacomb of 11th inst. it was ordered that Tenders be invited for the Iron Work and submitted to the Committee and that the remainder of the work be done by Messrs. Jackson & Shaw according to the Schedule of prices in their general Contract with the Company.

4261 *Way and Works Committee* *April 24 1873*

Locomotive Running Shed Nine Elms

Mr. Jacomb reported that upon further communication with the Contractors - Messrs. Jackson & Shaw, he found that the building would cost about £21,000 instead of his original estimate of £15,500, and he was instructed to reduce the cost as much as possible and submit an amended estimate at next meeting of the Committee, but in the meantime the work may be commenced and if any saving can be made by employing the Company's own Staff, the same to be done.

To be done.

4274 *May 8 1873*

Locomotive Running Shed Nine Elms

Referring to Minute of 24 April, read report from Mr. Jacomb of the 5th inst as to the arrangements which he proposes to make for the above work with a rider to a reduction of the cost as far as possible including the free conveyance of Bricks by the Company from Fareham to Nine Elms.

Approved.

THE EXPANSION 1865 -1878

4457 Locomotive & Traffic Committee   Dec 18th 1873.

<u>Nine Elms New Loco. Running Shed.</u>

Read report of Mr. Jacomb of 12th Dec. as to the two Turn tables required at the above Shed and the arrangements proposed for the same including the supply of wrought iron Girders and plates for covering over the whole of the Table Pit so as to avoid breakdowns and delays etc.

To be further considered by Mr. Beattie and Mr. Jacomb, and the best plan to be adopted.

4483   Jan 15 1874

<u>Nine Elms. New Loco. Yard.</u>

Referring to Minute of 8th May 1873 read report of Mr. Jacomb of 13th inst with his Plans of the Tank House and Coal Stage required in connection with the new Locomotive Running Shed at Nine Elms.

Approved at a cost of £500 for the necessary Water Mains and Hydrants and £2007 for the Tank House and Coal Stage (Builders work) making £2,507 on Capital Account.

Tenders for the Ironwork to be obtained.

4510   Feb 12 1874

<u>Nine Elms Loco: Running Shed</u>

Referring to the Loco: Committee Minute of 18th Dec. Mr. Jacomb submitted two sets of Tenders received from various Firms for the two Engine Turntables required at the above new Shed as arranged between him and Mr. Beattie, and he was authorised to accept the Tender of Lloyds Fosters & Co. at £900. Subject to modifications in some particulars which he will settle with them.

4767 Way and Works Committee   October 8 1874

<u>Nine Elms. New Running Shed</u>

Read Minute of Locomotive Committee of 24th ulto: recommending the erection of Foremens Offices and a Clock Tower in connection with the above Shed.

Approved and Tenders to be invited for the buildings, as also for the clock.

4888   Feb 11 1875

<u>New Loco: Shed Nine Elms</u>

Referring to Minute of 3rd Dec. last read report of Mr. Jacomb of 8th inst with an amended plan of the proposed new furnaces for lighting up Engines and drying Sand at the above Shed at a reduced cost of £668.

5081 Way & Works Committee   October 21 1875

<u>Nine Elms. Water Tanks at New Running Shed.</u>

Read report of Mr. Jacomb of 18 inst. as to the failure of the above erection for reason of an unexpected subsidence which threw some of the Columns out of place, and explaining his plan for rebuilding on another site for the Tanks near the new Engine Shed at a cost of about £600.

The work to proceed and Mr. Stratton to supply the necessary Boiler Plates for the new Tanks. Etc.

The extra cost to be reported and the difference between cast and wrought iron to be charged to Capital.

THE LSWR AT NINE ELMS

Fig. 141. Ilfracombe Goods number 282, photographed after duplication in 1899 as 0282.

6
LOCOMOTIVE and ROLLING STOCK PROCUREMENT
1873 - 1878

W. G. Beattie - Locomotives

William George Beattie succeeded his father, Joseph Beattie, as Mechanical Engineer on 23rd November 1871, and resigned his position in the Company on 20th December 1877, ostensibly on the grounds of ill health. However he lived until 1918, so it was more likely that his departure was due to his performance as Mechanical Engineer being less than satisfactory. In spite of having the benefits of a brand new workshop, all of the new locomotives, coaches and wagons for which he was responsible were obtained from outside contractors, who were also responsible for a lot of the design.

Even design decisions that he did make were of dubious merit. He chose to purchase Metropolitan tanks from Beyer Peacock & Co, which although they gave good service in suburban applications on the Metropolitan Railway, were ill suited to the higher speeds that they would be expected to cope with on the Lydford and Okehampton line in the West Country. They proved to be unstable at higher speeds, even dangerous it was suggested, and this lead to tests being made in 1877 on two locomotives, one fitted with a bogie designed by William Adams (before he joined the LSWR) and one with a Crewe-type Bissell truck. The results were satisfactory, but as there was little to chose between the performance of the Adams bogie and the Bissell truck, the latter was chosen as it was cheaper. However, the Adams bogie remained with No 318 until it was withdrawn. Minute number 4267 of 8th May 1873 on page 131, records the authorisation for Beyer Peacock & Co to build six engines of this type for the Lydford line.

Another serious design failure initiated by W. G. Beattie was the 348 class of 4-4-0, alternatively known as the "Sharp's Expresses" after the company Sharp Stewart who made them. It has been commented upon that five companies were approached to tender; one refused to supply to the design, and two suggested major modifications. Twenty were eventually delivered, and most of them suffered from numerous mechanical failures, as a result of both poor design and poor workmanship and materials used. William Adams made a number of modifications to the class with some improvement in reliability and performance, but they were never very satisfactory, and had an average life of only 19 years.

The company had much better success with the three goods classes, but only because W. G. Beattie had little to do with their design. The Locomotive Committee Chairman became so dissatisfied with Beattie's attempts at designing an 0-6-0 tender engine for working the Barnstaple to Ilfracombe line that he instructed him to send the relevant parameters to the Beyer Peacock Company, and let them produce the design. The resultant "Ilfracombe Goods" engines were very successful. Minute number 4608 of the 5th February 1874 on page 132 records the ordering of two further locomotives of this type for the Sidmouth

TABLE 7

Build Period	Number Built	Builder	Wheel Arrangement	Class	Withdrawal Period	Figure Numbers
3/1873-11/1880	8	Beyer Peacock & Co.	0-6-0	Ilfracombe Goods	1/1905-12/1913	141,142,143, 144,145,146
7/1874-5/1878	36	Beyer Peacock & Co.	0-6-0	Single Frame Goods	12/1889-12/1925	147,148,149, 150,151,152
1/1875-6/1882	6	Beyer Peacock & Co.	4-4-0T	Metropolitan	9/1906-12/1913	153,154,155, 156
5/1876-6/1882	20	Beyer Peacock & Co.	0-6-0ST	Shunter	9/1924-8/1932	157,158,159, 160,161
2/1877-6/1877	20	Sharp Stewart & Co.	4-4-0	'348'	12/1889-3/1905	162,163,164, 165,166,167

line.

Just before he died, Joseph Beattie had ordered six more double framed 0-6-0 locomotives as a repeat order from Beyer Peacock & Co, but his son changed this order into one for a single-frame version, for no apparent reason as the double framed version had been very successful. Minute number 4107 of 21st November 1872 on page 131 is believed to be Beyer Peacock & Co's tender for six of these locomotives. The single-frame locomotive was, however, a successful Beyer Peacock & Co design, and a total of 36 were delivered. The final "goods" order was for a standard 0-6-0 saddle-tank, also a Beyer Peacock & Co standard design, so Beattie's doubtful influence was again avoided. They were successful engines, twenty being delivered, and all lasting for between forty and fifty years.

The contents of minute 4158 page 131 implies that tax liability manipulation happened even in 1873.

The locomotive production is summarised as in Table 7 on the previous page.

Minute number 4781 on page 110 refers to an acceptance by the Company of an offer by Beyer Peacock & Co to supply a light engine, with copper tubes, for £2750; I can find neither evidence of it being supplied, nor of the order being cancelled.

We have a few more items from the minute book, of a general nature. Minutes 4002 and 4743 on page 132 give information on the price of coal supplied to the company and also the quantity supplied in a half-year.

The "Broken Tyres and Axles" book yields two more relevant records. Figure 168 shows the broken axle from Ilfracombe Goods locomotive number 282, and Figure 169 shows a diagram relating to the axles from Single Framed Goods locomotives numbers 337 and 341.

Page 132 shows minute number 4021 of 8th August 1872 containing a complaint about the poor dividends paid on investments in the company, and the actions that were recommended. 18 months later, minute number 4533 on page 132 records the fact that copper tubes are to be used in the Company's engines. One can only assume that they had previously used steel tubes, and it is surprising that the increased cost was considered worthwhile. We do not know for how long the practice was continued.

Up to this time, in the early 1870s, continuous braking systems had not been fitted to the company's trains, and stopping a train depended upon the ability of the brakesman in the train and the locomotive staff. There were frequent over-runs of signals and platforms, but the seriousness of such incidents was kept within acceptable limits because of the low speeds involved. However speeds were bound to rise, and from about this time consideration began to be given to more satisfactory ways of stopping trains. Minute number 4001 on page 111 gives details of an offer by the Westinghouse Company to test their air brake system on this company's trains. The opposing system is represented in minute number 4858 on page 110 by "Smith's Vacuum Break", and another system is offered in minute number 4612, also on page 110. Minute number 4327 on page 111 contains an offer of a passenger communication system invented by Sir J. Macwill.

W. G. Beattie - Rolling Stock

As I have mentioned earlier, there is little information regarding the procurement of carriages and wagons. Although there are some parts of the works, both on the north and on the south side of the main line that were labelled as being allocated to these items, there is no evidence that any rolling stock was actually built there. They were probably used for carrying out repairs, refurbishments and modifications. As evidence to this theory, we have a series of minute book extracts dealing with the processing of tenders from a number of companies regarding the manufacture of most types of rolling stock for the LSWR. They cover the period from 8th August 1872 to 7th October 1875, when W.G. Beattie was in power, and are shown on pages 110 to 115.

There are seven different companies involved, and the choice appears to have been made only on the basis of lowest price in each case. Table 8 is a summary of those purchases that were made.

Minute number 4745 on page 110 shows a tender from the "Patent Shaft & Axletree" company for carriage wheels and axles. We do not know whether these items were intended for assembly at Nine Elms or for supply to the coachmakers. Minute 4629 on page 110 shows that even in 1874 there was quality control on what passengers sat on.

The total expenditure of £156,695 shown in Table 8 was over a period of 3 years only, whereas £246,760 spent on locomotives covered a period of 9 years. On these figures, and over this time period, the annual spending (for items that W.G. Beattie authorized) on carriages and wagons was double that for locomotives, and all new locomotive and rolling stock manufacturing that he ordered was performed by outside contractors. It should be realised, however, that there were a number of locomotives initiated by his father that were completed in the period covered by the Table 8. These were 12 Standard Well Tanks built by Beyer Peacock & Co at a total cost of £30,000 and three Lion, three Volcano, and 11 Vesuvius class loco-

LOCOMOTIVE and ROLLING STOCK PROCUREMENT 1873-1878

motives built in-house for a total of £55,225. If we include the cost of these locomotives, the average annual expenditure on coaches is about the same as that on locomotives for the period of Table 8.

The subject of a new "Queen's Coach" was discussed by the Court of Directors, and by the "Special Committee on Queen's Coach", starting on 14th May 1874 with minute number 4698 in which Mr. Portal is obviously concerned at the state of the existing coach. There appeared to be a fair amount of discussion on the matter, as reported in minutes 4616 and 4644, resulting in detailed estimates for a replacement being drawn up, only for minute 4698 to curtly report the decision to do nothing about it! These minutes are shown on page 115.

TABLE 8

Date	Company	Item	Class	Finish	Quantity	Price each (£ s d)	Total (£)
10/10/1872	Metropolitan Carriage Co	Open goods wagons			200	66-5-0	13,250
24/10/1872	Metropolitan Carriage Co	Carriages	1st	Teak	20	425-10-0	8,510
24/10/1872	Metropolitan Carriage Co	Carriages	2nd	Teak	10	361-0-0	3,810
24/10/1872	Metropolitan Carriage Co	Carriages	3rd		10	275-15-0	2,757
24/10/1872	Metropolitan Carriage Co	Break vans	3rd		10	282-0-0	2,820
24/10/1872	Oldbury Co	Carriages	2nd	Painted	50	320-0-0	16,000
4/12/1873	Oldbury Co	Horse boxes			12	186-0-0	2,232
4/12/1873	Oldbury Co	Carriages	2nd		20	365-0-0	7,300
4/12/1873	Oldbury Co	Timber trucks			50	72-0-0	3,600
4/12/1873	Metropolitan Carriage Co	Carriage trucks	Composite		30	420-0-0	12,600
4/12/1873	Metropolitan Carriage Co	Carriages			4	160-0-0	640
4/12/1873	Metropolitan Carriage Co	Passenger guards vans			25	294-0-0	7,350
10/09/1874	Oldbury Co.	Carriages	1st	Painted	20	440-0-0	8,800
10/09/1874	Britannia Co.	8 ton goods wagons		Painted	200	75-0-0	15,000
10/09/1874	Metropolitan Carriage Co	Carriages	1st		20	462-0-0	9,240
10/09/1874	Metropolitan Carriage Co	Carriages	2nd		8	378-0-0	3,024
10/09/1874	Metropolitan Carriage Co	Break vans	3rd		8	330-0-0	2,640
10/09/1874	Metropolitan Carriage Co	Carriages	3rd		12	283-0-0	3,396
10/09/1874	Oldbury Co	Break vans	3rd	Painted	12	307-0-0	3,684
10/09/1874	Oldbury Co	Carriages	Composite	Painted	20	376-0-0	7,520
19/11/1874	Metropolitan Carriage Co	8 ton goods wagons		Painted	100	75-0-0	7,500
7/01/1875	Britannia Co	Covered goods wagons			50	107-10-0	5,375
7/10/1875	Metropolitan Carriage Co	Break vans	3rd	Painted	10	305-0-0	3,050
7/10/1875	Metropolitan Carriage Co	Carriages	Composite	Painted	18	386-10-0	6,597

The total expenditure from 10/10/1872 to 7/10/1875 was £156,695. The total number of passenger vehicles was 263. The total number of goods vehicles was 656. (Note, the use of the word 'break' in these and other minutes was the then common reference to what were later referred to as brake-vehicles.)

THE LSWR AT NINE ELMS

4612   May 26 1874

<u>Patent Railway Break</u>

A letter from Mr. E. Stevens of 16th inst calling attention to his Patent Railway Break was referred to Mr. Beattie.

4629   June 4 1874

<u>Messrs Peters Account for "Horse Hair"</u>

Read report of Mr. Stratton of 3rd inst upon the claim of Messrs. G. Peters for £93. 6. 8 for Curled Horse hair delivered to the Co. in Oct. 1872 and rejected by the Carriage Dept as being of inferior quality to the sample upon which Messrs. Peter's tender had been accepted.

Claim declined and Messrs. Peters Consignee to be communicated with if necessary.

4745   <u>Locomotive Committee</u>   Sept 24 1874

<u>Carriage & Wagon Wheels & Axles</u>

A tender from the Patent Shaft & Axletree Co. dated 2nd inst for supply of the Carriage and Wagon Wheels and axles required for the Company's New Rolling Stock was submitted as under.

80 sets 3' 6" Carriage Wood Wheels & Axles as per Tracing No. 1952	£45 per set
20 sets 3' 6" Solid Wrought Iron Break Van Wheels & Axles as per Tracing No. 1945	£46.10 per set
200 sets of 3' Wagon Wood Wheels & Axles as per Tracing No. 1983	£37 per set

Approved subject to the inspection of sections of Axles of other Companies by Mr. Beattie.

4781   October 8 1874

<u>New Light Engine</u>

Read letter from Messrs Beyer Peacock & Co. of 7th October offering to construct a light Engine with copper tubes for £2,750.

Offer to be accepted.

4858   <u>Officers Committee</u>   January 18 1875

<u>"Smiths" Vacuum Break</u>

Mr. Beattie having called the attention of the Committee to the above Break and asked their opinion as to the advisability of introducing it on this Line, it was resolved to postpone the consideration of the matter until the result of the forthcoming experiments about to be made on the G.E. Railway is known.

LOCOMOTIVE and ROLLING STOCK PROCUREMENT 1873-1878

4001 Locomotive & Traffic Committee   July 11th 1872

Engine & Carriage Breaks

Read letter from Mr. G. Westinghouse of the 9th int. proposing to apply his system of Air Breaks upon some of the Company's Engines and Carriages upon terms of payment including Royaltys.

To await trails on other Railways.

4327 Officers Committee   July 7th 1873

Train Communication between Passengers and Guards

A pamphlet was submitted from Sir J. Macwill describing a new invention of his for communicating between Passengers and Guards which was referred to Mr. Beattie for examination and report.

4022 Traffic Committee   August 8th 1872

Rolling Stock

Mr. Scott reported that during the Spring and Summer months it had been found impossible to meet the requirements of the line for Carriages and great inconvenience had been caused thereby especially on Monday last. He recommended that at least 50 additional Carriages should be obtained before the spring of next year.

Recommend 50 additional Carriages to be ordered, the same as last received, and Tenders to be obtained from the Metropolitan, the Oldbury and Ashbury Companies and from Brown Marshall Cos. Not to be made of Teak Wood, but of Bay Wood and painted.

4080 Court of Directors   October 10th 1872.

Goods Wagons

With reference to the Locomotive Committee minute of today. Mr. Scott reported that the Metropolitan Carriage Co. will undertake the supply of 200 open Goods Wagons at the price of £66.5.0 each.

To be accepted subject to the delivery of the whole number by the 1st March next.

4061 Court of Directors   September 12th 1872

Rolling Stock

Referring to Traffic Committee Minute of 5th ulto it was agreed to order 100 New Carriages instead of 50 as therein recommended, half of that number being built as Second Class Carriages and the other half in the Block Train principal.

4081 Locomotive & Traffic Committee   October 10th 1872

Carriage & Wagon Stock

Read letter from Mr. Wright in the part of the Metropolitan Carriage & Wagon Co. of 25th ulto: offering this Company 50 eight Tons Wagons upon hire for 12 months at the rate of £11.10.0 per wagon.   To be accepted.

The following Tenders were submitted for the supply of 100 open Goods Wagons according to a drawing & Specifications by Mr. Beattie the Wheels & Axles, Axle Boxes, Bearings and Bearing Springs being supplied by this Company viz

Oldbury Carriage Co.	£67.17.6 per wagon
Metropolitan Carriage Co.	67.0.0 per wagon

An order to be given to the Metropolitan Carriage Co. for 200 Wagons if they will supply them at £66.0.0 per Wagon. The whole to be delivered by 1st March next.

THE LSWR AT NINE ELMS

4090   Locomotive & Traffic Committee   October 24th 1872

New Carriages

Referring to the Board Minute of the 12th ulto the following Tenders were received for the supply of 100 Carriages therein named

Vehicle	Metropolitan Carriage Co.	Oldbury Carriage Co.	Brown Marshall Co.
20 First Class	£425.10.0 each	£449.0.0 each	£433.0.0 each
10 Second Class (Teak Wood)	£331.0.0 each	£352.10.0 each	£350.0 each
20 Second Class (Painted)	£320.0.0 each	£299.0.0 each	£320.0.0 each
10 Third Class	£257.15.0 each	£289.0.0 each	£277.10.0 each
10 Third Break Vans	£282.0.0 each	£307.10.0 each	£330.0.0 each

The 50 carriages forming the Block Train Stock of Teak to be ordered from the Metropolitan Carriage Co. and the 50 second class painted Carriages to be ordered from the Oldbury Co. at the above price.

Invalid Carriage

Referring to Minute of last Meeting read Minute of Officers Committee of 14th inst recommending that another of the small saloons be converted into an Invalid Carriage at the cheapest possible cost.

Mr. Beattie to submit a plan and estimate.

4444   Locomotive & Traffic Committee   Dec. 4th 1873

New Carriages & Vans etc.

Referring to Minutes of 9th and 23rd October the following Tenders were received viz:

	Railway Carr. & Wag. Co.	Metropolitan Carr. & Wag. Co
12 Horse Boxes	£186 each	£189 each
20 Second Class Carr.	£365 each	£372 12/- each
50 Timber Trucks	£72 each	£75 each
30 Composites	£433 each	£420 each
4 Carriage Trucks	£163 each	£160 each
25 Pass. Guards Vans.	£299 each	£294 each

The Oldbury (Railway Carriage &) Cos. Tender to be accepted for the Horse Boxes, Second Class Carriages and Timber Trucks if satisfactory as to time of delivery.

The Metropolitan Co's Tender to be accepted for the Composite Covered Carr Trucks and Guards Vans.

The above numbers of Vehicles (141) are in substitution for those (179) named in the Minutes referred to.

4697   Court of Directors   August 6th 1874

New Rolling Stock

Read Minutes of the Locomotive Committee of 16th and 30th July recommending the purchase of the following new Vehicles viz:

      200 Goods Wagons
      20 First Class Carraiges
      20 Composites
      12 Guards Vans

Also 4 new Block Trains each consisting of 12 Vehicles as follows

      2 Vans with 3rd Class Compartments   2 Seconds
      3 Thirds   5 Firsts

Agreed to and ordered to be carried out.

LOCOMOTIVE and ROLLING STOCK PROCUREMENT 1873 -1878

4728 *Locomotive Committee*   *September 10th 1874*

<u>*New Rolling Stock*</u>

Referring to Minute of last Meeting the following Tenders were submitted for the new Vehicles required by the Company according to the Drawings & Specifications prepared by Mr. Beattie viz.

20 First class (painted) Carriages	Oldbury Co.	£440 each	6 months delivery
	Metro. Carr Co.	£449 each	9 months delivery
	Britannia Co.	£450 each	10 months delivery
200 Goods Wagons (painted) 8 tons	Oldbury Co.	£76 15/- each	6 months delivery
	Metro. Carr Co.	£75 10/- each	4½ months delivery
	Britannia Co.	£75. each	5 months delivery
20 First Class Carriages	Oldbury Co.	£680 each	6 months delivery
	Metro. Carr Co.	£462 each	6 months delivery
	Britannia Co.	£470 each	8 months delivery
8 Second Class Carriages	Oldbury Co.	£384 each	4 months delivery
	Metro. Carr Co.	£375 each	6 months delivery
	Britannia Co.	£390 each	8 months delivery
8 Break Vans (3rd Class)	Oldbury Co.	£334 15/- each	5 months delivery
	Metro. Carr Co.	£330 each	6 months delivery
	Britannia Co.	£340 each	8 months delivery
12 Third Class Carriages	Oldbury Co.	£287 10/- each	5 months delivery
	Metro. Carr Co.	£283 each	6 months delivery
	Britannia Co.	£284 each	8 months delivery
12 Break Vans (painted) 3rd Class	Oldbury Co.	£307 each	5 months delivery
	Metro. Carr Co.	£312 each	9 months delivery
	Britannia Co.	£314 each	10 months delivery
20 Composites (painted)	Oldbury Co.	£376 each	6 months delivery
	Metro. Carr Co.	£383 each	9 months delivery
	Britannia Co.	£380 each	10 months delivery

The <u>lowest</u> Tenders to be accepted, but Mr. Beattie to remonstrate with the Oldbury Co. upon the state of the last stock delivered by them and inform them that if these Coaches are not superior they will not have any more tenders sent to them by this Company.

4745 Locomotive Committee   Sept 24th 1874

<u>Carriage & Wagon Wheels & Axles</u>

A Tender from the Patent Shaft & Axlebox Co. dated 2nd instant for supply of the Carriage and Wagon Wheels & Axles required for the Company's New Rolling Stock was submitted as under

80 sets 3'6" Carriage Wood Wheels & Axles as per tracing No. 1952	£45 per set
20 sets 3'6" Solid Wrought Iron Break Van Wheels & Axles as per tracing No. 1945	£46.10.0 per set
200 sets of 3ft Wagon Wood Wheels & Axles as per tracing No. 1983	£37 per set.

Approved subject to the inspection of Sections of Axles of other Companies by Mr. Beattie.

4762   <u>Wagons for Stone Traffic</u>   Oct 8th 1874

Read Minute of Officers Committee of 28th ulto recommending that 50 of the Wagons now building at Nine Elms be constructed with low sides for the purpose of the above traffic.
Approved.

4802 Locomotive Committee   Nov 19th 1874

<u>New Goods Wagons</u>

Read letter from Mr. J. Wright of 17th inst. offering, on the part of the Metropolitan Carriage & Wagon Co. to build another 100 Goods Wagons for this Company at the price of £75 each, and commence the delivery of the same in February 1875.
This offer to be accepted.

4870 Locomotive Committee   Jan. 7th 1875

<u>Covered Goods Wagons</u>

The following Tenders were received for 50 Covered Goods Wagons pursuant to Minute of last Meeting viz:-

Britannia Co.	£107.10.0 each
Oldbury Co.	£109.10.0 each
Midland Co.	£110.0.0 each
Metropolitan Co.	£111.8.0 each
Ashbury Co.	£117.10.0 each

The Tender of the Britannia Co. at £107.10.0 to be accepted.

4924 Court of Directors   March 18th 1875

<u>Second & Third Class Carriages</u>

With reference to the Locomotive Committee Minute of the 11th inst. read further Minute of the Officers Committee of 15th inst. recommending that as many of the old Third Class Carriages with raised roofs as are fit to run with safety should be turned out by Mr. Beattie after giving them as good an outside appearance as possible.
Approved and referred to the Locomotive Committee to carry out.

LOCOMOTIVE and ROLLING STOCK PROCUREMENT 1873 -1878

5069   Locomotive Committee   October 7th 1875

Carriages and Vans

The following Tenders were submitted for the new Carriages and Guards Vans required by the Company viz:

	Ashbury Carr. Co.	Brown Marshalls	Metro Carr. Co.
6 Painted Composite Carriages	£370	£369	£365
6 Painted Third Class Break Vans	£291	£296	£290 10/-
20 Painted Six Wheeled Second Class Carriages	£379	£386	£376
10 Painted Third Class Break Vans	£305 10/-	£310	£305
18 Painted Composite Carriages	£390	£407	£356 10/-

The Metropolitan Carriage Co's tender to be accepted for the 10 Break Vans @ £305 and 18 Composites @ £356 10/- each.

The question whether the 20 Second Class Carriages should not be of 4 Compartments with 4 wheels to be referred to the Officers Committee for consideration and report.

The 12 Short Buffer Carriages with Breaks also to be reconsidered.

4698   Court of Directors   May 14th 1874

Queen's Carriage

Mr. Portal having called attention to the age and condition of the above Carriage upon which he had been in communication with Mr. Beattie it was referred to a Committee consisting of Mr. Portal, Mr. Serjt Gaselee, Mr. Mortimer and Col. Campbell to report on the accommodation for the Queen.

4616   Special Committee on Queens Carriage   May 28th 1874

Mr. Beattie attended the Committee and stated that the height of the present coach is 6' 8" and proposed 7' 6" as the height in any new Royal Saloon.

1.   Mr. Scott reported that the accommodation required by her Majesty was a Saloon for her own accommodation with retiring room on one side, and one apartment for Male Attendants and another for Female Attendants with retiring room.
         Agreed to.
2.   It was agreed that the present Royal Carriage cannot be made available for the Queen and her attendants.
3.   That Mr. Beattie see the new South Eastern Royal Carriage, and lay before this Committee a tracing giving the required accommodation.
4.   That the Secretary make enquiries as to the South Eastern Royal Carriage being inspected by this Committee.
5.   That Mr. Beattie be prepared with an estimate of the cost of the proposed new Carriage.
6.   That this Committee meet again this day fortnight.

4644   Queens Carriage Committee   July 2nd 1874

Mr. Beattie attended and submitted four designs he had prepared with various accommodation.

No. 1 plan   Same as Great Western Railway Carriage viz. Royal Saloon, 2 attendants compartments, 3 Retiring Rooms. Estimate £2,250

No. 2 plan   Royal Saloon and Retiring Room, 2 attendants compartments £1,650

No. 3 plan   Royal Saloon, 1 attendants compartment, 2 Retiring Rooms £1,750

No. 4 plan   Royal Saloon and Retiring Room, 1 attendant compartment. In this design it is proposed to connect another carriage with it by a Gangway, for other attendants. £1,700

These 4 designs to be referred to the Board.

4698   August 6th 1874

Queens Carriage

Referring to Minute of 14 May the report of the Special Committee, on this subject, of 2 July, was brought up, and it was ordered that a new Royal Carriage be not built by this Company.

THE LSWR AT NINE ELMS

LOCOMOTIVE and ROLLING STOCK PROCUREMENT 1873-1878

Opposite page, top: Fig. 142. Beyer Peacock's works photograph of "Ilfracombe Goods" locomotive.

Opposite page, bottom: Fig. 143. "Ilfracombe Goods" No 282 at Nine Elms, rebuilt with Adams boiler, cab, and stove-pipe chimney, between 1889 and 1899.

This page: Fig. 144. "Ilfracombe Goods" No 394 with original boiler and cab but with stove-pipe chimney.

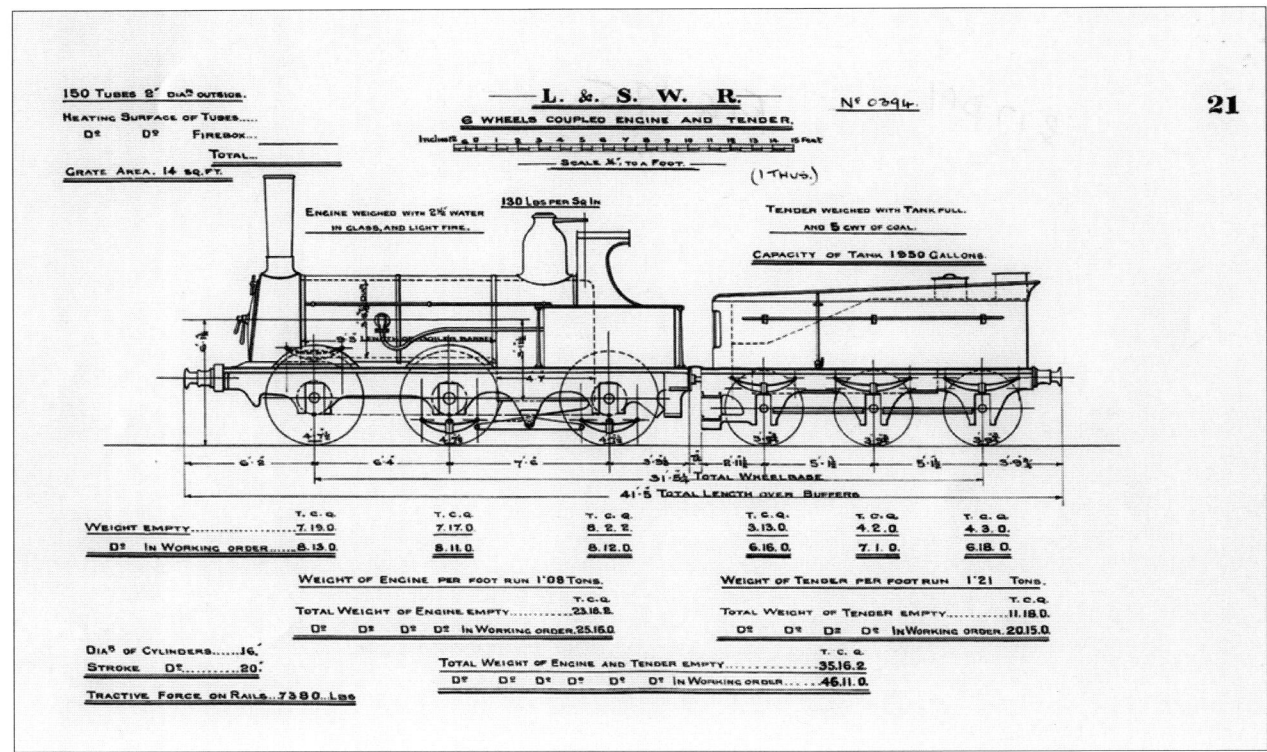

Fig. 145. Ilfracombe Goods engine diagram showing locomotive as built except for stove-pipe chimney.

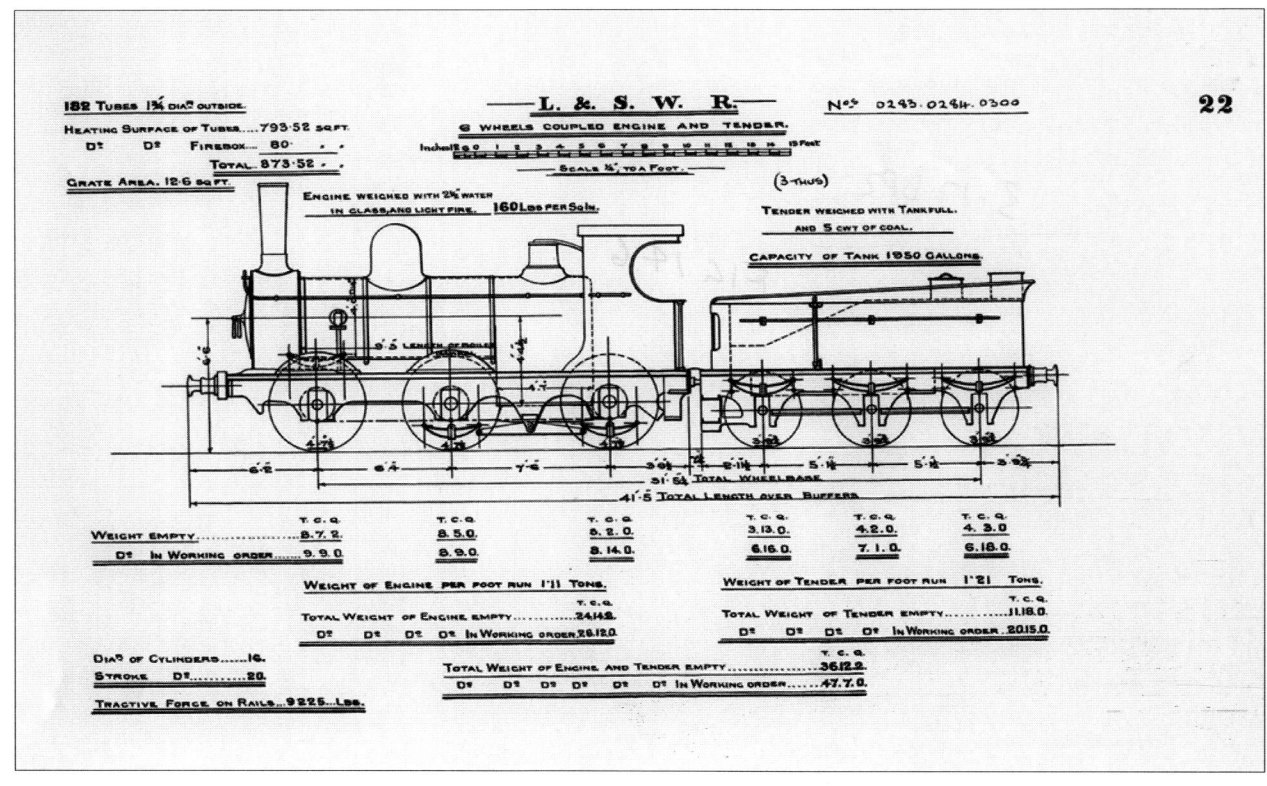

Fig. 146. Ilfracombe Goods engine diagram showing locomotive after Adams modifications.

LOCOMOTIVE and ROLLING STOCK PROCUREMENT 1873 -1878

Fig. 147. Beyer Peacock's works photograph of Single Framed Goods locomotive.

Fig. 148. Single Framed Goods locomotive No 345, as originally built except for removal of feedwater heater. Circa 1880.

Top: Fig. 149. Single Framed Goods locomotive No 151 "Montrose", as originally built except for removal of feedwater heater. No vacuum brake fitted. Circa 1882.

Right: Fig. 150. Single Framed Goods locomotive number 152, rebuilt with Adams boiler and cab, and Drummond chimney. Circa 1902.

LOCOMOTIVE and ROLLING STOCK PROCUREMENT 1873 -1878

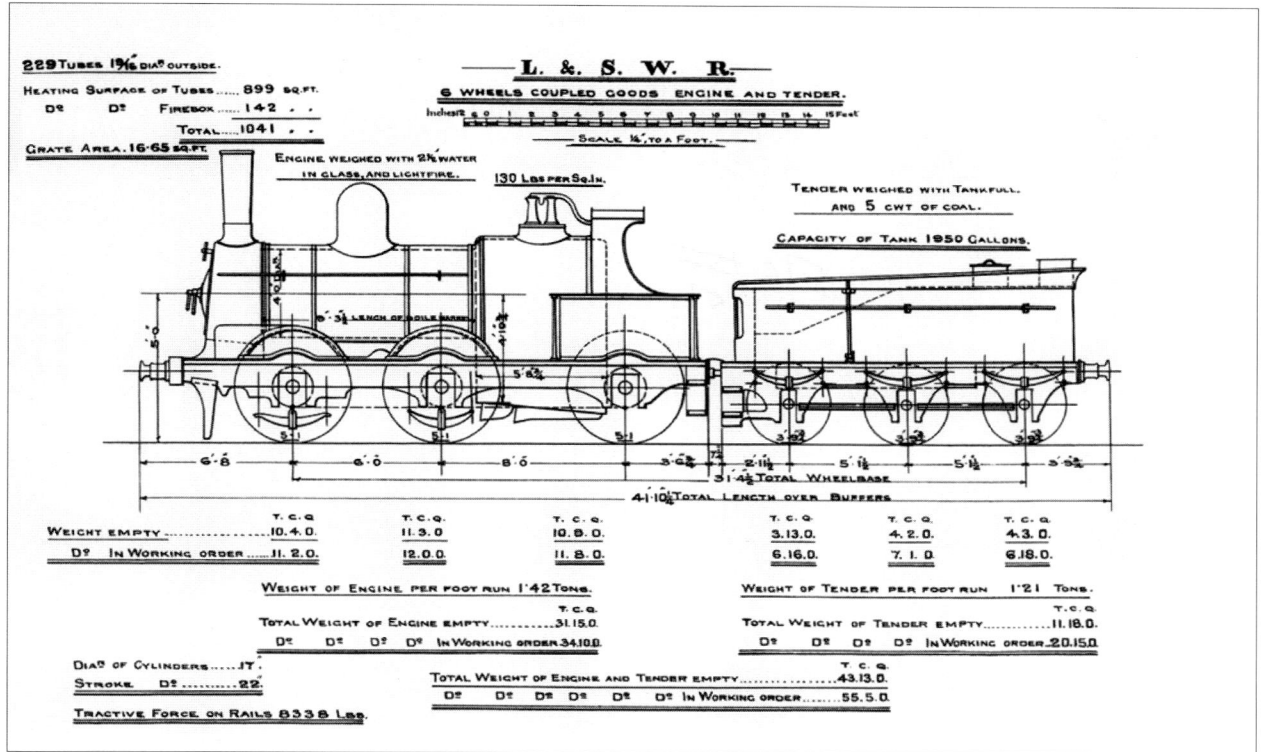

Fig. 151. Engine diagram of Single Framed Goods locomotive, as originally built but with stove-pipe chimney.

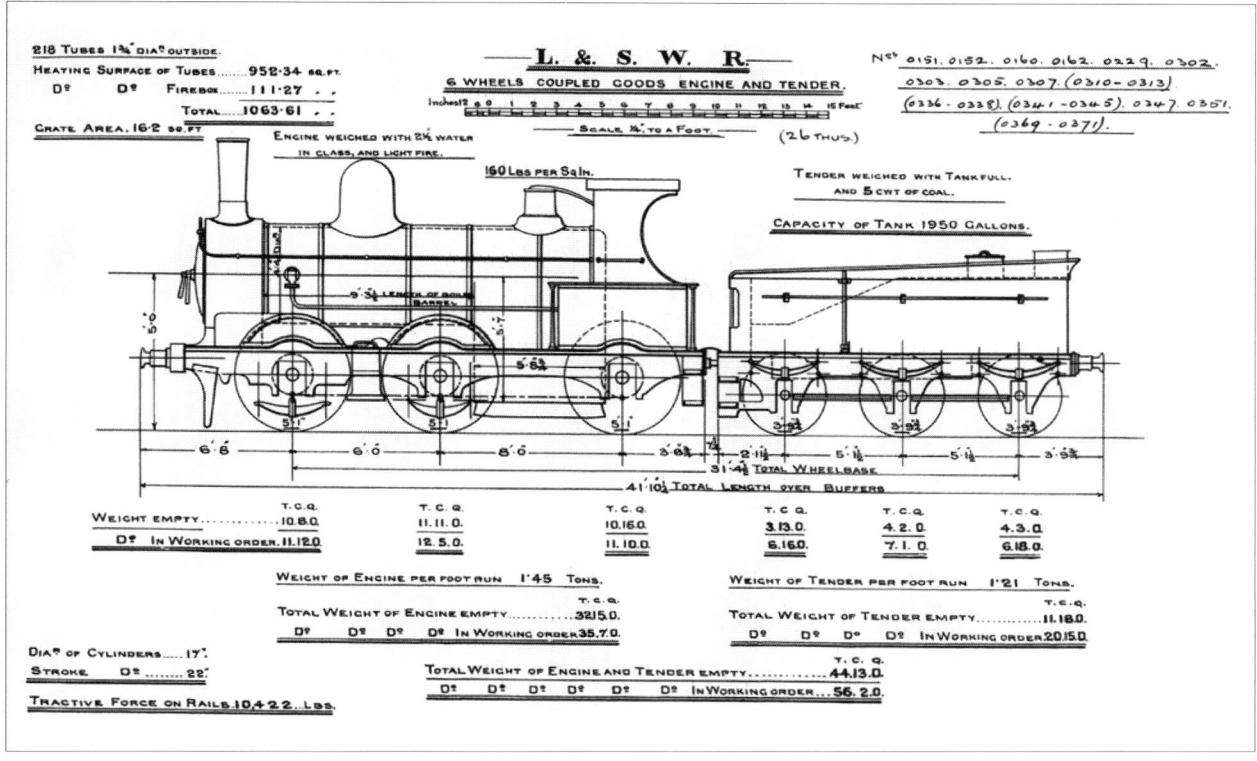

Fig. 152. Engine diagram of Single Framed Goods locomotive with Adams boiler and cab.

Fig. 153. Beyer Peacock's works photograph of Metropolitan class locomotive.

Fig. 154. Metropolitan class locomotive No 319, later duplicated as 0319. Circa 1900.

LOCOMOTIVE and ROLLING STOCK PROCUREMENT 1873 -1878

Fig. 155. Metropolitan class locomotive number 318, fitted with Adams patent bogie. Taken between 1890 and 1900.

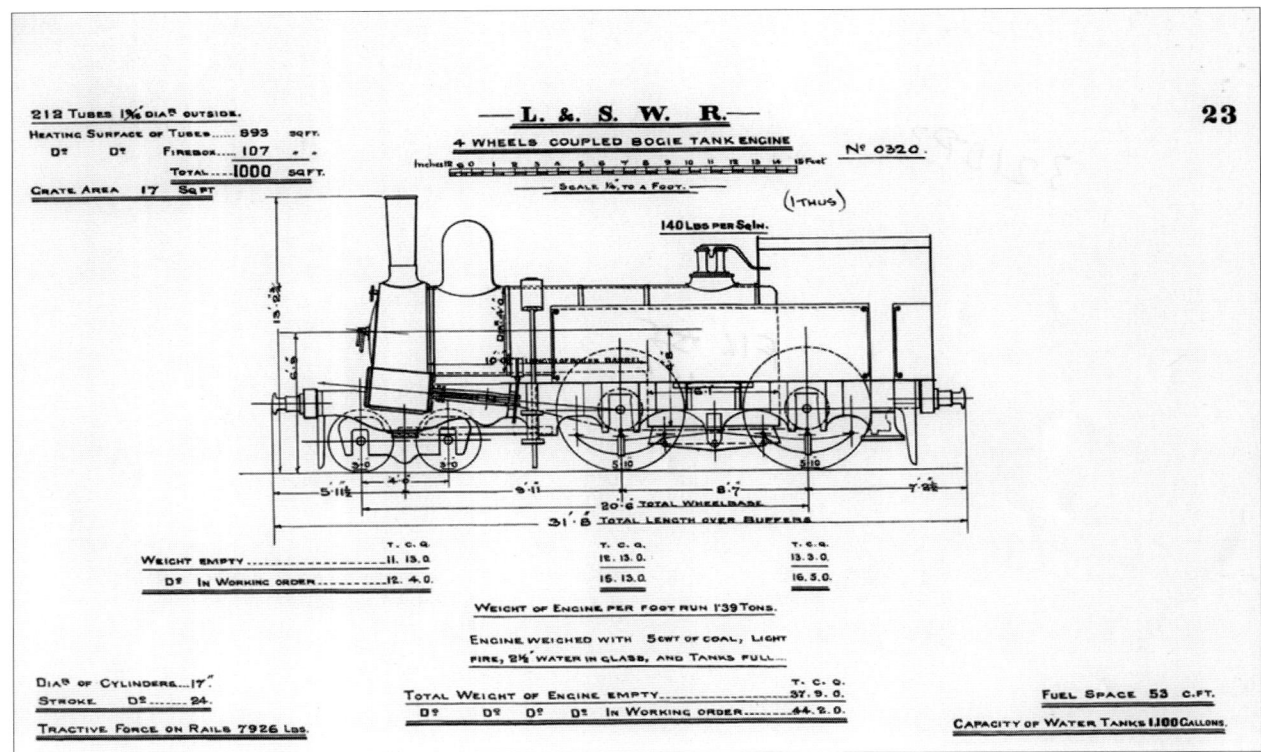

Fig. 156. Metropolitan class locomotive engine diagram, as originally built.

Fig. 157. Beyer Peacock 330 class shunter No 227, after being duplicated and then being returned to capital stock as No 316. Seen shunting wagons at an unknown location, sometime between 1899 and 1912.

LOCOMOTIVE and ROLLING STOCK PROCUREMENT 1873-1878

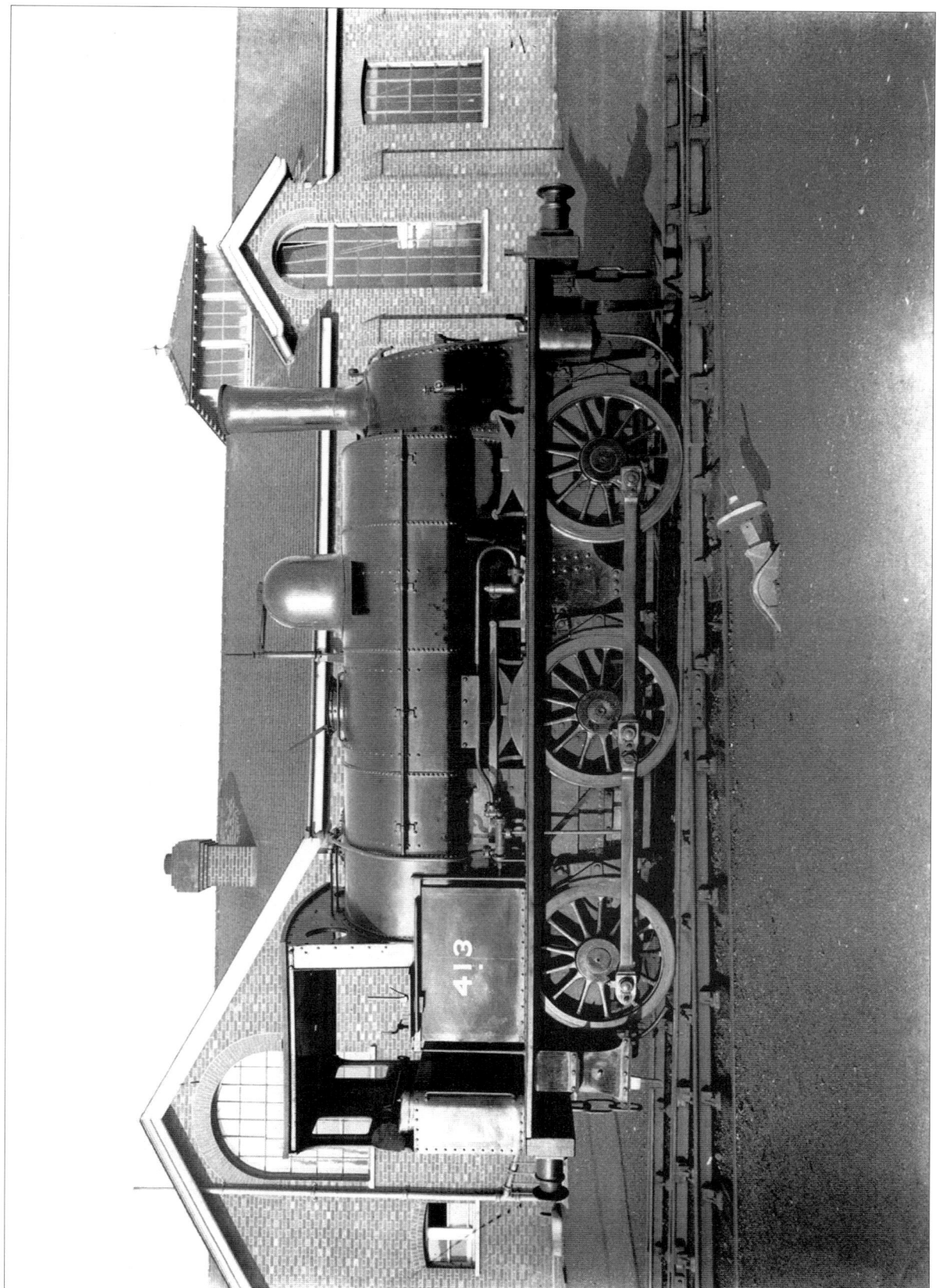

Fig. 158. Beyer Peacock 330 class shunter No 413, as originally built.

Fig. 159. Beyer Peacock 330 class shunter No 413, with added side sheets to cab.

LOCOMOTIVE and ROLLING STOCK PROCUREMENT 1873 -1878

Fig. 160. Beyer Peacock 330 class shunter No 409 at Nine Elms, showing collision damage to front nearside.

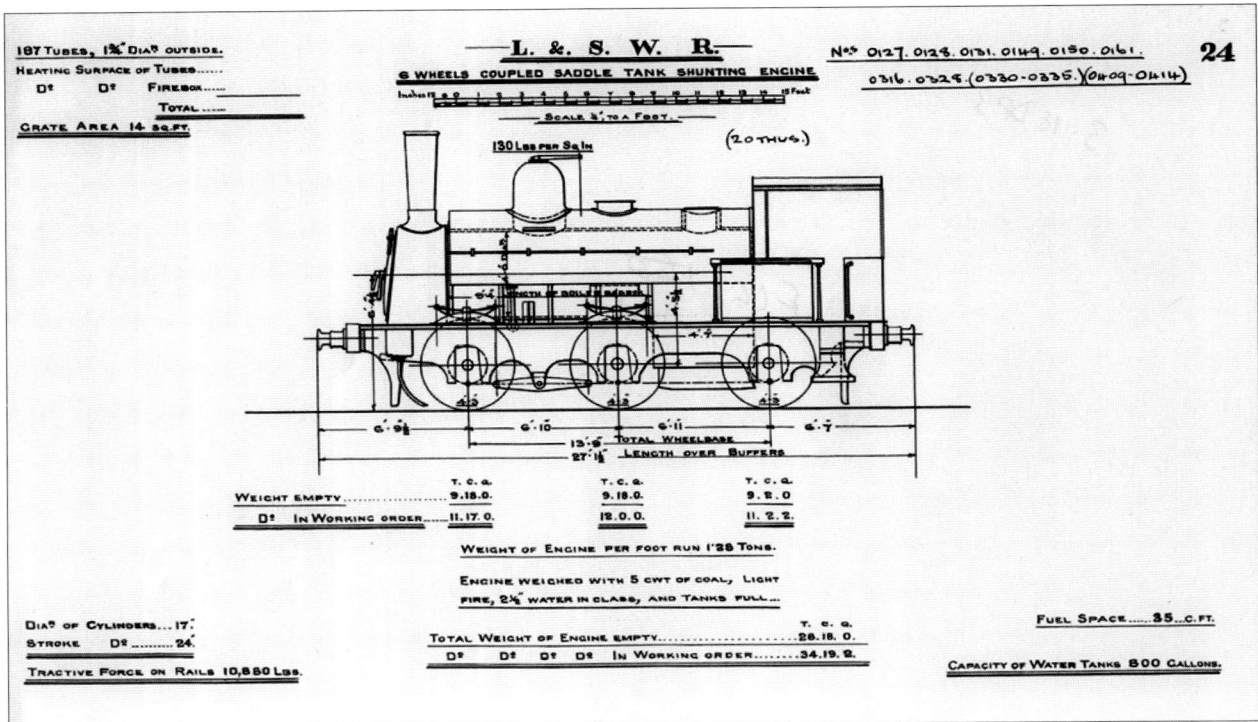

Fig. 161. 330 class shunter engine diagram as originally built.

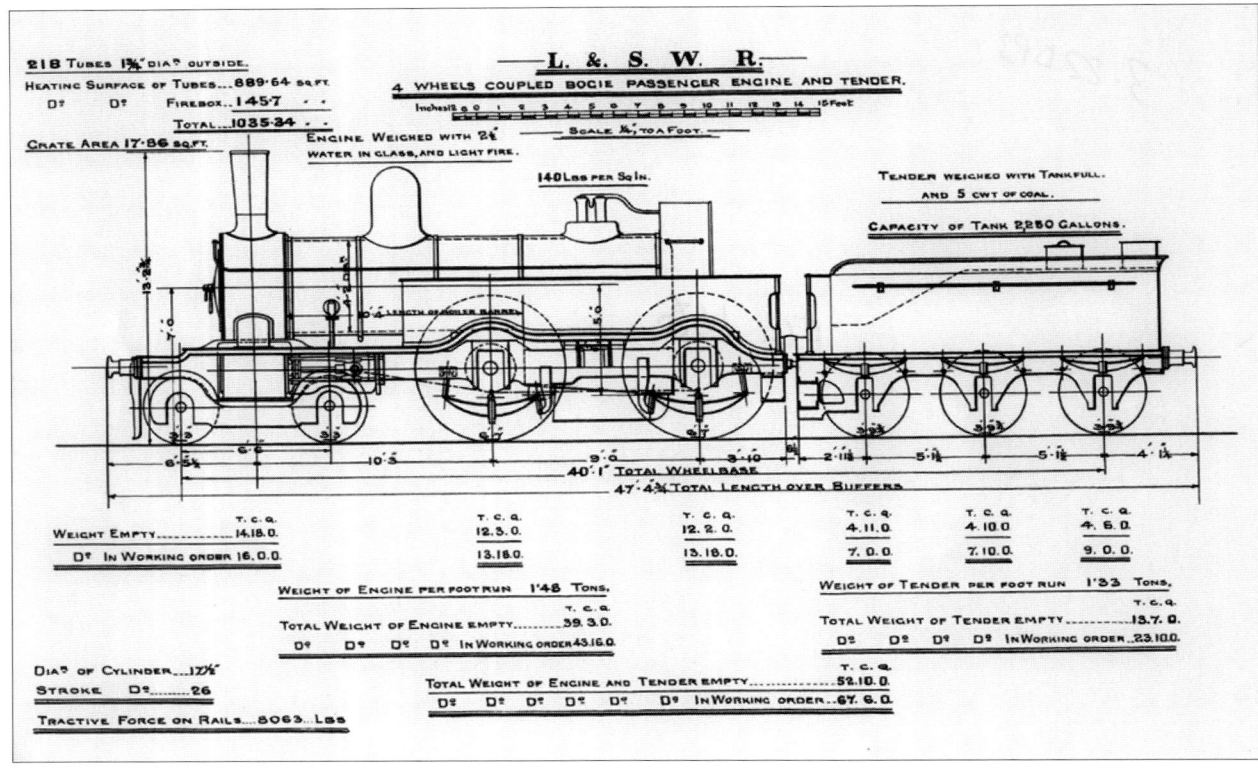

Fig. 162. 348 class engine diagram in original condition.

LOCOMOTIVE and ROLLING STOCK PROCUREMENT 1873 -1878

Fig. 163. 348 class number 364 at Eastleigh on a stopping train after modifications involving outside steam pipes. Photograph taken between 1880 and 1890. The leading vehicle is a 30ft Passenger Brake Van possibly 7ft 9ins wide, which can be seen to also have an arc roof. All that can be discerned of the second vehicle is that it is of the six-wheeled type.

Fig. 164. 348 class duplicated as No 0348 with Adams boiler, cab, stove-pipe chimney and modified splashers. 1900.

Fig. 165. 348 class No 348 after being fitted with a Drummond chimney in 1901. This locomotive was one of the last of the class to be withdrawn (in 1905) and is still duplicated (see Figure 164), but the zero before the number has been replaced by a line under it - albeit hard to see on the print.

THE LSWR AT NINE ELMS

Fig. 166. 348 class No 0365, in near-original condition, apart from having had fluted coupling rods fitted. Circa 1893.

LOCOMOTIVE and ROLLING STOCK PROCUREMENT 1873-1878

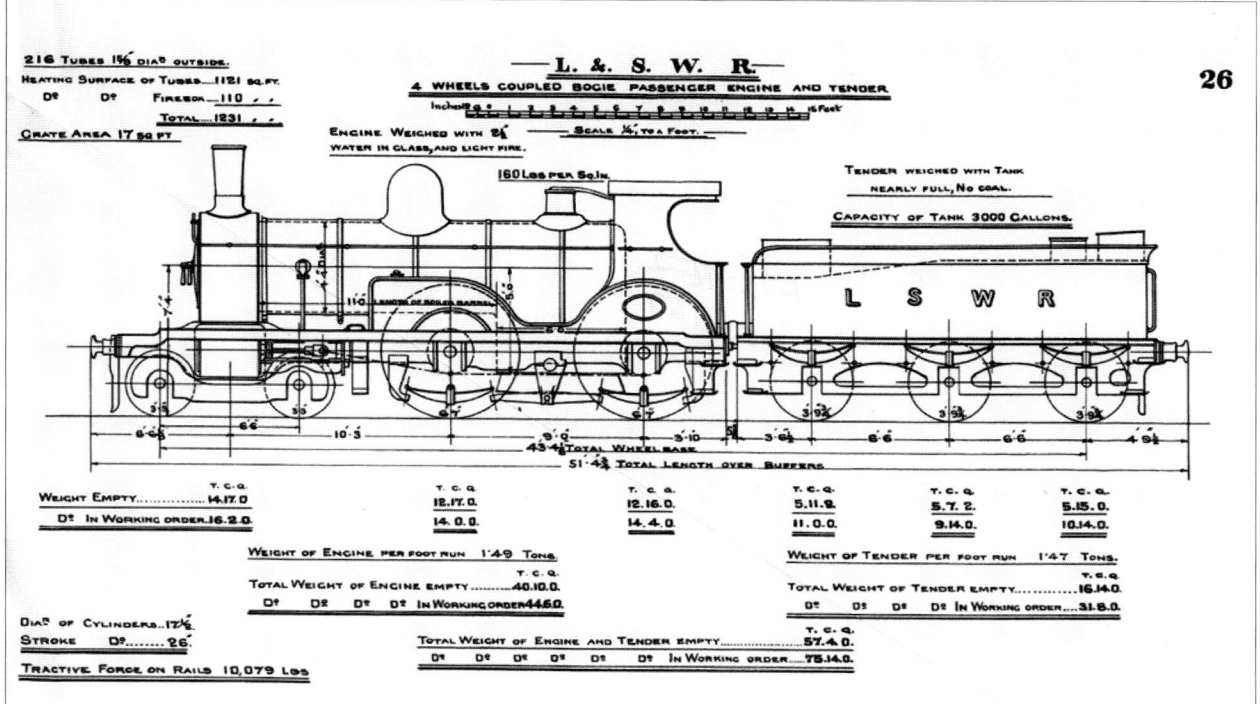

Fig. 167. 348 class engine diagram with Adams modifications.

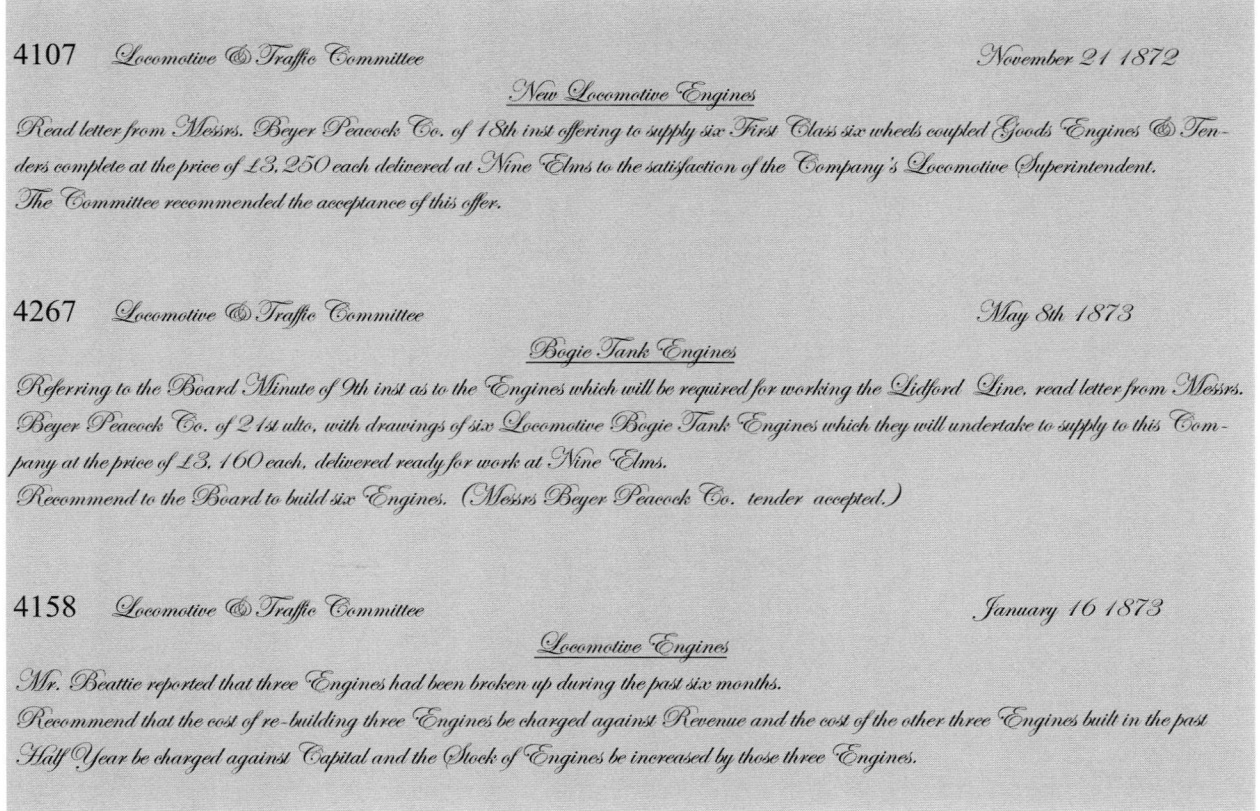

4107   *Locomotive & Traffic Committee*   *November 21 1872*
New Locomotive Engines

Read letter from Messrs. Beyer Peacock Co. of 18th inst offering to supply six First Class six wheels coupled Goods Engines & Tenders complete at the price of £3,250 each delivered at Nine Elms to the satisfaction of the Company's Locomotive Superintendent.
The Committee recommended the acceptance of this offer.

4267   *Locomotive & Traffic Committee*   *May 8th 1873*
Bogie Tank Engines

Referring to the Board Minute of 9th inst as to the Engines which will be required for working the Lidford Line. read letter from Messrs. Beyer Peacock Co. of 21st ulto, with drawings of six Locomotive Bogie Tank Engines which they will undertake to supply to this Company at the price of £3,160 each, delivered ready for work at Nine Elms.
Recommend to the Board to build six Engines. (Messrs Beyer Peacock Co. tender accepted.)

4158   *Locomotive & Traffic Committee*   *January 16 1873*
Locomotive Engines

Mr. Beattie reported that three Engines had been broken up during the past six months.
Recommend that the cost of re-building three Engines be charged against Revenue and the cost of the other three Engines built in the past Half Year be charged against Capital and the Stock of Engines be increased by those three Engines.

4608   Court of Directors   February 5th 1874

Engines for Sidmouth Line

Referring to the Minute of Loco. Committee of 29th ulto: read letter from Messrs Beyer Peacock Co. of the 30th ulto: offering to supply 2 Engines with Tenders complete for working the above line at the price of £2,750 each, and deliver the same by June next at Nine Elms. Two Engines to be ordered.

4021   Court of Directors   August 8th 1872

Company's Receipts & Expenses

Read letter from Mr. Spinks and Mr. G. Dickson of 3rd inst stating their disappointment at the rate of dividend for the past half year and suggesting the adoption of increased rates and fares for Goods and Passenger Traffic.

The Secretary to reply and it was ordered that a circular be issued to the Station Agents intimating the opinion of the Board that the expenditure of the Company has been excessive and the Heads of the several Depts. be informed of the views of the Board hereon with the hope that it will lead to such economy and reduction of expenses as will place the Account of the Company in a more satisfactory state for the future.

4533   Officers Committee   March 2nd 1874

Engine Tubes

Referring to the Minute of 19th ulto Mr. Beattie reported the result of the enquiries which he had made of other Co. as to their experience in the above matter upon consideration of which it was resolved to recommend that Copper Tubes be in future used in this Company's Engines.

4002   Way & Works Committee   July 11th 1872

Loco: Steam Coals

Read letter from Mr. Stratton of 10th inst with statement showing the following results viz:

Loco Steam Coal in Stock 1 January 1872	2,114 tons	15/6½d average price
Purchased during the last half year	51,648 tons	17/3½d average price
Stock 1 July 1872	3,867 tons	17/7d average price.

4743   September 24th 1872

Locomotive Coals

Read letter from Messrs. Stephenson Clark Co. of 18th instant offering to supply the Company with Locomotive Coals as under:-

Annersley Best Hards	20/2 per ton @ the Colliery
Barker Macker Hards	20/2 per ton @ the Colliery
Blackwell Hards	19/- per ton @ the Colliery
Best Fothergills handpicked	19/- per ton @ Basingstoke
Loco: Steam Coals	19/- per ton @ Basingstoke
Best South Wales	18/3 per ton @ Fremington
Steam Coals	18/3 per ton @ Fremington

This tender to be accepted for 3 months with an option to this Co to extend the period for another 3 months at the same price.

LOCOMOTIVE and ROLLING STOCK PROCUREMENT 1873-1878

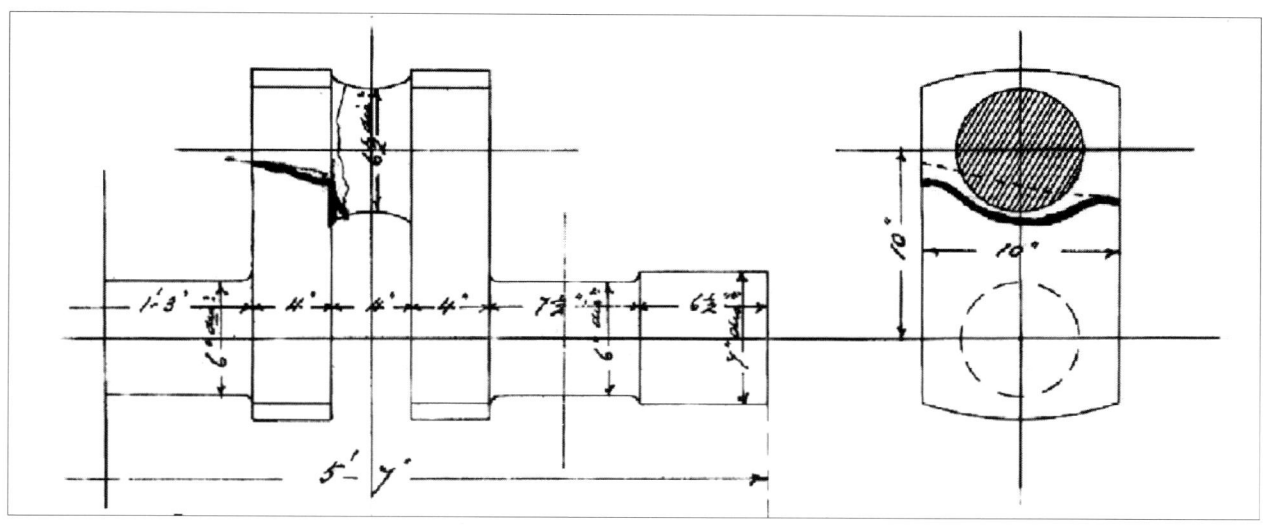

Fig. 168. Extract from "Broken Tyres and Axles" book recording a broken axle on Ilfracombe Goods locomotive No. 282. The incident occurred at Ilfracombe with the 8.29 pm train from Barnstaple on 14th February 1881.

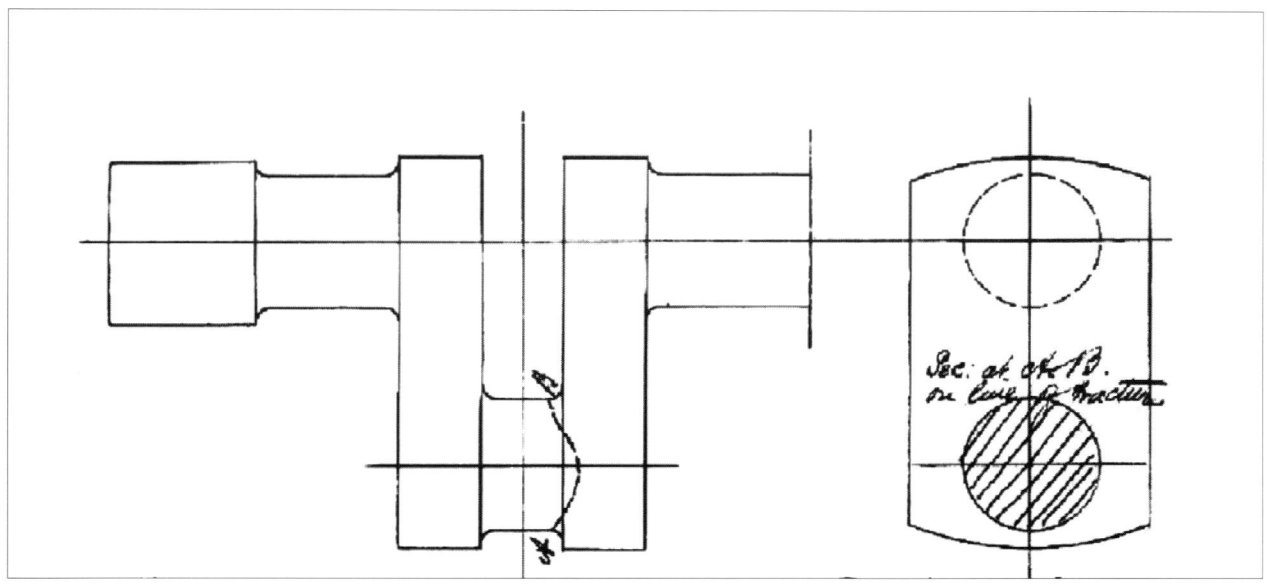

Fig. 169. Extract from "Broken Tyres and Axles" book recording broken axles on Single Framed Goods locomotives Nos. 341 and 337 on 2nd August and 5th August 1878. No 341 was on the 6.10 pm Exeter to Yeovil service, and No 337 was reported as hauling the 6.30 pm up Torrington Goods.

THE LSWR AT NINE ELMS

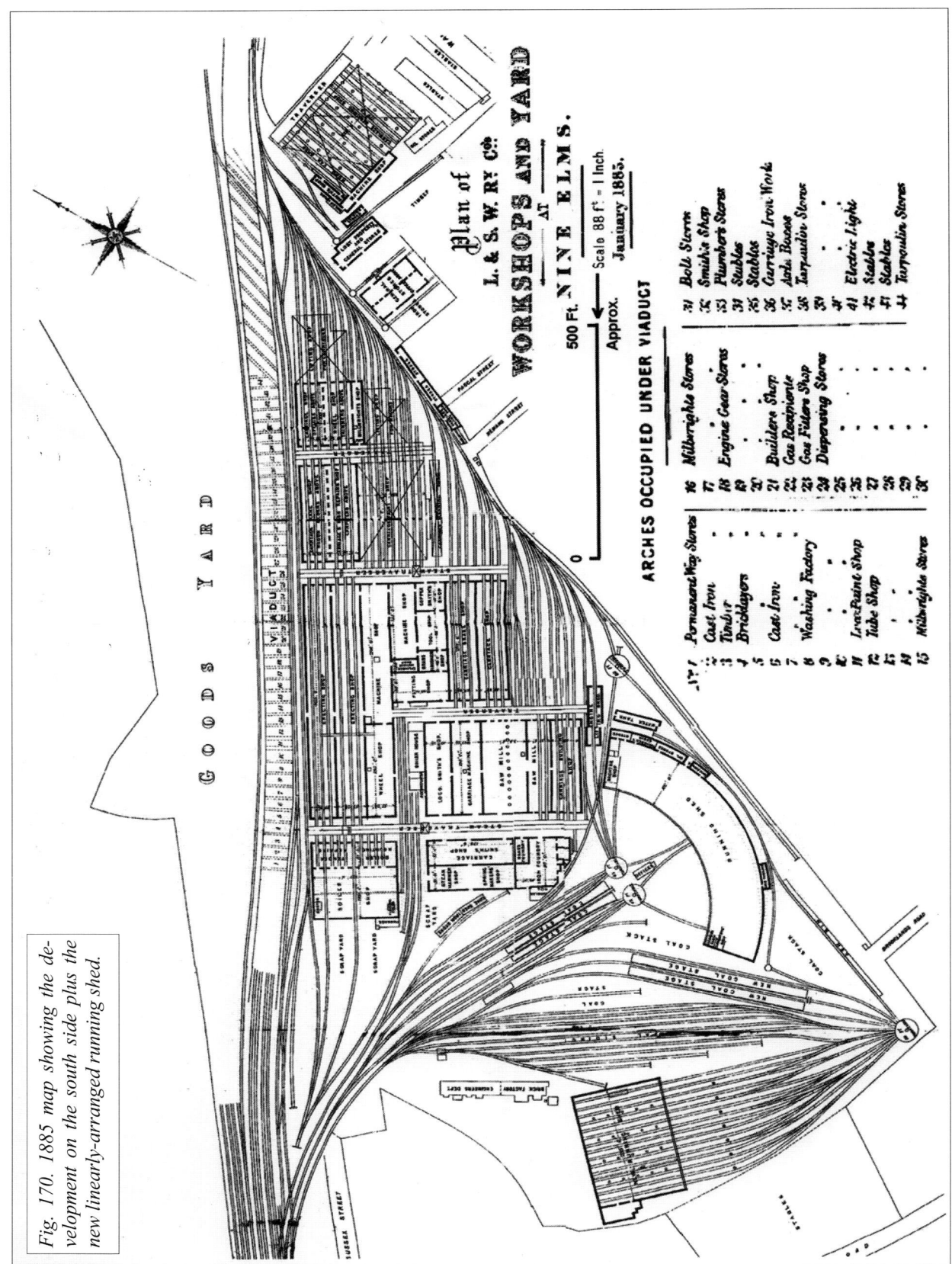

Fig. 170. 1885 map showing the development on the south side plus the new linearly-arranged running shed.

7
ENVIRONMENTAL and HUMAN ASPECTS

The Railway's Influence on its Environment

As mentioned in Chapter 5, the industrialisation of the area by the 1870s had become immense. The next article, entitled *The Impact of the Railway in Wandsworth* by Tim Sherwood, contains some information relevant to these years of expansion, and some to the later years. The Article was originally published in the author's book *Change at Clapham Junction* to which the reader is referred.

Some of the process of change in the Borough of Wandsworth during the 19th century, and especially the years 1861 to 1881, can be associated with the railway. Of all the parishes in the Borough, it is true to say that the railway's greatest environmental impact has been in Battersea.

When construction started on the London & Southampton in the winter of 1834/35, Battersea (apart from the riverside village) consisted of an unenclosed field, market gardens and farms such as Longhedge. This estate was doomed; first, bisected by the L&S, then diminished by the WECPR in 1857 and, finally, obliterated by the LCDR in 1860. Only the house and its ornamental garden was left.

By 1870 the lines had reached their greatest extent and around the Battersea "Tangle" was the paraphenalia of the steam railway: two locomotive works and one depot, five goods depots and five passenger stations - including the biggest in the United Kingdom, Clapham Junction. Most parts of Battersea and Wandsworth were within half a mile of a station; the railway was very much part of local life. The social aspirations of Park Town Estate had been spoilt by the proximity of Longhedge Works. A grid of terraced housing was spreading, bounded sometimes by the railway lines; Battersea, less famous than Swindon or Crewe, had become a railway town.

Mention has already been made of the effects of the viaducts, the smoke and the noise. The LBSCR and LCDR presented an east-west barrier and St George's parish at Nine Elms, already isolated by the mill pond and gasworks, became a separate community. The L&S created a barrier that remains to this day; although paths and farm tracks were preserved, there was, and is, no north-south road crossing between Queenstown and Latchmere Road, and no crossing between Heathfield Road and Garratt Lane. Likewise, Wandsworth Common was mutilated by the L&S and WECPR and lateral communication disrupted.

At Wandsworth, the Thames bank and the Wandle were already industrialised, so the railway made little difference. The railways, however, were not built for local people - they were trunk lines and tourist lines on their way to central London and, out of self-interest, they took the least disruptive routes. Yet they brought three advantages to local people: firstly, cheaper commodities such as coal, fresh food and milk; secondly, by the last quarter of the century, they were providing fast and safe travel for a significant number of local people (apart from workmen's trains to Waterloo and Victoria, one could get day excursions to the south coast); thirdly, they provided employment.

After small beginnings - only 17 staff were engaged for the Richmond line, it will be recalled - by 1871 the railway had become an important employer: 1348 men were employed at Nine Elms, of whom 780 were in the locomotive department, 568 in the carriage department, out of which 100 were based at Clapham Junction; thus, it has to be said, "bringing industrial work to an area that had been market gardens less than 20 years earlier". Longhedge, in 1881, was smaller, with 395 men in all departments (both were modest in comparison with Swindon Works which employed 4000). It was regular work with above-average wages.

The railway did not attract other industries - most of the sub-contracting was to engineering firms outside the area and other industries preferred the river bank where raw materials could be brought in cheaply. The railway in Battersea did, however, attract the distributive trades: firstly, goods trains were not allowed into the vicinity of Victoria, so depots had to be provided south of the River; secondly, the West London Extension Railway was primarily a goods line.

Where did the workers live? From the 1871 census we know that there were concentrations around Nine Elms and Clapham Junction. Near the former, 162 lived in Battersea New Town, 105 around the depot itself and 386 in the estates south of the LSWR main line. Of the latter, 97 lived in the Park Town Estate, including 15 in Brighton Terrace, which had been compulsorily purchased by the LBSCR because it was next to the south London line viaduct. 205 workers lived near Clapham junction, many in the new estates north of Grant Road. Of course, some of these people may have been employed elsewhere, eg. Victoria station, just as many of those working in Battersea travelled in from neighbouring areas.

It is as well to remind readers that the population of Battersea increased dramatically during this period, from 19,600 in 1861 to 107,262 in 1881, or by 547%. In the decade 1861/71, railway employment increased threefold (more than even the building trade) and the number of railwaymen living in Battersea fivefold, i.e. faster than the overall population for that decade.

Putney was not seriously disrupted or affected by the Richmond railway; Roehampton was untouched, the line running to the north of the large private estates. The arrival of the MDR (Metropolitan & District Railway), at the north end of the bridge was a more significant event, with its bus service feeding passengers on to a line which ran directly in to the West End and City. When the MDR was extended in 1889, the viaducts dominated east Putney and caused some dislocation, but it was minor in comparison with Battersea. Residents on the eastern side of Putney Hill then had a generous service with two stations to choose from. Indeed, of all the communities in the Borough, Putney has been favoured with the best train services (excepting Clapham Junction). This is the same situation as in the days of the short-stage coaches before the railway had been introduced.

It has been suggested that Balham, Streatham and Tooting were relatively unaffected by the railway in 1855, though the occupants of the Priory and Bedford Hill House might not have agreed when their view from the high ground of the village was interrupted by the embankment and bridges of the WECPR. The railway began to divide Balham: the cheaper land to the north of the line was sold for residential and commercial development, whereas to the south the estates and farms lasted to the end of the century, when there was a flurry of building at Tooting.

The change wrought by the railway in Balham and, for that matter, Putney, - as well as the snobbery of Victorian England - is illustrated by The Builder in 1875:

[...it might be that a locality had become dotted over with gentlemen's residences, occupied by persons of good means, all able to keep their carriages and saddle horses, and that the comparative remoteness of the neighbourhood from a station was an element of value ... The establishment of a new railway station in the immediate vicinity of this select locality would obviously much lessen the value of the existing house property. Vacant sites would no doubt improve in value ... to be occupied by clerks and business people ... and ... the old residents would leave the neighbourhood...]

At Streatham Hill, residential development was advancing down the Brixton Road in the 1850s, preceding the railway, part of which was in tunnel. The northern part of Tooting Common was mutilated by the railway - to which there was little opposition by landowners, though in 1859 there was opposition to the "cut-off" taking more of the Common and demolishing oak trees, The LBSCR had been forced to modify their plans in order to overcome the resistance. It is doubtful if local people still needed to exercise their grazing rights by the mid-19th century, so the loss of common land may not have been calamitous. Tooting village was little affected by the steam railway from 1868 as the trams and the underground railway in 1926 were of far more benefit.

From around 1880 the railways began to lose their supremacy in suburban transport and access to central London which they had enjoyed for the previous 20 years. Horse trams were introduced in Clapham in 1871 and Battersea and Wandsworth in 1881, providing a door-to-door service that many working class people could afford; they did not reach Balham and Tooting until 1890 and penetrate the Brixton Road and Streatham Hill until two years later. The horse tram never reached Putney.

Although there was an increase in the number of workmen's trains at the turn of the century, the tram was a far more useful and cheaper mode of transport than the local train services. Moreover, by 1910, the tramways, largely under the progressive control of the LCC, were electrified: Clapham 1903, Tooting 1903 (where the LCC had built the Totterdown Estate), Streatham 1904, Battersea and Wandsworth 1906 and Putney 1909. The effect on suburban railways was considerable; in 1908 the LSWR admitted that they had lost 1.5 million passengers in their London district in the previous six months. Like the MDR (1905), and the LBSCR (1909/11), they were forced into electrification (1915/16), a long overdue improvement which, with the exception of the TM&WR, (Tooting, Merdon & Wimbledon Railway) restored patronage.

The SECR lines were not electrified at this time, and in 1916 the Company withdrew their Victoria Ludgate Hill services and closed their stations at Battersea Park Road, Wandsworth Road and Clapham High Street. As already mentioned, the Clapham Junction-Kensington, and Waterloo-Wimbledon via East Putney services were withdrawn in the Second World War.

It has been from the 1960s, however, that the railway in Wandsworth has assumed its present size, though in the 1990s it looks as though the WLER may regain something of its former glory. It has been electrified so that it can carry "Eurostar" trains from Paris and Brussels to Edinburgh and Glasgow, International freight trains, and empty stock from Waterloo International to the new maintenance depot at Acton (using the re-instated "creep-up" spur). As already noted, the intensive orbital suburban services are being re-introduced. Had it survived, one wonders

ENVIRONMENTAL and HUMAN ASPECTS

what Punch, which lampooned the WLER so harshly in the 1840s, would have made of all this.

There is a reference to the "Battersea Tangle" in this article, which has been described in more detail in Chapter 5, together with a map in Figure 137. The increase in the population of Battersea mentioned in the article of 547% from 1861 to 1881 is incredible. Tim Sherwood offers the opinion that the railways were not built for local people, they were trunk lines, but they did have advantages where the supply of goods locally was concerned, and local passenger traffic did develop at a later date; but it is also noted that horse trams were introduced to some areas between 1871 and 1881, and that trams in general were more successful in providing local services than were the trains.

The quote from *The Builder* given in the article mentions the advantages of having properties that were remote from the railway, and this attitude persisted in later years, only to prove a disadvantage when daily commuting developed, and local transport systems disintegrated due to the arrival of the motor car. In most cases railway stations did not have sufficient room for car parking, but in later years when goods traffic disappeared, goods yards could be converted into parking areas.

The West London Extension Railway (WLER) is mentioned, and this line has had an interesting history. It is described in more detail under "Services to the Public" later in this chapter.

The following information has been extracted from an article by Keith Bailey, entitled *Railwaymen in Victorian Battersea* published in *The Wandsworth Historian No. 46*. It gives a lot more detail about railway employment in the area, including some figures from the 1851, 1861, and 1871 census results. Here are some of its findings:

Together with the building industry, railways formed one of the most important sources of employment in Battersea as it developed from a village into a

TABLE 9

Occupation	1851		1861		1871	
Overall	**Number**	**%**	**Number**	**%**	**Number**	**%**
Traffic	55	69.62	159	77.18	858	75.53
Engineering	24	30.38	47	22.8	278	24.47
Total	**79**	**100.00**	**206**	**100.00**	**1136**	**100.00**
Trades						
Clerk	-	-	8	3.90	54	4.75
Signalman	-	-	8	3.90	53	4.70
Porter	-	-	20	9.71	155	13.60
Guard	-	-	-	-	80	7.00
Platelayer	-	-	20	9.71	54	4.75
Engine Driver	10	12.66	36	17.50	173	15.22
Fireman	-	-	20	9.71	60	5.30
Engine Cleaner	-	-	-	-	50	4.40
Turner / Fitter	-	-	17	8.20	129	11.40
Engineers	7	8.86	-	-	-	-
Labourers	12	15.19	-	-	76	6.70
Unspecified	50	63.29	77	37.37	252	22.18
Total	**79**	**100.00**	**206**	**100.00**	**1136**	**100.00**

THE LSWR AT NINE ELMS

suburb after 1840. Tim Sherwood's articles on the early history of the London & South Western Railway (LSWR) [1] show the importance of the area which lay astride the south-western approaches to London. Between 1838 and 1867 Battersea was criss-crossed by railways and their associated installations, not only of the LSWR, but also of the London, Brighton & South Coast Railway (LBSCR) and the London, Chatham & Dover Railway (LCDR). Since the area was relatively undeveloped, even in the early 1860s, two of the companies set up their locomotive, carriage and wagon building works there - the South Western at Nine Elms and the Chatham at Longhedge Farm. These, together with engine sheds, freight facilities and passenger stations provided a very large amount of employment, only part of which was met by men living locally, others coming from adjacent parishes such as Lambeth and Clapham, or from further afield.

The Census Enumerators's returns for 1851, 1861 and 1871 give an insight into the development of railway employment in mid-Victorian Battersea. Despite the possession of travel concessions which might have encouraged separation of home and workplace, many railwaymen chose to live close to their work. Table 9 sumarises the growth in railway workers over the twenty year period.....

There are some inconsistencies between figures due to the different methods of categorization adopted over the years- some grades are individually categorized in later years whereas they are included under "Unspecified" in earlier times – and differences appear between the two articles, but a good general idea can, nevertheless, be achieved of the increase in the various types of employment that occurred. It is also difficult to understand why it appears that there are between 2 and 3 times the number of drivers as firemen. In 1861 there were an additional 158 workers employed on building the WLER not shown in the above table.

Keith Bailey continues:-

....Despite having been served by the LSWR for almost fifteen years in 1851, there was relatively little railway employment in Battersea.(-I think the author means that in 1851, few railway employees lived in Battersea...Editor). The works and sheds at Nine Elms, together with the original terminus, which had by then become a goods depot, were not yet surrounded by housing development. Indeed, the Census shows that many of the workers lived in the buildings associated with this station. In 1851, the only other railway facility in the parish was the station at Clapham Common (actually Battersea Rise)....

....Amongst the individual workers was the level crossing keeper at Plough Lane, Thomas Knowles, a 51-year-old married man born in Halifax, Novia Scotia. One wonders how he had come to be in this job. As in subsequent years, the majority of railwaymen were young, with 71% aged under 40 and 42% less than 30 - a common feature, then as now, of new, technologically-oriented industries. Another feature of local railway employees already apparent in 1851 is the relatively low proportion of heads of household. Of the 79 men recorded in the census of that year, only 41 (51.9%) came into this category, whereas 25 (31.6%) were lodgers, many living in the LSWR's own premises at Nine Elms station. The remainder were either relatives of householders, or visitors. The spread of railwaymen's birthplaces is also similar to that in later decades, as shown in Table 10.

TABLE 10

	1851	1861	1871
Region	%	%	%
Surrey/Middlesex	26.60	25.20	33.10
Home Counties	24.10	37.10	28.60
South West England	13.90	8.00	11.20
East Anglia	-	10.70	5.30
Northumberland/ Durham	-	-	4.30
Others	35.40	18.90	17.50

A few extracts from Keith Bailey's article follow because they contain relevant information to the railway industry:

....The main change was a diminution in the proportion coming from outside the south of England, offset by an increase in those born in Surrey and Middlesex. This reflects not only the growth in the population of the London area over the twenty years, with many second-generation workers born in the area, but also the fact that the early railways perforce drew many skilled workers from the north of England, where steam railways had first developed. For example, three of those living in Battersea in 1851 were born in Lan-

ENVIRONMENTAL and HUMAN ASPECTS

cashire and two in North-East England....

.....*In what was, of course, an all-male industry, most workers were younger men, less than 40 years old (308, 85%). Railways had existed only for a generation, so it is not surprising that few men were older than this, which was in its way a high-technology industry in the 1850s. Still only 60% of railwaymen were heads of households in 1861, about 25% lodgers and boarders, the rest visitors or relations. This further underlines the evolving nature of the industry at that time, and also the relative sparsity of housing close to the workplace.*

As might be expected, few railway workers were born in Battersea. The great majority came from the rural counties of southern England and East Anglia, notably Kent, Sussex and Hampshire. Even amongst the navvies on the WLER there is only one born in Ireland, compared with twenty from Hampshire. The old stereotype of the railway navvy needs correcting here at least. It seems that the lure of high wages shifting dirt on the new lines was very tempting to landless labourers in depressed agricultural areas....

...The relatively large number of railway workers born in north-east England - the cradle of railways - is surprising at this date, given the number of employment opportunities between Battersea and the Tees. It is a far higher proportion than for the population of Battersea as a whole [2] and suggests a conscious policy of attracting such skilled workers to the southern railways....

"...Although the total number of railway employees had increased (by 1871) by more than fivefold since 1861 (excluding those working on the WLER in the former year), the increase had not been uniform across the board. Drivers, for example, had increased by less than fivefold, although this in itself indicates the very substantial growth in railway traffic in the 1860s as the network was completed and train services improved. Firemen, on the other hand, had increased by less than three times. Porters and fitters show the largest growth in the decade, by more than seven times. Overall, the growth in the traffic departments was about five-and-a-half times and in engineering about six-fold. It must be emphasised, however, that many hundreds of men employed on the railways within the parish of Battersea lived outside the area. By way of comparison, the number of building workers increased by less than fourfold in the 1860s, even though this was a boom period for house-building. During the twenty years after 1851, the rate of growth in the railway industry was roughly three times that in building. In broad terms, almost one household in four derived all or part of its income from these two industries in 1871. This characteristic of local employment marked its development as a suburb for many decades in the late nineteenth and early twentieth century.

References
1. "A Preliminary Note on the London & Southampton Railway", Wandsworth Historian No.40, March 1984, p 13-15; "Nine Elms as a Passenger Station, 1838-1848", Wandsworth Historian, No.41, June 1984, p 14-18; "The London & South Western Railway 1838-1856", Wandsworth Historian, No.42, September 1984, p 3-7.
2. In 1871, only 0.7% of a sample of household heads in Battersea were born in Northumberland and Durham.

Workers' Welfare

This section deals with various items connected in one way or another with the welfare of the workers. It is easy to be cynical about the motives behind the apparent care that the management provided in various ways. Firstly there were the elaborate fire precautions that were maintained in the works. These are described in the section of the article *All about Battersea, 1882* by Simmonds, which follows, and in the description of the new works in *The Engineer* featured on page 95 and the following pages. How much motivation stems from the protection of the worker, and how much from the desire to avoid disruption of production and the consequent financial loss can only be surmised.

The last paragraph of this section of the article reminisces about the "good old days" of early Nine Elms, but even in these writings one senses the callousness by which the 1840 equivalent of today's "Big Brother" in the guise of various governing bodies takes ordinary people's properties from them in return for inadequate compensation, just as they do today.

"...About forty years ago, when Mr. Gooch was Locomotive Superintendent a fire broke out at the London and South Western Railway Works, Nine Elms Lane, which caused great destruction of property, including a very handsome clock tower. Various metals were fused and mingled into shapes fantastic, portions of which were substituted for chimney-piece ornaments in the homes of workmen and kept as mementoes of this conflagration! A man of the name of Dover who it is said accidentally set the stores on fire was so frightened that it turned the hair of his head grey in one night! At Nine Elms, Locomotive, Carriage and Stores Departments are fire precautions which the Railway Company insist upon being strictly observed. A fire engine with hose and all necessary appliances is kept in a building set apart for it adjoining Heman's Street Entrance gate. A properly-

qualified fireman is appointed to look after the whole of the buildings by night, as a precaution against fire. The fireman's name is Thomas Lemon, and his residence is 51, Thorne Street, Wandsworth Road. His hours of duty are from 5.30 p.m. to 6.30 a.m. It is the fireman's duty to perambulate the whole of the works during the night, and to make a daily report of the circumstances in the book provided for that purpose. He is responsible that the fire engine, hose, hydrants, etc, are kept in working order and tried once a week. A statement of the trial is to be made in the fireman's report book with any suggestions or remarks. Positions of hydrants at Nine Elms Works: There are 120 hydrants (always charged) distributed as follows: 15 in the offices, paint loft and shops beneath; 4 in the general stores; 4 in wheelwrights' and signal shops; 2 in bonnet shop; 5 in waggon shop; 4 in new waggon shop and saw mill; 5 in smiths' and carriage fitting shops; 9 in erecting shops; 2 in turning shop; 3 in tender shop; 4 in new erecting shop; 1 in permanent way shop; 4 in arches under the Viaduct ; 52 in running shed; 4 at outlets of water tanks, and 2 on the coal stage. Positions of Tell-tale Clocks: 1 in the office; 1 in general stores; 1 in wheelwrights' shop; 1 in paint shop; 1 in saw mill. It is the fireman's duty to commence to "peg" each of these clocks four times every night at the following hours, viz., 8 p.m., 10.30 p.m., 1 a.m. and 3.30 a.m.

    Facing the Goods Station are the Company's Wharves with an extensive river frontage. Here also formerly stood Francis' Cement Works, adjoining is Nine Elms Steamboat Pier. The South Western Railway Locomotive Works and Goods Department occupy a vast area. It is computed that about 2,000 persons are employed in the various departments. Here were formerly orchard grounds—many a goodly tree bearing fruit and pleasant to the eye has been felled, "Woodman spare that tree!" though spoken by feminine lips would have no force of appeal in this fast age of iron railways and steam locomotives, when Railway Companies scruple not by virtue of Act of Parliament to pull down by hundreds the dwellings of the poor, it is not to be supposed for an instant that a few fruit trees however delicious their produce or delightful their shadow should prove a peculiar obstacle in the way of this March of Civilization! On payment of sixpence, children at half-price, persons might enter these orchards with full liberty to eat as much fruit as they liked on condition that they brought none away. The old Spring Well near Nine Elms Lane, Wandsworth Road, is within the recollection of many, who by descending some six or eight steps reached with their hands the iron ladle out of which they often drank cooling draughts of nature's sparkling acquatic refreshment"

The following extract from the minute book records an incident that the internal fire precautions did not appear to prevent:

> 4036   26 August 1872
> *Nine Elms Yard*
>
> Read report from Mr. Beattie of 19th inst as to a stack of wood having a fire in the above Yard on the previous day which is believed to have been caused in connection of a fire being made too near to it, for the purpose of burning some old Wagon Timbers to get the ironwork.
> Recommend that letter of thanks be forwarded to Messrs. Hewitt for sending the Fire Engine with a gratuity of £4 to be divided between their men.
> Also that the following rewards be given to the under mentioned men for their praiseworthy conduct and actions on the occasion.
> Policeman Langley £1 Inspector May £1
> Inspector Dungate £1
> The above amounts to be charged to the Fire Insurance Fund.
> It was further ordered that Inspector Hamshare be cautioned not to make these fires as near the stacks that Mr. Beattie be requested to deal with the other men who assisted in extinguishing the Fire.

The next minute, number 3993, deals with another question of security, that of requiring staff to deposit amounts of money, of varying amounts, presumably in proportion to their level of responsibility, with the Company. The object, it would seem was to encourage them to work more diligently, otherwise Company failure might involve them in personal financial loss. Minute number 4213 on page 89 shows the salaries of Messrs. Sedgwick and Ortton as being raised from respectively £190 to £200 and £300 to £350 per year, whilst the securities are £200 and £300 in that order. The securities appear therefore, to be of the order of one year's salary, no small amount.

The next minute, number 4908, deals with a complaint from Mr. Ashmore, via Mr. Scott, about the apparent increase in the number of employees, compared with the increase in train miles, from January 1872 to January 1875. From inspection of these figures it seems that an increase of 49% in number of employees has resulted from an increase of only 13% in the train miles worked over the same period; also the increase in route miles was only 5%.

ENVIRONMENTAL and HUMAN ASPECTS

3993   27 June 1872
Finance & Accounts Committee

Securities of Company's Officers

A Minute of the Board dated 20th. June 1872, ordering all Salaried Officers to find Security, and leaving the question of Amount to be fixed by the Finance Committee, was submitted.

Securities proposed as follows:-

H. Clark	£1000	L. Groundlie	£1000
W. J. Beattie	£1000	W. Jacount	£1000
W. G. Beattie	£350	E. Andrews	£200
W. H. Sedgwick	£200	A. H. Langley	£400
J. Gratton	£300	B. J. Fisher	£400
E. Bore	£200	W. Brady	£400

4908   1 March 1875
Officers Committee

Company's Staff

Mr. Scott stated that his attention had been called by Mr. Ashmore to the increase in the numbers of the Staff employed in the Traffic, Loco, and Permanent Way Depts as shown in the following table which had been prepared by him in the years 1871 & 1874 as to which he was desirous of having some explanation.

Miles worked in 1871	704.40	Miles worked in 1874	741.58
Train Miles run in 1871	3,631,915	Train Miles run in 1874	4,153,787
Men Employed on		1 January 1872	1 January 1875
Loco. Dept.		1400	1754
Carriage Dept		550	633
Traffic Dept		3200	4617
Per. Way. Dept		1650	3136
		6800	10140
			Increase 3340

Divided between the above Depts as follows.

	1 January 1873	1 January 1875	
Loco Workshop	540	772	Increase 232
Drivers & Firemen, Cokemen, Cleaners	480	571	Increase 91
Steam Fitters etc.	330	411	Increase 31
Carriage Dept	550	633	Increase 83
Traffic Dept	3200	4617	Increase 1417
Per. Way	1650	3136	Increase 1436
		Increase 3340	

Referred to the Heads of the respective Depts. for comment at next meeting of the Committee.

The contents of minute number 4927 may have been in response to the above complaint:

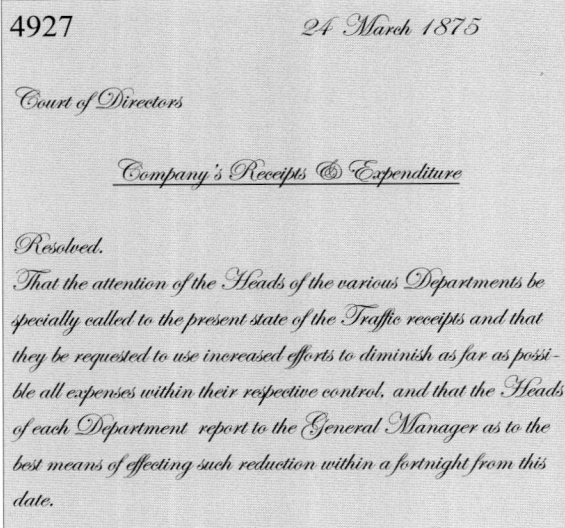

Remuneration to employees is probably considered by most people to be high on the priority list. The following sequence of minutes records the negotiations between the engine drivers and the Locomotive Committee which took place between May and August 1874. The use of the word "Memorial", apparently meaning a request for a wage increase, is interesting. The last minute (Number 4713) is of particular significance, since it records a request from the District Secretary of the Amalgamated Society of Railway Servants asking for an interview. The curt reply is that the Society is not recognised by the Board.

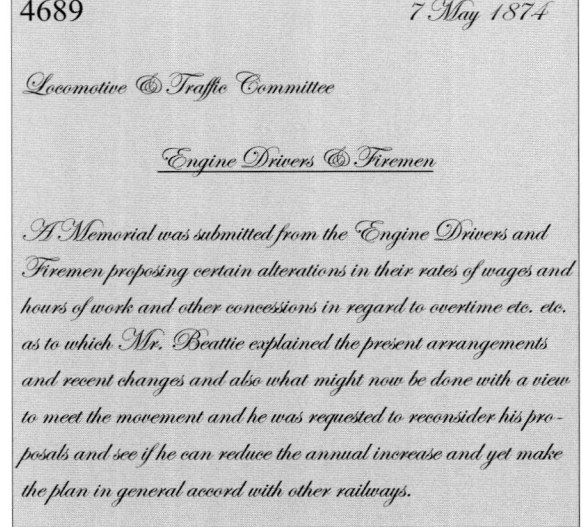

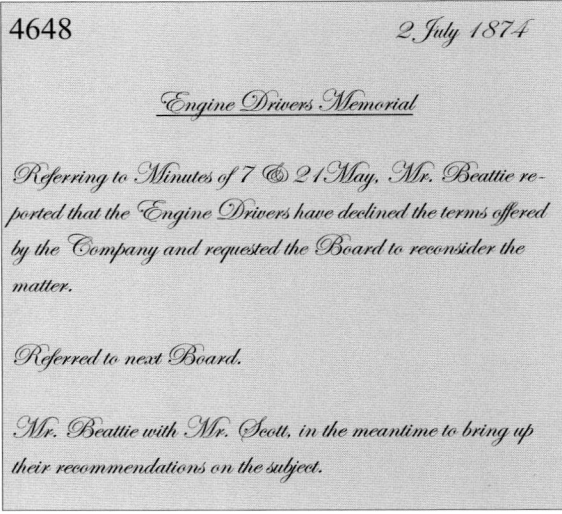

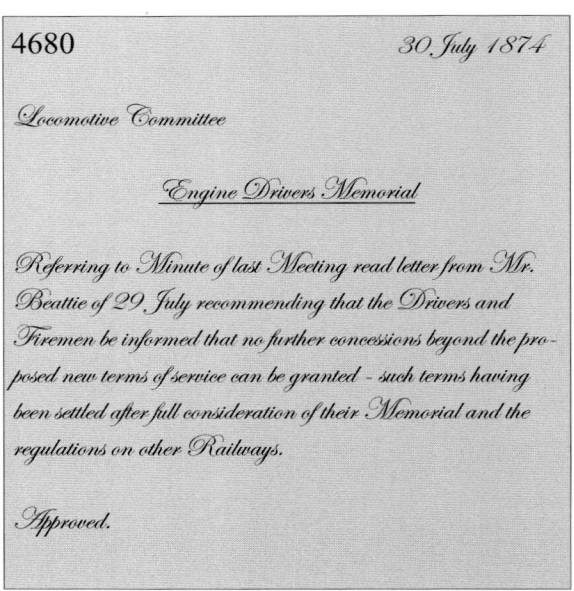

ENVIRONMENTAL and HUMAN ASPECTS

The Company was, sometimes, generous, as would appear from minute number 4125:

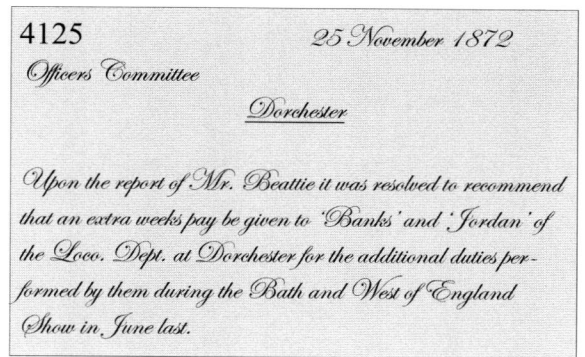

4125   25 November 1872
Officers Committee
Dorchester

Upon the report of Mr. Beattie it was resolved to recommend that an extra weeks pay be given to 'Banks' and 'Jordan' of the Loco. Dept. at Dorchester for the additional duties performed by them during the Bath and West of England Show in June last.

The Court of Directors appoints a salary committee as recorded in minute number 4856, which soon acted to increase the salaries of four employees, as shown in minute 4885. The range of increases is quite large, from 6% to 11%.

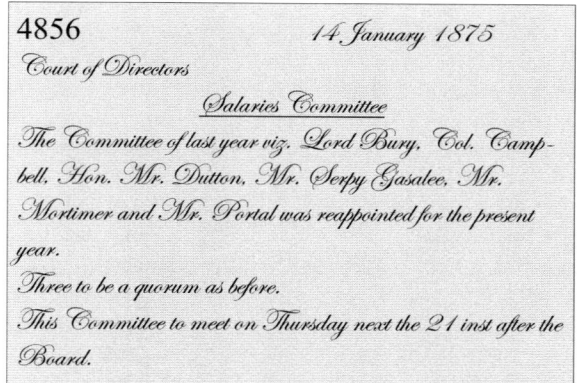

4856   14 January 1875
Court of Directors
Salaries Committee

The Committee of last year viz. Lord Bury, Col. Campbell, Hon. Mr. Dutton, Mr. Serjy Gaselee, Mr. Mortimer and Mr. Portal was reappointed for the present year.
Three to be a quorum as before.
This Committee to meet on Thursday next the 21 inst after the Board.

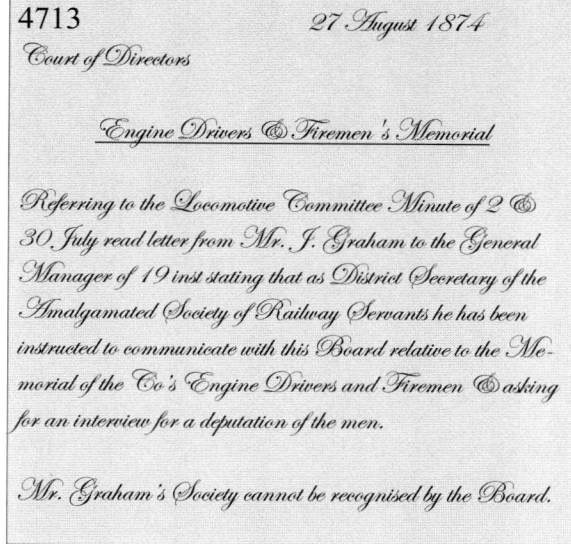

4713   27 August 1874
Court of Directors

Engine Drivers & Firemen's Memorial

Referring to the Locomotive Committee Minute of 2 & 30 July read letter from Mr. J. Graham to the General Manager of 19 inst stating that as District Secretary of the Amalgamated Society of Railway Servants he has been instructed to communicate with this Board relative to the Memorial of the Co's Engine Drivers and Firemen & asking for an interview for a deputation of the men.

Mr. Graham's Society cannot be recognised by the Board.

Finally, there did appear to be efforts made to assist employees with solving health problems. The St. John Ambulance Shield shown in Figure 171 on the next page, was provided at a later date (1900) but does indicate the Company's interest in health, although how much this interest results from compassion for the employees, and how much from maintaining a full work force will never be known. The minutes on page 145 are relevant, numbers 3958 and 3959 indicate there was praise for the "satisfactory management" of the dispensing business, which could mean either the financial success (for the Company) or the benefit to employees. Minute 4801 is possibly significant because it records the objections of employees to paying contributions to the facility.

4885   4 February 1875

Salaries Committee Report

Referring to Minute of 14 ulto, the report of the above Committee was brought up and approved and ordered to be carried out.
Extract from Salaries Committee Report referred to.

21 January 1875

It was resolved to recommend the following increases of Salary, to date from 1 February 1875.

Loco & Carr Depts.	Present Salary	Proposed increase
Mr. G. Wood	£99	£11
Mr. W. Conway	£85	£5
Mr. T.W. Parmiter	£70	£5
Mr. A. Matthews	£70	£5

Fig. 171. Shield awarded in 1900 for the annual competition of the St. John Ambulance Brigade.

ENVIRONMENTAL and HUMAN ASPECTS

3958 — 15 May 1872
Court of Directors

Medical Arrangements. Nine Elms

Referring to Minute of 11 ulto: the Secretary reported an interview which he has had with Mr. Suter and read letters from Mr. W. G. Beattie of 14 inst and Dr. Vine of same date with reference to Mr. Suter's satisfactory management of the Dispensing Business at the Nine Elms Surgery.

Dr. Vine to be requested to see the Directors on the subject at 1pm tomorrow.

3959 — 16 May 1872
Court of Directors

Medical Arrangements. Nine Elms

Referring to Minute of last Board, read letters from Mr. W. G. Beattie & Dr. Vine of 14 inst as to Dr. Vine having attended and given explanation as to Mr. Suter's duties, and having engaged him as a qualified assistant shall attend the Co's Staff at Nine Elms, it was agreed that Mr. Suter may be employed as dispenser at the Nine Elms Surgery. A duly qualified practitioner being engaged by Dr. Vine to attend to the Staff.

Upon this understanding the Board resolution of 11 ulto is hereby rescinded.

4714 — 27 August 1874

Hospital Saturday Fund.

Read letter from Mr. Beattie of 17 inst asking for instructions as to allowing placards and collecting boxes to be put up by the Committee of the above Fund on the walls of the Company's Locomotive & Carriage Yard, it being understood there is to be no canvassing of the men for subscriptions.

The Notices and 4 boxes may be placed in the Yard as proposed.

4785a — 19 November 1874
Court of Directors

Medical Arrangements. Nine Elms

Referring to Minute of last Board read letter from Mr. Beattie of 17 inst recommending that the weekly pence monies for the Medical Fund be not deducted from the Company's Workmen at Nine Elms & Clapham Junction.

Approved

4801 — 12 November 1874
Court of Directors

Medical Arrangements. Nine Elms

A Memorial from the Company's Mechanics against the present Medical arrangements at Nine Elms and objecting to the weekly de-

Services to the Public

We have talked about the products emanating from the works in terms of the locomotives etc that it produces. The ultimate products, however, are the services it provides to the general public in terms of railway transport. We can only "scratch the surface" in this domain, as the extent of the services provided is so great. The public have available to them timetables that list the passenger services provided by the various companies, but within these companies are what is known as "Working" timetables which give far more information including details of all movements, including goods trains, light engines, etc and additional points at which trains are timed. A range of these timetables was salvaged from Eastleigh covering periods from November 1879 to November 1883.

Firstly, Figures 172 to 175 show part of the

NOVEMBER, 1879.

DOWN PASSENGER & GOODS TRAINS ON THE MAIN LINE, FROM LONDON TO SOUTHAMPTON, &c.

(Continued on next Page.)

Miles.	WEEK DAYS.	21 Passenger Hampton Court. arr.	dep.	22 Passenger Southton, Mail. A arr.	dep.	23 Passenger Aldershot. arr.	dep.	24 Empty Foreign Wagons. arr.	dep.	25 Passenger Roundabout Norbiton, Kingston, Twickenham Waterloo. arr.	dep.	26 Passenger Hampton Court. arr.	dep.	27 Passenger Exeter Fast. arr.	dep.	28 Passenger Epsom. arr.	dep.	29 Empty. arr.	dep.	30 Passenger Portsmth. Direct. B arr.	dep.
		a.m.	a.m.	a.m.	a.m.	a.m.	a.m.	a.m.	a.m.	a.m.	a.m.	a.m.	a.m.	a.m.	a.m.	a.m.	a.m.	a.m.	a.m.	a.m.	a.m.
...	Waterloo Bridge	..	7 45	..	8 5	..	..	..	..	...	8 30	..	8 40	..	9 0	..	9 5	..	9 25	..	9 30
1¼	Vauxhall	....	7 50	8	9	....	....	...	...		8 35	..	8 45	9	3	9	9	9	20	9	34
	Nine Elms Yard	..	....	..	..	..	..	..	8 10	...	...	..	....	..	..	....	....	....	....	..	..
3	Queen's Road Junction	7	53	8	11	....	....	8	12	8	37	8	47	9	5	9	11	9	31	9	36
3¾	Clapham Junction	....	7 57	8	14	..	..	8	15		8 41	..	8 51	9	8	9 14	9 15	9	34	9 38	9 39
7	Wimbledon Junction	8	2	8	18	....	....	8	25	8	46	8	56	9	12	9	19	9	39	9	43
7¾	Wimbledon	8 3	8 5	8	19	..	..	8 26	8 32	...	...	8 57	8 58	9	13	...	...	9 40	..	9	44
9¾	Coombe and Malden	..	8 10	8	23	..	..	8	36	...	...	..	9 4	9	17	...		....	....	9	48
12	Surbiton	8 15	8 16	8 27	8 28	....	....	8 44	9 0	...	...	9 9	9 10	9 20	9 21	...	Fast Passenger from London. See No. 27	..	..	Sig.	9 51
13¼	Hampton Court Junct.	8	19	8	30	..	..	9	3	...	...	9	13	9	24	...		....	....	9	53
14¼	Esher			8	32	....	....	9 8	9 15	...	...			9	26	...		..	..	9	55
17	Walton	..	..	8	36	..	..	9 25	10 8	...	...	..	..	9	29	...		....	....	9	58
19	Weybridge	....	....	8	39	..	..	Foll. 10 12	No 30 10 29	...	...	....	....	9	32	...		..	..	10	1
24¼	Woking	....	....	8 46	8 48	..	8 52			...	...	..	..	9 39	9 40	...		....	....	10 8	10 10
27¾	Brookwood Necropolis	..	..	Sig.	8 56		8 58	This Train to stop at Clapham on Mondays to take up stores for Clapham Lading Box.		...	...	....	....	9	46	...		..	..	..	..
29¾	Pirbright Junction	....	....	8	59	9	1			...	...	....	....	9	49	...		....	....	....	....
33	Sturt Lane Junction	....	....	9	4	....	....			....	....	....	....	9	53	....		..	..	....	....
33	Farnborough	..	..	9 6	9 7	....	....			...	...	..	..	9	54	...		....	....	..	....
36½	Fleet	....	....		9 14					...	...	..	..	9	59	...	...	..	..	....	....
39	Winchfield	..	..	..	9 26	Goods from Guildford. See page 84.				...	...	....	....	10	3	...	...	....	....	..	..
47¾	Basingstoke	....	....	9 35	9 39					...	...	..	..	10 13	10 17	..	10 20	..	..	....	....
51	Worting Junction	..	....	9	45			....	....	...	...	....	....	10	21	10	24	..	..	..	..
58	Micheldever	....	..	....	9 59	C	..	..	..	...	...	..	..	..	..	10	36	....	....	....	....
64¼	Winchester Junction	..	....	10	11	10 45	10 53	....	....	...	...	....	....	....	....	10	48	..	..	..	..
66½	Winchester	....	..	..	10 15	Af No 10 57	28 Dn. 11 5	..	..	...	...	..	..	..	..	10 51	10 52	....	....	....	....
73¼	Bishopstoke	..	..	10 28	10 30	11 25	....	....	....	...	...	....	..	....	....	11 5	11 6	..	..	..	..
77	St. Denys	....	....	Sig.	10 37	..	..	..	..	...	...	....	....	..	..	11	13	....	....	....	....
8½	Northam	..	..	10 39	10 41	...	....	....	....	...	...	....	....	....	....	11 16	11 17	..	..	..	..
79¼	Southampton	....	....	10 45	..	..	..	...	..	...	..	....	....	..	..	11 20	....	....	....	....	....

A No. 22 Train will stop at Brookwood to take up Passengers only.

B No. 29 Train will stop at Surbiton to take up Passengers only.

C Note to Goods from Alton at bottom of column No. 23—This Goods must wait at the Stop signal on branch at Winchester Junction and follow No. 28.

On Mondays Wednesdays and Fridays an Engine and Van will leave Waterloo at 10.0 a.m. for Walton to do shunting (stopping at Esher when necessary) returning from Walton to Nine Elms at 12.46 p.m. or 2.5 p.m. as required, with Goods. See note B at foot of page 37.

NOVEMBER, 1879.

DOWN PASSENGER & GOODS TRAINS ON THE MAIN LINE FROM LONDON TO SOUTHAMPTON, &c.

(Continued on next Page.)

Miles.	WEEK DAYS.	31 Empty Train. arr.	dep.	32 Passenger Hampton Court. arr.	dep.	33 Passenger Godliming and Basing. arr.	dep.	34 Passengr Epsom. arr.	dep.	35 Passenger Aldershot, Farnham, Alton and Southampton. arr.	dep.	36 Passenger Hampton Court. arr.	dep.	37 Passenger Exeter Fast. A arr.	dep.	38 Passenger. Kingston New. arr.	dep.	39 Passenger. Southton. A arr.	dep.	40 Passenger Epsom. arr.	dep.
		a.m.	a.m.	a.m.	a.m.	a.m.	a.m.	a.m.	a.m.	a.m.	a.m.	a.m.	a.m.	a.m.	a.m.	a.m.	a.m.	a.m.	a.m.	a.m.	a.m.
...	Waterloo Bdge	..	9 32	..	9 35	..	9 45	...	10 10	..	10 15	..	10 25	..	10 45	..	10 50	..	11 20	..	11 25
1¼	Vauxhall	9	36	....	9 40	....	9 50	...	10 15	10	19	....	10 30	10	40	....	10 55	11	23	....	11 30
	Nine Elms Yd.			..	..	..	....	...	...	..	..	..	....	....	..	...	...	..	..	..	..
3	Queen's Road Jtn.	..	..	9	43	9	53	10	17	10	21	10	33	10	51	10	58	11	25	11	33
3¾	Clapham Junction	9	38	....	9 47	9 56	9 56	...	10 21	10 23	10 25	....	10 37	10	54	...	11 2	11	28	..	11 37
7	Wimbledon Jtn.	9	41	9	53	10	4	10	26	10	29	10	42	10	58	11	7	11	31	11	42
7¾	Wimbledon	9 45	9 46	9 53	9 54	10 5	10 6	...	...	10	30	10 43	10 44	10	59	..	..	11	33	..	..
9¾	Coombe and Malden	9	53	..	10 0	..	10 12	...	...	10	34	..	10 50	11	3	Through Train to Kingston.	...	11	37	..	..
12	Surbiton	9 56	....	10 5	10 6	10 18	10 19	...	...	10 37	10 39	10 55	10 56	Sig.	11 7		...	Sig.	11 40	....	....
13¼	Hampton Court Jtn.	..	..	10	9	10	23	...	...	10	41	10	59	11	9		...	11	43	..	..
14¼	Esher	....	....			....	10 26	...	...	10	43			11	11		...	11	45	....	....
17	Walton	Ascot Train.		Goods		..	10 32	...	...	..	10 40	...	...	11	15		...	11	48	..	..
19	Weybridge					10 37	10 38	...	..	10 53	10 54	...	...	11	18		...	11	51	....	....
24¼	Woking	...	10 10	..	10 15	10 48	10 53	...	...	11 3	11 8	...	...	11	25			11	59	..	..
27¾	Brookwood (Nerpls)	10 16	10 17	10 25	....	....	11 0	...	...	....	11 15	...	...	11	30	..	..	12	4	....	....
29¾	Pirbright Junction	10	20	..	..	11	4	...	...	11	18	...	...	11	33	..	..	12	6	..	..
33	Sturt Lane Junction	10	26	...	...	11	9	...	...	...	...	...	...	11	37	...	...	12	10	...	...
33	Farnborough	....	....	....	....	....	11 11	...	...	....	....	...	...	11	38	...	...	12	12	....	....
36½	Fleet	..	..	..	..	....	11 19	...	...	..	..	...	...	11	43	..	..	12	16	..	..
39	Winchfield	...	....	....	....	....	11 25	...	...	....	....	...	...	11	47	....	....	12	20	....	....
47¾	Basingstoke	..	....	..	..	11 42	....	...	...	..	..	...	...	11 57	12 2	..	..	12 31	12 35	..	..
51	Worting Junction	....	..	....	....	..	..	...	...	....	....	...	...	12	7	...	...	12	40	....	....
58	Micheldever	..	..	..	..	....	....	...	...	...	...	...	...	...	...	..	..	Stop Sat.	12 52	..	..
64¼	Winchester Junction	....	....	....	....	..	..	...	...	12	48	...	...	...	...	...	....	1	5	....	....
66½	Winchester	..	..	..	..	....	....	...	...	12 52	12 54	...	...	...	...	....	....	1 8	1 10	..	..
73¼	Bishopstoke	....	....	....	....	..	..	...	...	1 8	1 10	...	..	...	...	...	....	1 23	1 25	....	....
77	St. Denys	..	..	..	..	....	....	...	...	..	1 17	...	..	...	...	..	..	1	30	..	..
78¼	Northam	....	....	....	....	..	....	...	...	1 21	1 22	...	...	...	...	...	...	1 33	1 35	....	....
79¼	Southampton	..	..	..	..	....	....	...	....	1 25	..	...	...	...	...	..	..	1 40	..	..	..

Sig. Nos. 30, 37, 39 & 41 Trains will stop at Surbiton by Signal to take up Passengers only. They will not convey Horses and Carriages.

A No. 39 Train will Stop at Micheldever on Saturdays.

Fig. 172. November 1897 Working Timetable for the Waterloo to Southampton route, covering trains 21 - 40.

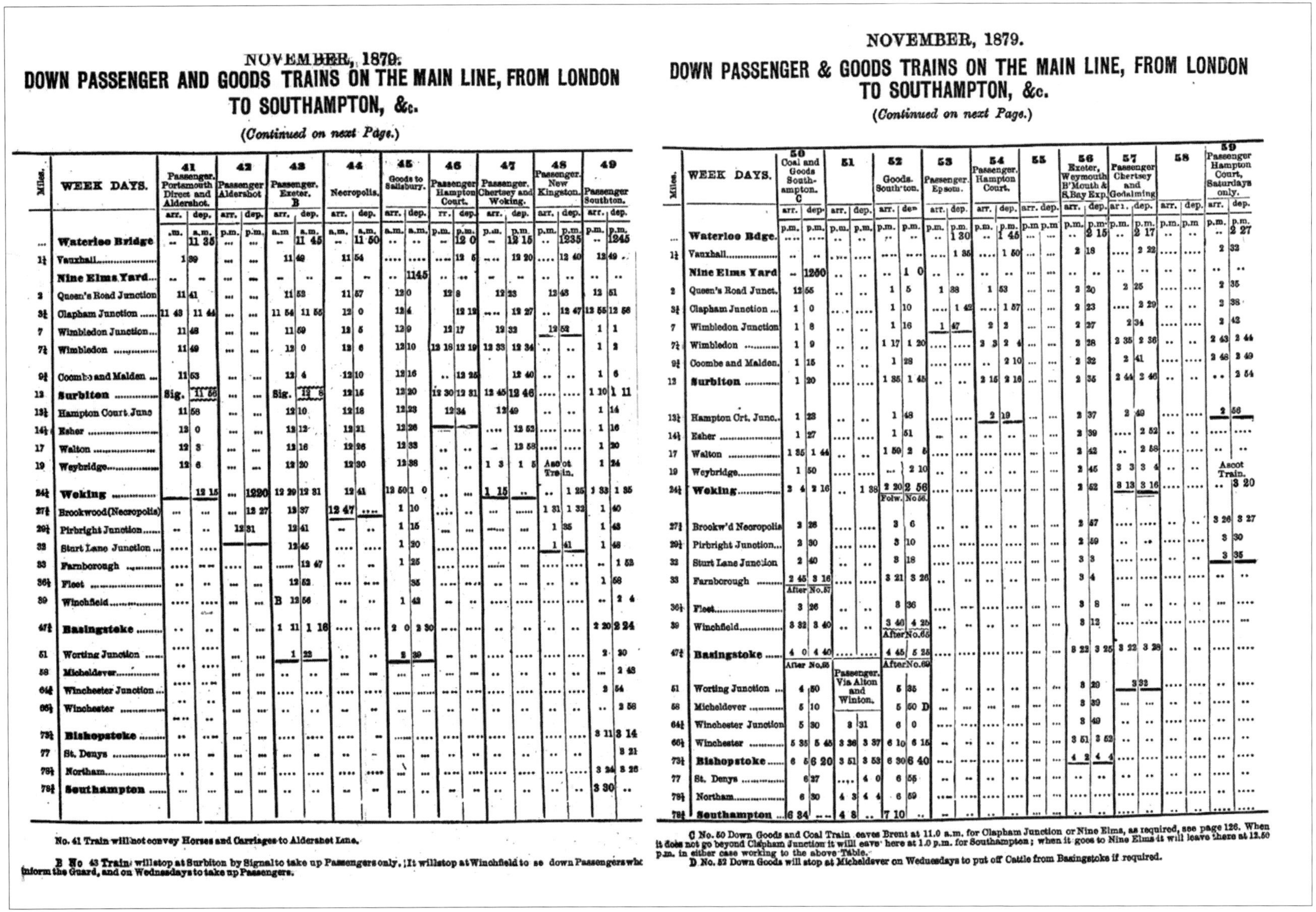

ENVIRONMENTAL and HUMAN ASPECTS

Fig. 173. November 1897 Working Timetable for the Waterloo to Southampton route, covering trains 41 - 59.

NOVEMBER, 1879.

UP PASSENGER & GOODS TRAINS ON THE MAIN LINE, FROM SOUTHAMPTON, TO LONDON.

(Continued on next Page.)

Miles.	WEEK DAYS.	30 Local Basingstoke and Woking Train. arr.	30 dep.	31 Passenger Southampton. arr.	31 dep	32 Alton and Aldsht. Pas. dep.	33 Passenger Yeovil and Salisbury, via Andover. arr.	33 dep.	34 Epsom Train. arr.	34 dep.	35 Passenger Hampton Court. arr.	35 dep.	36 Passengers Alton. arr.	36 dep.	37 Mail Southampton A arr.	37 dep.	38 Passenger Aldershot arr.	38 dep.	39 Passenger Direct Portsm'th. arr.	39 dep.
		a.m.	a.m.	a.m	a.m	a.m.	a.m.	a.m.	a.m.	a.m.	a.m.	a.m.	a.m.	a.m.	a.m.	a.m.	a.m.	a.m.	a.m.	a.m.
...	**Southampton**	..	..	...	8 5	..	..	..	..	..	..	..	..		—	8 45	..	..	..	..
0½	Northam	....	....	...	8 8	....	....	....	....	....	....	....	....	....		8 47	....	....	....	....
1¼	St. Denys	....	....	...	8 11	....	....	....	....	....	....	....	....			8 50	....	....	....	....
5¼	**Bishopstoke**	..		8 17	8 19	..	..	..	..	..	..	..	..	..	8 57	9 1	..	..	..	..
12¾	Winchester	Local Trains.	....	...	8 31	....	....	....	....	....	....	....	....	....	9 15	9 16	....	....	....	....
14	Winchester Junction		..		8 35	..	..	..	..	..	..	..	..	..		9 20	..	..	..	..
20½	Micheldever		....	...	8 47	..	..	..	....	....	....	....	....	..		9 32	....	....	....	....
27¾	Worting Junction		..		8 58	....		9 3	..	..	..	..	..	...		9 44	..	..	..	..
31	**Basingstoke**	....	8 32	9 3	9 11	..	9 8	9 11	....	....	....	....	....	....	9 49	9 52	....	....	....	....
39¼	Winchfield	..	8 46	See No. 32	...	....		9 24	..	..	..	..	..	..		10 2	..	..	..	..
42¼	Fleet	....	8 51		...	..		9 27	....	....	....	....	....	....		10 6	....	....	..	..
45½	Farnborough	..	8 58	Ascot Train.		....		9 31	..	..	..	..	..	..		10 10	..	..	....	....
46¾	Sturt Lane Junction		8 59		9 21	..		9 33	...	...	....	....	....	....		10 11	....	....	....	....
49¼	Pirbright Junction		9 3		9 25	9 29		9 36	...	...	...	...	...	...		10 15		10 30	...	...
51	Brookwood Necropolis	..	9 7	9 27	9 28	9 33		9 38	...	...	...	...	..	..		10 17	10 32	10 33	...	...
54¼	**Woking**	9 13	...	934	...	9 39	9 45	9 48	...	...	...	...	9 55	10 0		10 22	10 39	....	10 46	10 48
59¼	Weybridge			...	...	..		9 56	—	..	—	..	10 9	10 11		10 29	..	..		10 56
61½	Walton	Passngr. New Kingston.		...	...	....		9 59	...	....	....	....	10 15	10 16		10 32	Passngr. Surbiton to London.			10 59
64½	Esher			...	...	..		10 2	—	..	..	..	10 21	10 23		10 35				11 3
65¼	Hampton Court Junction			...	...	....		10 4	....	....		10 16		10 25		10 37	....	...		11 5
66½	**Surbiton**	...	...	...	...	....		10 6	..	..	10 18	10 19	10 27	10 29		10 39	..	10 50		11 7
69	Coombe and Malden	...	...	...	...	....		10 10	....	....	....	10 24		10 33		10 42		10 54		11 11
71¼	Wimbledon	...	...	...	...	..		10 14	...	...	10 29	10 30		10 37		10 46	....	10 58		11 15
71¾	Wimbledon Junction		10 8	...	...	....		10 15		10 25		10 31		10 38		10 47		10 59		11 16
75	Clapham Junction	...	10 14	...	...	..		10 20		10 30	..	10 37		10 43		10 51	11 4	11 5	11 19	11 20
76¾	Queen's Road Junc.		10 17	...	...	....		10 23		10 33		10 41		10 47		10 54		11 7		11 22
77	**Nine Elms Yard**	...	...	...	...	..	..	...	...	...	...	..	..	..	...	...	....	....	....	....
77¼	Vauxhall	10 19	10 21	...	...	....	10 25	10 27	10 35	10 37	10 43	10 45	10 49	10 51	10 56	1 58	11 9	11 10	11 24	11 26
78¼	**Waterloo**	1026	..	...	...	..	1032	..	10 41	..	1050	..	10 55	..	11 2	...	11 16	....	1130	....

A No. 37 Train will not convey Horses and Carriages.

NOVEMBER, 1879.

PASSENGER & GOODS TRAINS ON THE MAIN LINE, FROM SOUTHAMPTON, &c., TO LONDON.

(Continued on next page.)

Miles.	WEEK DAYS	40 Passengs. Basingstoke. A arr.	40 dep.	41 Goods. Southampton when required. arr.	41 dep.	42 Goods. When necessary. arr.	42 dep	43 Passenger Epsom. arr.	43 dep.	44 Goods. arr.	44 dep.	45 Passengr's New Kingston. arr.	45 dep.	46 Passenger Direct P'rtsmt'h arr.	46 dep.	47 Passenger from Ascot. arr.	47 dep.	48 Passenger from Aldershot. arr.	48 dep.	49 Exeter fast Passenger arr.	49 dep.
		a.m.	a.m.	a.m	a.m.	a.m.	a.m.	a.m.	a.m.	a.m.	a.m.	a.m.	a.m.	a.m.	a.m.	p.m.	p.m.	p.m.	p.m.	a.m	a.m.
...	**Southampton**	..	..	—	8 55	..	..	...	...	..	..	..	..	..	..	..	..	...	...	..	..
0½	Northam	....	....		9 1			...	...	....	....	....	....	....	....	....	....	...	...	....	....
1¼	St. Denys	..	..		9 5	When necessary.		...	...	..	..	..	..	..	..	.	....	...	...	..	..
5¼	**Bishopstoke**	....	....	9 15	9 20			...	...	....	....	....	....	....	....	..	..	...	...	....	....
12¾	Winchester	..	..		9 40			...	...	..	..	..	..	..	..	....	....	...	...	..	..
14	Winchester Junc.	....	....		45			...	...	....	....	....	....	....	....	..	..	...	...	....	....
20½	Micheldever	..	..		10 5	....	....	...	...	..	..	..	..	..	..	..	....	...	...	..	..
27¾	Worting Junction	....	....		10 25		10 10	...	...	....	....	....	....	....	....	See No. 49.	..	...	...		11 35
31	**Basingstoke**	..	1010	10 35	1040	10 20	10 30	...	...	..	..	..	..	..	..		....	...	...	11 40	11 44
39¼	Winchfield	....	10 25		10 55		10 50	...	...	....	....	....	....	....	....		..	...	...		11 54
42¼	Fleet		10 29		11 5		10 58	...	...	..	..	..	..	..	..	....	....	....	...		11 58
45½	Farnborough	10 34	10 35		11 15		11 6	...	...	....	....	....	....	....	....	..	..	...	....		12 2
46¾	Sturt Lane Jun.		10 36		11 16	11		....	....	....	....	....	....	....	....		11 40	....	....		12 3
49¼	Pirbright Junctn.		10 40		11 25		11 16	...	...	....	....	..	..	..	..		11 46		12 0		12 7
51	Brookwood (Nec.)		10 44		11 35		11 21	...	...	....	11 10	..	....	....	....	11 50	11 51		12 3		12 9
54¼	**Woking**	10 50	1052	1125	11 50	11 33 After	12 15 No 49	...	..	11 20	..	....	..	11 31	1132	11 57	12 15	12 9	....	1214	1215
59¼	Weybridge	11 1	11 4		12 0		12 28	...	...	Passeng'rs Hampton Court.		....	....	....	11 42	..	..	Hampton Court.			12 22
61½	Walton	11 9	11 11		12 5		12 33	...	...			..	..		11 46	Passengers from Wimbledon.					12 25
64½	Esher		11 16		12 11		12 37	...	...	....	§	....	....		11 50			...	...		12 28
65¼	Hampton Ct. Junc.		11 18		12 14		12 41	...	...		11 26	..	..		11 52				12 10		12 30
66½	**Surbiton**	11 21	11 23	12 18	12 30		12 45	...	...	11 29	11 30	....	....		11 54			12 13	12 14		12 33
69	Coombe & Malden		11 26		12 35		12 50	...	...	..	11 35	..	..		11 57			...	12 19		12 35
71¼	Wimbledon	A	11 31		12 43	1 0	1 16	...	...	11 41	11 42	....	....		12 0	....	12 10	12 23	12 24		12 38
71¾	Wimbledon Junc.		11 32		12 44	AfNo. 1	53 up. 17		11 38		11 43		11 50		12 1	12	11		12 25		12 39
75	Clapham Junction	11 36	11 38		12 50		1 23	....	11 42	....	11 49	....	11 56	12 6	12 7	12 16	12 17	12 30	12 31		12 43
76¾	Queen's Rd. Junc.		11 42		12 54		1 27		11 45		11 53		12 1		12 9	12	19		12 34		12 46
77	**Nine Elms Yd.**	....	....	1259	..	1 32	....			....	....	....	....	..	....	....	....	...	...	....	....
77½	Vauxhall	11 44	11 46	..	..	..	..	11 47	11 49	11 55	11 57	12 3	12 5	12 10	12 12	12 21	12 23	12 36	12 38	12 48	12 50
78¼	**Waterloo**	1150	....	....	....	....	....	1153	...	12 2	..	12 9	..	1216	..	1227	....	1243	...	1254	....

A—This Train will stop at Wimbledon to set down Passengers for Epsom and Leatherhead Line who inform the Guard.

Fig. 174. November 1897 Working Timetable for the Southampton to Waterloo route, covering trains 30 - 49.

ENVIRONMENTAL and HUMAN ASPECTS

Fig. 175. November 1897 Working Timetable for the Southampton to Waterloo route, covering trains 50 - 69.

THE LSWR AT NINE ELMS

coverage of the main line from Waterloo to Southampton and return services for November 1879. The fastest down times, Waterloo to Southampton are 2hr 20min (3 stops, train no 39), 2hr 40min (6 stops train no 22), and 2hr 45min (6 stops, train no 49). From information in the Southampton-Dorchester-Weymouth sections (not reproduced here) trains for these destinations either diverted from Bishopstoke, and called at Southampton West (train no 56) or appeared to divide from the Southampton train there (departing there 10.35 a.m. from no 22 and 1.30 p.m. from no 39), the other section of the train continuing to Southampton Terminus. The up trains are arranged similarly.

It should be noted that at this time there was still no direct link to Bournemouth (from Brockenhurst). Passengers had to either change at Ringwood and travel via the Ringwood-Hurn-Christchurch-Bournemouth East service (about 6 trains per day), or change at Wimborne and travel via Poole-Parkstone-Bournemouth West (about 15 trains per day, including those of the Somerset & Dorset Railway). There was no direct connection between the East and West Bournemouth stations. The link from Brockenhurst was not opened until 5th March 1888.

Secondly, the convenience of through routes to and from other railway companies began to be realised. One of the most interesting is the link between Willesden junction on the LNWR, and the LSWR near Clapham Junction. Figure 176 shows a map of this route. The lines splits at Battersea, (Latchmere Junction) one link going to Clapham Junction, the other towards Queen's Road, enabling through trains to Waterloo. The route commenced life as part of the Birmingham, Bristol and Thames Junction Railway, in the name of the West London Railway, and began at an existing junction between the GWR and the LNWR just south east of Willesden Junction, and proceeded to Chelsea. It was opened in 1844. This line was extended by the West London Extension Railway from Chelsea to a junction with the West End and Crystal Palace Railway at Longhedge on 2nd March 1863. Several other connecting links were built enabling trains from Willesden Junction and from Earl's Court to travel to either Clapham Junction or Waterloo.

This route was used by a number of goods trains in the early days, and then a variety of passenger services evolved. Minute number 4183 of 10th February 1873, on page 151, records the agreement between officers of the LSWR and the LNWR, regarding a service connecting the two railways. The 1879 working timetable shows such a service which links Clapham Junction with Kensington (then known as Addison Road, it is now Olympia). This service is shown in Figure 177. Here it links with the L&NWR service

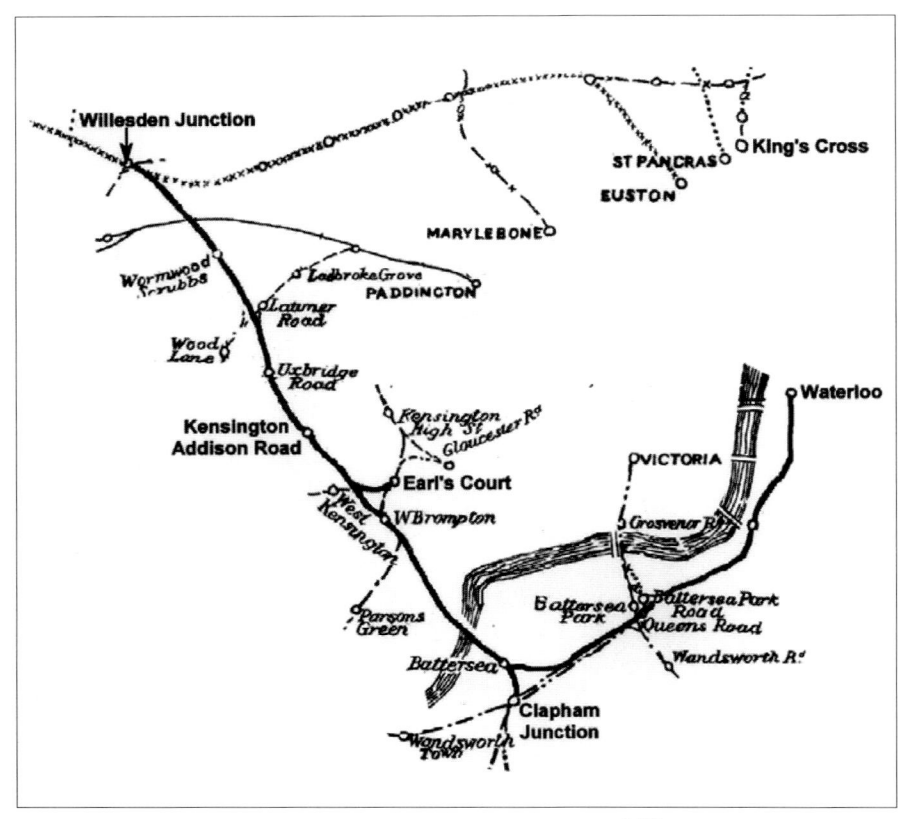

Fig. 176.

Map showing the route of the West London Extension Railway which provides a connection between Waterloo or Clapham Junction and Kensington (Addison Road) thence to Willesden Junction.

ENVIRONMENTAL and HUMAN ASPECTS

4183 — 10 February 1873
Officers Committee

Train Service Willesden & Waterloo

Referring to Board Minute of 6 inst appointing Mr. Mortimer, Capt. Johnston and Col. Campbell to meet the Committee as to a proposed Service of Trains between Willesden Junction and Waterloo via Kensington. Mr. Scott explained the necessity for providing a better connection of Trains between the Systems of the London & North Western Co. and the Company either by the Service above proposed or by stopping some of this Company's Main Line trains at Clapham Junction in connection with a new service of trains via Kensington to Willesden.

Mr. Mortimer having expressed his views on the subject, it was after full discussion with Messrs. Verrinder, Copus, Thompson, Green and Wansborough who attended the Committee.

Resolved.

That as an experiment, a new service should be established between Willesden & Clapham Junction and that a certain number of this Company's trains should stop at Clapham Junction to effect the interchange between the two Co's systems.

4969 — 3 June 1875
Court of Directors

Train Service between Willesden & Waterloo

The Traffic Committee Minute of today and proposals therein referred to as discussed between Mr. Scott and Mr. Frindlay of the North Western Co for a Train Service between Willesden Junction & Waterloo Station were brought up, and approved and ordered to be carried out, as from the 1 July next.

WEST LONDON EXTENSION LINE. NOVEMBER, 1879.

DOWN TRAINS.—WEEK DAYS

NOTE.—Trains marked S are South Western Trains, and run to and from the South Western Platforms at Clapham Junction, and Trains marked B are Brighton Company's Trains, and run to and from Brighton Company's Platforms at Clapham Junction.
All Trains are 1st, 2nd, and 3rd Class between Clapham Junction and Kensington both on Week Days and on Sundays.

STATIONS.	S.	N.W. Gds.	S.	S.	B.	S	B	S.	B.	S.	B.	S.	B.	S	B	S.	B.	S.	B.	S.
	a.m.	a.m.	a.m.	a.m.	a.m.	a.m.	a.m.	a.m.	a.m.	a.m.	a.m.	a.m.	p.m.	p.m.	p.m.	p.m.	p.m.	p.m.	p.m.	p.m.
Clapham Jn.(L.&S.W) dep.	5 35	6 40	6 36	7 50	...	8 50	...	9 53	...	10 50	...	11 53	...	12 40	...	2 10	...	3 55	...	4 4
Do (L.B.&C.) ,,	...	...	...	...	8 10	...	9 13	...	10 10	...	11 13	...	12 15	...	1 5	...	3 10	...	4 18	...
Latchmere Junction pass.	5 37	6 43	6 38	7 52	8 12	8 52	9 15	9 55	10 12	10 52	11 15	11 55	12 17	12 42	1 7	2 12	3 12	3 57	4 20	4 4
Battersea dep.	5 38	...	6 39	7 53	8 13	8 53	9 17	9 56	10 13	10 53	11 16	11 56	12 18	12 43	1 8	2 13	3 13	3 58	4 21	4 4
Chelsea ,,	5 40	...	6 42	7 56	8 16	8 56	9 19	9 59	10 16	10 56	11 19	11 59	12 21	12 46	1 11	2 16	3 16	4 1	4 24	4 4
West Brompton ,,	5 43	...	6 46	8 0	8 20	8 59	9 23	10 3	10 20	11 0	11 23	12 3	12 25	12 50	1 15	2 20	3 20	4 5	4 28	4 4
Kensington arr.	5 46	...	6 48	8 3	8 23	9 1	9 27	10 6	10 23	11 3	11 26	12 6	12 28	12 53	1 18	2 23	3 23	4 8	4 31	4 4

DOWN TRAINS.—WEEK DAYS.—Continued.

STATIONS.	B.	S.	B.	S.	B.	S.	B.	S.	B.	S.	B.
	p.m.	p.m.	p.m.	p.m.	p.m.	p.m.	p.m.	p.m.	p.m.	p.m.	p.m.
Clapham Jn.(L.&S.W) dep.	...	5 40	...	6 47	...	7 35	...	8 45	...	9 50	...
Do (L.B.&C.) ,,	5 13	...	6 10	...	7 17	...	8 15	...	9 9	...	10 30
Latchmere Junction pass.	5 15	5 42	6 12	6 49	7 19	7 37	8 17	8 47	9 11	9 52	10 32
Battersea dep.	5 16	5 43	6 13	6 50	7 20	7 38	8 18	8 48	9 12	9 53	10 33
Chelsea ,,	5 19	5 46	6 16	6 53	7 23	7 41	8 21	8 51	9 15	9 56	10 36
West Brompton ,,	5 23	5 50	6 20	6 57	7 27	7 45	8 25	8 55	9 19	10 0	10 40
Kensington arr.	5 26	5 53	6 23	7 0	7 30	7 48	8 28	8 58	9 22	10 3	10 43

Fig. 177.

from Willesden Junction to Earl's Court.

Minute number 4969 of 3rd June 1875 on page 151 records a similar discussion regarding a service between Waterloo and Willesden Junction and the resultant timetable is shown in Figure 178. The 1879 timetable also shows a service between Waterloo, Chelsea, Kensington, Hammersmith, and Richmond, via the WLER with an approximately hourly interval of trains. This service was apparently removed in World War II.

Tim Sherwood's article in the previous section mentions the high aspirations held for this link as a through long-distance link to the North, but in-spite of electrification throughout, they did not mature. However, today there is a frequent service of trains over the WLER, from Clapham Junction to Willesden Junction (2 trains per hour), and as far as Watford (1 train per hour), at both of these stations one can change into trains from Euston to the Midlands and the North West.

Fig. 178.

NOVEMBER, 1879

LONDON AND NORTH WESTERN COMPANY'S SERVICE OF TRAINS,

BETWEEN WATERLOO, KENSINGTON, AND WILLESDEN.

		a.m.	a.m.	a.m.	p.m.	p.m.	p.m.	p.m.	p.m.			
Willesden	dep.	9 39	10 28	11 50	1 6	2 25	4 3	5 20	7 10	...	...	...
Kensington	arr.	9 46	10 36	11 58	1 14	2 33	4 11	5 27	7 19	...	...	...
"	dep.	9 47	10 37	11 59	1 15	2 34	4 13	5 28	7 20	...	...	...
West Brompton	"	9 50	10 40	12 2	1 19	2 36	4 15	5 32	7 23	...	...	...
Chelsea	"	9 52	10 42	12 4	1 22	2 38	4 17	5 34	7 25	...	...	...
Battersea	"	9 56	10 46	12 8	1 26	2 41	4 20	5 37	7 29	...	...	...
Latchmere Junc.	pass	9 58	10 48	12 10	1 27	2 43	4 22	5 39	7 31	...	...	...
West London Junc.	"	9 59	10 49	12 10	1 28	2 43	4 23	5 39	7 31	...	...	...
Queen's Road Junc.	dep.	10 1	10 51	12 12	1 30	2 45	4 25	5 41	7 33	...	...	...
Vauxhall	arr.	10 4	10 53	12 16	1 33	2 48	4 27	5 44	7 36	...	...	...
"	dep.	10 5	10 55	12 17	1 34	2 49	4 29	5 45	7 37	...	...	...
Waterloo	arr.	10 10	11 0	12 21	1 39	2 54	4 34	5 49	7 41	...	...	...

		a.m.	a.m.	p.m.	p.m.	p.m.	p.m.	p.m.	p.m.			
Waterloo	dep.	10 30	11 28	1 12	2 30	3 20	5 15	6 15	8 22	...	...	...
Vauxhall	"	10 34	11 32	1 16	2 34	3 24	5 19	6 19	8 27	...	...	...
Queen's Road Junc.	"	10 38	11 36	1 20	2 38	3 28	5 22	6 22	8 31	...	...	...
West London Junc.	pass	10 39	11 37	1 21	2 39	3 29	5 23	6 23	8 32	...	...	...
Latchmere "	"	10 40	11 38	1 22	2 40	3 30	5 24	6 24	8 33	...	...	...
Battersea	dep.	10 41	11 39	1 23	2 41	3 31	5 25	6 25	8 35	...	...	...
Chelsea	"	10 43	11 41	1 26	2 44	3 34	5 28	6 28	8 38	...	...	...
West Brompton	"	10 47	11 45	1 31	2 48	3 38	5 32	6 32	8 42	...	...	...
Kensington	arr.	10 49	11 47	1 34	2 50	3 40	5 34	6 34	8 44	...	...	...
"	dep.	10 50	11 48	1 35	2 51	3 41	5 35	6 35	8 45	...	...	...
Willesden	arr.	10 59	11 57	1 44	3 0	3 51	5 43	6 44	8 54	...	...	...

8
LOCOMOTIVE PROCUREMENT
1878 - 1895

William Bridges Adams, Part 1 (1878 -1890)

William Bridges Adams was a very widely travelled man in his engineering life, and his fertile mind produced a number of important inventions. On joining the London & South Western Railway as a successor to W.G. Beattie, whose performance in equipping the railway with locomotives and rolling stock had been poor, he tackled the situation with inspiration, and the railway benefited from his expertise in the form of a number of new designs that performed in an excellent manner. Most of the locomotives produced by him up to 1890, with the exception of the O2, A12, and T1 types, although designed "in house" were manufactured by outside contractors. This was due to the expansion in public services which had occurred giving rise to an amount of repair work that fully occupied the workshops, even in their expanded form.

In researching Adams's history, I have encountered some difficulty and much confusion. Briefly, the problem appears to be that there were two gentlemen with the name "William Bridges Adams", one lived from 1797 to 1872, and one from 1823 to 1904. Both had railway careers, the earlier man went to Chile for some time for health reasons but returned in 1836 and wrote the book *English Pleasure Carriages* which dealt with lightweight steam carriages that could run on normal railways, but could be lifted off the track by four people when a "real" train approached! It appears that the histories of the two men have been dovetailed by various people to some extent.

The confusion is fuelled from a number of sources: Hamilton Ellis states in *British Railway History* (1956), that William Bridges Adams was unrelated to the William Adams of the North London Railway, but does agree with all the other information about him in Table 9 including the design details. However in his book *Twenty Locomotive Men*, (1958), the first chapter is on "William Bridges Adams" but his life span is given as 1797 to 1872. Later in the article he credits this man with inventing the fishplate, and radial axlebox. (I have tried researching the Internet, and one site, www.steamindex.com has two consecutive articles, one on William Adams, one on William Bridges Adams, but they repeat the confusion, and another site is from a Spanish language source, which

Fig. 179. The gracefulness of the Adams designs is typified by Beyer Peacock 135 class locomotive No 141 as originally built but with the addition of a Drummond chimney.

gives details on the earlier man, and credits him with inventing the fishplate in 1847, and the radial axlebox in 1863. I would suggest interested readers may wish to undertake further research in order to fully solve the enigma.)

A photo of Adams is shown in Figure 181, along with part of a works test specification. The date of the document is not known, but it is obviously produced by Adams, and is the first example I have of serious attempts being made to ensure the quality of materials at Nine Elms. The table below affords a list of what I believe to be his professional career.

William Bridges Adams was a prolific inventor and was responsible for raising many patents. I have in my possession 20 of his patents, spanning the years from 1835 to 1870. Some of them are extremely complex, for example specification number 13,653 of 1851, entitled *Construction of Roads and Ways, Buildings, Bridges, Locomotive Engines and Carriages, &c.*

In 1847 he invented the fishplate, which had little to do with locomotive design, but which was to become a very important item in railway building throughout the world. This invention is included in patent number 11,715 of 1847 entitled, confusingly, *Railways, Engines, Carriages, &c. &c.* He appears to have invented it early in his entry into the railway industry. A fishplate is used to connect the ends of rails together and it was a substantial improvement on the previous method which was to fit a chair to the end of each rail and mount them both on the same sleeper with the rail ends butting together. We might have hoped that Adams benefited well financially from this very important contribution to rail safety, but he was far less of a businessman than he was an engineer, as is often the case, and other interested parties, including, apparently, Robert Richardson, listed as a co-inventor, reaped the benefit of his invention.

Figure 185 shows an arrangement of his next invention - his radial axlebox. This drawing may relate to one of the two locomotives mentioned in this paragraph. The idea behind the design is to cause the wheels to more accurately align themselves tangentially to the rails, as the locomotive rounds a curve, and as the axle moves sideways in the frames. This is achieved by the use of axleboxes with cylindrical sides moving in similarly curved hornblocks. Another advantage stems from the fact that with this arrangement the use of a pair of "reigns" one from each axlebox to a pivot towards the centre of the locomotive, necessary with a simple "pony truck" is dispensed with, enabling the axle to be placed nearer to an obstacle, such as the firebox back, or a driving axle. The patent was allo-

TABLE 11

Date	Employment	Design Details
Circa 1839	Commenced work for his father at the East and West India Docks Company.	None known.
Circa 1840	Worked with Miller & Ratcliffe, Engineers and Millwrights. Served an apprenticeship and then assembled marine engines at Blackwall.	None known.
March 1845 to 1853	Assistant Works Manager with Philip Taylor & Co. Worked in Marseille and Genoa before being appointed Engineer in Chief of the Sardinian Navy.	1847, patented the 'Fishplate' used for joining lengths of rails.
1853 to 1863	Returned to England and worked at various places including Cardiff Docks, the Isle of Wight, and upon equipping the North London Railway Works at Bow.	1863, patented the 'Radial' Axlebox and used this on a 2-4-2T locomotive.
1863 to 1873	Mechanical Engineer of the North London Railway Company.	Circa 1865 modified an old 0-4-0 tank locomotive into an 0-4-2T using radial axleboxes. 1868 designed a 4-4-0T locomotive using his patent radial bogie.
1873 to 1878	Locomotive Superintendent of the Great Eastern Railway.	Introduced the 2-6-0 type of locomotive to the UK.
January 1878 to May 1895	Mechanical Engineer, LSWR.	Designed and had built 16 new classes of locomotive.

LOCOMOTIVE PROCUREMENT 1878 - 1895

Fig. 180. A Neilson built 395 class locomotive No 27. This was one of the later, longer-frame versions. It is depicted with shunter step-boards, but with the handrails having been removed from the tender. Circa 1900.

THE LSWR AT NINE ELMS

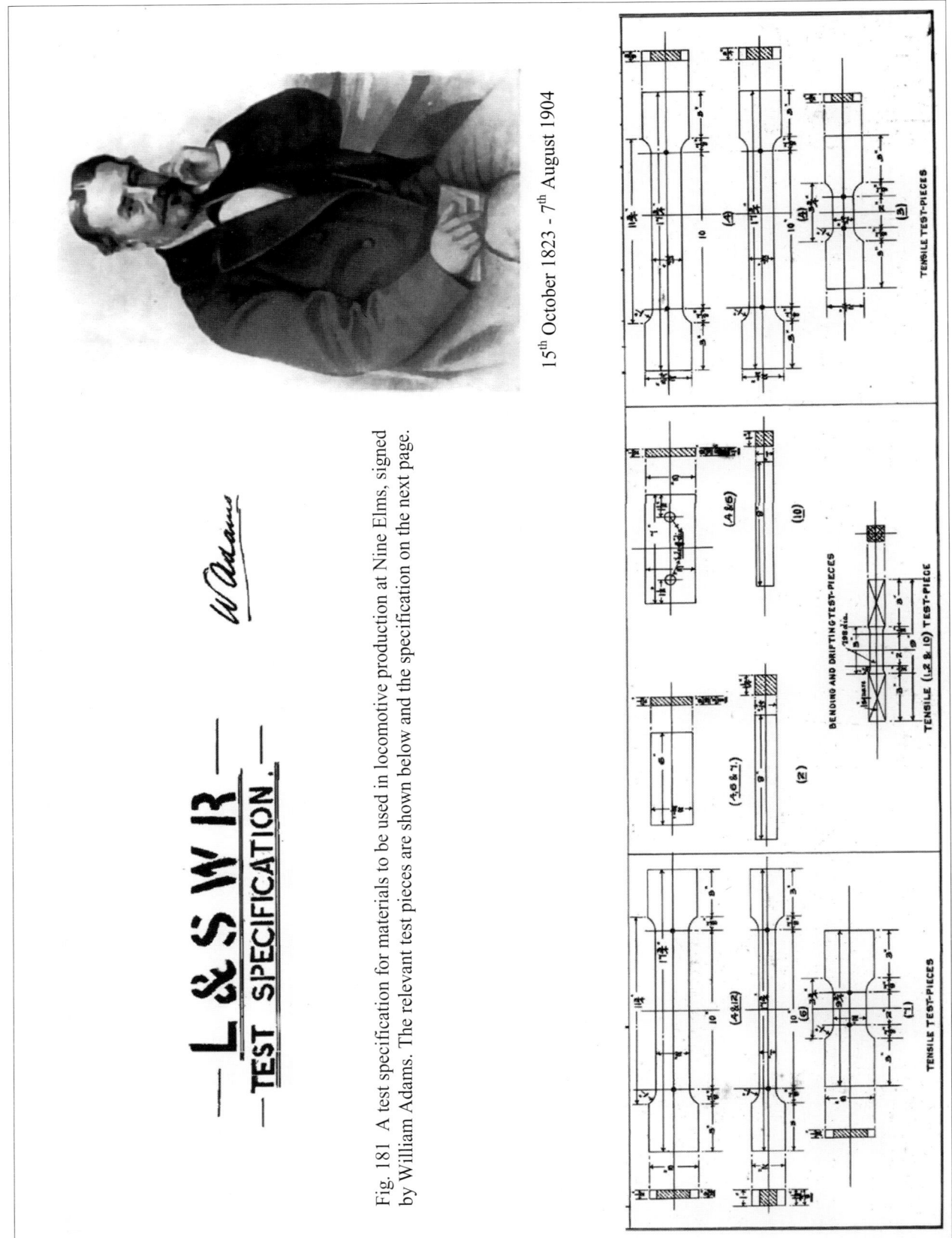

Fig. 181 A test specification for materials to be used in locomotive production at Nine Elms, signed by William Adams. The relevant test pieces are shown below and the specification on the next page.

15th October 1823 - 7th August 1904

	MATERIAL		TESTS APPLIED, INSPECTION, ETC.	TENSILE TESTS			BENDING TEST	DRIFTING TEST	ANALYSIS				
				Elong % in 2"	Ult Stress in 16" Tons ☐"	Contraction of Area %			C	Si	P	S	Mn
1	TYRES	Engine and Tender	Falling Weight Test — 1 ton Tup — dropped 10 to 30 feet (rising 5 feet per blow) successively on to the Tyre. until deflected ⅛ of external diameter without fracture. 1 in 51, or 1 from each charge to be tested; Test pieces to be machined cold from the Tyre.	15	45 to 49		—	—					
2	AXLES	Engine and Tender Crank	Nil Makers to state the mileage each Axle is guaranteed to run without showing signs of failure.	25 25	29 to 32 29 to 32	— —	Close Close	— —					
3	SPRINGS	Bearing Buffer	Each Spring after being weighted with a load 33% in excess of the working load must resume its original camber. Nil.	— —	— —	— —	— —	— —					
	SPRING STEEL	Ordinary Weldable	A piece 2·6 long, 1 at 1 radius·20 times thickness pushed straight 7 times must show no signs of permanent set after first time. Nil.	15 —	45 —	— —	— —	— —					
4	BOILER PLATE	Steel Iron	Inspected for surface defects. Every plate to be Tested. Inspected for surface defects.	— —	25 to 30 —	23 —	Close —	5/8.16 —	Free	Free	Free	Free	
5	BOILER TUBES	Steel Brass	Inspected for surface defects. Ends to fit gauges supplied by Company. 1 in 101 tested externally, to 2500 lb☐ and internally to 800 lb☐ Ditto.	— —	— —	— —	— —	— —					
6	FRAME PLATE	Steel Iron	Inspected for surface defects. A test to be made from each charge and thickness of plate. Inspected for surface defects.	— —	24 to 30 —	20 —	Close —	5/8.16 —	Free	Free	Free	Free	
7	COPPER PLATE		Every plate to be tested, and inspected for surface defects.	40	14	—	Close	—					
8	BARS FOR FIREBOXSTAYS	Copper Steel	Nil. Nil.	40 —	14 —	— —	— —	— —	Analyses not specified				
9	MERCHANT IRON	Common Best Best, Best, Best, Best, Best Yorkshire	Nil. Nil. Nil. Nil. Nil.	— — — — —	— — — — —	— — — — —	— — — — —	— — — — —					
10	STEEL CASTINGS	Wheel Centres Roof Girders	Inspected for surface defects, and 1 in 40 tested to destruction: Wheel dropped from 10-15-20-25-30 feet, no defects must be shown at the two lower heights. Each Wheel and rebolted by fall from 4ft 6 ins. on to wooden block without signs of defect. Each roof girder subjected to a transverse stress calculated from working load.	20 —	28 —	— —	90° —	— —					
11	IRON CASTINGS		Nil.	—	—	—	—	—					
12	MILD STEEL PLATES		One in fifty to be Tested.	—	24 to 30	18	—	—	Free	Free	Free	Free	
13	BEST YORKSHIRE IRON RIVETS		Nil.	30	22	—	—	—					

cated in 1863, number 3195, entitled *Locomotive Engines &c.* and the first locomotive to use the system was a 2-4-2 tank engine called "White Raven", built for the St. Helens Railway by Cross & Company in 1863. Adams was associated with the North London Railway at this time and it was tested on that railway before being despatched to its owners. Adams then used the radial axlebox on one locomotive belonging to the North London Railway – an 0-4-0 tank locomotive, which was the only one to have previously belonged to the North and South Western Junction Railway and which had been used on the South Acton to Hammersmith branch. Around 1865 he converted it to an 0-4-2 tank and fitted it with a steam operated crane on the rear end. This locomotive lasted until after World War II, and must have been his inspiration for a similar crane engine that he proposed in 1894 for the LSWR, illustrated later in Figure 277.

Figure 186 refers to his 415 class 4-4-2T locomotive, of which 71 were manufactured, all by outside contractors, during the period 1882 to 1885. This particular drawing is by Dubs & Co, one of the contractors, and indicates the use of radial axleboxes on that class of engine.

Another invention was the radial bogie, which performed a similar function to the radial axlebox but utilised two axles on the bogie frame. He patented this item in 1865, specification number 404, entitled *Bogie frames for Locomotives and Carriages*. The centre pivot in previous designs of bogie was fixed, with a simple bearing surrounding it, enabling the bogie to turn, but when the locomotive encountered a curve, it caused the wheels to be misaligned with the rails because the bogie could not move laterally. With the Adams bogie, the bearing is slotted, allowing the whole bogie to move sideways when encountering a curve, controlled in its initial designs by rubber side "springs", allowing the wheels to remain substantially tangential to the rails, as with his patent radial axlebox. Adams used this type of bogie in 1868 on the No 1 class of 4-4-0 tank locomotives designed for the North London Railway, which gave good service until the end of the independent existence of that company. A drawing of the patented bogie as previously used on the North London Locomotive is shown in Figure 187.

I have tried to ascertain which inventions were used on the various classes in this section by reference to available drawings, with only moderate success. The results are depicted in Table 12.

Yet another invention of his was the "Vortex" exhaust blast pipe. This enabled a better draught to be obtained by spreading the vacuum achieved more evenly over the whole smokebox tubeplate. This resulted in better steam production and was another successful design.

A summary of the locomotive types designed by Adams during in the period 1878 to 1890 is shown in Table 13.

The 46 class, delivered as 4-4-0 tank locomotives, were rebuilt between 1883 and 1886 into the 4-4-2T configuration by the addition of a rear axle with radial boxes. This was done for two reasons, the riding qualities of the locomotive as original had been poor, and its coal and water carrying capacity inadequate, so the extra axle enabled the bunker to be extended. This is an example of where the use of the radial type of axlebox enabled the axle to be placed a lot nearer to the rear driving axle than would have been possible if pony reigns had been necessary.

From 1896, some new boilers were fitted to the 380 class, and to one of the 135 class (number 136), and as these were of slightly different dimensions to the originals, it required the substitution of new cab frontplates with round windows. The bogies on these two classes had 2ft 6in diameter wheels with solid centres, and the axles were spaced at 6ft 6in. It is thought that these bogies were not of Adams's patent radial pattern, but confirmation has eluded me. The later ones with 3ft 4in diameter wheels and a spacing of 7ft fitted from class 415 onwards, have been

TABLE 12

Class	46	380	135	415	445	460	A12	O2
4-wheel bogie type	FP	FP	?	R	RP	R	-	R
Rear axle type	R*	-	-	R	-	-	F	-

R   Axle or bogie with radial characteristics, allowing lateral movement.
F   Axle or bogie with no lateral movement permitted.
P   Probably.
-      Does not exist.
*   After conversion to 4-4-2T configuration.

LOCOMOTIVE PROCUREMENT 1878 - 1895

TABLE 13

Build Period	Number Built	Builder	Wheel arrangement	Class	Withdrawal period	Figure Numbers
6/1879-8/1879	12	Beyer Peacock & Co	4-4-0T (1)	46	2/1914-7/1925	188,189,190, 191,192
9/1879-12/1879	12	Beyer Peacock & Co	4-4-0	380	7/1913-12/1925	193,194,195, 197
11/1880-1/1881	12	Robert Stephenson & Co	4-4-0	135	12/1913-12/1924	179,196,198, 199
11/1881-12/1887	70	Neilson & Co	0-6-0	395	8/1916-9/1959	180,200,201, 202,203,204, 205,207
8/1882-11/1882	12	Beyer Peacock & Co	4-4-2T	415	6/1916-11/1925	206,210,214
3/1883-10/1885	28	Robert Stephenson & Co	4-4-2T	415	11/1921-7/1961	208,209,212
4/1883-8/1883	12	Robert Stephenson & Co	4-4-0	445	5/1923-12/1925	182,183,216, 217,218,219, 220
4/1884-10/1887	33	Nine Elms	2-4-0	(2)	6/1888-11/1898	221,222,223, 224,225
11/1884-12/1885	20	Dubs & Co	4-4-2T	415	11/1921-1/1961	213
9/1884-10/1884	10	Neilson & Co	4-4-0T	460	12/1924-4/1929	226,227,229
6/1884-12/1887	11	Robert Stephenson & Co	4-4-0T	460	2/1926-4/1929	224
2/1885-3/1885	11	Neilson & Co	4-4-2T	415	9/1917-1/1928	211,215
5/1887-5/1895	50	Nine Elms	0-4-2	A12	11/1928-7/1947	228,231,232, 233,234,235, 238
6/1888-7/1896	50	Nine Elms	0-4-4T	T1	10/1931-5/1951	240,241,243, 244,245,246
12/1889-3/1895	60	Nine Elms	0-4-4T	O2	2/1933-3/1967	247,248,249, 250,251
11/1892-4/1893	40	Neilson & Co	0-4-2	A12	5/1932-12/1948	230,236,237, 239

Notes:

(1) All rebuilt as 4-4-2T locomotives, 1883 to 1886.

(2) Rebuild of 33 Beattie Well Tanks into 2-4-0 tender engines.

In preservation: 415 class, number 488, O2 class, number 209 (W24 Calbourne). In addition a T1 class replica is being constructed using a genuine T1 boiler.

checked from drawings to be of the patent pattern, but no drawings of the 135 or 445 classes have been available.

In the 1880s the London and North Western Railway had been experimenting with compound locomotives, and it wasn't long before William Adams began to consider the possible advantages of using the system on the route to Salisbury. One of the 445 class, Number 446, was converted and ready for trials on 10th February 1888. The locomotive is shown in Figure 183, and a diagram of the Worsdell & Von Borries system used is shown in Figure 182, the diameter of the right hand cylinder being increased from 18in to 26in However, the results were not startling. On test runs to Salisbury the performance was compared to a unmodified locomotive, number 448, and the average fuel consumption of number 446 was only 4.4% lower than the standard engine, and its consumption of lubricating oil was 30% higher. It was therefore decided not to adopt compounding, and number 446 was converted back in March 1891.

The Vortex blast pipe invention has been mentioned. The invention is reputed to have been patented, but I have not been able to locate the patent documents as I have the other Adams inventions mentioned. The Locomotive Committee was becoming worried about the rising costs of the locomotive department in 1885, which probably initiated the compounding experiment, but it also gave rise to a series of experiments with the vortex blast pipe. It was fitted to a goods engine, number 403 of the 395 class, and an express passenger engine, number 463, of the 460 class. The performances of these locomotives were compared to those of numbers 165 and 466, respectively. The reduction in the consumption of fuel by 12% in the case of the goods engine, and 8.5% for the passenger engine was considered well worthwhile, so it was ordered that all new passenger tender engines from 1885 be fitted with this form of blast pipe.

It appears, however, from research made at the National Railway Museum, that not only was a significant proportion of locomotives in use after 1885 fitted with the Vortex blast pipe (including some of the Vesuvius and Ilfracombe Goods classes), but that Adams exported his design to other railways, both in Britain and abroad. The invention did not find favour with Drummond for some reason, and he removed most of them when he came to power.

The previous locomotive to be built inside Nine Elms Works was a Beattie Standard Well Tank that left the works in November 1875. The rest of the time, the works had been fully occupied with repairs

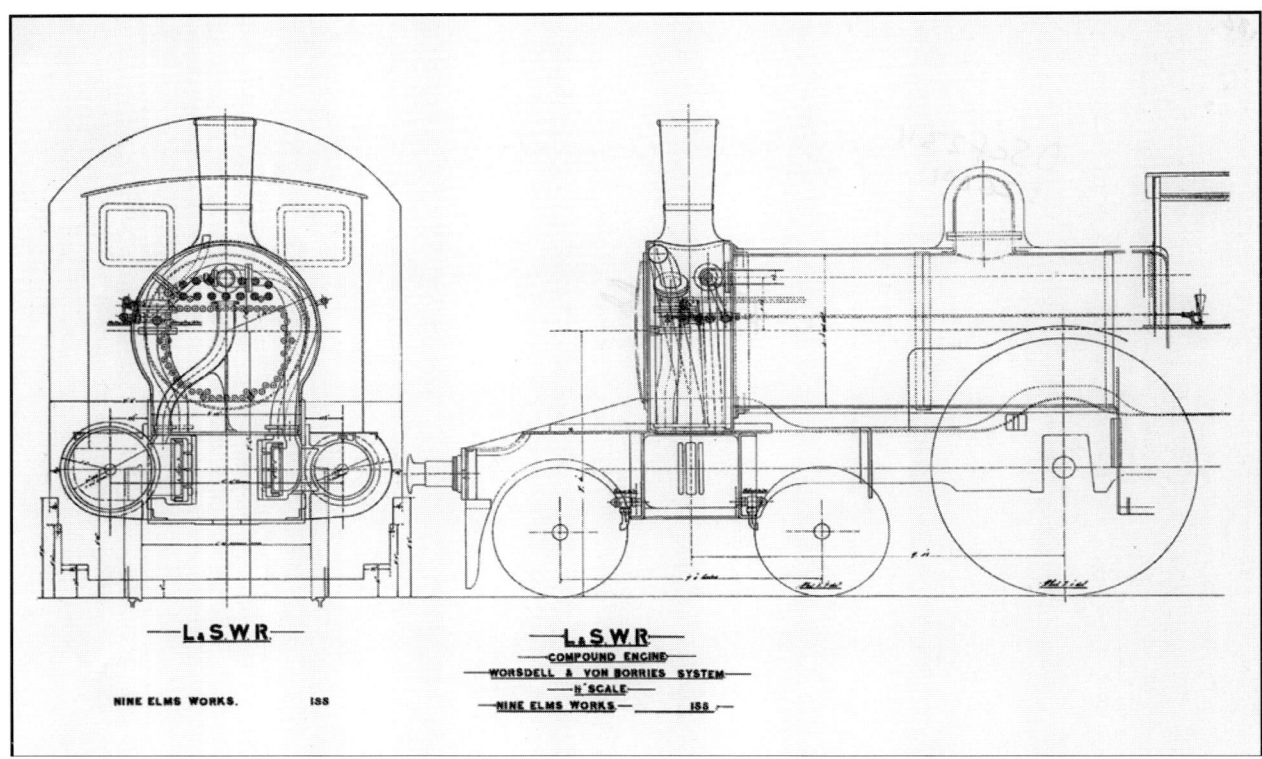

Fig. 182. Diagram of the Worsdell & Von Borris system of compounding applied to locomotive No 446.

LOCOMOTIVE PROCUREMENT 1878 - 1895

Fig. 183. 445 class locomotive No 446 at Basingstoke after conversion to a compound. The low pressure 26in diameter cylinder is shown on the side nearest the camera. The oval plate on the cab sheet is in recognition of Worsdell & Von Borris.

and modifications, in spite of the expansion that had taken place. This break in new construction was ended after 12 years, when the first A12 locomotive, number 527, left the works in April 1887. At this time it was decided to introduce a new works order numbering system, two characters consisting of a letter followed by a number, starting with A1. The letter advances first up to Y, then the number advances to 2 and the letters are sequenced again. I, J, Q, U, W, and Z are not used. The numbers were used to identify a range of products, such as cylinders, etc, and usually the order number of the first batch of each locomotive type was used as the overall class number. However, it is not known why the first locomotive to be produced after the break was given the number A12, instead of A1, (the next one was T1, then O2).

A short lived experiment in April 1905 consisted of fitting A12 engines numbers 618 and 638 with the Whitaker token exchange equipment, and trials were performed on the Barnstaple to Yeoford line. The trials were successful but it was not considered worthwhile, as there were so few non-stop trains that would benefit from it.

As early as 1902 an attempt was made to use oil fuel in a locomotive. The price of coal had been rising, and the developing oil companies saw that the railway industry could provide a large previously untapped source of revenue, so several of them were offering to modify locomotives on a trial basis to use oil as a fuel. On the LSWR an O2 was selected, number 180, and fitted with equipment supplied by M. Samuel & Co. Figure 184 shows the "Holden's Patent" apparatus for burning liquid fuel that was probably applied to this engine. The engine was based at Nine Elms and used on several passenger services around Clapham Junction during the tests. However, although the thermal efficiency was probably higher than with coal, the price of the fuel was even higher, and the economics prevented its future use. In addition there were environmental objections even at that time in history, as the passengers and engine crews objected to the effects of the fumes and preferred the smoke and smell of coal.

A number of the O2 locomotives found their way to the Isle of Wight, either in parts, or by means of the Southampton Dock floating crane, as the deck loading of the ferries during that period was insufficient to transport them assembled. They were given an I.O.W. number, prefixed by "W", and had extended bunkers fitted to reduce the number of visits to the refuelling depot.

410 locomotives were built to Adams's design during this period (1878 to 1890), 160 at Nine Elms and 250 by subcontractors. (These figures exclude the rebuilding as tender locomotives of the 33 Beattie Well Tanks.) They were of 10 different classes and are illustrated in the following pages. From this time, it appears that the works photographer was given the

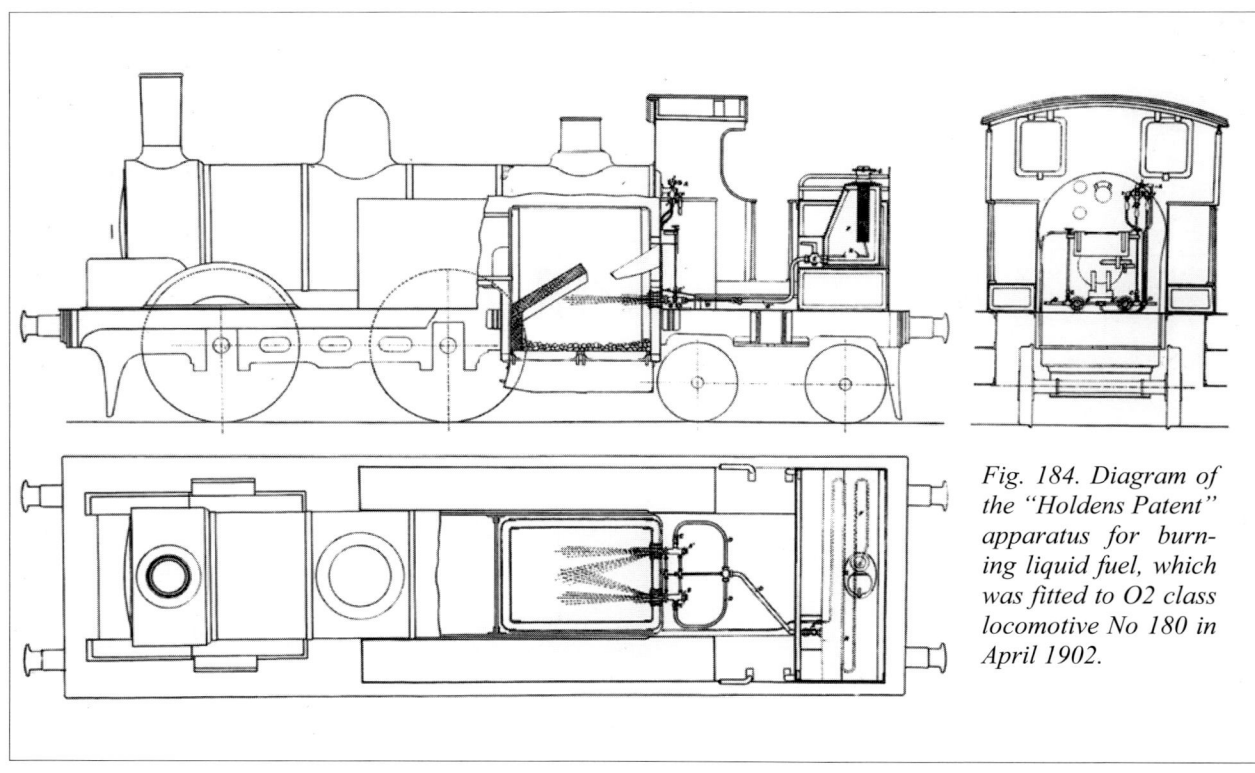

Fig. 184. Diagram of the "Holdens Patent" apparatus for burning liquid fuel, which was fitted to O2 class locomotive No 180 in April 1902.

LOCOMOTIVE PROCUREMENT 1878 - 1895

task of recording locomotives that had been involved in collisions, and some of the examples are shown here. It would appear that the A12 class was particularly prone to such incidents, or maybe it was just as a result of their frequent use as "maids of all work". Two examples of the locomotives in this section have been preserved, one each of the 0415, and O2 types.

As we have reached the era of the 395 locomotive, a little light relief may be appropriate. Many years ago, when I was an impoverished student, my father, who was employed at Eastleigh works, managed to get me a job during my vacation with the adjacent Motive Power Department as a locomotive cleaner. Unfortunately for the railway, but fortunately for me, they were desperately short of firemen, as few people were interested in taking up a career living on dirty steam engines. My father, in fact, told me that this was the real reason why they had begun to replace steam with diesel and nothing to do with increased efficiency etc. The shortage was so great that every cleaner who was over the legal limit of 16 years of age was put through a "test" and promoted to a "Passed Cleaner" which qualified him to do firing duties. So, as I was aged 18, I was immediately entered for the test, which consisted of being taken to a room in the office block and being asked by the examiner to recite two rules from the many hundreds in the rule book which your foreman had previously primed you about. I managed to pass this test, and was allocated to do one week on "Preparation and Disposal" (sorting out the locomotives before and after their duty), one week on "Steam Raising" (looking after the fire and water levels on locomotives on shed), and then one week as "third man" with a crew out on the footplate. My first tour of duty as third man was on the O2 class locomotive used as a coach and parcel van shunter at the north end of Eastleigh station.

After that training I was qualified to perform as fireman in my own right, and the following week I was allocated to the Eastleigh works shunter. There were two of them, one a Brighton "Terrier", but I was to look after one of the last remaining 0395 0-6-0 tender locomotives, number 30566.

The driver had been a main line driver, who had been "put back" onto shunting duties because he had failed the eyesight test. He was a tall, severe, Dickensian looking man, with a long flowing, raincoat.

We had to prepare the locomotive early in the morning in the Motive Power Department before going over to the works, and whereas most drivers preparing for a shunting duty did not give full attention to all the rules regarding the presence and the state of the lamps, tools, flags, etc, this man was totally pedantic about the state of the locomotive before we left the shed. His argument was that you never knew when an engine on the main line will break down and we will be called to assist. I was fearful of what standards he might require of me but shunting on an 0395 turned out to be quite pleasant.

On the fourth firing day, it was a Thursday, which was pay-day, and our wages were issued (in cash) from a corrugated iron lean-to on the office wall of the Motive Power Depot across the way; mine would be £3 7s 6d for a week. We were shunting up and down, when all of a sudden the driver stopped, stood up, and said to me "Take over mate, I'm going to get my pay". With that, he climbed down, and all I could see was his flowing coat tails.

I was suddenly aware of what seemed to be a multitude of screaming shunters surrounding the hissing locomotive. There were probably only about four of them, but they all seemed to be shouting that we had to get a move on, as "all this lot had to be done by lunchtime". I had never, ever, driven a steam locomotive before, and I was scared.

I went over to the driver's side. I knew what the regulator and reverser did, but I was confused by the brake (I cannot remember what type was fitted). After fiddling with the controls, I thought I heard the brakes release, so I gingerly opened the regulator, checking that the reverser was pointing the right way. We moved, slowly, but we moved. Could we stop? I had visions of a 70-ton 0395 crashing its way into one of the works roads somewhat before its scheduled overhaul date. When the shunter yelled to stop, I lowered the most likely looking lever on the brake, and we shuddered to a halt and a wagon went off on its own. I had achieved a movement. I then pointed the reverser the other way, and we retraced our steps. However, after a couple of attempts like this, the shunters declared that they couldn't carry on at this rate, and they were going to have their lunch and finish the job when the real driver returned. I sat down on my seat, very relieved, and could not believe what had just happened. I think I had just visited the "deep" end.

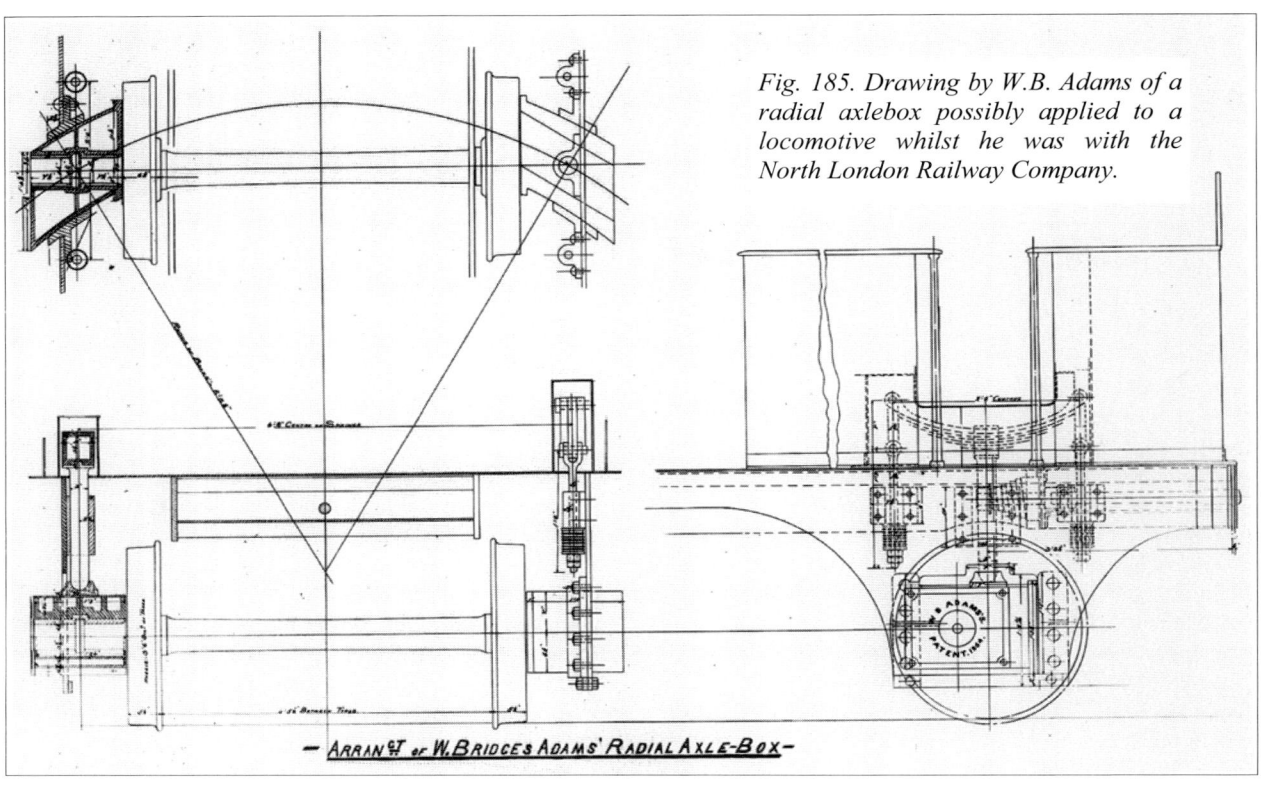

Fig. 185. Drawing by W.B. Adams of a radial axlebox possibly applied to a locomotive whilst he was with the North London Railway Company.

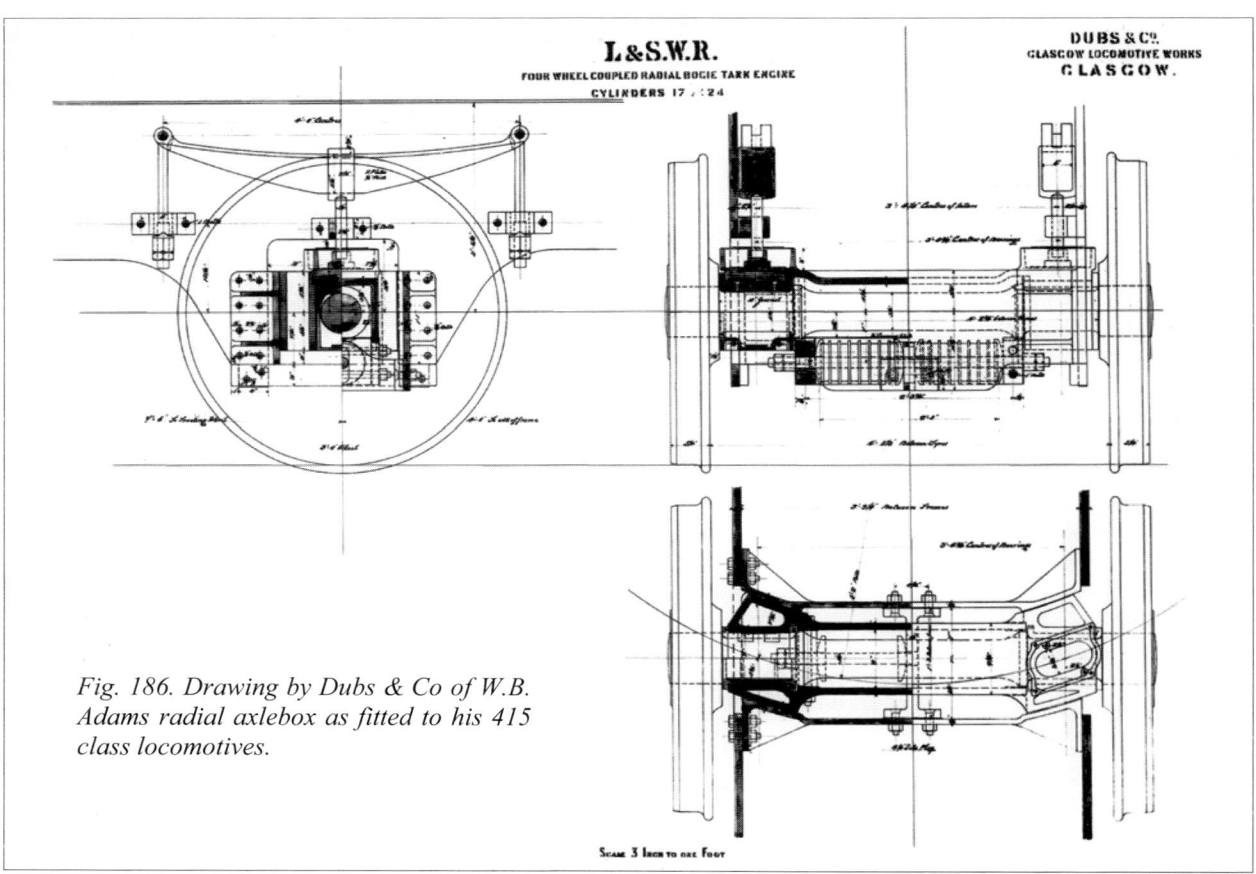

Fig. 186. Drawing by Dubs & Co of W.B. Adams radial axlebox as fitted to his 415 class locomotives.

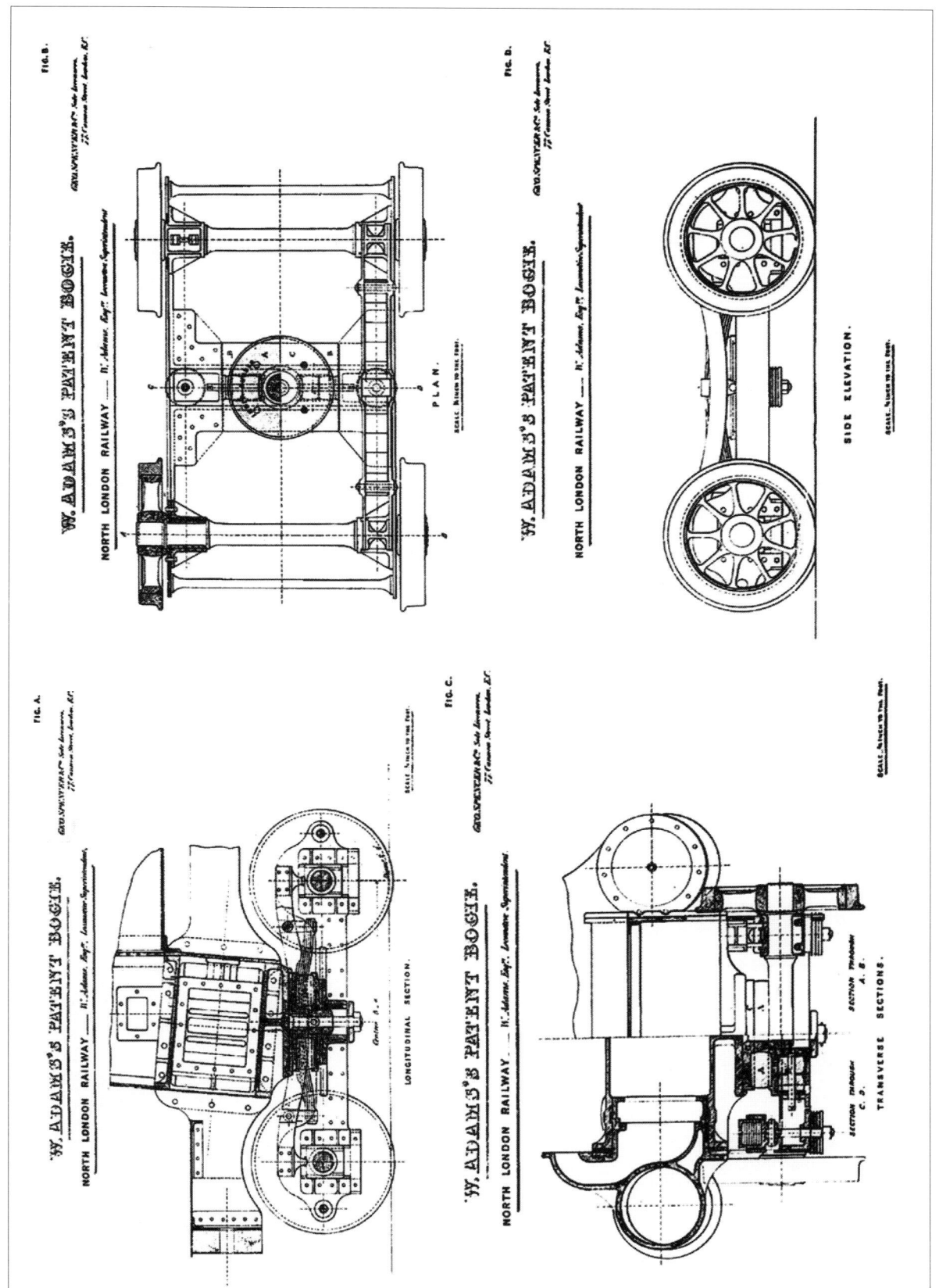

Fig. 187. Drawing of W.B. Adams Patent Radial Bogie registered at Geo. Spencer & Co, sole licencees, when he was employed by the North London Railway Company.

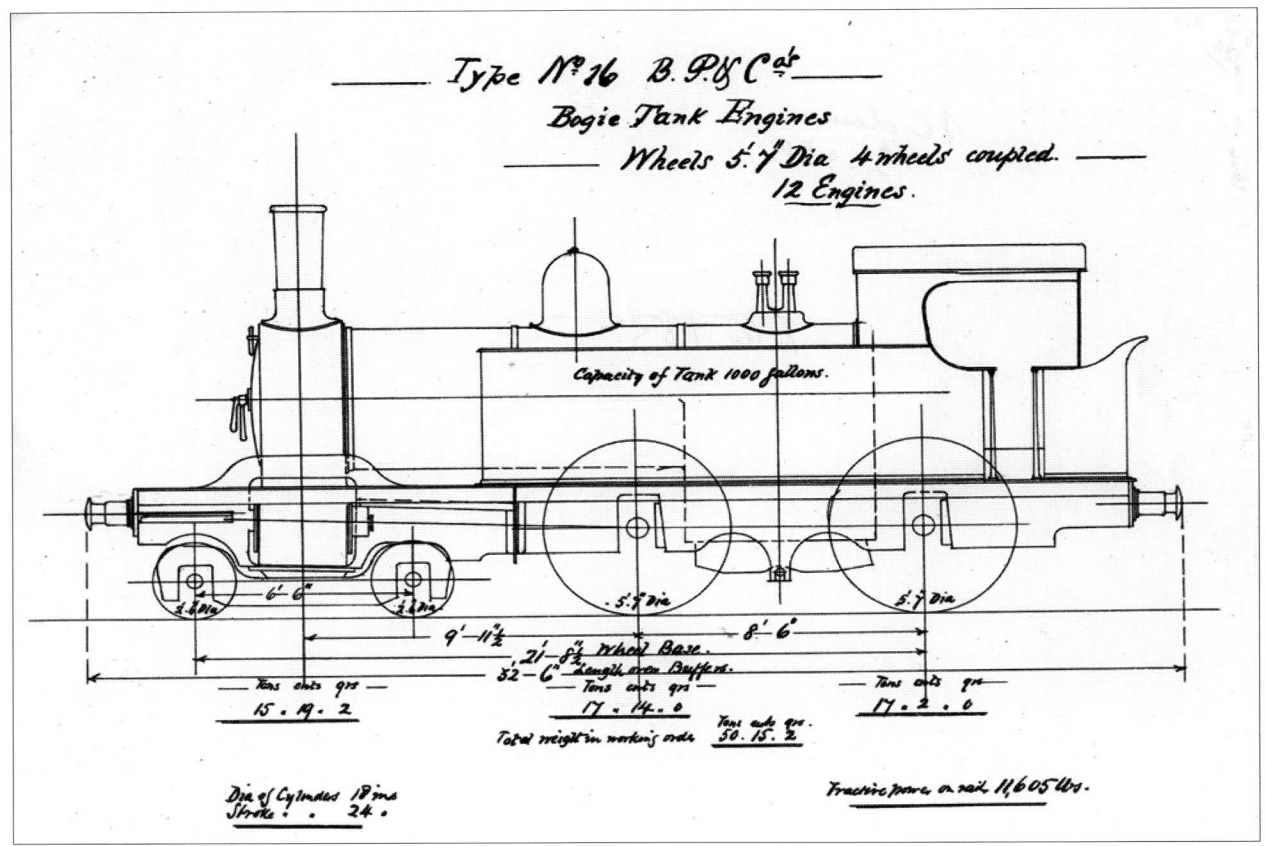

Fig. 188. Diagram of the 46 class 4-4-0T locomotive, as supplied by Beyer Peacock & Co.

Fig. 189. Works photograph of Beyer Peacock & Co 46 class locomotive No 379 as a 4-4-0T.

LOCOMOTIVE PROCUREMENT 1878 - 1895

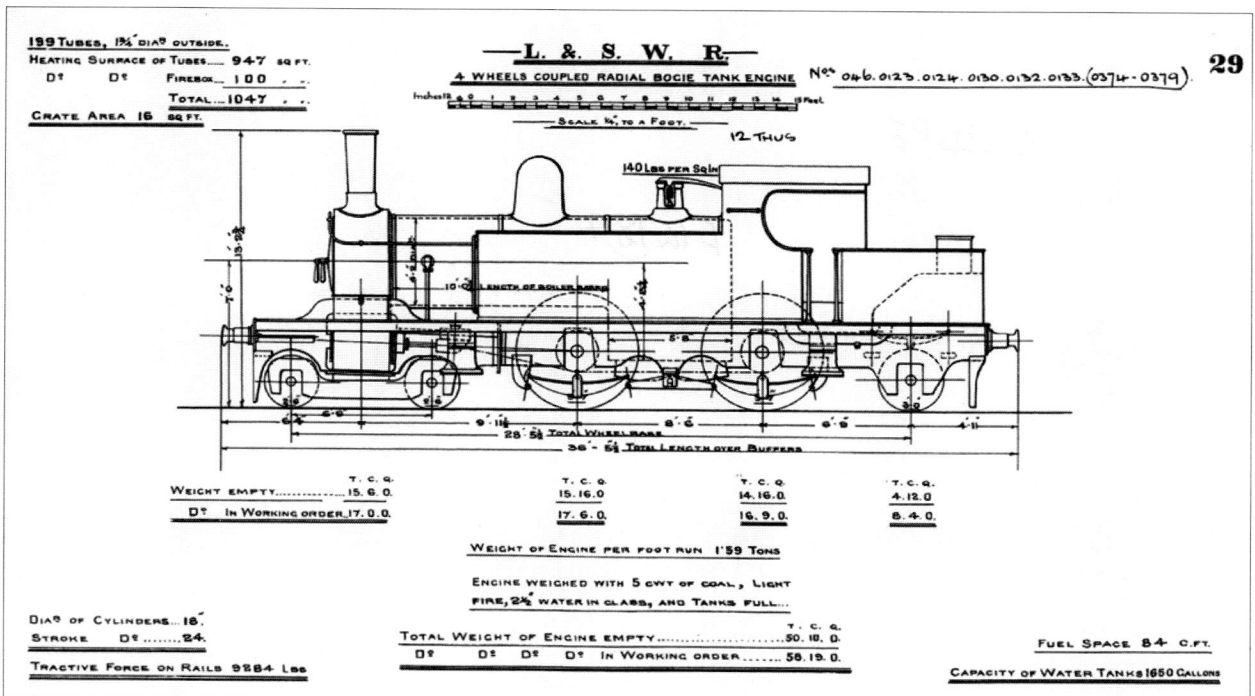

Fig. 190. Diagram of the Beyer Peacock & Co 46 class locomotive as modified at Nine Elms into a 4-4-2T type.

Fig. 191. Beyer Peacock & Co 46 class locomotive No 374, after the addition of a trailing radial axle and extended bunker. The small hole provided in the solid bogie wheel was provided to assist in lifting when necessary.

Fig. 192. Beyer Peacock & Co 46 class locomotive No 124 after modification to a 4-4-2T, with a Drummond chimney.

LOCOMOTIVE PROCUREMENT 1878 - 1895

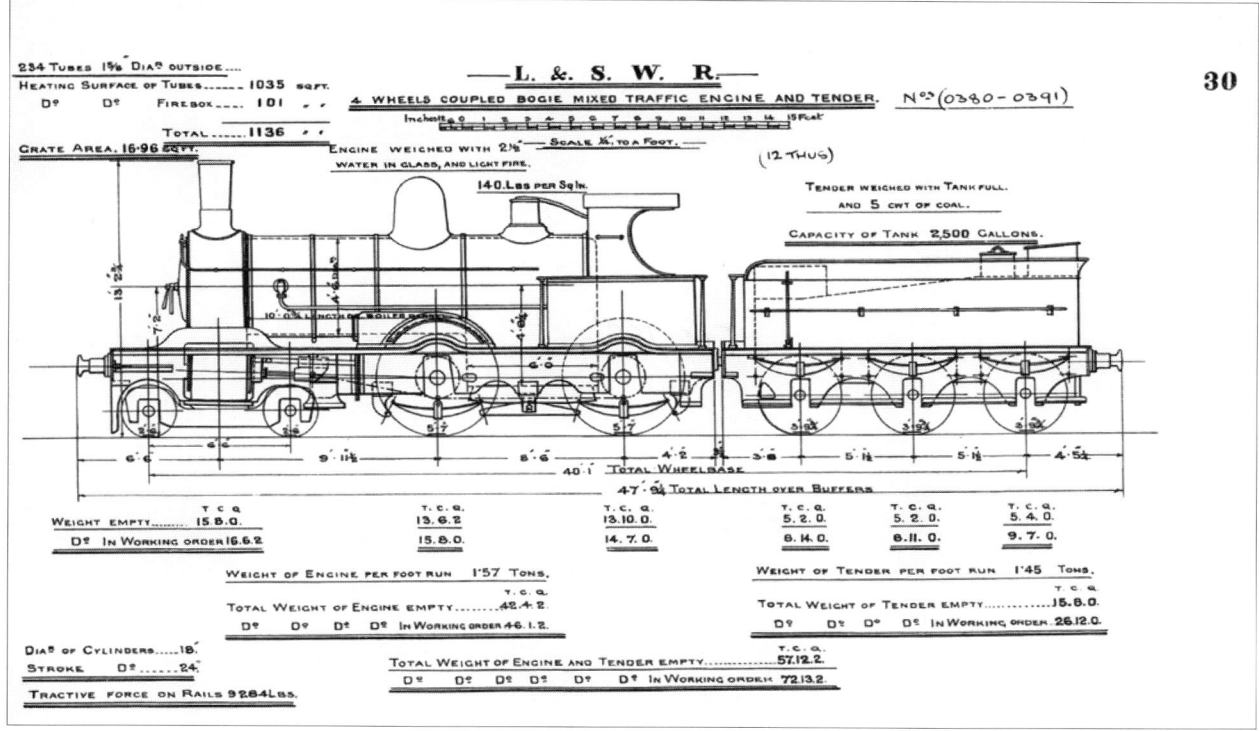

Fig. 193. Diagram of the Beyer Peacock & Co 380 class locomotive, but with the newer replacement Adams boiler.

Fig. 194. Beyer Peacock & Co 380 class locomotive No 391 as originally built, but with a lubricator on the dome and square windows.

Fig. 195. Beyer Peacock & Co 380 class locomotive No 386 as originally built, but with front-end damage and awaiting repair following the accident at Tresmeer on the North Cornwall line on 19th November 1898 when it was in collision with A12 No 535.

LOCOMOTIVE PROCUREMENT 1878 - 1895

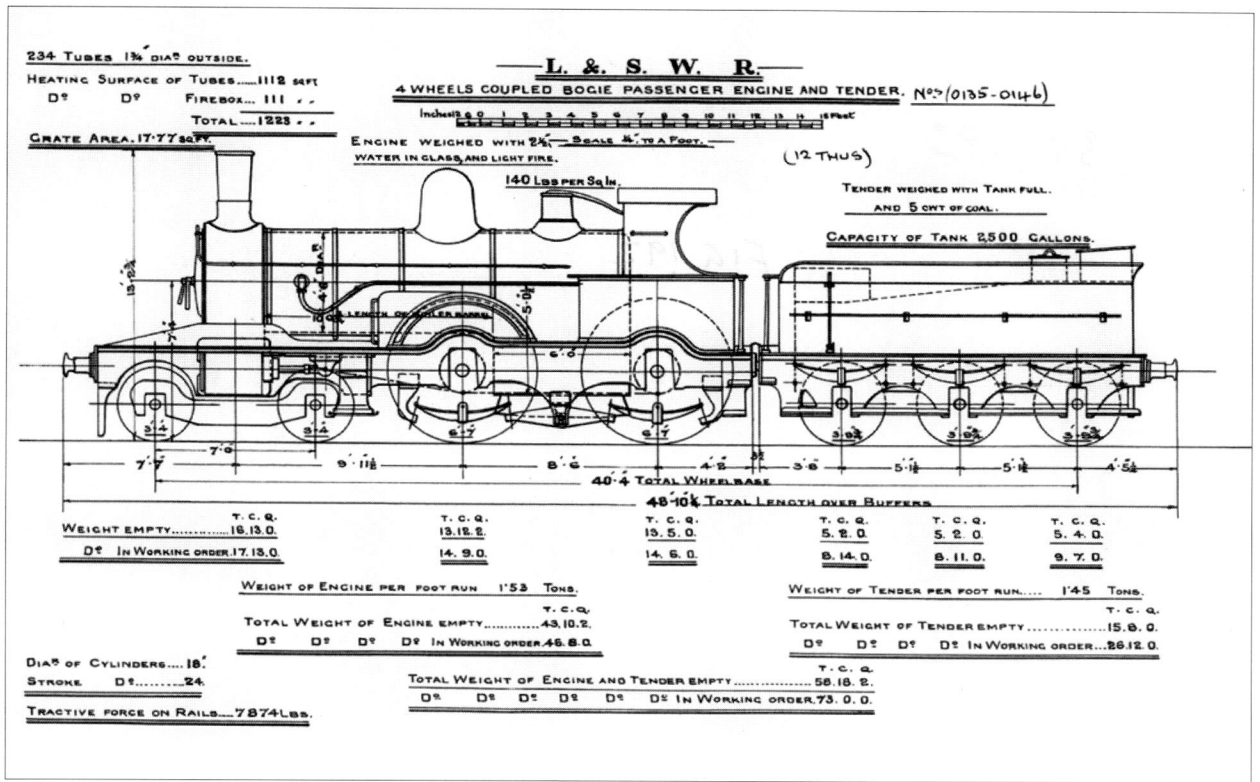

Fig. 196. Diagram of Beyer Peacock & Co 135 class locomotive.

Fig. 197. Photograph of Beyer Peacock & Co 380 class locomotive No 380, (duplicated with a line under the number), and fitted with replacement Adams boiler and Drummond chimney, circa 1902.

THE LSWR AT NINE ELMS

Fig. 198. Beyer Peacock& Co 135 class locomotive No 135, as originally built.

LOCOMOTIVE PROCUREMENT 1878 - 1895

Fig. 199. Beyer Peacock & Co 135 class locomotive No 126, duplicated with a line through the number, and fitted with an Adams replacement 4ft 4in boiler. This necessitated a new cab front, which had round windows. At the same time, an Adams patent spark arrester was fitted, requiring a conical smokebox door. This latter feature was removed in October 1903. Photograph taken between September 1902 and October 1903.

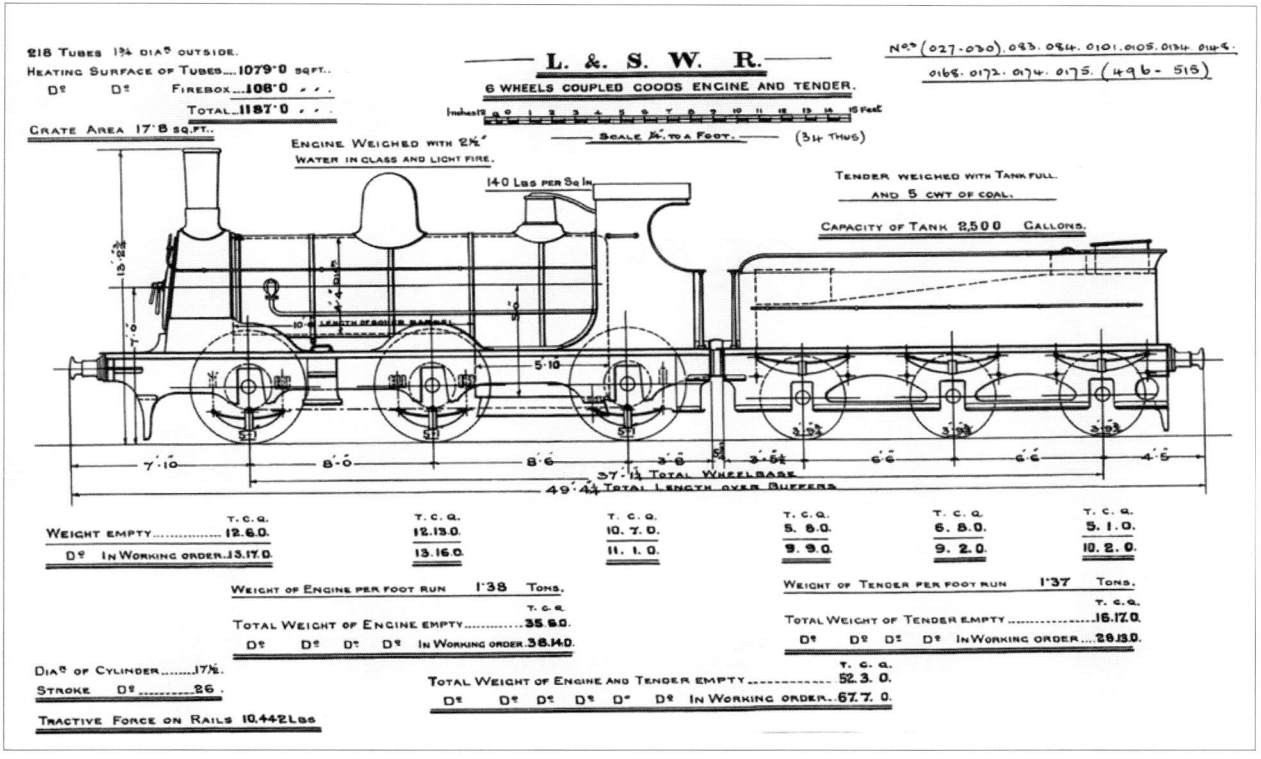

Fig. 200. Diagram of a Neilson 395 class locomotive. This shows the dimensions of the longer frame, 1885/6 series.

THE LSWR AT NINE ELMS

Fig. 201. Neilson 395 class locomotive No 434, one of the earlier, shorter frame versions. Shown in original condition with the shunter step-boards and handrails on the tender that were removed in Adams's later years. This engine was one of several of the type sent to the Middle East in March 1917 for the First World War and worked on the Palestine Military Railway. It ended its days as Iraq State Railways stock.

LOCOMOTIVE PROCUREMENT 1878 - 1895

Fig. 202. A Neilson 395 locomotive, No 502, one of the later, longer frame versions. Shown with shunter step-boards and handrails removed from the tender, circa 1900. This particular machine was another of the type sent to Palestine.

Fig. 203. 395 class locomotive, No 513, depicted after suffering a derailment having "split the points" possibly in Nine Elms yard. Assistance is being provided by a K10 or L11 type.

LOCOMOTIVE PROCUREMENT 1878 - 1895

Fig. 204. Neilson 395 class locomotive No 167 after a frontal collision, seen on the Nine Elms turntable. The engine is as originally built, apart from the lack of shunter step boards and hand rails.

Fig. 205. A Neilson 395 class locomotive on a passenger train, including a 4-coach suburban block-set and some 49ft stock passing Nine Elms Junction. The headcode in the 1911 list indicates a journey from Windsor, Feltham, or Barnes to Waterloo, via the loop line (Kew Bridge). The alternative for the same code is Southampton Docks to Waterloo but this would be unlikely.

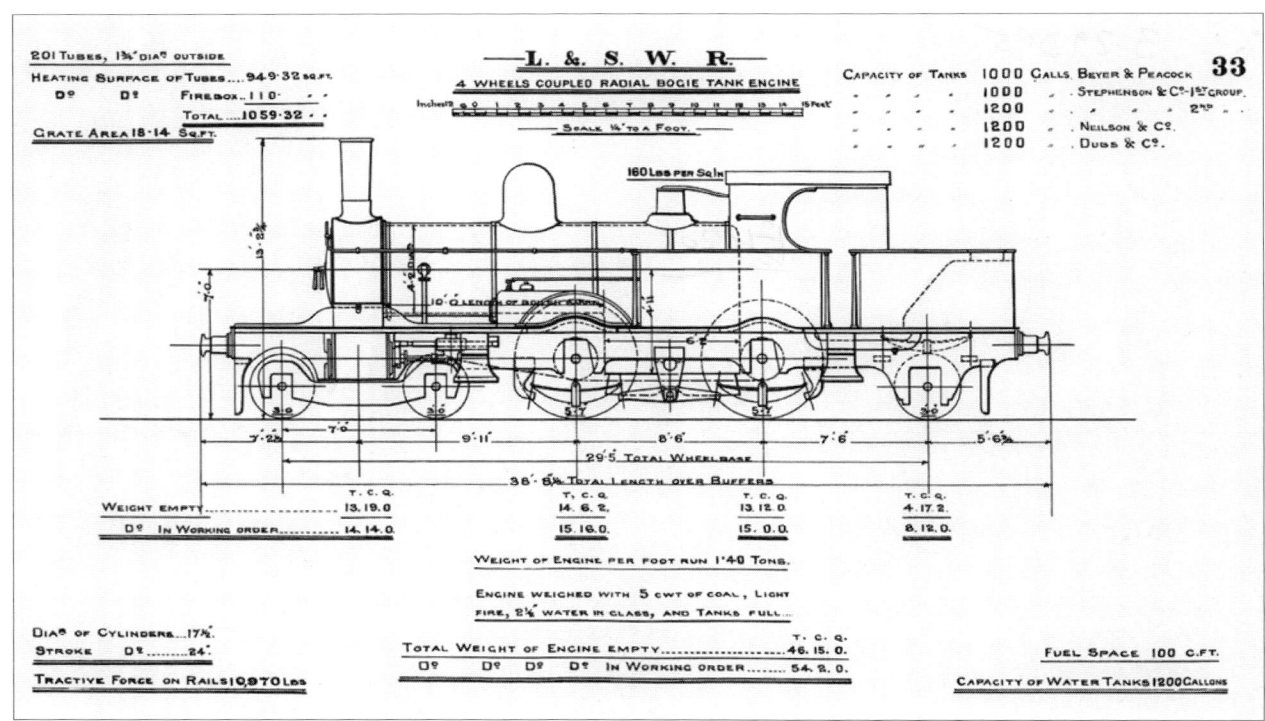

Fig. 206. Diagram of the 415 class of locomotive shown with the 1895 replacement boiler.

LOCOMOTIVE PROCUREMENT 1878 - 1895

Fig. 207. Neilson 395 class locomotive on a goods train. (Webpraxis)

THE LSWR AT NINE ELMS

LOCOMOTIVE PROCUREMENT 1878 - 1895

Opposite page top: Fig. 208. 415 class locomotive No 427, one of the Robert Stephenson & Co series, shown as originally built.

Opposite page bottom: Fig. 209. 415 class locomotive No 48, another of the Robert Stephenson & Co series, shown as originally built.

This page: Fig. 210. 415 class locomotive 427, one of the Beyer Peacock & Co series, shown as originally built.   (HMRS)

Fig. 211. 415 class locomotive No 482, one of the Neilson & Co series. Shown as originally built.

LOCOMOTIVE PROCUREMENT 1878 - 1895

Top: Fig. 213. 415 class locomotive No 517, one of the Dubs & Co series with 1895 boiler and added coal rails. Taken at Bournemouth, August 1902. (D.L. Bradley)
Centre: Fig. 214. 415 class locomotive No 415, one of the Beyer Peacock & Co series, with original boiler, but with added coal rails and with double slidebars. September 1907. (D.L. Bradley)

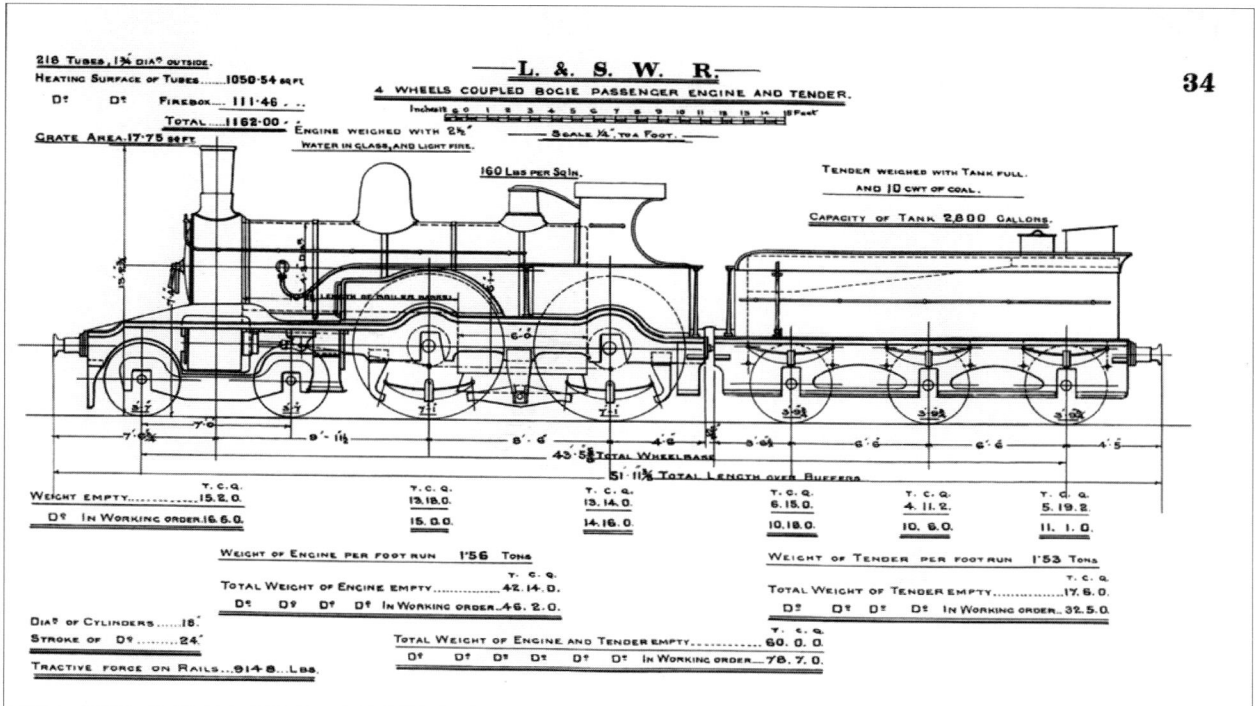

Fig. 216. Diagram of the 445 class of locomotive shown with original boiler

Above: *Fig. 217. 445 class locomotive No 448, in original condition.*

Opposite page, bottom: *Fig. 215. 415 class locomotive No 3488 (originally 488), one of the Neilson series, with Drummond boiler and chimney at Eastleigh in August 1949. This locomotive had been sold to the Government in 1917, and was then passed on to the East Kent Railway, who then resold it back to the Southern Railway in 1946. It was overhauled at Eastleigh and worked until July 1961, when it was preserved by the Bluebell Railway.*

(D.L. Bradley)

THE LSWR AT NINE ELMS

Fig. 218. 445 class locomotive No 455, in original condition. Many of the views seen in this book were naturally recorded by the official LSWR photographer, with the equipment referred to in a minute of the Locomotive and Stores Committee for 26th March 1890, which approved a proposal from the Locomotive Superintendent as to, "...the purchase of photographic apparatus." Possibly earlier "official" views of LSWR subjects had either been taken by commercial photographers to order, or even by approved amateurs.

LOCOMOTIVE PROCUREMENT 1878 - 1895

Fig. 219. 445 class locomotive No 448 with replacement boiler fitted in October 1894, necessitating a new cab front with round windows. The shunter step boards and handrails have been removed, but the Adams chimney remains.

THE LSWR AT NINE ELMS

Fig. 220. 445 class locomotive No 448 as in Figure 219, but with the substitution of a Drummond chimney.

LOCOMOTIVE PROCUREMENT 1878 - 1895

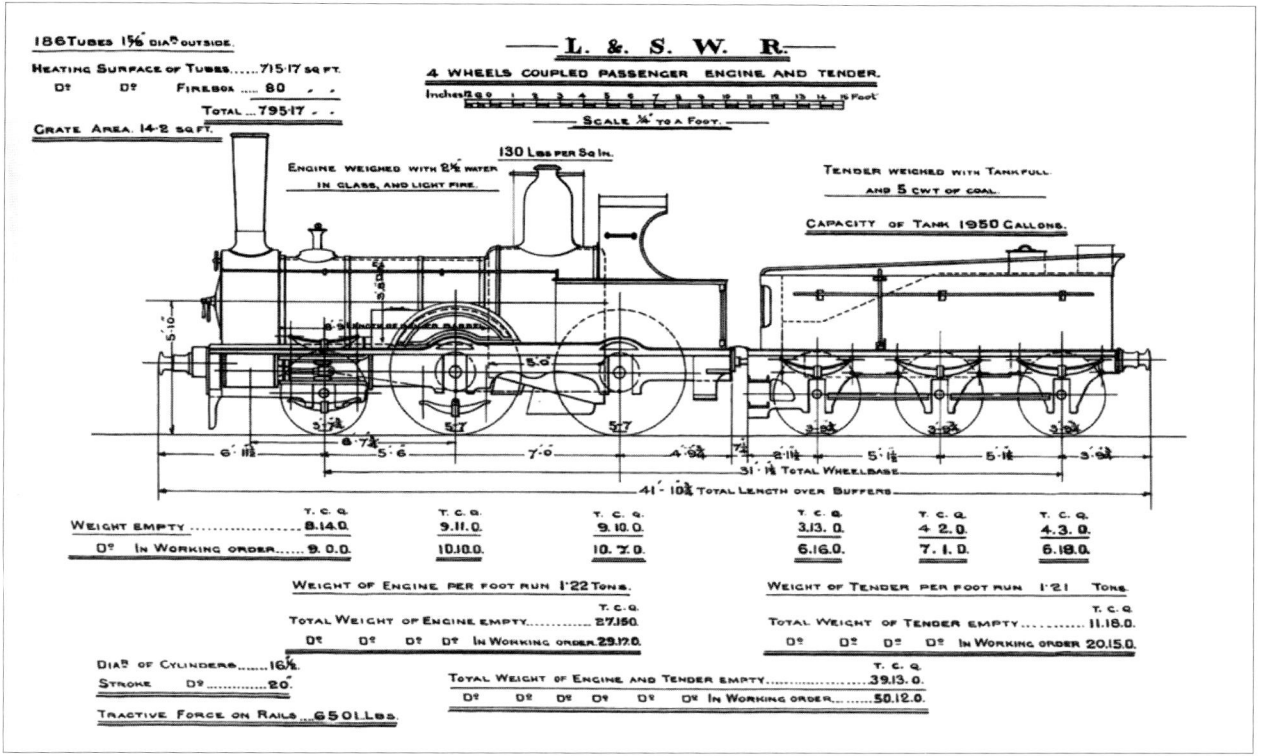

Fig. 221. Diagram of a Beattie Well Tank locomotive, rebuilt by Adams into a tender engine, with original boiler.

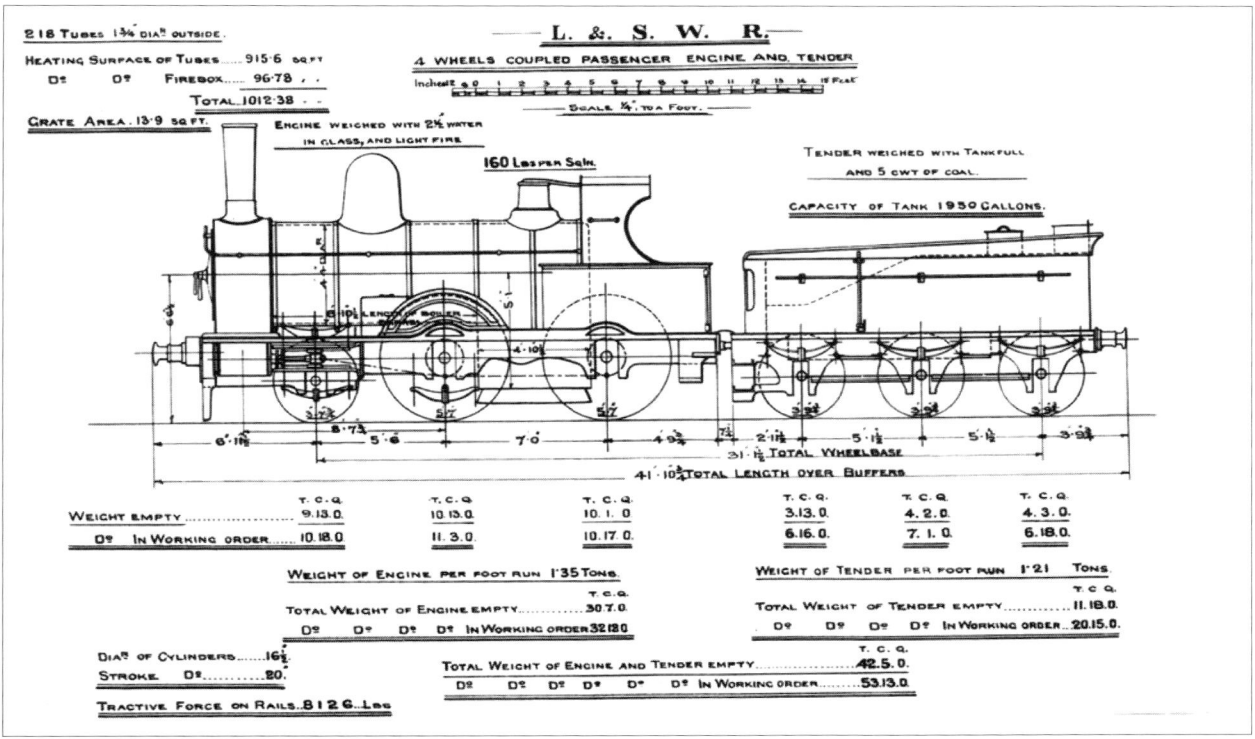

Fig. 222. Diagram of a Beattie Well Tank locomotive, rebuilt by Adams into a tender engine, with an Adams boiler.

Fig. 223. Rebuilt and duplicated Beattie Well Tank No 0214, with original boiler, but stovepipe chimney, circa 1894. (HMRS)

Fig. 224. Rebuilt Beattie Well Tank No 196, with Adams boiler and chimney, circa late 1880s. (South Western Circle)

LOCOMOTIVE PROCUREMENT 1878 - 1895

Fig. 225. Rebuilt Beattie Well Tank with duplicated number 0186, and with Adams boiler and chimney. Photographed between 1890 and 1895.
(South Western Circle)

Fig. 226. 460 class locomotive by Neilson & Co, No 468 with Drummond chimney. Photographed between 1900 and 1912.

LOCOMOTIVE PROCUREMENT 1878 - 1895

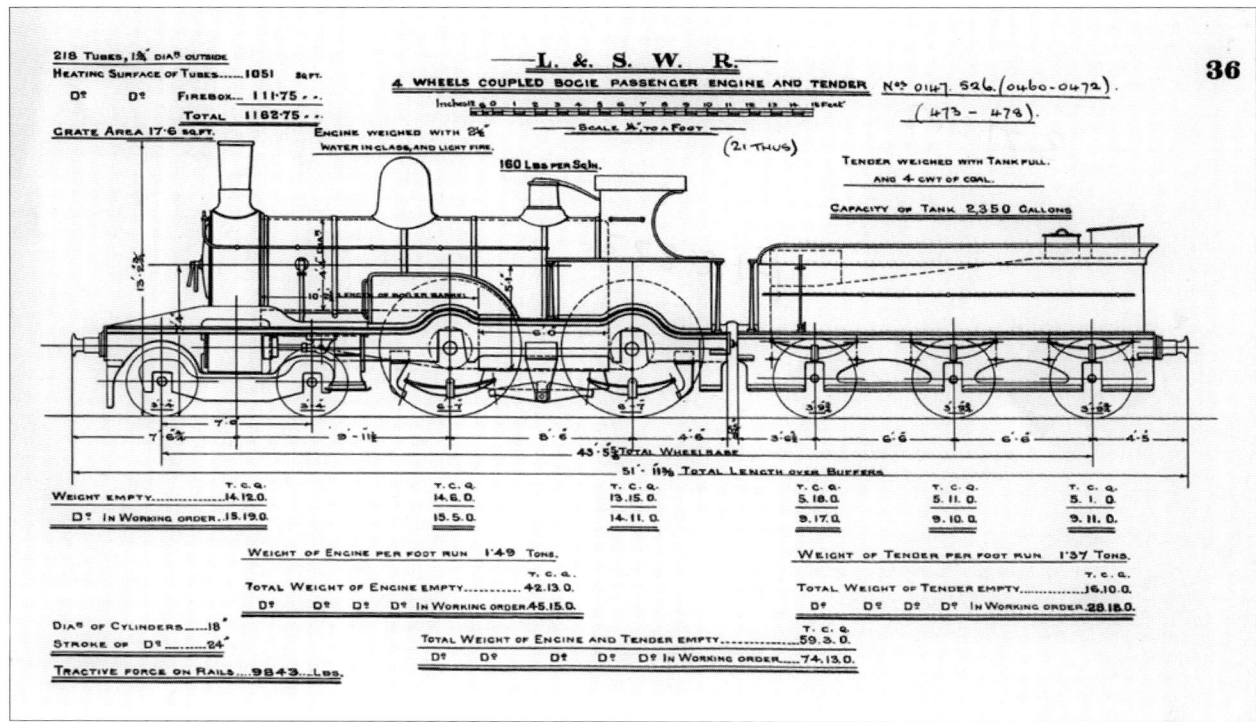

Fig. 227. Diagram of 460 class locomotive in original condition.

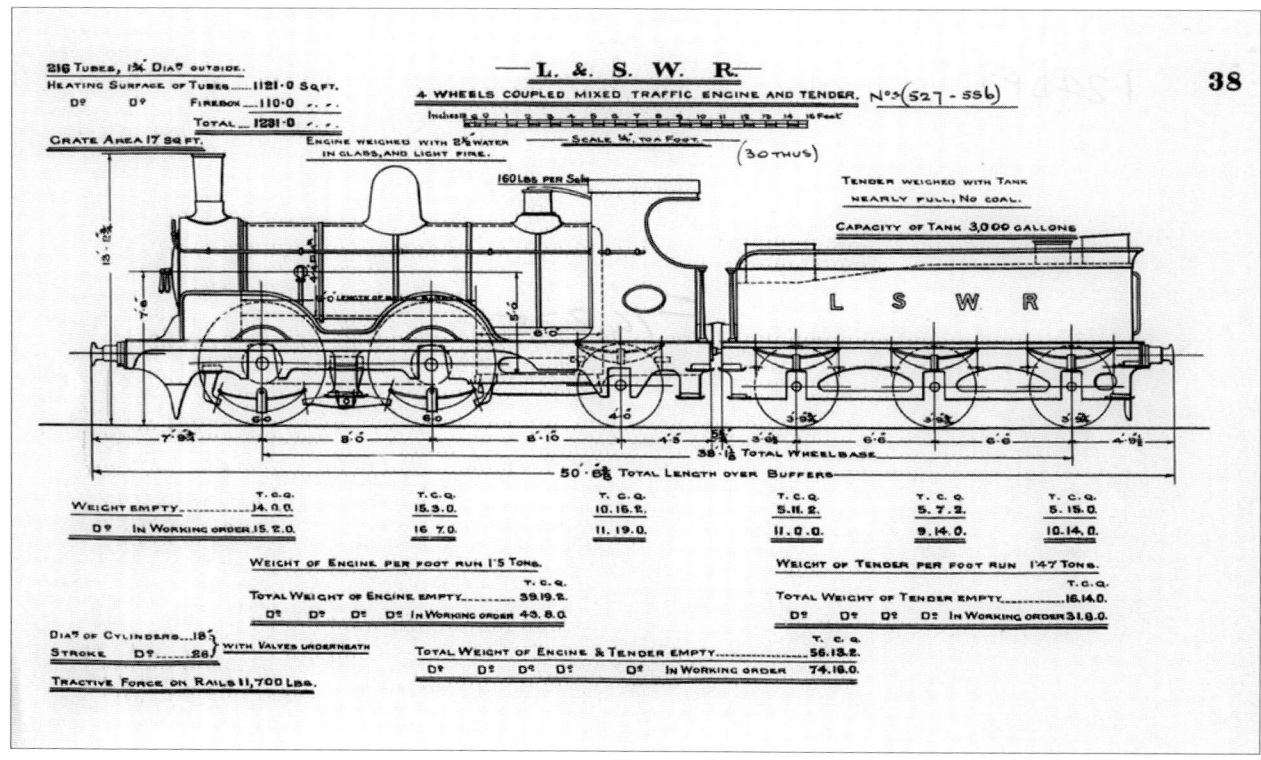

Fig. 228. Diagram of the first series of A12 class locomotive.

LOCOMOTIVE PROCUREMENT 1878 - 1895

Fig. 229. Unidentified 460 class locomotive (No 472?) at speed, with a Waterloo to Bournemouth West via Sway passenger train consisting of a 44ft Passenger Brake Van, 48ft Third, 48ft Lavatory Composite of 1898 (which unusually shows the pale interior reveals of the First Class compartments). After this is a 48ft Third, a 46ft Lavatory First, another 48ft Lavatory Composite also of 1898 (again with pale window reveals). These are followed by a 44ft Passenger Brake Van, another 48ft Lavatory Composite as described previously, a 48ft Third, a 30ft Passenger Brake Van, and finally what appears to be a block set of four-wheeled vehicles. The location is near Wimbledon with the Putney line in the foreground.

THE LSWR AT NINE ELMS

Fig. 230. A12 locomotive No 637, one of the third series by Neilson & Co. The boiler is an Adams original, but a Drummond chimney has been fitted. Many Adams tender engines carried a small bracket on the front nearside top of the tender, sometimes used to carry a headcode disc, as in this picture. If it was also for another use this is not known.
Bottom: Fig. 231. A12 locomotive No 536, one of the first Nine Elms series, in works grey for photographic purposes. The engine is obviously in original condition, and probably photographed around its completion date, December 1887.

LOCOMOTIVE PROCUREMENT 1878 - 1895

Fig. 232. The A12 class appeared to be prone to collisions. No 528 in this photograph, one of the first Nine Elms series, is shown with frontal damage, probably on a Nine Elms turntable, but the procedure of blanking out the background of official photographs, which started to become fashionable about this time, unfortunately inhibits confirmation.

Fig. 233. Another damaged A12, No 535, again of the first Nine Elms series, is shown in this photograph, probably at the rear of the Nine Elms roundhouse.

5023　　　　　　　　　　　　　　　　　　　　　　2 August 1875

Officers Committee　　　　　　　　　　　　　　　　Nine Elms

Read letter from Mr. J. Kirk of 30th ulto complaining of the Company's men trespassing on his premises when leaving their work at Nine Elms.

Mr. Jacomb to be requested to fix the gate at Sussex Street forthwith as ordered by Minute of 13th April 1874 and Mr. Potter to report as to the Police arrangements.

LOCOMOTIVE PROCUREMENT 1878 - 1895

Fig. 234. *A12 No 601, a Nine Elms second series engine, is being repaired in the Nine Elms workshops after what must have been an interesting collision.*

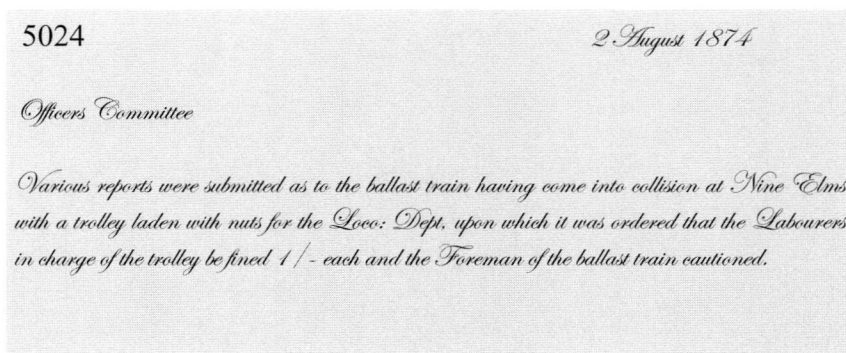

5024 2 August 1874

Officers Committee

Various reports were submitted as to the ballast train having come into collision at Nine Elms with a trolley laden with nuts for the Loco: Dept. upon which it was ordered that the Labourers in charge of the trolley be fined 1/- each and the Foreman of the ballast train cautioned.

Fig. 235. A second Nine Elms series A12 locomotive, possibly No 605, "straining at the leash" on a seven-coach train consisting of three 42ft Thirds, a 48ft Brake Third, 48ft Lavatory Composite of 1898, a 48ft Lavatory Tri-composite of 1897, and finally a 48ft Brake Third.

LOCOMOTIVE PROCUREMENT 1878 - 1895

Fig. 236. Neilson series A12, No 646, near Wimbledon with a Waterloo - Southampton service. At the head is an 18ft Passenger Luggage Van dating from 1887, then a 24ft Passenger Luggage Van from 1896, a 30ft Passenger Brake Van, a 48ft Lavatory Tri-composite also of 1896 build, a 48ft Lavatory Composite from 1898, a 48ft Brake Third, 48ft Lavatory Tri-composite, after which comes a 48ft Brake Third. The view was taken from a point on the opposite side of the track to the photograph of the 460 class in Figure 229 on page 195.

Fig. 237. Neilson series A12, number 617, on a goods train passing Guildford. (Webpraxis)

Fig. 238. An A12 of the first Nine Elms series photographed with a four-coach 'main line set' of 1904-9. Identification is made more difficult as there is no set number visible.

LOCOMOTIVE PROCUREMENT 1878 - 1895

Fig. 239. A12, possibly No 618 or 638, with an unidentified outside-cylindered 4-4-0 (possibly an X2) photographed speeding past what might be Nine Elms Junction. Note the 30ft Passenger Brake Van with caboose at the front, followed by a 48ft Lavatory Tri-composite of 1896. The formation also contains a Pullman car.

Fig. 240. Works photograph of T1 class, No 68, taken around March 1889.

LOCOMOTIVE PROCUREMENT 1878 - 1895

Fig. 241. T1 No 18 with added coal rails at the Nine Elms roundhouse.

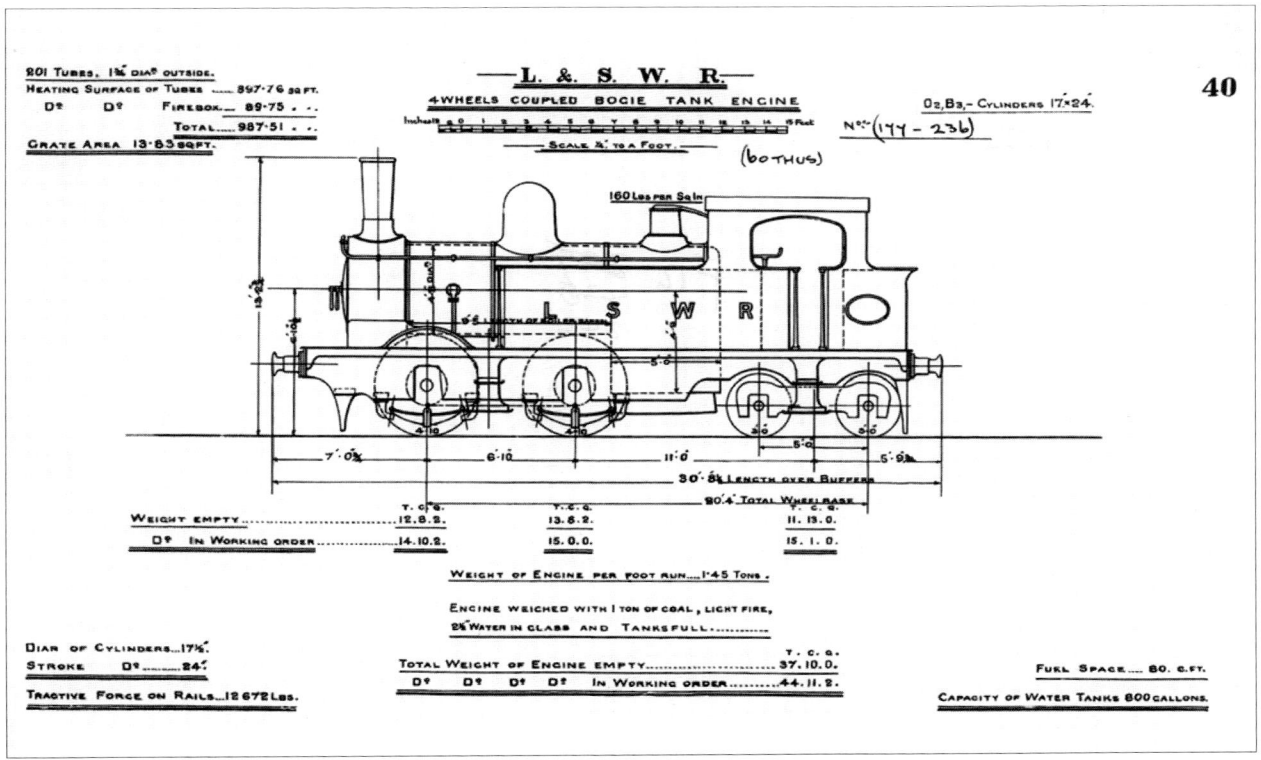

Fig. 242. Diagram of an O2 locomotive.

Fig. 243. T1 No 78 with added coal rails and Drummond livery at Nine Elms roundhouse. Photographed taken in the early 1900s.

LOCOMOTIVE PROCUREMENT 1878 - 1895

Fig. 244. Damaged T1 class No 64 at Nine Elms.

Next page: top, Fig. 245. Close-up of damage to rear of T1 No 64.

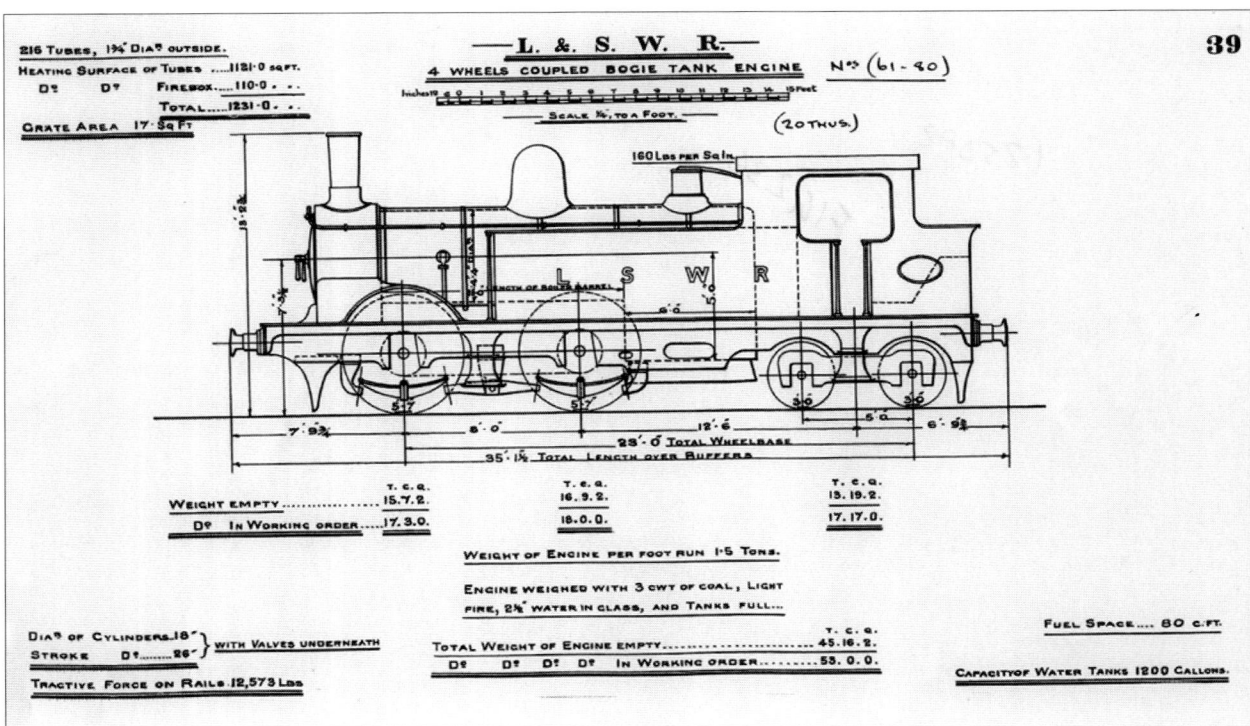

Fig. 246. Diagram of a T1 0-4-4T locomotive relating to order numbers T1 and D2.

LOCOMOTIVE PROCUREMENT 1878 - 1895

Fig. 247. O2 locomotive No 207, with Adams boiler, but Drummond chimney. Coal rails have been added, and the date of the photograph is between 1903 and 1923.

Fig. 248. O2 locomotive No 201, as originally built, in works grey for photographic purposes. Photograph taken around its completion in July 1891.

LOCOMOTIVE PROCUREMENT 1878 - 1895

Fig. 249. O2 locomotive No 216, with frontal damage. Original boiler and chimney. Photograph taken between 1892 and 1905.

LOCOMOTIVE PROCUREMENT 1878 - 1895

Fig. 250. O2 locomotive No 211 with a passenger train near Oreston on the Plymouth to Turnchapel branch. The locomotive has been fitted with a Drummond chimney and coal rails. Compressed air equipment is also fitted for motor train working. Circa 1920. *(Maurice Dart Collection)*

Fig. 251. O2 locomotive No W31 with a passenger train arriving at Ryde St. John's Road on the Isle of Wight. Photograph taken in 1967, until when a number of these locomotives had survived in regular everyday service. Note the extended bunker fitted to all the engines on the Isle of Wight, in order to reduce the frequency of their visits to the fuelling point.

THE LSWR AT NINE ELMS

Top: Fig. 252. X2 class locomotive No 591, pre 1900 with tail rods and bogie splashers.

Bottom: Fig. 253. X2 class locomotive No 582 with footplate staff, pre 1900 with tail rods and bogie splashers.

LOCOMOTIVE PROCUREMENT 1878 - 1895

Changes in the Works

The organisers of the Nine Elms Works were continually fighting with the problems of a rapidly expanding industry trying to operate within a constricted site. Since the site was last discussed on page 104 the linear locomotive shed had been built and extended as shown on the 1889 map in Plate 9 on page 39, as described in another extract from the *Railway World* article that appears below. A major decision was then made on 22nd December 1888 to move the whole of the carriage and wagon department to a brand new site, on an area of waste land at Bishopstoke (which in later years became Eastleigh) near Southampton. This vacated a number of areas within the works that were immediately swallowed up by the locomotive department.

One can compare Plate 9 with Figure 139 on page 102. Plate 9 shows the erecting shop extended across the (removed) traverser, and joined to the old Carriage and Wagon department. The old (Figure 139) wheel shop was combined with the machine shop (the modifications are shown in red in Plate 9). Similarly the old tool shop was converted into a machine shop, and the C & W department below became the wheel shop. The other half of the C & W department to the right became the loco paint shop. To the left, wood machining shops, employed previously on coach work have been converted into a pattern shop. Other minor changes are shown.

The improvement in workshop facilities enjoyed by the locomotive department as a result of these moves enabled all of William Adams future designs (169 locomotives of 7 classes) to be built at Nine Elms. The following extract from the *Railway World* article describes the period up to the next major change in 1909.

When built, the roundhouse could house well over 100 engines, but with the introduction of longer wheelbase machines such as the Adams 415 4-4-2Ts, and the rapid growth of suburban traffic, it was not long before the need for additional facilities became imperative. The plan on (p102, this book) shows the depot as it was in 1885 when the first part of a new fifteen-road "straight" shed with its own coaling facilities had just been completed. The second stage, which consisted of doubling the length from 180ft to 360ft, was carried out in 1889. The layout was most unusual for a shed of this size in that all movements in and out were controlled via the 50ft turntable an arrangement that was by no means without its troubles. The other 50ft table just east of the roundhouse was put in earlier, probably in 1883 when Adams introduced his 445 7ft 1in 4-4-0s which had a wheelbase of 43ft 5 1/2in and were therefore too large for the existing 42ft tables. It is interesting to notice that the 1885 plan shows the two 50ft turntables linked together by a road running behind the roundhouse. Evidently this was put in to provide an alternative exit in emergencies, but in any case the second turntable was unnecessary and was removed shortly afterwards for use elsewhere.

With the completion of the new shed in 1889 the capacity of the depot was well in excess of 200 engines, but it was not until the end of the century that the allocation actually reached this figure.

After 1883 the routine of working the depot underwent a radical change. The new shed was reserved for main line duties worked almost exclusively by tender engines, while the roundhouse dealt with suburban traffic and other local duties mostly worked with tank engines. This still left the roundhouse with a fair amount of surplus capacity, which was then used to relieve pressure on the erecting shop by handling light repair work and the storage of engines due for overhaul.

The method of working the new shed was that engines off up workings entered the depot via the coaling stage chimney first, and were then reversed and turned on the table so that they entered the shed chimney first. Thus on leaving the shed they backed on to the turntable tender first, reversed, and then proceeded to the main line with the engine "right way round" for down workings out of Waterloo and Nine Elms goods. In later years this became standard practice for the entire depot and remained so until its closure in 1967.

The next major change occurred in 1890 when the carriage and wagon works was transferred to Bishopstoke, later to be better known as Eastleigh. This was immediately followed by another period of upheaval when the main line was widened from four to six tracks in 1891, while most of the redundant C & W shops were quickly adapted to serve the needs of the goods department. This was just as well because by 1899 the goods depot had become one of the largest and most important in the country, with an annual throughput of roughly 1,250,000 tons, of which 70% was general merchandise. At that time the goods depot covered 37 acres, employed a staff of 1,700, and worked to a timetable which provided for 55 outward and 30 inward workings a day - although most of this activity took place between 18.00 and 06.00, when trains arrived and departed at the rate of one every 10 minutes!

Reverting to 1890; in addition to expanding the goods facilities, the removal of the C & W works also permitted some long overdue and very necessary improvements to the locomotive works. The main trouble here was that Beattie's old erecting shop could no longer cope with a workload that had more than doubled since 1865. Other shops had been modernised to keep pace with the increased demand, but the erecting shop remained a bottleneck because little could be done until extra space was made available for its enlargement. This probably explains why all new construction was put out to private builders between 1876-86, and it is significant that its resumption in 1887 only occurred after the availability of the roundhouse for repairs had eased matters. However, this was only an interim measure, and as soon as the C & W repair shop to the east became redundant, the intervening steam traverser was removed and the erecting shop was extended by an additional 255ft. A contemporary account describes it as having two bays, each 750ft long by 57ft wide, and providing accommodation for 100 engines. Each bay had three tracks with pits throughout, and two travelling cranes of 30-ton capacity. The description adds that at any given time it was usual for about 80 to 90 engines to be undergoing repairs, while a further 10 to 20 new locomotives would be under construction. The general offices connected with the Locomotive Department, including those of the design staff and the drawing office, were on the first floor above one of the former carriage shops just east of the new extension, and on an eye level with the main line. These offices survived the closure of the works by more than 50 years, and their lighted windows at the far end of the great erecting shop were probably noticed by thousands of daily travellers without so much as a second thought. But for the author it always created a fleeting vision of draughtsmen in purgatory - dim figures confined to their boards by the spirit of Dugald Drummond - until such time as they had sorted out what really went wrong with No 720!

By 1902 the Locomotive Department at Nine Elms (including the running sheds) employed about 2,400 "men and boys" at a cost to the Company of £3,600 per week.

Although somewhat ambiguous the term "men and boys" does highlight the extensive use at that time of what would now be regarded as child labour. Nevertheless it was a well-founded arrangement whereby the boys acquired a skilled trade in exchange for several years of cheap labour, usually at the rate of a few shillings a week.

William Bridges Adams, Part 2 (1890-1895)

Whilst the carriage works was moving to Eastleigh, William Adams's mind was already working on new designs to be built in the further-expanded workshops. All of his future designs would be built at Nine Elms with no recourse to outside contractors. The locomotive types designed by Adams during the period 1890 to 1895 are shown in Table 14.

The X2 design represented the first of his 60 very attractive 4-4-0 outside-cylindered locomotives built between 1890 and 1896. During the initial construction of the X2 batch, Adams realised that the firebox was not going to be long enough, and he also had complaints from the drivers about the narrow cabs and tenders with inadequate capacity, but as some of the construction had started, these faults were only rectified on some of them. This design had 7ft 1in diameter wheels, and he followed it with a batch of 20 engines, class T3, with 6ft 7in wheels, in which the aforementioned faults were corrected, including a 6in longer firebox.

In between these designs, at the other end of the power spectrum, he designed the B4 yard shunter. These became necessary as a result of the increasing amount of goods traffic in establishments such as Southampton Docks, where a number of them were

TABLE 14

Build Period	Number Built	Builder	Wheel arrangement	Class	Withdrawal period	Figure Numbers
6/1890-5/1892	20	Nine Elms	4-4-0	X2	12/1930-11/1942	254,255,256,257,258
10/1891-6/1908	25	Nine Elms	0-4-0T	B4	5/1948-10/1963	259,260,261,262,263,264
12/1892-11/1893	20	Nine Elms	4-4-0	T3	4/1931-8/1945	265,266,267,268,269,270,271 273,274
6/1894-6/1900	34	Nine Elms	0-6-0T	G6	8/1948-12/1962	280,281,282,283
9/1895-5/1896	10	Nine Elms	4-4-0	T6	2/1933-4/1943	284,285,286,287,288,289, 290,291
12/1895-6/1896	10	Nine Elms	4-4-0	X6	3/1933-12/1946	292,293,294,295,296,297,298

In preservation: "T3" class number 563, "B4" class numbers 96 and 102.

LOCOMOTIVE PROCUREMENT 1878 - 1895

allocated, and where the sharp curves precluded the use of larger wheelbase engines. I can bear witness that during my short spell on the footplate in the Eastleigh area, when I was sometimes allocated to serve on these engines, they were often called upon to perform tasks much in excess of those that they were designed for.

This was not helped by the poor quality of coal available in the 1950s, and by the fact that the Southampton site (a secondary depot) always received the poorest quality coal from Eastleigh. In spite of this hard treatment, their average lifetime was around 60 years, and two of them are still working in preservation. The cabs were modified on some of the Southampton Docks engines, with the front and back plates being cut away to give the crew better visibility, but later on, when it was decided that better weather protection was more necessary, they were plated in with just small square windows provided.

On page 158, I referred to the 0-4-0T locomotive that Adams had converted into a crane locomotive, whilst he was with the North London Railway. In November 1894 he designed a very similar machine at Nine Elms, based upon a B4 class locomotive, with a lifting capacity of 6 tons. It is shown in Figure 277, and there were plans to build three of them for use at Nine Elms, Northam, and the Engineer's department at Wimbledon. However, it was decided that the work could be done more cheaply by other means.

Adams then designed the G6 class 0-6-0T yard shunter to cope with the ever-increasing goods traffic that he found could not be handled by the B4 locomotives.

Then in 1893, for some reason, Adams became attracted to the use of single driving axle locomotives. They had been used on a number of railways in the country, but not with universal success. His first step was to commission a survey of some of the single locomotives being used on other railways, and compare them with his own four coupled engines. The results of this survey are shown in Figure 275. Unfortunately, in common with most other documents from Nine Elms, it is not dated, but it was most probably produced in 1893. As a result of his investigations, Adams drew up a design for a single driving axle locomotive in March 1893, which is shown in Figure 276. To back up his ideas, he arranged for the Midland Railway to loan a similar locomotive for trials on the Waterloo to Bournemouth line. However the Civil Engineer realised that the weight on the driving axle was substantially in excess of that allowed, both for the Midland engine and Adams's proposed design. The proposal was therefore dropped around August 1893.

Following these investigations, Adams was still in favour of large-diameter wheel locomotives, so, not to be out-done, he put forward a proposal for a 4-4-0 locomotive with 7ft 7in diameter wheels. His proposal is shown in Figure 278. This was also not accepted because it would limit the use of the locomotive to the less heavily-graded lines. He then designed his last two locomotives, the T6 and X6 classes with 7ft 1in and 6ft 7in diameter wheels respectively. The proposal for the locomotive with 7ft 1in wheels is shown in Figure 279. However, William Adams resigned his position on 29th May, 1895, before any locomotives of these two classes were completed, and their introduction to service was overseen by the next Chief Engineer, Dugald Drummond.

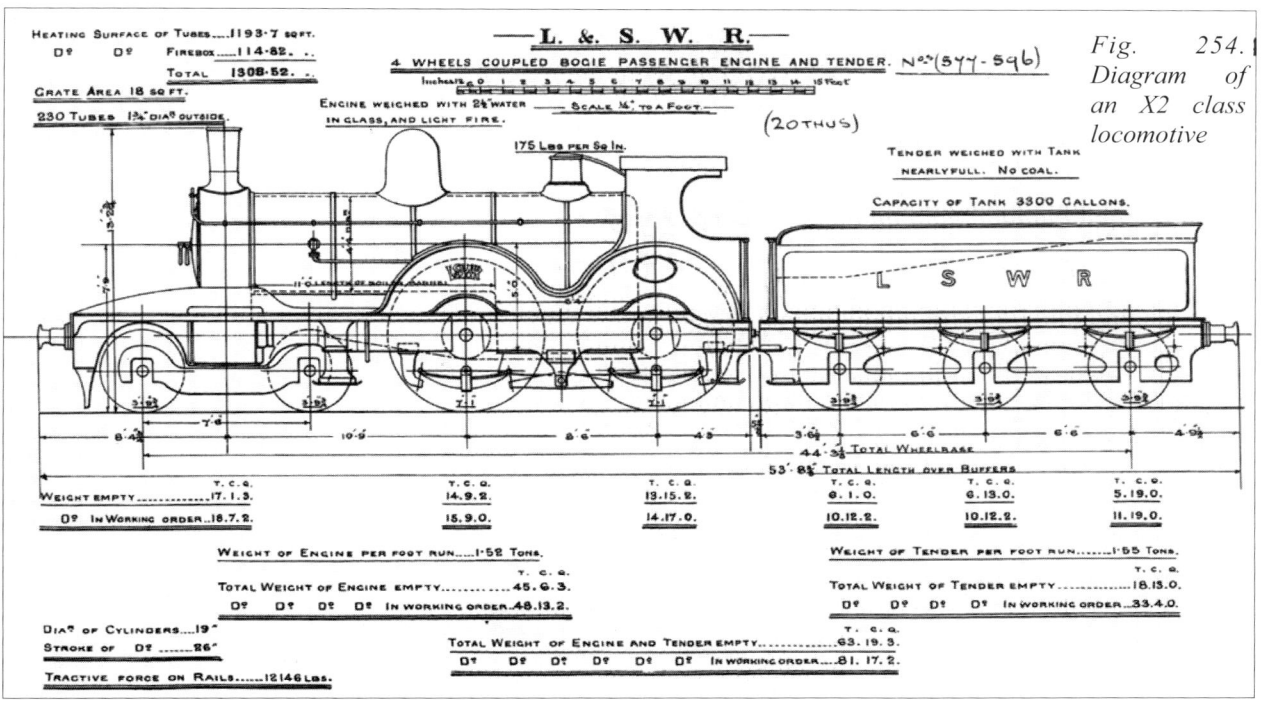

Fig. 254. Diagram of an X2 class locomotive

THE LSWR AT NINE ELMS

Top: Fig. 255. X2 class locomotive No 577 with a 30ft Passenger Brake Van and the 47ft 6in "Eagle" Saloons when new, October 1892.
Bottom. Fig. 256. X2 class locomotive on a Waterloo to Dorchester train passing Nine Elms Junction. Bogie splashers and tail rods have been removed, and Drummond chimney and coal rails fitted. Circa 1905. The stock commences with a 30ft Passenger Brake Van, 48ft Lavatory Third, 48ft Lavatory Composite, 48ft Lavatory Tri-composite, and a 48ft Brake Third.

LOCOMOTIVE PROCUREMENT 1878 - 1895

Fig. 257. X2 class locomotive No 582 possibly just east of Wimbledon, passing an early travelling crane possibly dating from the 1860s. At the head of the ballast train is a G6 locomotive. The X2 has had its bogie splashers and tail rods removed and coal rails have been added, but the stove-pipe chimney has been retained. Behind the passenger locomotive is what appears to be a very new 48ft Lavatory Brake Third built in 1899, a 48ft Lavatory Tri-composite, a 48ft Lavatory Third, a 48ft Lavatory Composite of 1898, and then a 44ft Passenger Brake Van.

THE LSWR AT NINE ELMS

Fig. 258. Two X2 class locomotives double-heading a train at speed. The combination shows one example of each of the two types, one with a wide and one with a narrow cab. Coal rails have been added, so this was probably photographed post-1900. The train is bound for Waterloo and has just passed Clapham Junction with the lines of the rival LBSCR to the left. At the head of the stock is the ubiquitous 24ft Passenger Luggage Van followed by a 30ft Passenger Brake Van.

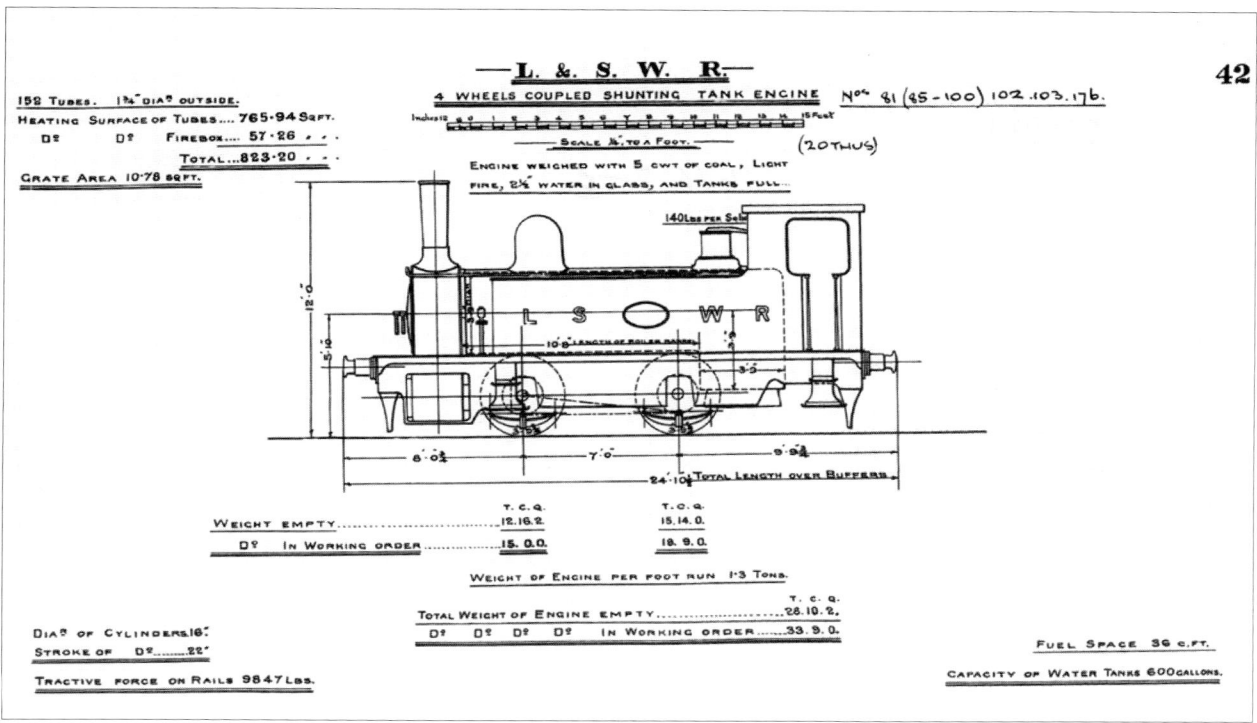

Fig. 259. Diagram of a B4 class locomotive.

Fig. 260. B4 class locomotive No 90, as originally built in works grey paint, November 1892.

Fig. 261. B4 class locomotive No 87, as originally built in Adams goods livery.

Fig. 262. B4 class locomotive No 30096 with van shunting Southampton Town Quay, 9th June 1961. The cutaway cab sheets have been filled in and small square windows provided. This locomotive was later sold to the fuel distributors "Corrals" in Southampton, to work their connection with Northam Yard, and was then preserved by the Bluebell Railway in Sussex. *(The late David Fereday-Glenn)*

LOCOMOTIVE PROCUREMENT 1878 - 1895

Fig. 263. B4 class locomotive No 94 as originally built, at Eastleigh, still with stove-pipe chimney, but painted with a lined livery and approximately 22 inch high numerals. Photographed between 1923 and 1940.

Fig. 264. B4 class locomotive No 91 with a goods train believed to be travelling along the Town Quay Railway in Southampton. *(Maurice Dart Collection)*

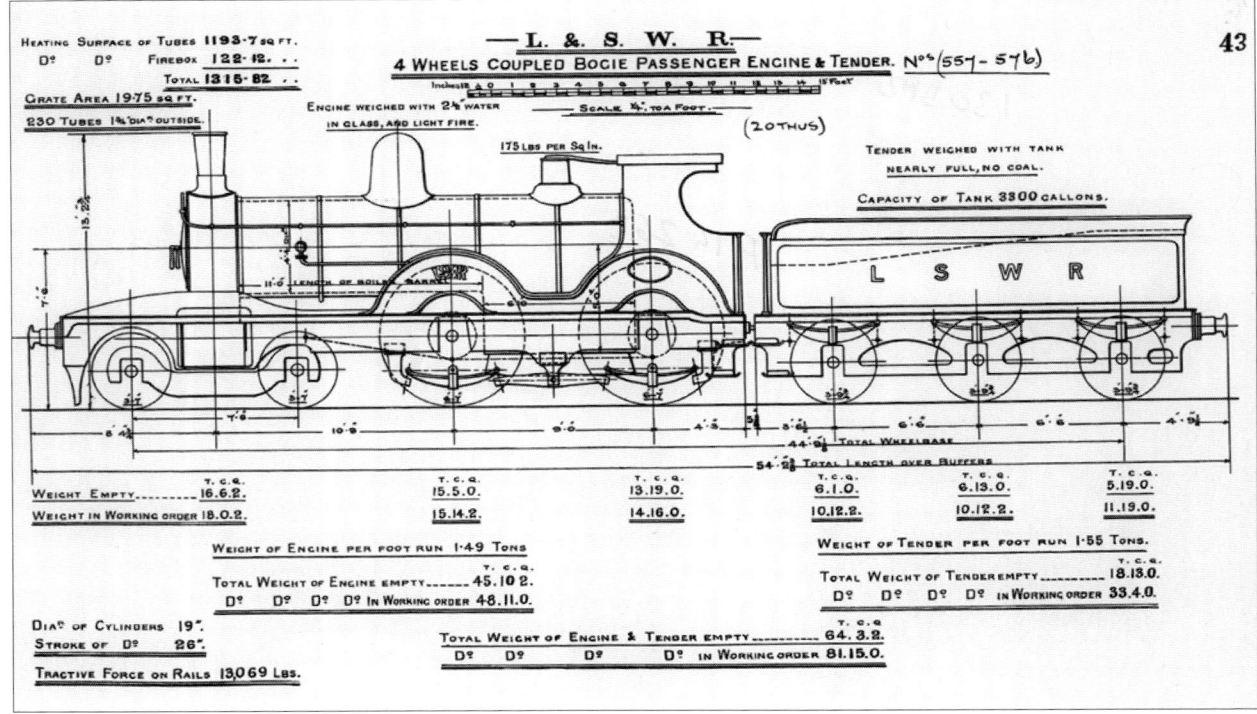

Fig. 265. Diagram of a T3 class locomotive, as originally built.

LOCOMOTIVE PROCUREMENT 1878 - 1895

Top: Fig. 266. T3 class locomotive No 563 and 56ft Tri-composite No 847 coach, as preserved for the National Railway Museum, York.
Bottom: Fig. 267. T3 class locomotive No 561 as originally built and in works grey paint.

Fig. 268. Frames of T3 class locomotive No 573 being riveted together in Nine Elms Works in 1893. The tank locomotive is a T1 class, either being built, or in for repairs.

Fig. 269. T3 class locomotive No 573 with boiler, cab, cylinders, and wooden lagging fitted.
Opposite page, bottom left: Fig. 273. Boiler of the type that would have been fitted to T3 locomotive No 573.

LOCOMOTIVE PROCUREMENT 1878 - 1895

Fig. 270. T3 class locomotive No 573 with steel cladding sheets, smokebox, and splashers added.

Centre left: Fig. 271. Adams bogie of the type that would have been fitted to T3 locomotive No 573.

Above: Fig. 272. Set of wheels and crank axle of the type that would have been fitted to an inside cylinder locomotive. The massive size of the axle is obvious, and at maximum speed it would be turning at around 4 revolutions per second.

Fig. 274. Inside of the cab of T3 locomotive No 573 under construction in Nine Elms Works, 1893.

LOCOMOTIVE PROCUREMENT 1878 - 1895

Name of Railway	Description of Engine	Cylinders	Wheel Diam-	Steam Pressures (Boiler Pressure Lbs. / Mean Effective Pressure Lbs.)	Tractive Effort	Adhesive Weight on Driving Wheels	Co. efficient	Length of Firebox	Length of Coupling Rod	Grate Area Sq. Ft.	Heating Surface Tubes Sq. Ft.	Heating Surface Firebox Sq. Ft.	Heating Surface Total Sq. Ft.
L S & W Ry.	Proposed Single Driver	19" x 26"	8'.0"	175 / 110	10,754 lbs.	19 tons	4.0	6'.10"	—	19¾	1264.3	126.4	1390.7
"	Proposed Four Coupled	19" x 26"	7'.1"	175 / 110	12,146	30.3	5.6	6'.10"	9'.0"	19¾	1193.7	126.4	1320.1
"	Existing Four Coupled	19" x 26"	7'.1"	175 / 110	12,146	30.3	5.6	6'.10"	8'.6"	18	1264.6	122.6	1387.7½
"	Existing Four Coupled	19" x 26"	6'.7"	175 / 110	13,069	30.3	5.0	6'.10"	9'.0"	19¾	1193.7	126.4	1320.1
G.W. Ry.	Existing Single Driver	20" x 24"	7'.8½"	160 / 100	10,378 lbs.	19 tons	4.1	6'.6"	—	20.8	1321	126	1445
G.N. Ry.	Existing Single Driver	18" x 28"	8'.1½"	160 / 80	8,505 lbs.	17 tons	4.4	6'.2"	—	17¾	936	109	1065
M. Ry.	Existing Single Driver	18¼" x 26"	7'.6"	160 / 100	9,887.22 lbs.	17.5 tons	3.9	6'.6"	—	19.6	1123.5	117	1260.6
G.E. Ry.	Existing Single Driver	18" x 26"	7'.0"	160 / 80	8,331.42 lbs.	16 tons	4.3	6'.0"	—	17.9	1124.96	105.5	1230.46
C. Ry.	Existing Single Driver	18" x 26"	7'.0"	150 / 90	9,527 lbs.	17 tons	3.9	5'.6"	—	17.4	973	112	1085

Fig. 275. List of proposed and existing single driver locomotives, with their major parameters, made at Adams's request around 1893.

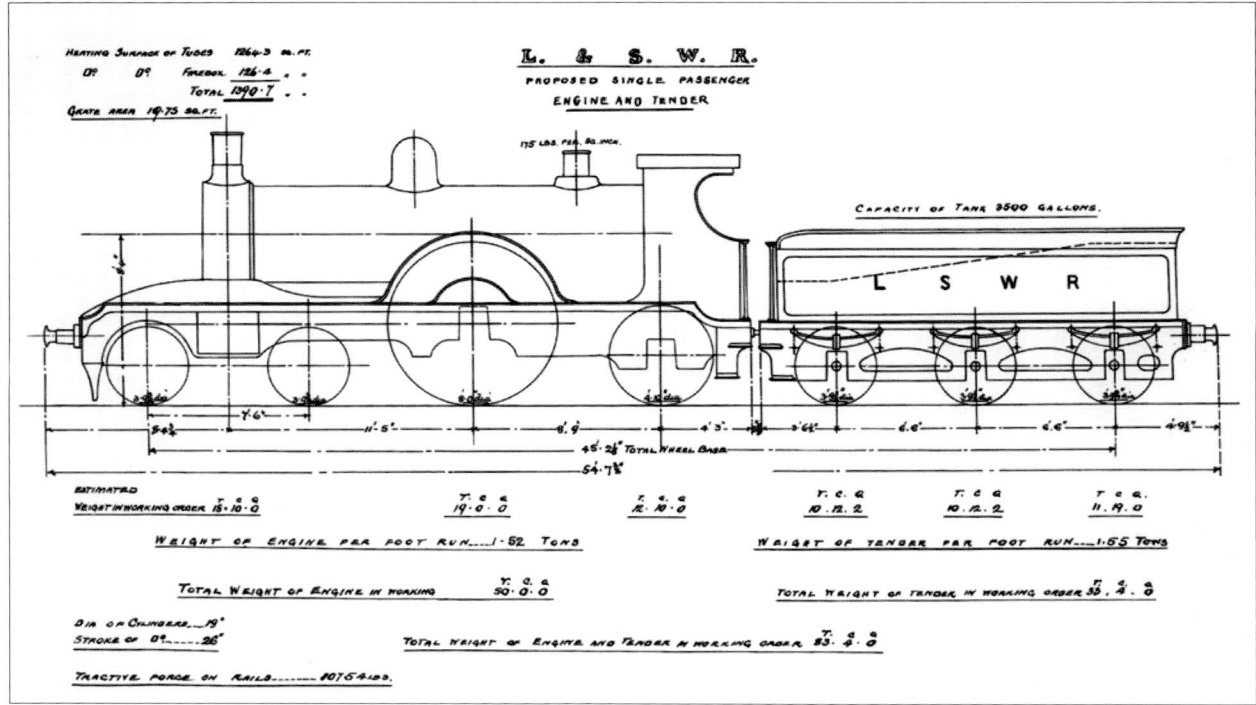

Fig. 276. Diagram of Adams's proposed single driver locomotive with 8ft diameter wheels, made in March 1893. This proposal was not built.

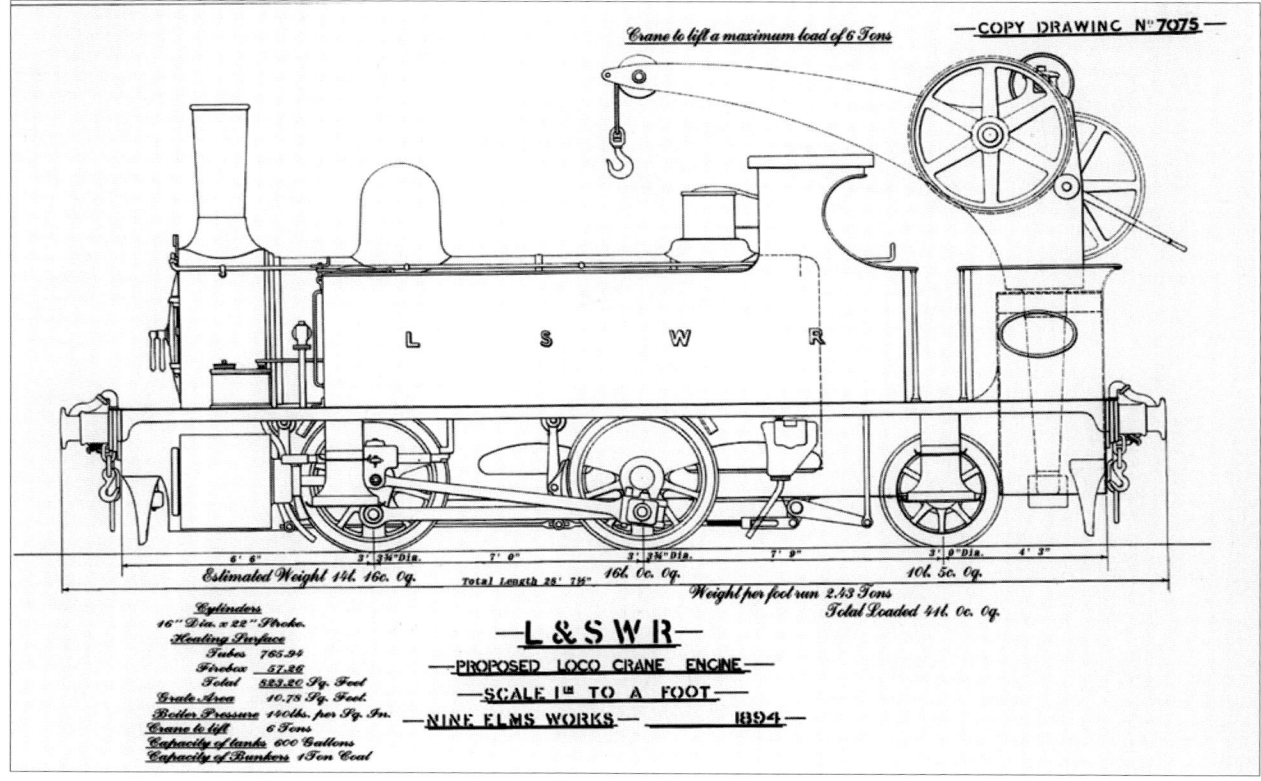

Fig. 277. Diagram of Adams's proposed 0-4-2 crane tank engine, based on his B4 0-4-0T and on his crane engine, modified for the North London Railway around 1865. This proposal was not built.

LOCOMOTIVE PROCUREMENT 1878 - 1895

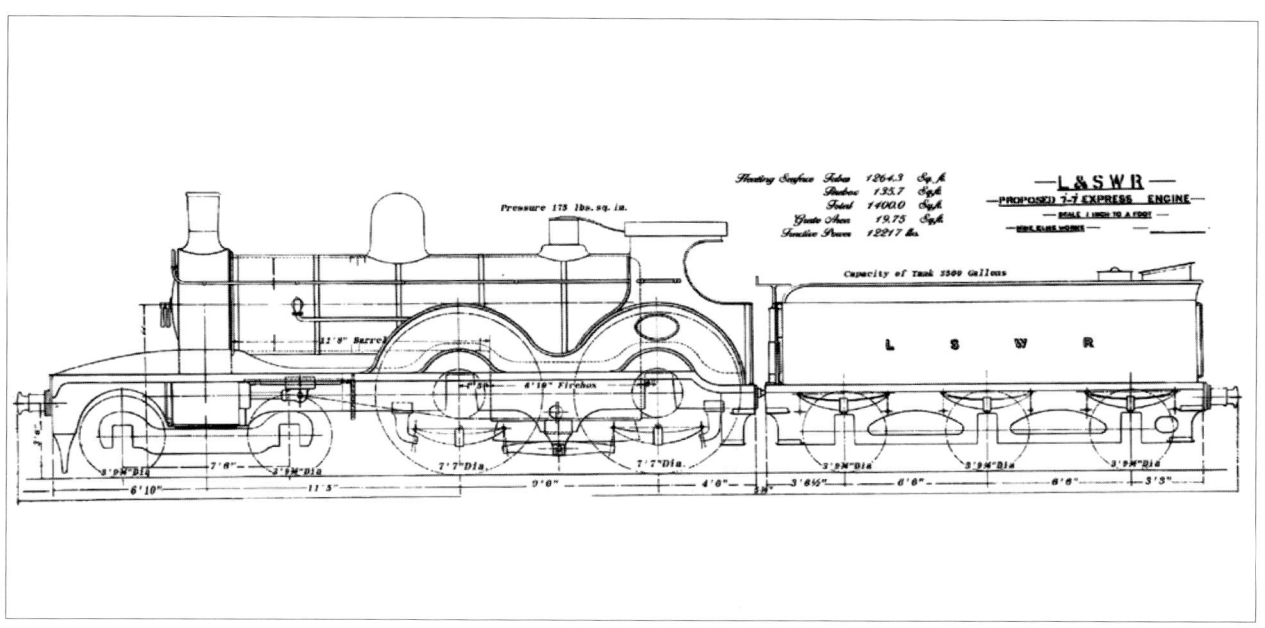

Fig. 278. Diagram of Adams's proposed 4-4-0 express locomotive with 7ft 7in wheels, which was not built, as it would be restricted to the less heavily graded sections of the system. Drawn in 1894.

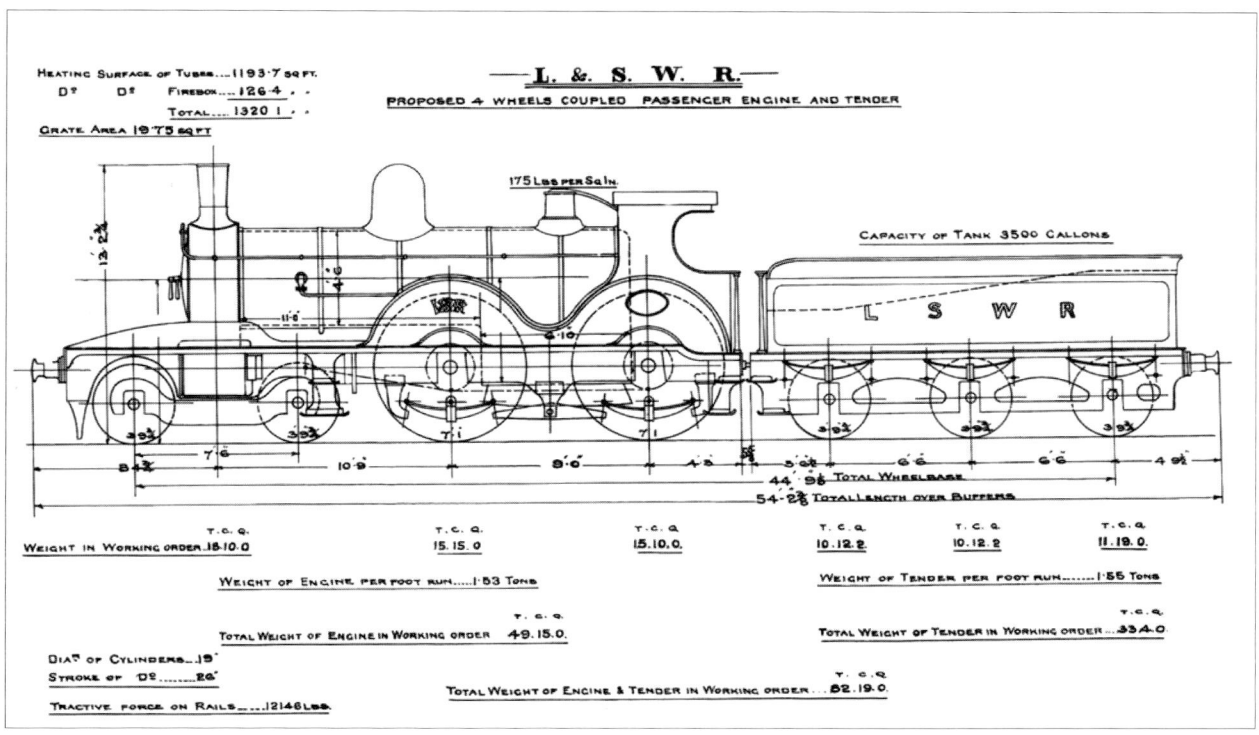

Fig. 279. Diagram of Adams's proposed 4-4-0 express locomotive with 7ft 1in wheels. This design formed the basis of the T6 design of which ten locomotives were built. Drawn in 1894.

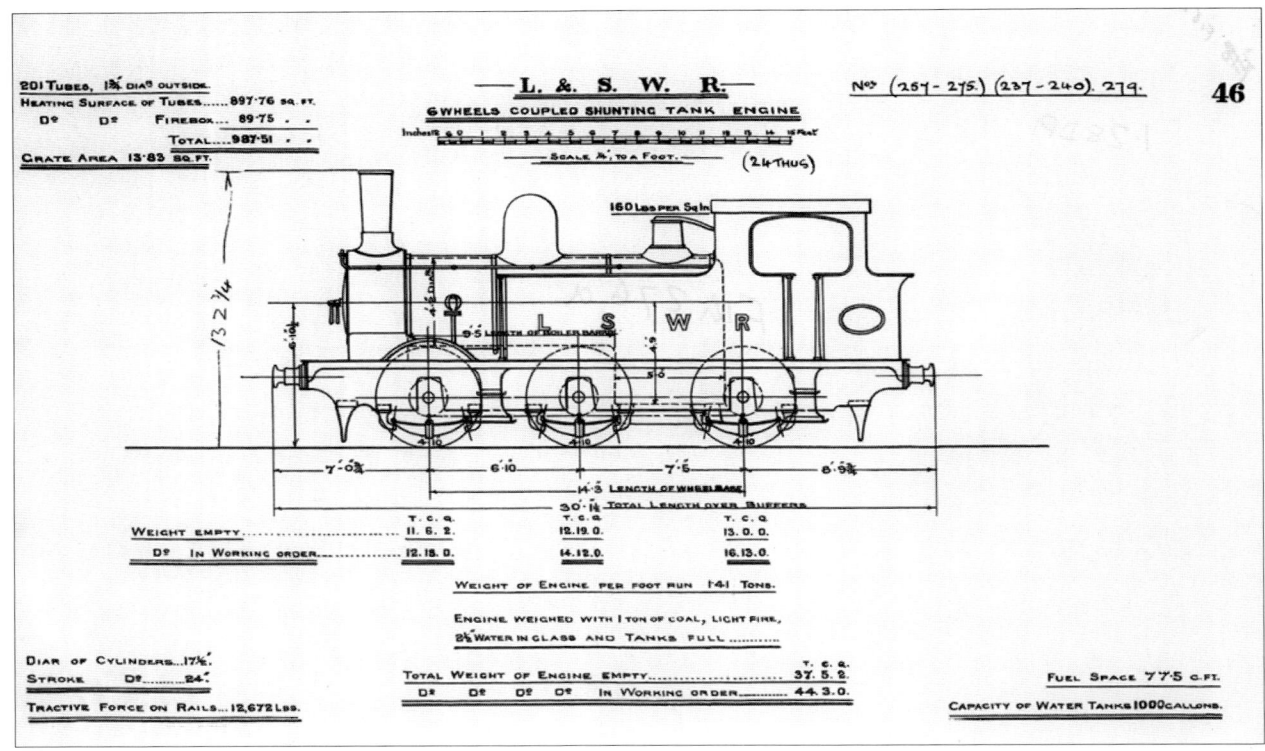

Fig. 280. Diagram of G6 class locomotive, first built in June 1894.

Fig. 281. G6 class locomotive No 258, as originally built in works grey colours. Photographed in 1894.

LOCOMOTIVE PROCUREMENT 1878 - 1895

Fig. 282. G6 class locomotive No 348 as built, with Drummond chimney and Adams type boiler as salvaged from Beattie Vesuvius class 2-4-0 locomotive No 35 "Vivid". As this boiler was slightly shorter than normal G6 boilers, the smokebox was made longer on this and other G6 locomotives similarly fitted. Shown with staff at Nine Elms. Date unknown.

Fig. 283. G6 class locomotive No 257, as originally built in Adams livery.

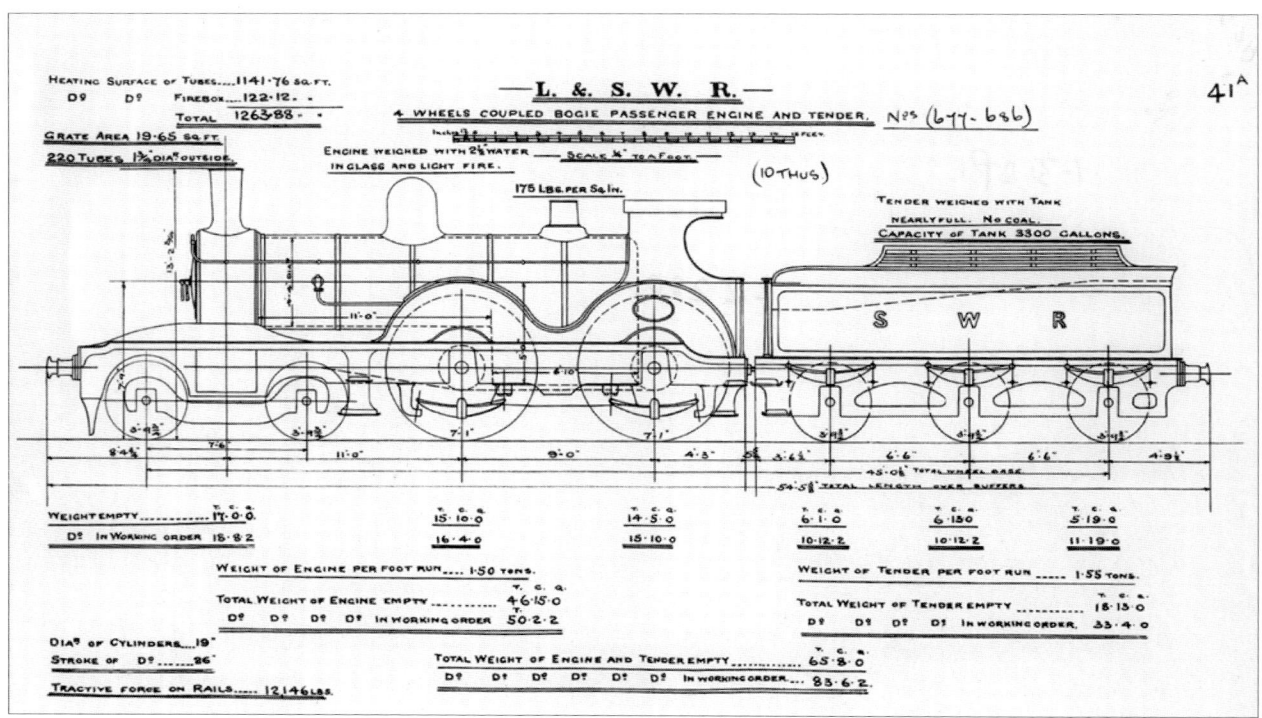

Fig. 284. Diagram of T6 class locomotive.

LOCOMOTIVE PROCUREMENT 1878 - 1895

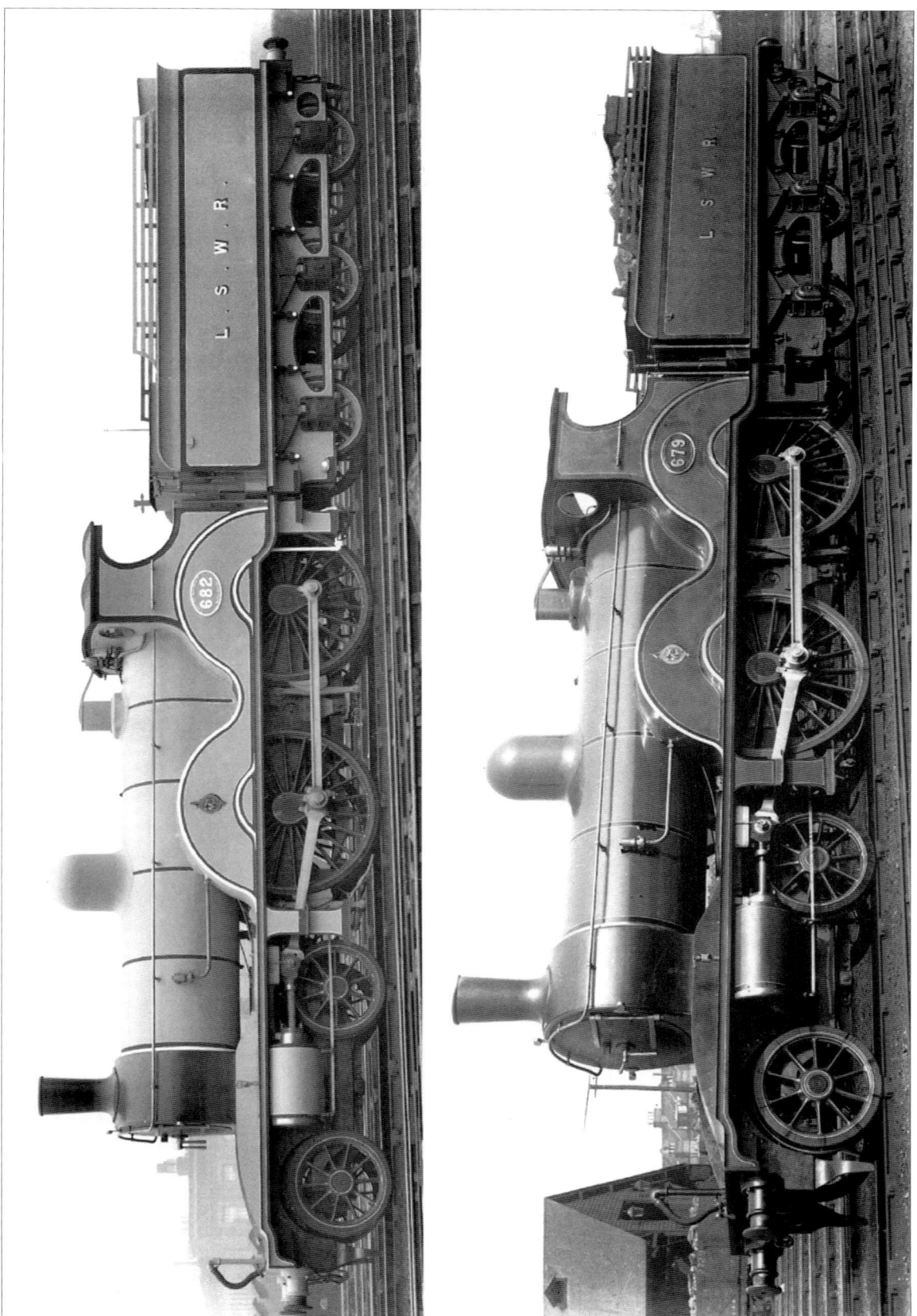

Top: Fig. 285. T6 class locomotive No 682, as originally built in works grey livery, December 1895.
Bottom: Fig. 286. T6 class locomotive No 679, as originally built in Adams livery, circa 1896.

Top: Fig. 287. T6 class locomotive No 682 on a Bournemouth West to Waterloo train - note the Pullman coach at the rear, believed to be approaching Wimbledon. The remainder of the stock would appear to be of non-corridor type, circa 1900.

Bottom: Fig. 288. T6 class locomotive No 682 on a Southampton train passing Nine Elms Junction, circa 1900.

LOCOMOTIVE PROCUREMENT 1878 - 1895

Fig. 289. T6 class locomotive on a London to Exeter train; unknown number and location, although we do know that the view was taken at 11.0 a.m., Friday 20th October 1898! The stock consists of a 44ft Passenger Brake Van, two 48ft Lavatory Composites, three 48ft Brake Tri-composites, another Composite, and finally a 30ft Passenger Brake Van.

Fig. 290. T6 class locomotive on a train, possibly just east of Wimbledon, circa 1900. The stock that can be identified commences with a 24ft Passenger Luggage Van, a 44ft Passenger Brake Van, two 48ft Lavatory Composites, 42ft Third, 30ft Passenger Brake Van (arc roof) and a 48ft Brake Third.

LOCOMOTIVE PROCUREMENT 1878 - 1895

Fig. 291. T6 class locomotive, possibly No 677, on a Waterloo to Bournemouth Pullman express (fourth vehicle in the train), near Wimbledon, circa 1900. The other vehicles from the front are a 44ft Passenger Brake Van, 48ft Third, and a 48ft Tri-composite.

LOCOMOTIVE PROCUREMENT 1878 - 1895

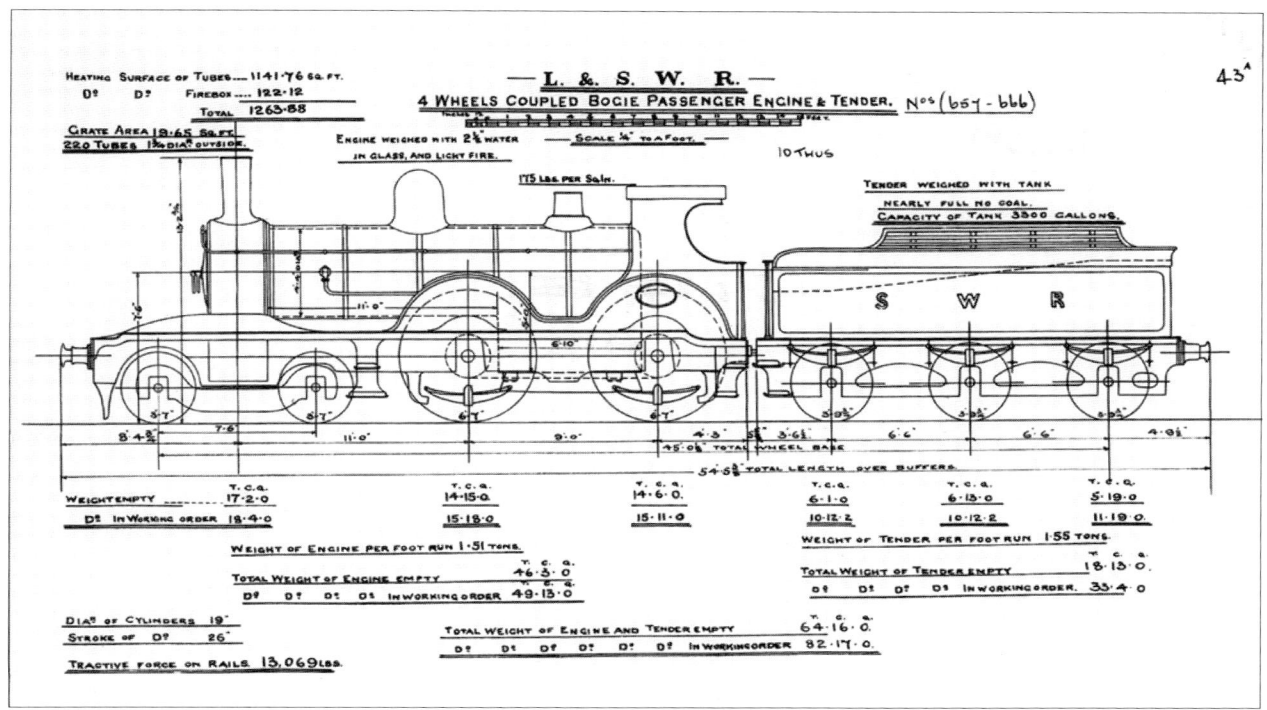

Fig. 292. Diagram of X6 locomotive No 661, in original condition.

Fig. 293. X6 locomotive No 661, in original condition. Coal rails, and smooth number plates were fitted from introduction under Drummond's supervision, and the lettering reduced to "S. W. R.".

Next page: top, Fig. 294. Setting up the frames of a new X6 locomotive in Nine Elms Works, 1896.
Next page: centre, Fig. 295. Adding components to an X6 frame. We know this to be No 666 from the chalked numbers on the brake hangers.
Next page: bottom, Fig. 296. The cab and splashers have been added and also the wooden lagging around the cylinders. The brake hangers indicate that this is No 665.

THE LSWR AT NINE ELMS

LOCOMOTIVE PROCUREMENT 1878 - 1895

Fig. 297. The boiler, with its wooden lagging, has been added to the frames of X6 No 666.

Fig. 298. The completed boiler, frames, cab, and splashers of the X6 locomotive are being lowered onto the wheels. Note the heavy lifting gear, using two travelling gantries. The total weight being supported would be somewhere between 30 and 40 tons.

THE LSWR AT NINE ELMS

9
AROUND THE WORKS AT THE TURN OF THE CENTURY

The Ordnance Survey performed another survey of the area in 1897, and Figure 301 on the next page, shows the result for the Nine Elms Works and its environs. One can only presume that the alterations to the usage of the buildings upon the move of the Carriage and Wagon department to Bishopstoke, proposed in Plate 9 (page 39) have been enacted. I have not been able to find an interior plan of the works subsequent to the move. The map shows what is probably the final stage in the development of the goods depot to the north of the main line, before it was extended to take over part of the works on the south side, when the locomotive section moved to Eastleigh in 1909. The motive power department was to be extended further by increasing the number of tracks in the linear shed from 15 to 25 in 1910, and this is on the final Ordnance Survey map shown in this book, (Figure 430) produced in 1913.

In 1902, the company photographer took a number of photographs of the inside of the works. The glass negatives have survived and his efforts are reproduced here. It should be remembered that photographic emulsion speeds were still very slow. This has the advantage, due to the small grain size, of excellent definition, but it does produce difficulties when people are included in the scene, because any movement of the subject is not arrested due to the long time exposures involved. On some of the plates the place and date were inscribed along the edge of the plate and this information is repeated as written (with accurate dates) where appropriate in the photographs that follow.

Opposite page: Fig. 299. The erecting shop No 1 bay (looking west), 11th June 1902.
Above: Fig. 300. Enlargement of part of the previous view, with what are believed to be locomotives of the K10 and M7 classes.

THE LSWR AT NINE ELMS

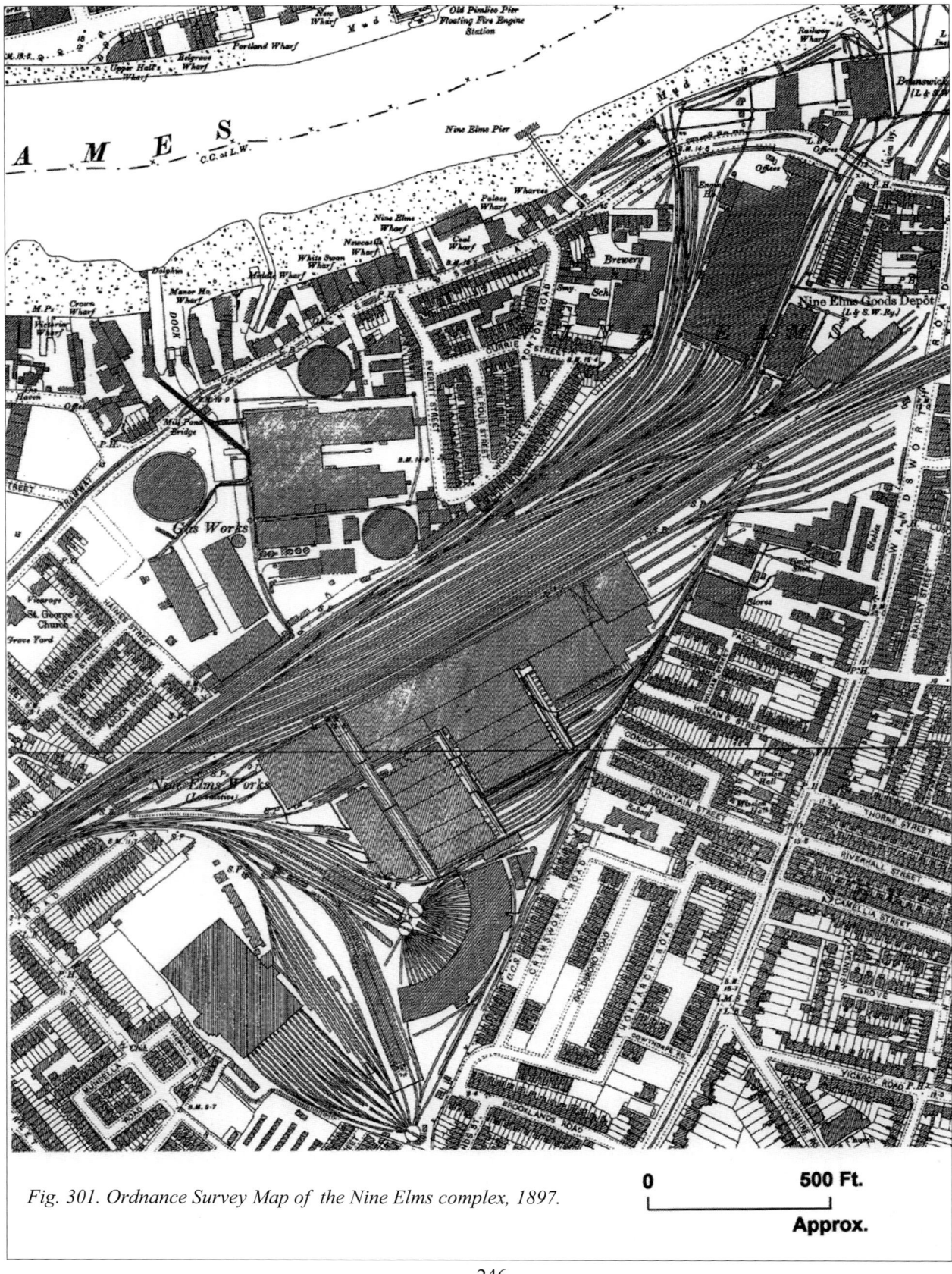

Fig. 301. Ordnance Survey Map of the Nine Elms complex, 1897.

AROUND THE WORKS AT THE TURN OF THE CENTURY

Fig. 302. Boiler shop (looking east), 9th June 1902. The "E11" markings refer to a batch of K10 locomotives.

Fig. 303. Part of the boiler shop, showing multi-head drilling machines used for making boiler tube plates.
(Rev. Brian Arman.)

Fig. 304. Foundry (looking west), 5th June 1902.

AROUND THE WORKS AT THE TURN OF THE CENTURY

Fig. 305. Foundry with staff.

Fig. 306. Long machine shop (looking east), 5th June 1902.

Fig. 307. Part of the smiths' shop, showing steam hammer and supply boiler on the right hand side. The method of firing the elevated boiler is not obvious.   *(Kidderminster Railway Museum)*

AROUND THE WORKS AT THE TURN OF THE CENTURY

Fig. 308. Smiths' shop (looking east), 12th June 1902.

Fig. 309. Machine shop.

AROUND THE WORKS AT THE TURN OF THE CENTURY

Fig. 310.   Machine shop with staff.

Fig. 311.   Machine shop with staff.

Fig. 312. Machine shop with staff.

Fig. 313. Heavy machine shop with staff.

AROUND THE WORKS AT THE TURN OF THE CENTURY

Fig. 314. Wheelshop, the wheel lathes are those which are seen in the distance in Figure 316.

Fig. 315. Fitting shop.
(Kidderminster Railway Museum)

Fig. 316. Wheelshop (looking east), 16th June 1902.

Fig. 317. Wheelshop, again the wheel lathes shown are those in the previous figures, but the photograph is of a later date. The numbered items, 702, 172, 516, are probably from a Dubs T9, a 395, and a 415 respectively. This would date the view between 1900 and 1909. The photograph also gives a good view of a 'monorail' mobile crane, with one rail in the ground and one in the roof. (Rev. Brian Arman)

Fig. 318. Pattern shop with staff. The large item on the right hand side is intriguing.

Above: Fig. 319. The same pattern shop as depicted on the previous page but with some changes.
(Kidderminster Railway Museum)

Left: Fig. 320. Enlargement of one of the gas lamps in the erecting shop, which were the only means of artificially illuminating the works.

Right: Fig. 321. The paint shop. Locomotives are (left), T1 No. 76, and (right) B4 No. 88. The large diameter pipes are for heating.

AROUND THE WORKS AT THE TURN OF THE CENTURY

THE LSWR AT NINE ELMS

Fig. 322 A view of the coaling stages. In the background can be seen the roundhouse and in the centre the clock tower that surmounts the offices. To the left is the foundry part of the works with its attendant chimneys and line of wagons, which would probably be supplying coal or scrap iron and also taking away rubbish associated with the process. The locomotives in the picture are, from left to right, a Beattie Well Tank, No 246, a G6 No 257, and T1 No 7.

10
LOCOMOTIVE PROCUREMENT
1895 - 1908

Dugald Drummond

Born in Ayrshire 1st January 1840, Drummond suceeded William Adams on 1st July 1895. He had previously worked for a number of companies including:
Forest & Barr of Glasgow (apprenticeship)
Caledonian Railway (two periods)
Glasgow & Edinburgh Railway
Thomas Brassey's Canada Works
North British Railway (two periods)
Highland Railway
London, Brighton & South Coast Railway
Australasian Locomotive Works (Sydney)
Glasgow Railway Engineering Company

Although a competent engineer, Drummond is perhaps better known for his fiery attitude towards anyone who displeased or crossed him. His first task was to oversee the introduction to service of Adams's last two locomotive types – the T6 and X6 passenger 4-4-0 locomotives. He immediately implemented changes to the design by removing the cylinder tail rods and bogie wheel splashers and adding coal rails to the tenders, before these 20 locomotives entered service. The last 10 Adams T1 class and the last 20 of his G6 class tank engines also entered service after Drummond had taken office. For some reason, Drummond was not in favour of the Vortex Blast Pipe (possibly because of increased maintenance costs) in use on many of Adams engines and he progressively removed this device from the locomotives that still carried the system.

Drummond's first designs for the LSWR were the M7 0-4-4 tank engine and the 700 class 0-6-0 goods engine. They were regarded as very successful designs with some of each type lasting until the early 1960s. Then however, and in similar fashion to the way in which William Adams went through a period of becoming besotted with the idea of large diameter single driving wheel locomotives, Drummond seemingly became obsessed with the idea of a means of eliminating coupling rods. His first attempt at this was the solitary T7 4-2-2-0 locomotive, which had two inside cylinders driving the leading axle and two outside cylinders driving the rear axle. Its only advantage, other than not having coupling rods, was the opportunity to fit a longer firebox between the two axles. It did not prove to be a success and was given progressively less onerous work schedules until withdrawn in April 1927.

There followed in 1898/9, two of his more successful designs, the C8 and T9 4-4-0 passenger locomotives. A total of 66 T9s were built, a mark of

Fig. 323. Dugald Drummond in his uniform as a Major in the Volunteer Regiment. Drummond died in service on 8th November 1912 aged 72. He is buried at Brookwood Cemetery within the sound of the former LSWR main line.

their success being that the first withdrawal did not take place until 1951. Around the same time Drummond designed, and had built his personal F9 class carriage (known as "Drummonds Bug"), consisting of a small locomotive with integral passenger compartment on the same framework. This he used to travel around the system when visiting the various depots. Such a combination was not unique, as the LBSCR had a similar vehicle engine and carriage combination as did the Highland Railway. No doubt enhanced by his reputation, the chance of a surprise visit was feared by many.

Drummond then appeared to have another engineering relapse and designed the E10 4-2-2-0 locomotive. Again this was a 4-cylinder "double single" with no coupling rods. Five were built in 1901, and all these engines exhibited a similar history of poor performance to the T7 locomotive and all were similarly withdrawn by 1927. More successful was the K10 class, another 4-4-0 type. Forty were produced, the last one withdrawn in 1951.

Perhaps Drummond now needed another challenge to occupy his mind and this came with the railmotor concept - did such an idea germinate from his own locomotive and carriage combination? The first version, class K11, consisted of two units which were used on the joint LBSCR/LSWR East Southsea line from Fratton. Despite having no trailing load, the vertical boilers originally fitted were quickly found to have insufficient steaming capacity and were substituted for larger horizontally placed boilers. (The East Southsea branch was a little over 1¼ miles in length and aside from two short sections with gradients at 1 in 100 was either level, or almost so.)

The H12 (2 units) and H13 (13 units) railmotors followed, again with larger boilers. They proved reasonably successful at operating on several lightly patronised branch lines. Even so they were rarely successful at tackling a trailing load, and the boilers were also prone to poor steaming in areas of hard water. The coach sections of all these units were constructed at the Eastleigh Carriage works and as such was probably the first time that Eastleigh had became involved in motive power construction.

Later, partly due to over-crowding and the fact that maintenance was difficult as a combined unit, Drummond introduced the C14 design of 2-2-0 tank locomotive that could be used on two-coach trains on similar services.

Three more classes of 4-4-0 locomotive, the L11, S11, and L12 classes, were designed and built at Nine Elms between 1903 and 1905. All were successful and lasted until 1949 -1955.

Drummond then turned his attention to larger 4-6-0 locomotives having four cylinders. The logic in this was understandable - train weights and speeds were increasing, accordingly five F13 locomotives appeared in 1905. All the F13 breed were destined to quickly gain a reputation for very poor steaming. The class were initially tried on the West of England fast services, but as they proved unsuitable in this application they were relegated to lighter passenger and goods services. One of the class (number 333) was superheated in June 1920, but without significant improvement. Not surprisingly, all were withdrawn in 1924, although some were rebuilt by Robert Urie (Drummond's successor), as the H15 class.

Surprisingly another similar 4-6-0 locomotive, this time classified E14, was produced in 1907. Fortunately only one was built as its performance was even worse and it is reputed that on one occasion, when hauling a heavy goods from Salisbury to Exmouth junction, it had to be pulled in from Whimple having run out of fuel! If the tender had been full at the start from Salisbury this would imply a coal consumption rate as high as 130 lbs per mile. The solitary E14 was withdrawn in 1914 but again rebuilt by Urie also as an H15.

Drummond's final 4-6-0 was another 4-cylinder type, ordered in 1908 and classified as class G14. Five were built at Nine Elms in 1908, to be followed by another five classified as P14, which were built at the new Eastleigh works in 1910/11. They performed better than all the previous 4-6-0 examples, but even then, seldom improved upon the performances of the T9 and L12 types. All were withdrawn in 1925.

Finally in 1907 some more small 0-4-0T shunters were required, and five locomotives classified K14 were ordered. The type were based upon the successful Adams B4 design, but fitted this time with a Drummond boiler. Two, named 'Dinan' and 'Dinard' were sent straight to Southampton Docks in April 1908. The other three, numbers 82, 83 and 84, were the last locomotives to be built at Nine Elms, and were delivered in June 1908. All of Drummond's 2-cylinder designs were very successful, but he did not appear to be able to equal their performance with his 4-cylinder locomotives produced at Nine Elms. It might be that his problem was simply that he could not estimate how much extra steam was required, and may not have had anything to do with wheel arrangement.

Table 15 lists his designs for the period 1897 to 1908. The total number of locomotives ordered by Drummond was 369, of 19 classes. Of these, 306 were built at Nine Elms over an 11¼ year period - an average of 27 per year. Two M7 class tanks have survived, numbers 53, and 245. The only example of a Drummond design tender engine remaining is T9 No 120. Additionally A1X No 734 and the carriage body from Drummond's bug also escaped scrapping.

LOCOMOTIVE PROCUREMENT 1895 - 1908

TABLE 15

Build Period	Number Built	Builder	Wheel arrangement	Class	Withdrawal period	Figure Numbers
2/1897 - 3/1906	95	Nine Elms	0-4-4T	M7	5/1948 - 5/1964	326.327.328.329
3/1897 - 8/1897	30	Dubs & Co	0-6-0	700	9/1957 - 12/1962(1)	330,331,332,333,334
8/1897	1	Nine Elms	4-2-2-0	T7	4/1927	335,336,337,338
6/1898 - 11/1898	10	Nine Elms	4-4-0	C8	2/1933 - 1/1938	339,340,341,433
1/1899 - 11/1901	31	Dubs & Co	4-4-0	T9	3/1951 - 7/1961	342,343,344,345,346, 347,348,349,434,436
6/1899 - 10/1901	35	Nine Elms	4-4-0	T9	3/1951 - 7/1963	250,351,352,353,354, 355,356,357,358,435
6/1899	1	Nine Elms	4-2-4T	F9	8/1940	359,360,361,362,363, 364,365
4/1901 - 7/1901	6	Nine Elms	4-2-2-0	E10	9/1926 - 4/1927	366,367,368
11/1901 - 1/1903	40	Nine Elms	4-4-0	K10	1/1947 - 7/1951	369,370,371,372,373
Purchased 3/1903	2	Brighton Works	0-6-0T	A1X	12/1936 - 11/1963	374,375
4/1903 - 5/1903	2	Nine Elms (2)	Railcar	K11	9/1919	377,378,379,380,381, 382,383,384
6/1903 - 12/1903	40	Nine Elms	4-4-0	L11	5/1949 - 6/1952	385,386,387
6/1903 - 12/1903	10	Nine Elms	4-4-0	S11	2/1951 - 10/1954	388,389,390,391,392, 393,394,395,396,397, 398,399,400
5/1904 - 6/1904	2	Nine Elms (2)	Railcar	H12	11/1916	401,402
6/1904 - 3/1905	20	Nine Elms	4-4-0	L12	2/1951 - 2/1955	403.404.405.406,407, 408,409
9/1905 - 12/1905	5	Nine Elms	4-6-0	F13	7/1924 - 10/1924	410,411,412.413
10/1905 - 6/1906	13	Nine Elms (2)	Railcar	H13	11/1916 - 7/1919	414,415
9/1906 - 2/1907	10	Nine Elms	2-2-0T	C14	12/1916 - 3/1959	416,417,418,419,420, 421,422
11/1907	1	Nine Elms	4-6-0	E14	1/1914	423,424
4/1908 - 5/1908	5	Nine Elms	4-6-0	G14	1/1925	425,426,432
4/1908 - 6/1908	5	Nine Elms	0-4-0T	K14	11/1948 - 11/1959	427,428,429

(1) A few 700 class locomotives were reinstated for use as snowploughs during the winter of 1962/3. See Figure 332.
(2) The carriage section of these railcars were built and fitted at Eastleigh Carriage Works.

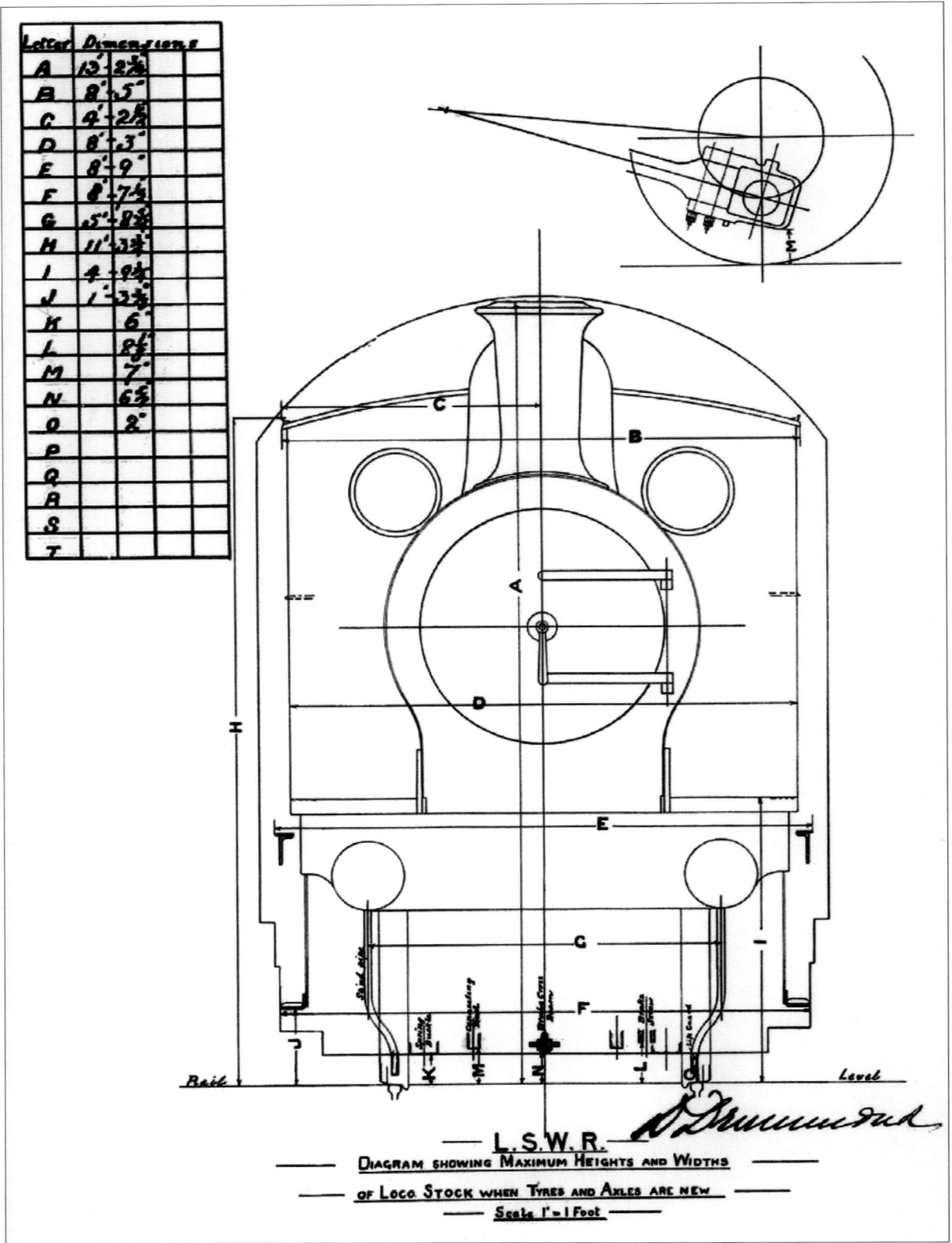

Fig. 324. Loading gauge diagram showing maximum dimensions to which locomotives can be built, signed by Dugald Drummond.

LOCOMOTIVE PROCUREMENT 1895 - 1908

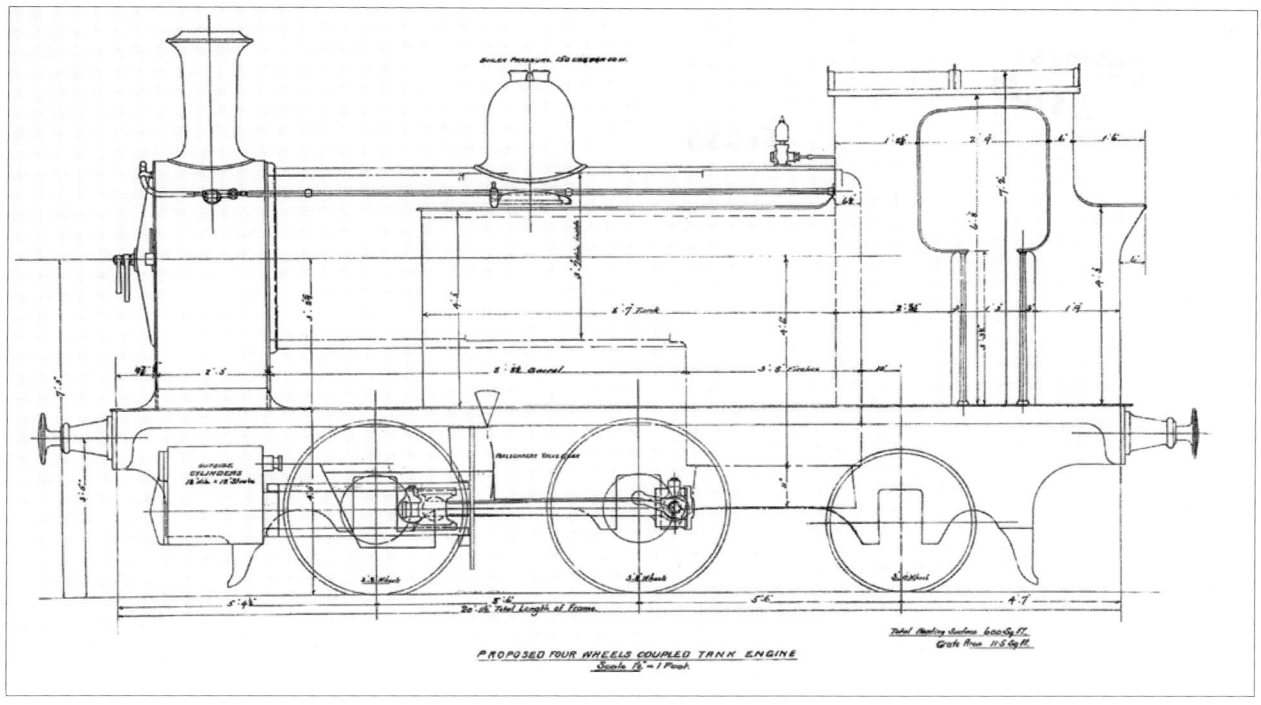

Fig. 325. Proposed 0-4-2 tank engine, similar to the C14 2-2-0T, date of drawing unknown, but it has Drummond type safety valves.

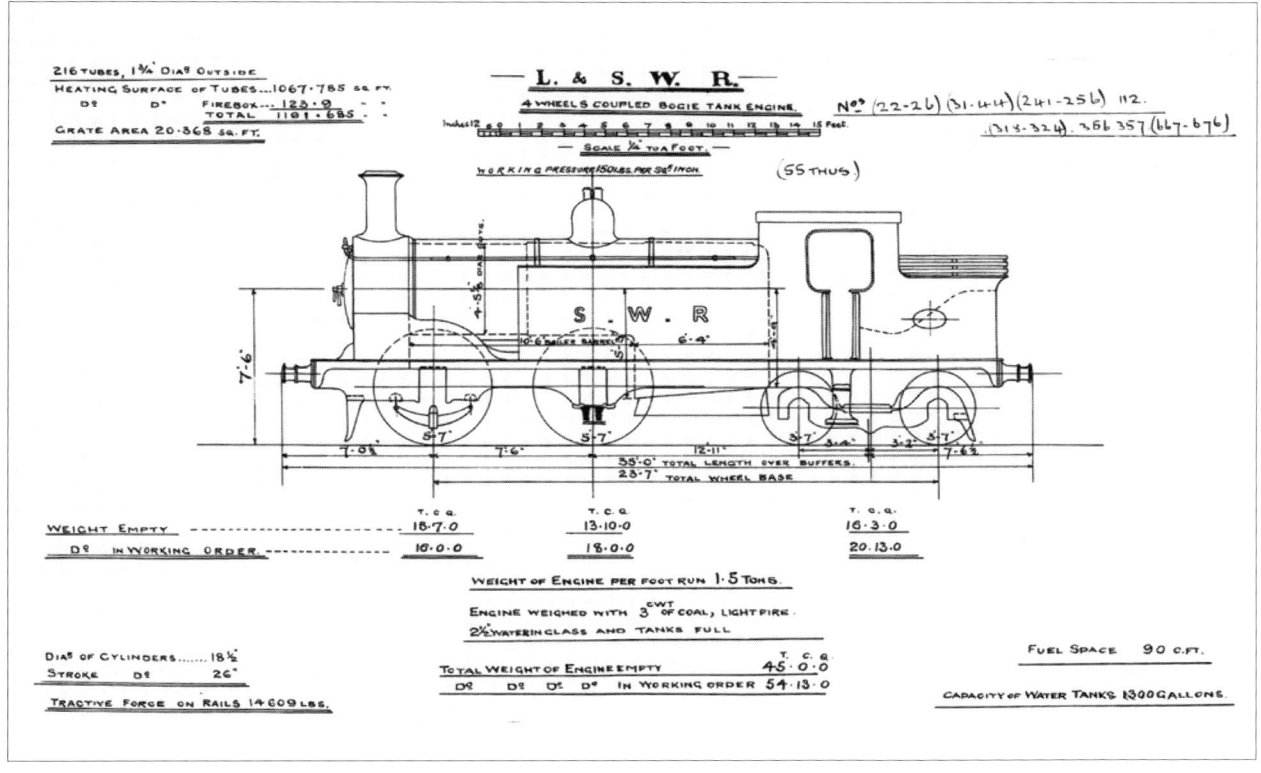

Fig. 326. Diagram of class M7 0-4-4 tank engine.

Fig. 327. M7 class locomotive No 59 in works grey livery as built in March 1906. Engines of this class built between 1904 and 1911 had feed water heating equipment as indicated by the pipe leading from the smokebox to the side tank. Boiler feed was by means of the steam driven pump shown below the side tank. When Robert Urie took office, he replaced these pumps with hot water injectors.

LOCOMOTIVE PROCUREMENT 1895 - 1908

Above: Fig. 328. M7 class locomotive No 58 with frontal damage at Nine Elms.

*Right: Fig. 329. M7 class locomotive No 111, as British Railways 30111, fitted with compressed air motor train equipment on the smokebox and water tank. Shown at Bishops Waltham on the 7th March 1959, engaged on a Branch line Society Special working.
(J. Spencer Gilks)*

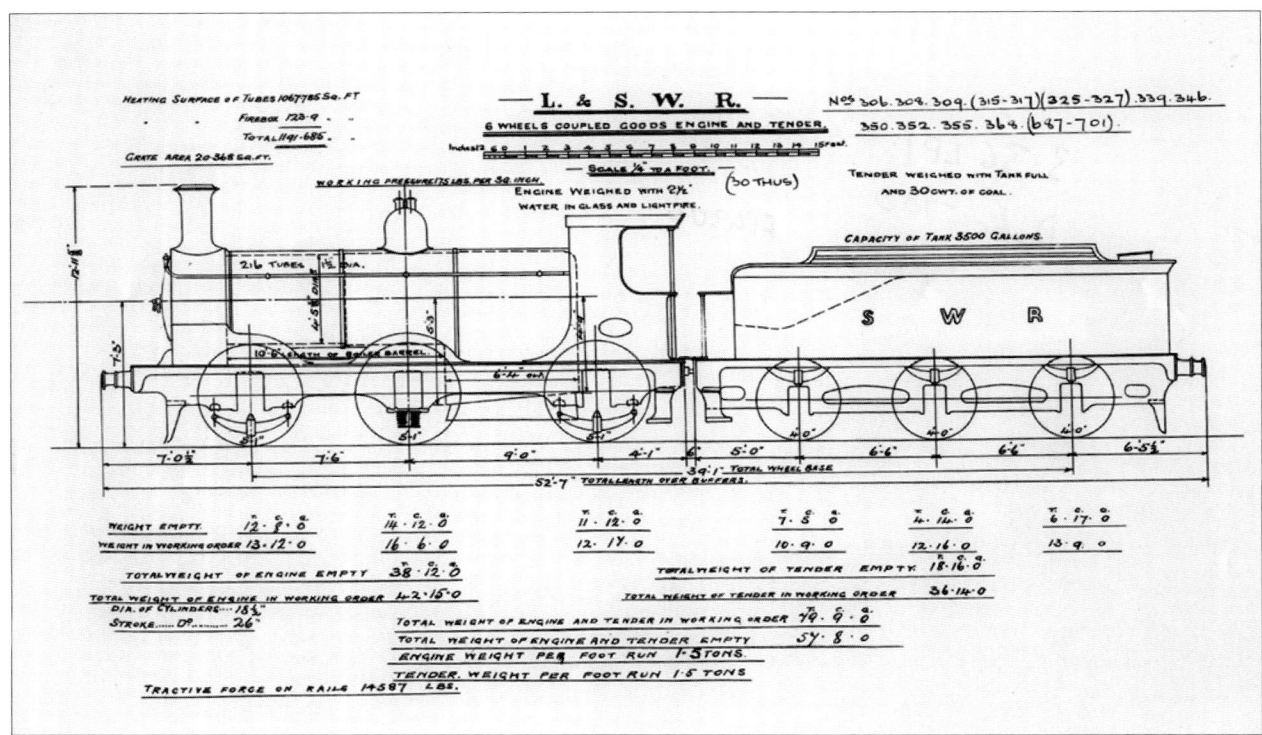

Fig. 330. Diagram of 700 class 0-6-0 locomotive.

Fig. 331. 700 class locomotive No 459 built by Dubs & Co.

LOCOMOTIVE PROCUREMENT 1895 - 1908

Fig. 332. 700 class locomotive No 702 (later 306) built by Dubs & Co running as British Railways 30306 and modified to operate as a snowplough in the severe winter conditions of early 1963.

Fig. 333. 700 class locomotive No 700 built by Dubs & Co showing damage between engine and tender. As there appears to be no damage at the rear end, and only minor bending of the front buffer beam, one could assume that the engine section fell off the end of a siding somewhere.

THE LSWR AT NINE ELMS

Fig. 334. 700 class locomotive No 701 built by Dubs & Co. Shown at Nine Elms fitted with performance test equipment. The rectangular box at the front end houses the equipment and the operator whilst the engine is operating.

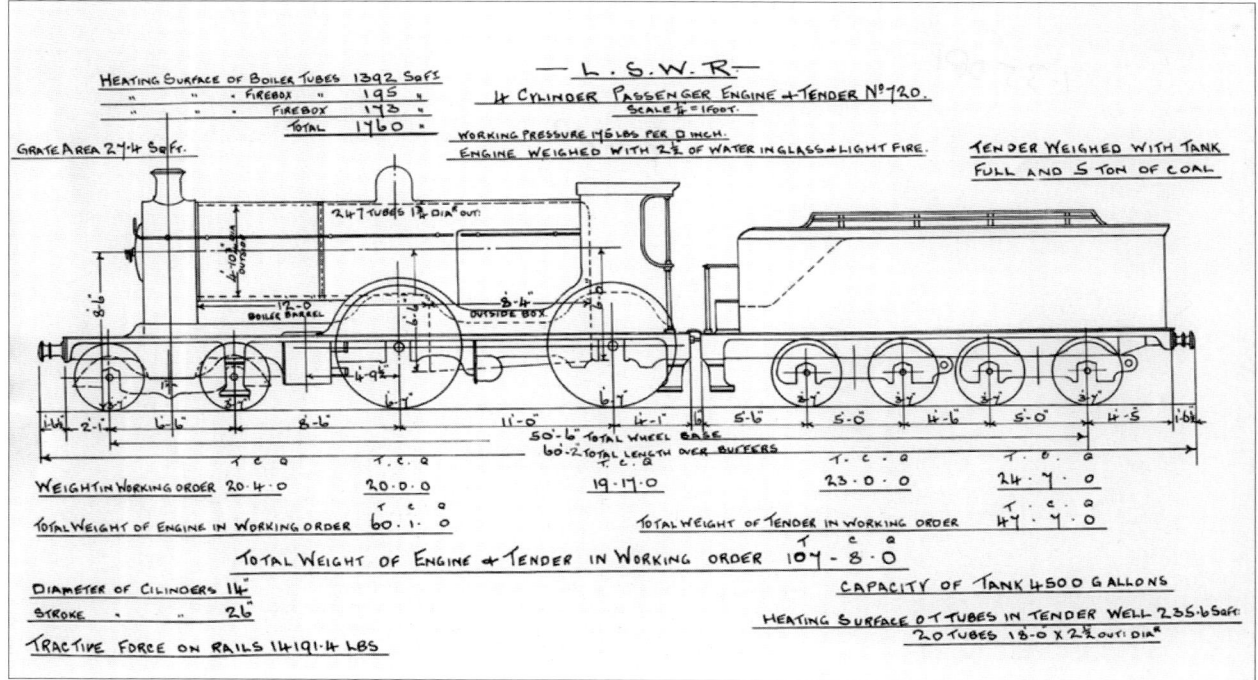

Fig. 335. Diagram of a T7 class locomotive.

LOCOMOTIVE PROCUREMENT 1895 - 1908

Fig. 336. T7 class locomotive No 720 at Nine Elms decorated for operating a special train (indicated by the white disc with black centre). The initials are not recognised, and it is surprising that this locomotive was used on a special journey in view of its reputation as a poor performer. Maybe the date of this journey was soon after its introduction to service (August 1897) and before its poor performance became evident.

LOCOMOTIVE PROCUREMENT 1895 - 1908

Fig. 337. T7 class locomotive No 720 as original in works grey livery, 1897.

Fig. 338. T7 class locomotive No 720 being tested on an 11-coach train of what appears to be very new stock. The train consists of a 56ft Brake Third Corridor, six corridor coaches, two Dining Saloons, and two other corridor vehicles. The temporary shelters at the front of the engine house test equipment and personnel, circa 1899.

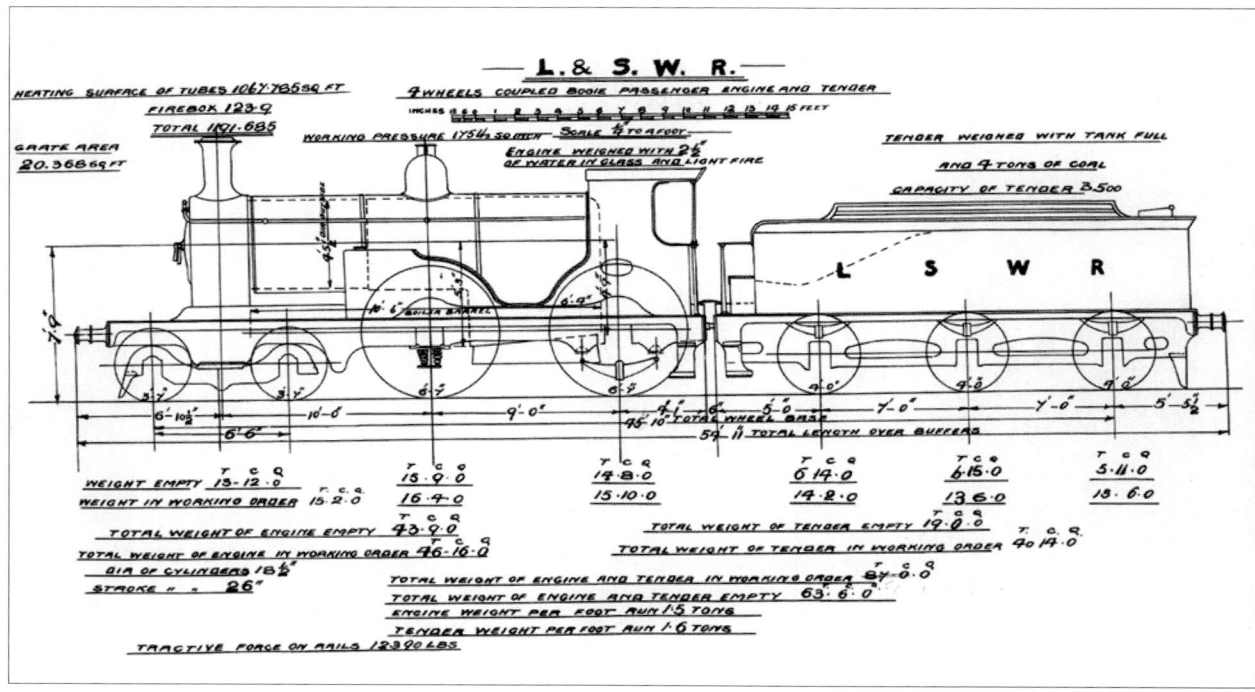

Fig. 339. Diagram of a C8 class locomotive.

LOCOMOTIVE PROCUREMENT 1895 - 1908

Above: Fig. 340. C8 locomotive No 292 as originally built in works grey livery, 1898.

Right: Fig. 341. C8 locomotive No 299 with original 6-wheeled tender on a train of miscellaneous stock: 44ft Passenger Brake Van, six-wheeled Composite (possibly 32ft), a 48ft Tri-composite (arc-roof version), a 48ft Third, and a 48ft Composite. The location is approaching Wimbledon, and it will be noted that no headcode is displayed. Date 1898-1903.

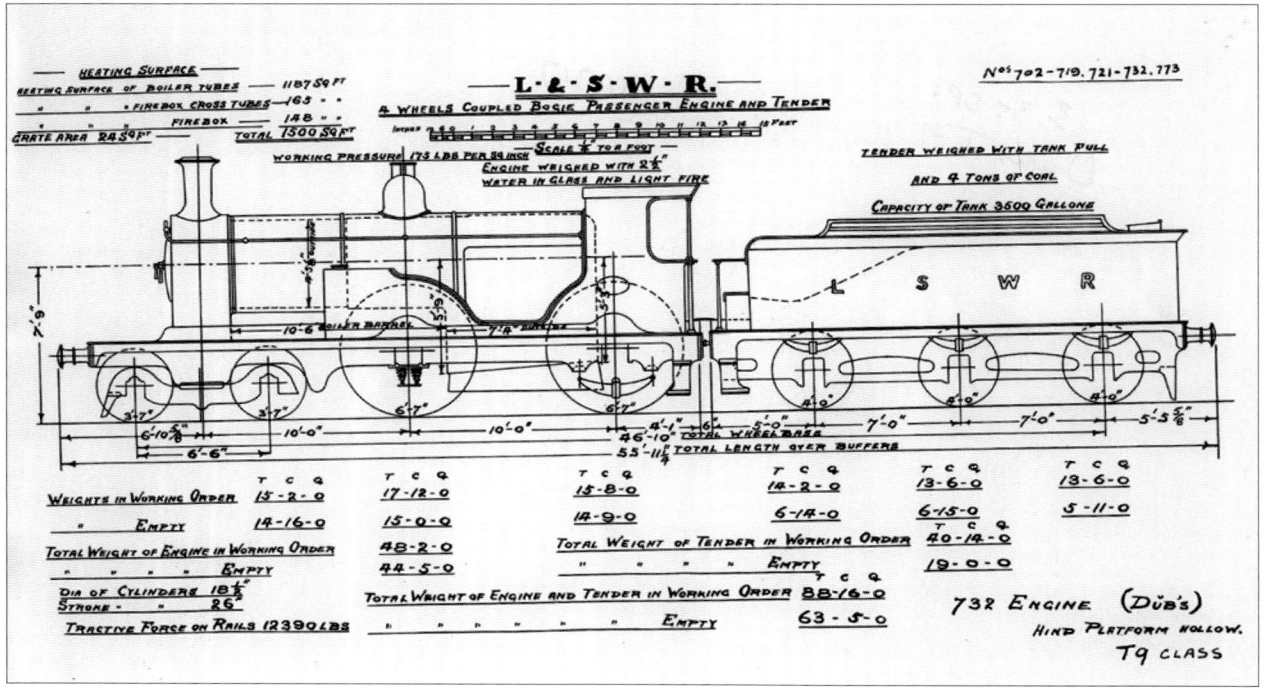

Fig. 342. Diagram of a Dubs-built T9 class locomotive.

Fig. 343. T9 class locomotive No 708 built by Dubs & Co. All of the Dubs' engines had firebox cross water tubes fitted.

LOCOMOTIVE PROCUREMENT 1895 - 1908

Fig. 344. T9 locomotive No 773 by Dubs & Co, decorated for a journey carrying a "special" person whose photograph is on the smokebox door. The significance of the "C" is not known. This locomotive was the "Exhibition engine" for which Dubs & Co had obtained permission from Nine Elms to exhibit at the Glasgow Trade Fair in 1900.

Fig. 345. Here the locomotive in Figure 344, T9 No 773, is shown operating a special working, bringing the Colonial Secretary, Joseph Chamberlain from Southampton to London in March 1903 on his return from negotiating the Treaty of Vereeniging that ended the Boer War. The vehicles consist of a 44ft Royal Kitchen Brake, 47ft 6ins Royal Saloon No 20, 47ft 6ins Royal Saloon No 17, possibly a 46ft First, and finally a 44ft Passenger Brake Van.

LOCOMOTIVE PROCUREMENT 1895 - 1908

4891 Officers Committee   15 February 1875
Romsey

Various reports were submitted as to a portion of the 11.40pm Goods train having broken away near the above Station on the 4th inst upon which it was ordered that Driver "Grainger" and Guard "Baker" be fined 2/6 each for going back after the missing wagons on the wrong line.

Fig. 346. T9 locomotive by Dubs & Co No 708, decorated on a special train passing an unidentified station. The initials "RB" refer to Robert Baden-Powell, with the working being his state return from the Boer War. The formation of the train is identical as described in Figure 348. Note the clarity of the communication cord running between train and engine.

LOCOMOTIVE PROCUREMENT 1895 - 1908

Fig. 347. The same train as seen on the previous page, again the communication between engine and train is apparent.

THE LSWR AT NINE ELMS

LOCOMOTIVE PROCUREMENT 1895 - 1908

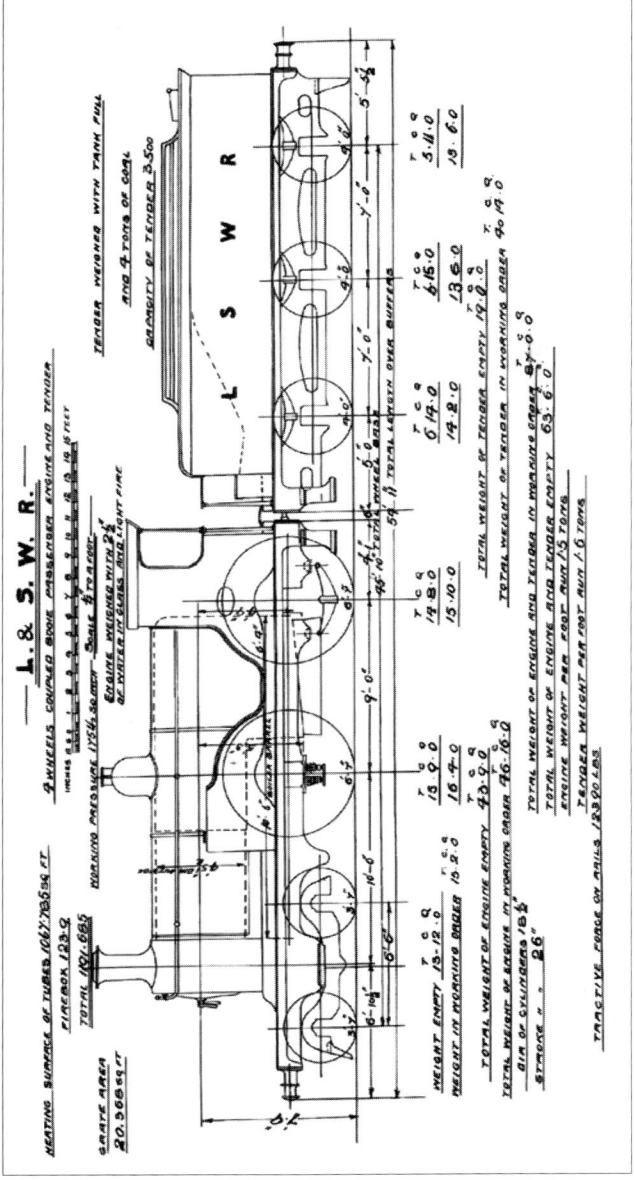

Previous page top: Fig. 348. T9 locomotive No 773, decorated, on a 6-coach train, the "K" standing for Lord Kitchener whose photograph is on the smokebox, on his state return from the Boer War. The coaches are a 44ft PBV, a 46ft First, 47ft 6ins "Eagle" Saloon, Royal Saloon No 20, a 50ft Double Family Saloon, and a 48ft Brake Tri-composite.

Previous page bottom: Fig. 349. A T9 locomotive by Dubs & Co with a 9-coach train passing Nine Elms Junction, consisting of a 44ft PBV, various 48ft Composites, a 48ft Third, and another 44ft PBV.

This page top: Fig. 350. Nine-Elms built T9 No 286 on a Channel Islands Flower Train in Eastleigh yard. The stock consists of 48ft Fruit Brake Vans and 24ft PLVs. This engine was one of the second series from Nine Elms and did not have cross water tubes or steam sanding with smokebox sandboxes.

This page right: Fig. 351. Diagram of a Nine Elms built T9 locomotive.

THE LSWR AT NINE ELMS

Previous page: Fig. 352. A T9 locomotive by Dubs & Co in the 721 to 729 range, on a special train, possibly an Epsom Race Special, just leaving Waterloo. The stock consists of a 30ft Passenger Brake Van, 43ft Third, 42ft 6ins Tri-composite and various others, all arc-roofed stock.

This page: Fig. 353. Nine-Elms built T9 No 300, one of the final Nine Elms series, with firebox cross water tubes and steam sanding.

4465 *Officers Committee*   *Hamworthy Junction*   *22 December 1873*

Various reports were submitted as to No. 262 engine having been thrown off the rails at the above Junction on the 18th inst. upon which it was ordered that Porter "Losham" be fined 5/- and Driver "Riddams" cautioned.

LOCOMOTIVE PROCUREMENT 1895 - 1908

Fig. 354. Nine Elms built T9 No 305 decorated for a special.

Fig. 355. Nine-Elms built T9 No 120 (now preserved) on a train of "emigrant" carriages. From the front, these are a 46ft 6ins Brake Third non-corridor, a 46ft 6ins Composite corridor, a 46ft 6ins Composite non-corridor, a 46ft 6ins Brake Third non-corridor, a 48ft Brake Tri-composite, and other vehicles that cannot be identified. Photographs of several "emigrant" cars together are fairly rare. Under the bridge, the train is one of meat vans on Open Carriage Trucks with a brake van. The location is unknown.

LOCOMOTIVE PROCUREMENT 1895 - 1908

Fig. 356. T9 No 300 on a special train for Lord Roberts at the time of his return from the Boer War. The vehicles are a 44ft Passenger Brake Van, a 46ft First, a 48ft Brake Tri-composite, a 47ft 6ins "Eagle" Saloon, 47ft 6ins Royal Saloon No 20, a Composite, and finally a further 44ft passenger brake van.

Fig. 357. Nine Elms T9 No 114 on the Birkenhead through train - the first three vehicles are of GWR origin, followed by LSWR stock. The first of these is a 56ft Brake Third Corridor, followed by a First Corridor, a Dining Saloon, and finally another 56ft Brake Third Corridor. The train was recorded at an unknown location. See also note re the photograph on the next page.

THE LSWR AT NINE ELMS

Fig. 358. Nine Elms T9 No 286, on a 7-coach train just south of Swaythling and apparently the same train as seen in Figure 357 - but in reverse order. It is likely then that these two views are of the Birkenhead to Bournemouth service. The Appendix to the Working Time Table for January 1911 states that the GWR express headcode of a lamp each side of the buffer beam were to be carried by through trains between Bournemouth and Oxford.

LOCOMOTIVE PROCUREMENT 1895 - 1908

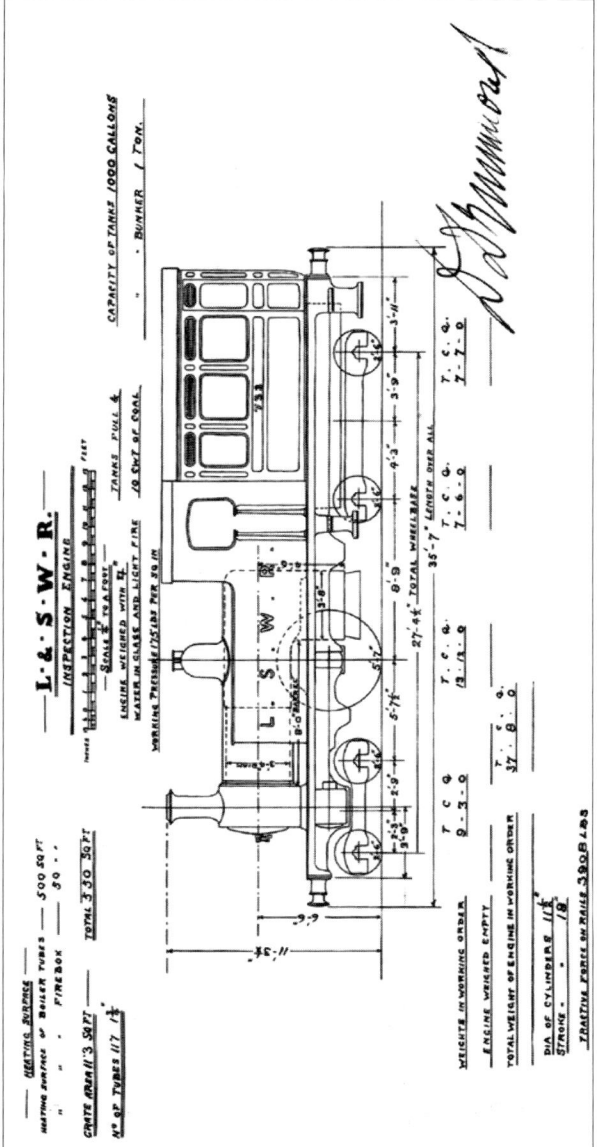

Top: Fig. 359. Drummond's inspection saloon, classified as F9, probably as built, in 1899.

Right: Fig. 360. Diagram of the inspection saloon class F9.

Fig. 361. *The frames of the F9 inspection saloon in the works, 1899.*

Fig. 362. *The boiler of the F9 inspection saloon in Nine Elms Works.*

LOCOMOTIVE PROCUREMENT 1895 - 1908

THE LSWR AT NINE ELMS

Previous page top: Fig. 363. The boiler mounted on the frames of the F9 inspection saloon in Nine Elms Works.

Previous page bottom: Fig. 364. The locomotive section of the F9 inspection saloon being built in Nine Elms, 1899.

This page: Fig. 365. Preparing for the removal of the carriage section of the F9 inspection vehicle to a preservation site in 1967. The location is Eastleigh Works where my father had found the body in 1967, in use as a timber inspector's hut at the back of the works. It is believed to have been used as such since about 1940.

4996 Officers Committee   22 June 1875
"H. Breaker" Fireman
Upon the report of Mr. Beattie it was ordered that the above man be fined 10/- for striking his Driver whilst on duty at Basingstoke on the 11th inst.

LOCOMOTIVE PROCUREMENT 1895 - 1908

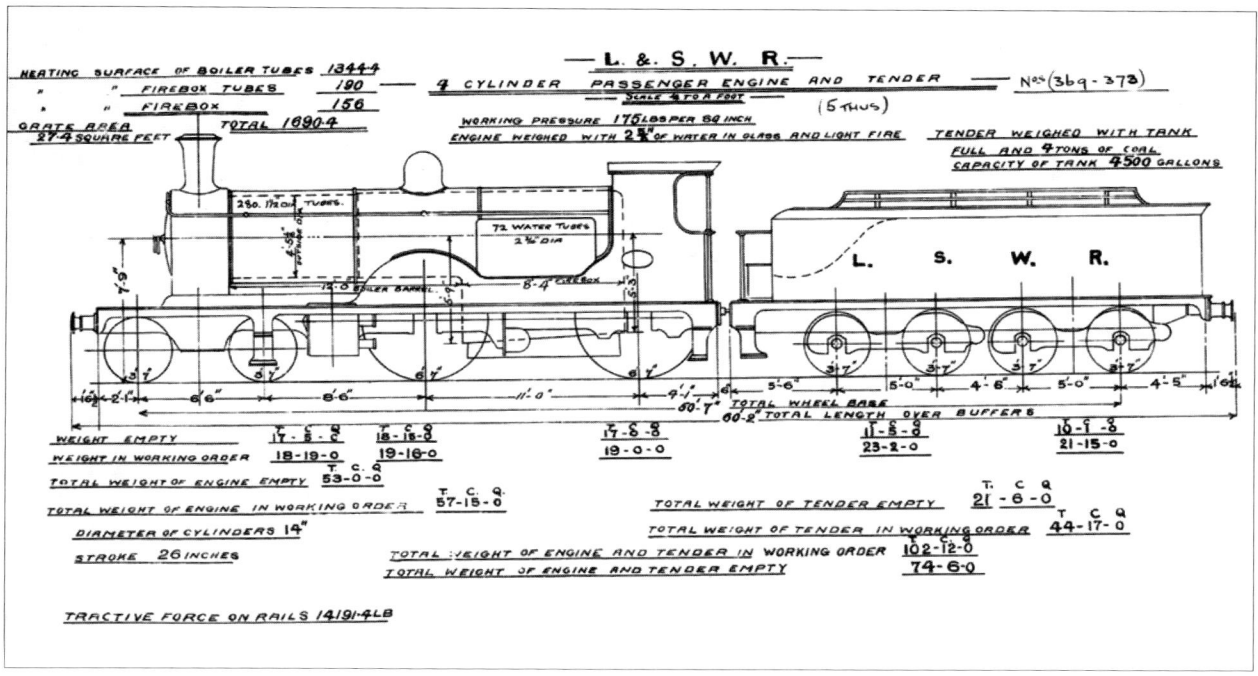

Fig. 366. Diagram of an E10 class 4-2-2-0 locomotive.

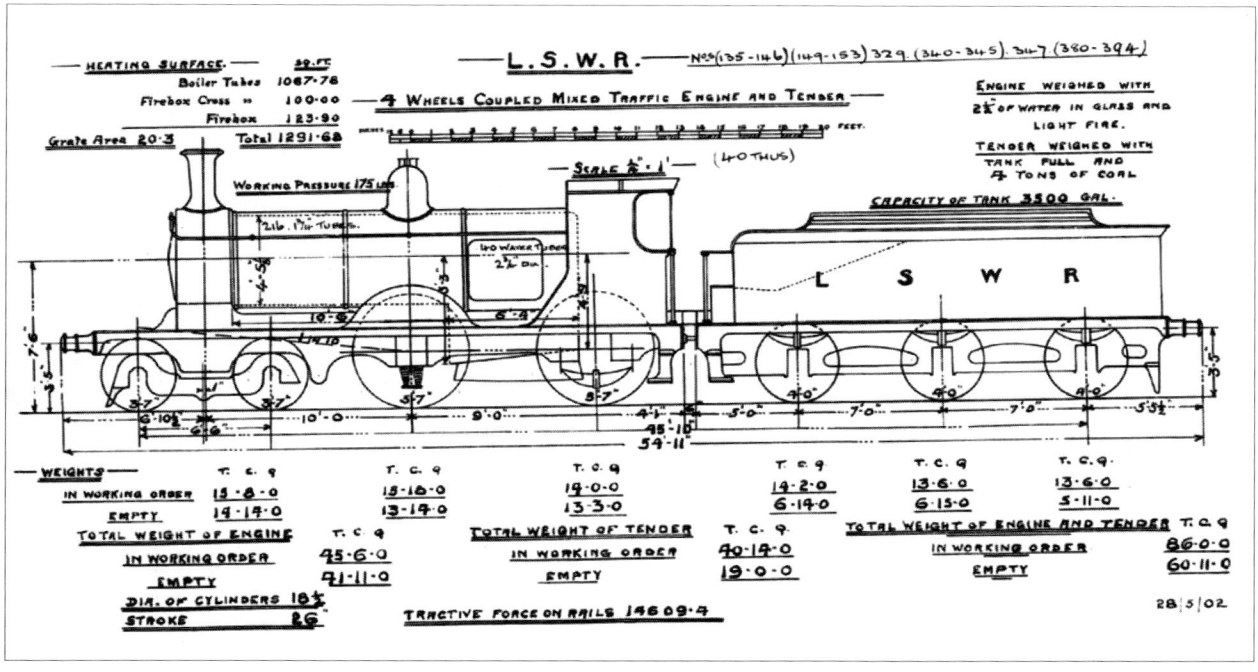

Fig. 367. Diagram of a K10 4-4-0 locomotive.

THE LSWR AT NINE ELMS

Fig. 368. E10 locomotive No 370 at Nine Elms in works grey livery, 1901.

4526 *Officers Committee*   23 February 1874

Side Lights on Engines

Mr. Scott called attention to the practice for some Engines to carry side lights whereas others worked without them, and having read letters which he had received from various Companies in reply to a communication which he had addressed to them thereon, it was ordered. That in future no side lights showing a white light to the rear be carried by any of this Company's Engines when attached to a train, but that when travelling empty a red tail light be placed on the Tender.

LOCOMOTIVE PROCUREMENT 1895 - 1908

Fig. 369. K10 locomotive No 343 in works grey livery, 1901/2, with steam sanding and smokebox sandboxes. It was fitted with a special water-tube boiler as shown in Figure 371.

Fig. 370. K10 locomotive No 136 with smokebox sandboxes and steam sanding removed.

THE LSWR AT NINE ELMS

Top: Fig. 371. The unique water tube boiler, destined for K10 locomotive No 343, under construction in Nine Elms Works.

Left: Fig. 372. Detail of this special boiler, with a number of cross tubes visible.

LOCOMOTIVE PROCUREMENT 1895 - 1908

Fig. 373. The completed water boiler for K10 No 343. The then recent practice of the Nine Elms photographer of blanking out the background is also apparent. When lagged and fitted to the engine there was little external difference to a contemporary boiler of the time.

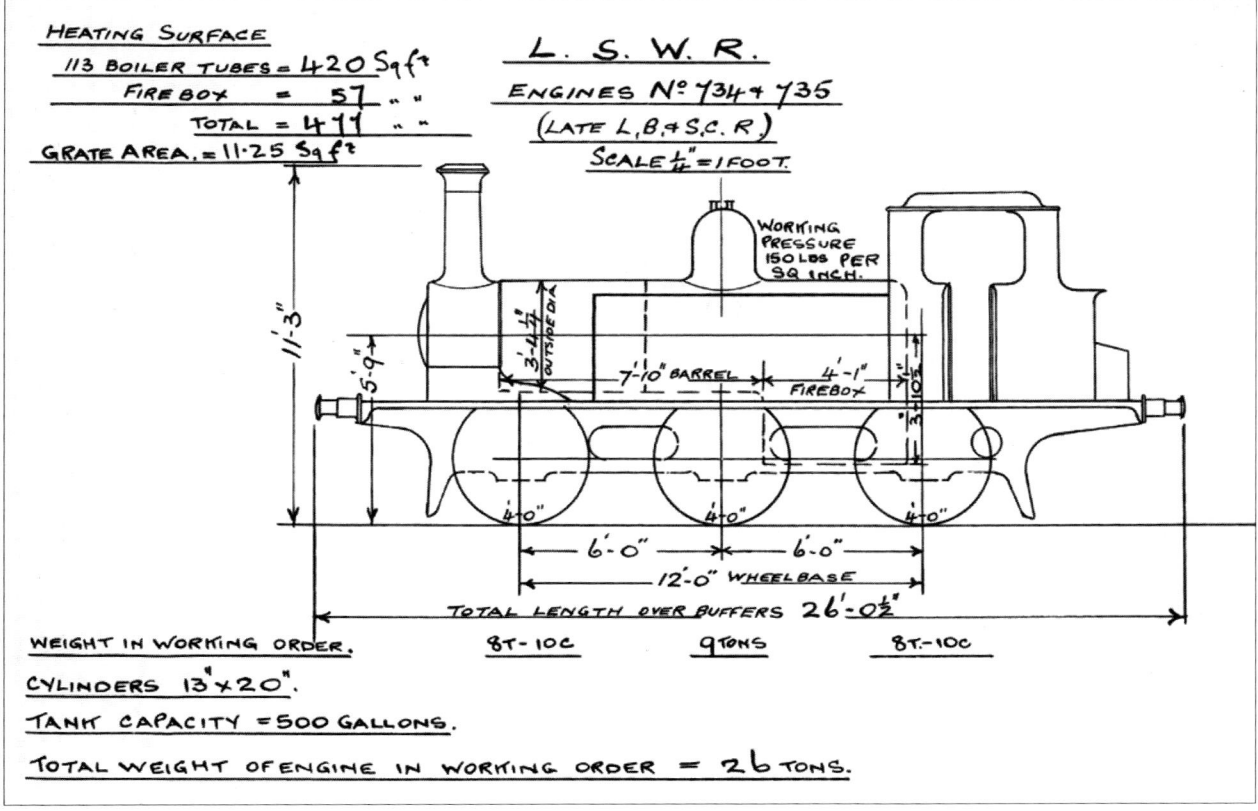

Fig. 374. Diagram of an A1X class locomotive.

Right: Fig. 375. A1X locomotive No 735, one of two purchased from the London, Brighton & South Coast Railway. This locomotive had exhaust-feed water heaters in the side tanks; the other engine, No 734, did not have this equipment.

Below: Fig. 376. K10 locomotive, possibly No 389, on a train of 44ft Passenger Brake Vans and 24ft Special Passenger Luggage Vans and also 32ft Special Milk Vans. The location is the yard adjacent to Eastleigh station. The actual working was described in the June 1911 "Railway Magazine" as being a Waterloo to Southampton special.

LOCOMOTIVE PROCUREMENT 1895 - 1908

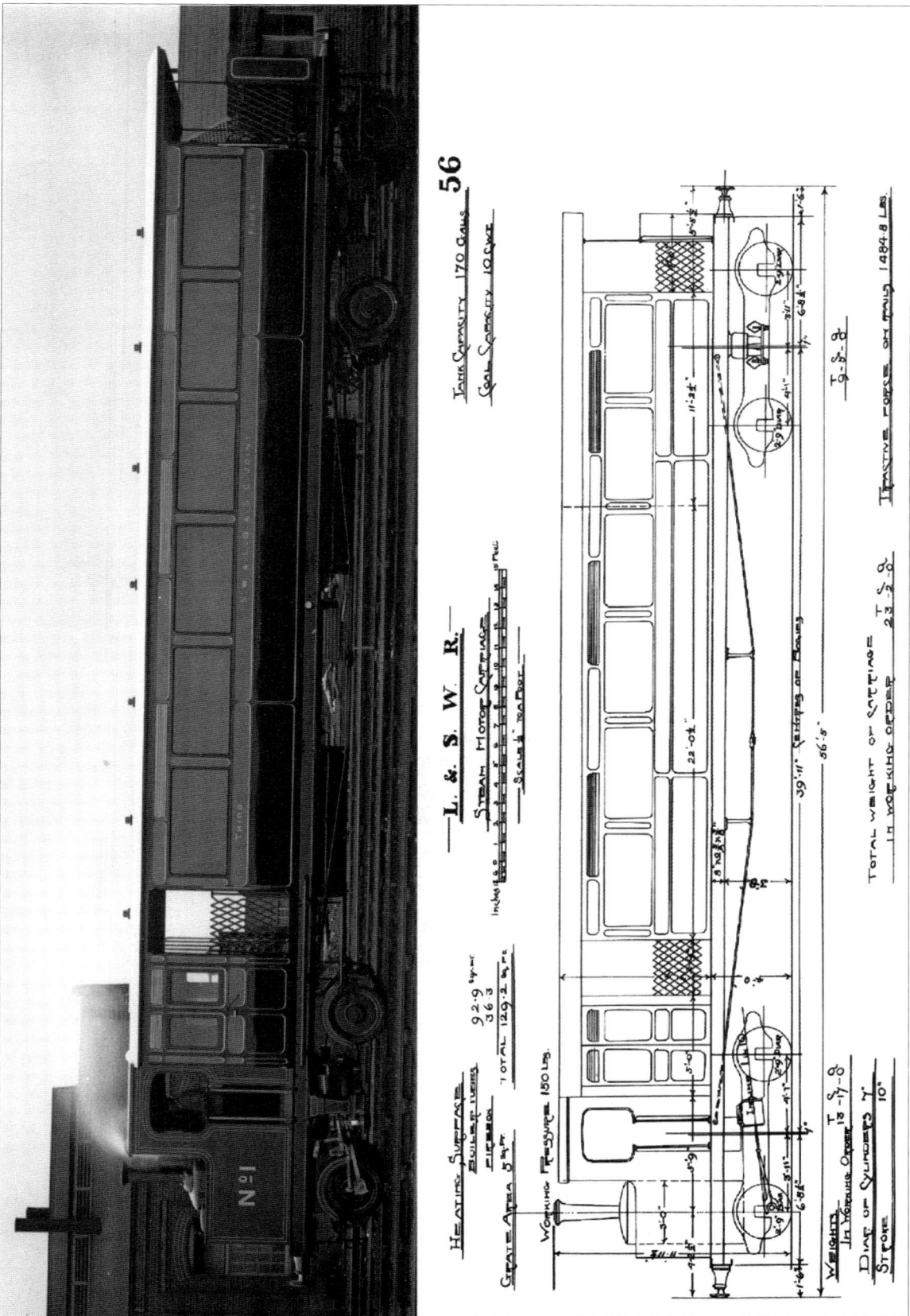

Top: Fig. 377. K11 railmotor No. 1, operated jointly by the South Western and the London, Brighton & South Coast Railways as fitted originally with a vertical boiler.
Bottom: Fig. 378. Diagram of a K11 class railmotor with vertical boiler.

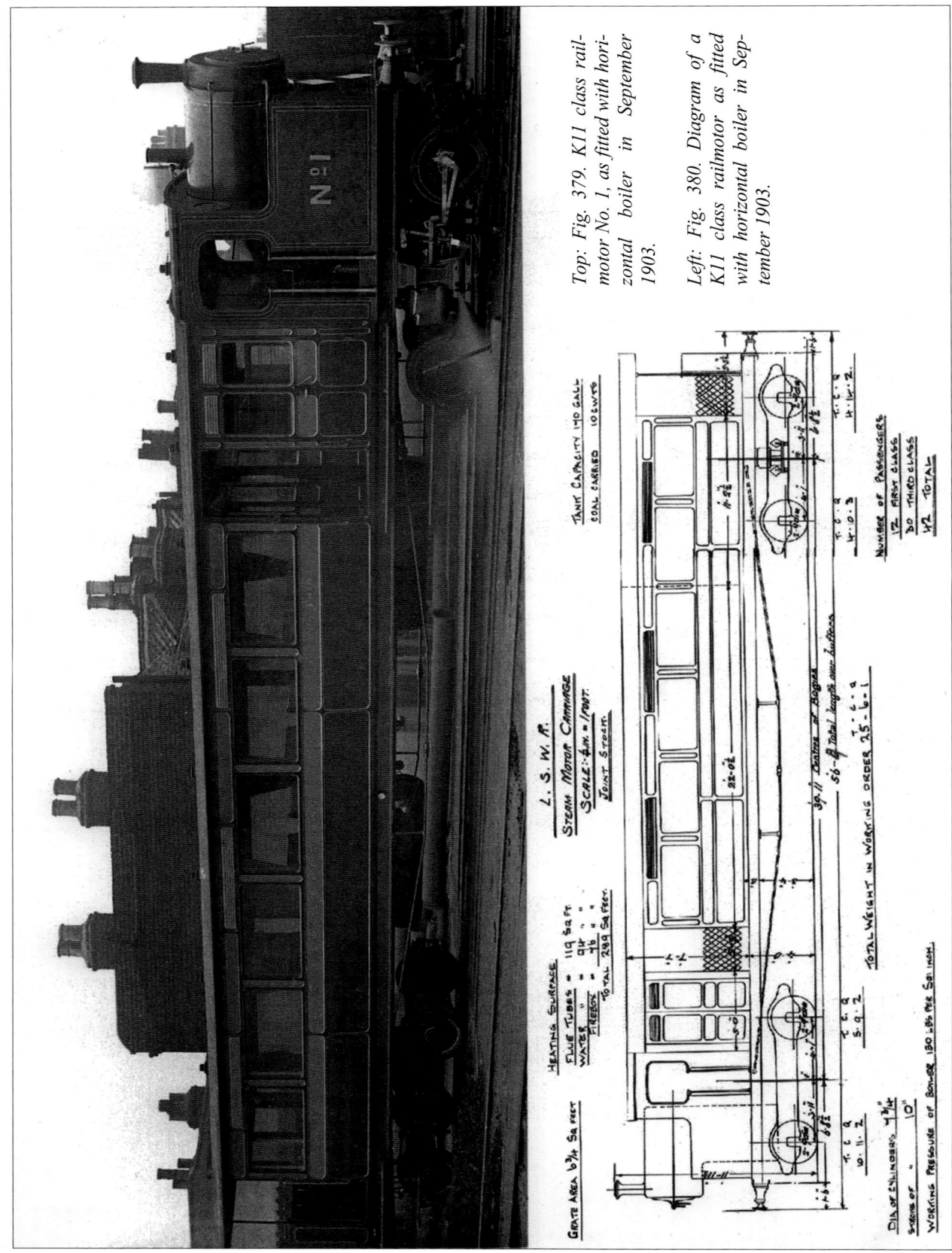

Top: Fig. 379. K11 class railmotor No. 1, as fitted with horizontal boiler in September 1903.

Left: Fig. 380. Diagram of a K11 class railmotor as fitted with horizontal boiler in September 1903.

LOCOMOTIVE PROCUREMENT 1895 - 1908

Top: Fig. 381. K11 class railmotor lagged boiler on power bogie, and trailing bogie, in Nine Elms Works.
Bottom left: Fig. 382. K11 class railmotor boiler under hydraulic test outside Nine Elms Works. This operation is usually performed in this position outside the works to minimise any inconvenience in the event of a fracture occurring.
Bottom right: Fig. 383. K11 class railmotor firebox under construction in Nine Elms Works.

Fig. 384. K11 class railmotor cab and frames on bogies in Nine Elms Works.

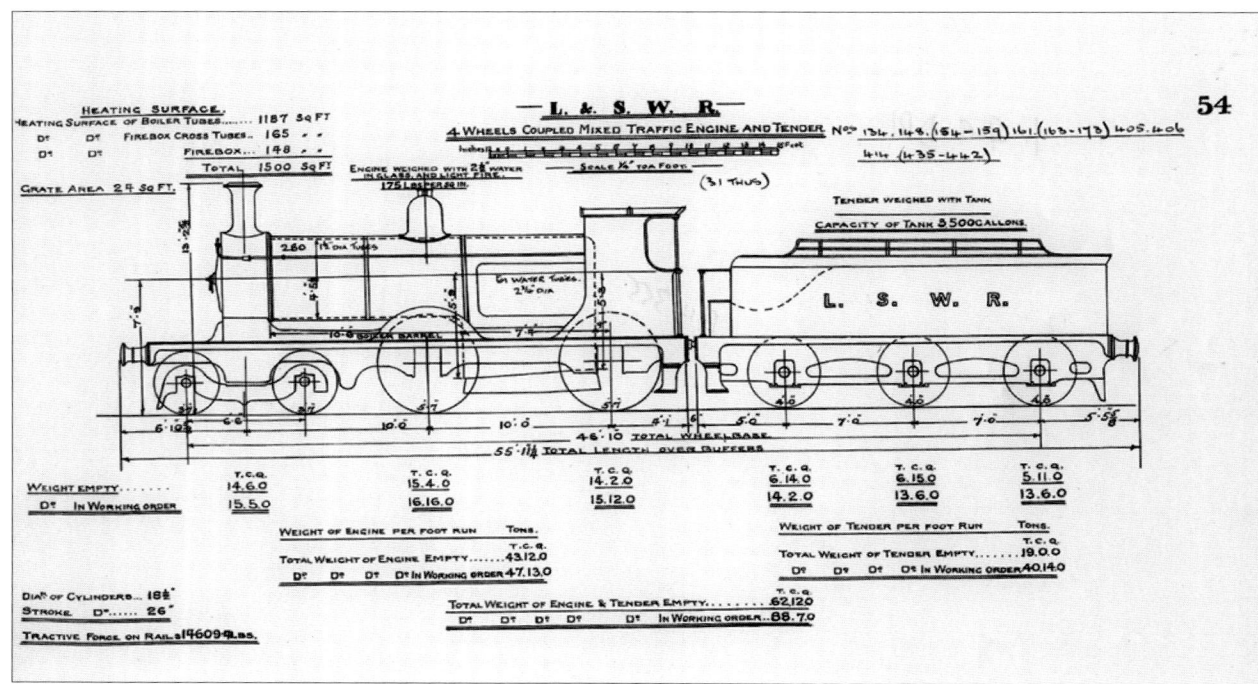

Fig. 385. Diagram of an L11 locomotive.

LOCOMOTIVE PROCUREMENT 1895 - 1908

Fig. 386. L11 locomotive No 408, as originally built with firebox cross water tubes. It was also fitted with the double bogie tender which had exhaust steam heaters, and Duplex pumps were fitted to the engines instead of injectors.

Next page: Fig. 387. L11 locomotive No 441 on a train of meat vans on Road Vehicle Trucks, Southampton Docks to Nine Elms.

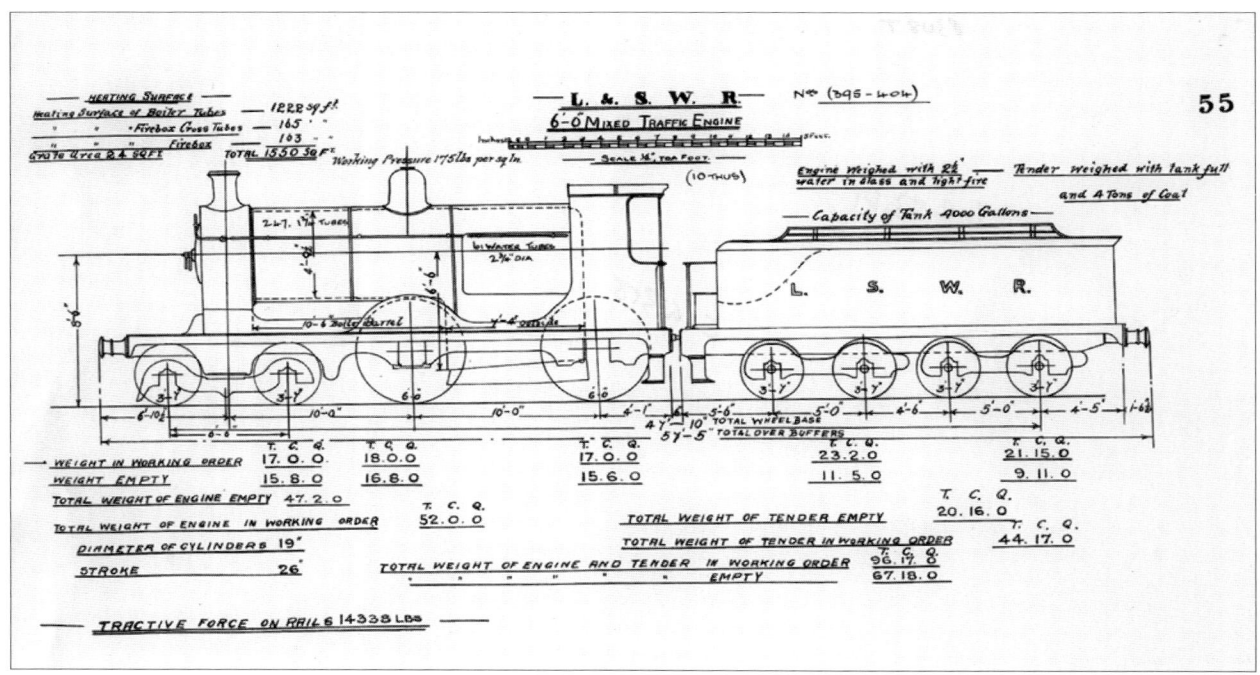

Fig. 388. Diagram of an S11 locomotive.

Fig. 389. S11 locomotive No 395 as original, in works grey livery, June 1903.

LOCOMOTIVE PROCUREMENT 1895 - 1908

Fig. 390. S11 locomotive No 396, carrying the special train disc with a black centre, on a 6-coach train. This black and white disc was supplemental to the conventional route indicating code, implying that this particular working was a West of England line train but could well be empty stock working to the sidings at Wimbledon. The coaches are a 56ft Dining Saloon, 44ft Passenger Brake Van, three non-corridor Composites, and finally a further 44ft Passenger Brake Van.

THE LSWR AT NINE ELMS

Top: Fig. 391. Figures 391-400 show stages in the manufacture of an S11 locomotive. This view of the boiler shop shows the boiler barrel for the fifth S11 locomotive, probably No 399.

Left: Fig. 392. Drilling the stay holes in an S11 inner firebox.

Above: Fig. 393. Tightening the nuts on the roof stays of the complete firebox. The segmented bar fixed temporarily in a horizontal position provides support for the long box spanner when force is applied to the end of the crow bar.

Fig. 394. With the cover plates removed from the access points on the side of the firebox, this view shows the holes into which the cross water tubes will be fitted and then expanded to form a seal that will withstand pressures in excess of boiler pressure.

Fig. 395. The boiler is now a complete pressure vessel, with the access point cover plates replaced and sealed. The boiler is set up for a hydraulic test, being completely filled with water, and pressure will be applied via the small bore pipe fitted into the front tube-plate via the chimney. A double pressure gauge is fitted so that two independent checks can be made on the pressure applied, which is normally about 1½ times normal working pressure. The vehicle carrying the boiler is also interesting.

Fig. 396. Here the two main frame plates are mounted in position, with the axlebox horn plates already in position. A neat pile of rivets await the next riveting operation.

Fig. 397. The stretchers, joining the frames together, buffer beams, and cylinder block have been fitted at this stage.

Fig. 398. The boiler has now been fitted to the frames.

LOCOMOTIVE PROCUREMENT 1895 - 1908

Fig. 399. The boiler lagging sheets, cab, and smokebox have been fitted.

Fig. 400. The unit seen in Figure 399 has now been lifted by means of two travelling gantries and lowered onto the wheels.

THE LSWR AT NINE ELMS

Top: Fig. 401. H12 railmotor No 1. Bottom: Fig. 402. Diagram of an H12 railmotor.

LOCOMOTIVE PROCUREMENT 1895 - 1908

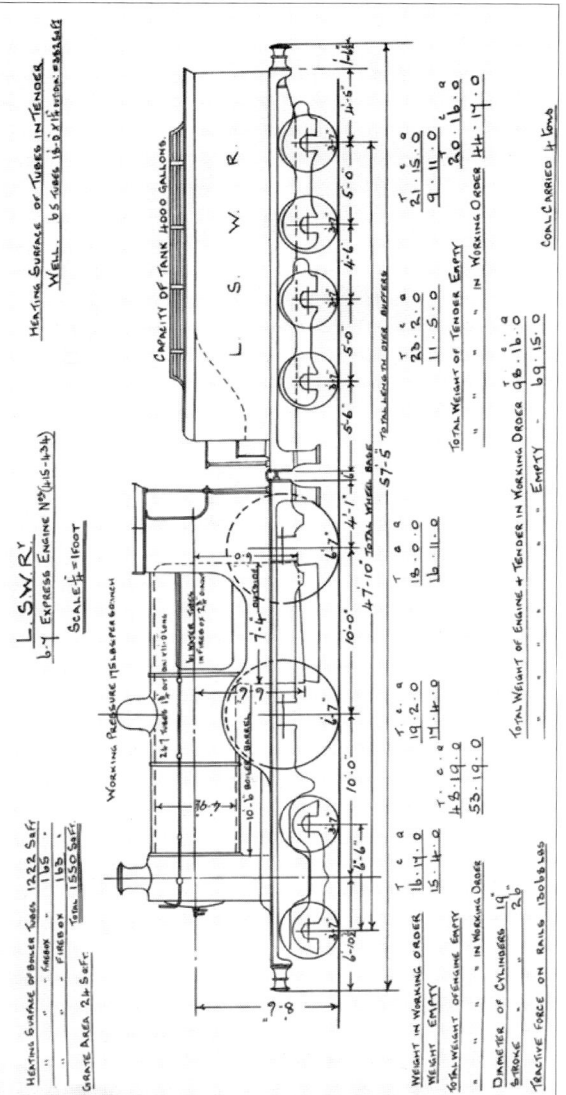

Top: Fig. 403. L12 locomotive No 421 after being superheated in July 1915, with extended smokebox.

Right: Fig. 404. Diagram of an L12 locomotive.

Fig. 405. L12 locomotive No 415 in works grey livery, circa June 1904.

LOCOMOTIVE PROCUREMENT 1895 - 1908

Figs. 406 and 407. Two views of L12 class locomotive No 421 removed to Nine Elms Works after the Salisbury accident of 30th June 1906 in which 29 people were killed.

THE LSWR AT NINE ELMS

Fig. 408. L12 class locomotive No 427 decorated for a special working.

LOCOMOTIVE PROCUREMENT 1895 - 1908

Fig. 409. L12 class locomotive No 427 at the head of the GWR Royal Train down from Waterloo, passing Nine Elms.

THE LSWR AT NINE ELMS

Top: Fig. 410. F13 class locomotive No 330 in original works grey livery at Nine Elms, circa September 1905.

Bottom: Fig. 411. F13 class locomotive No 333 after being superheated, necessitating an extended smokebox in June 1920.

LOCOMOTIVE PROCUREMENT 1895 - 1908

Top: Fig. 412. A set of frames for an F13 locomotive. The remaining sets are likely to be for engines from the same series.
Bottom: Fig. 413. An F13 boiler mounted on its frames. Wooden lagging has been applied.

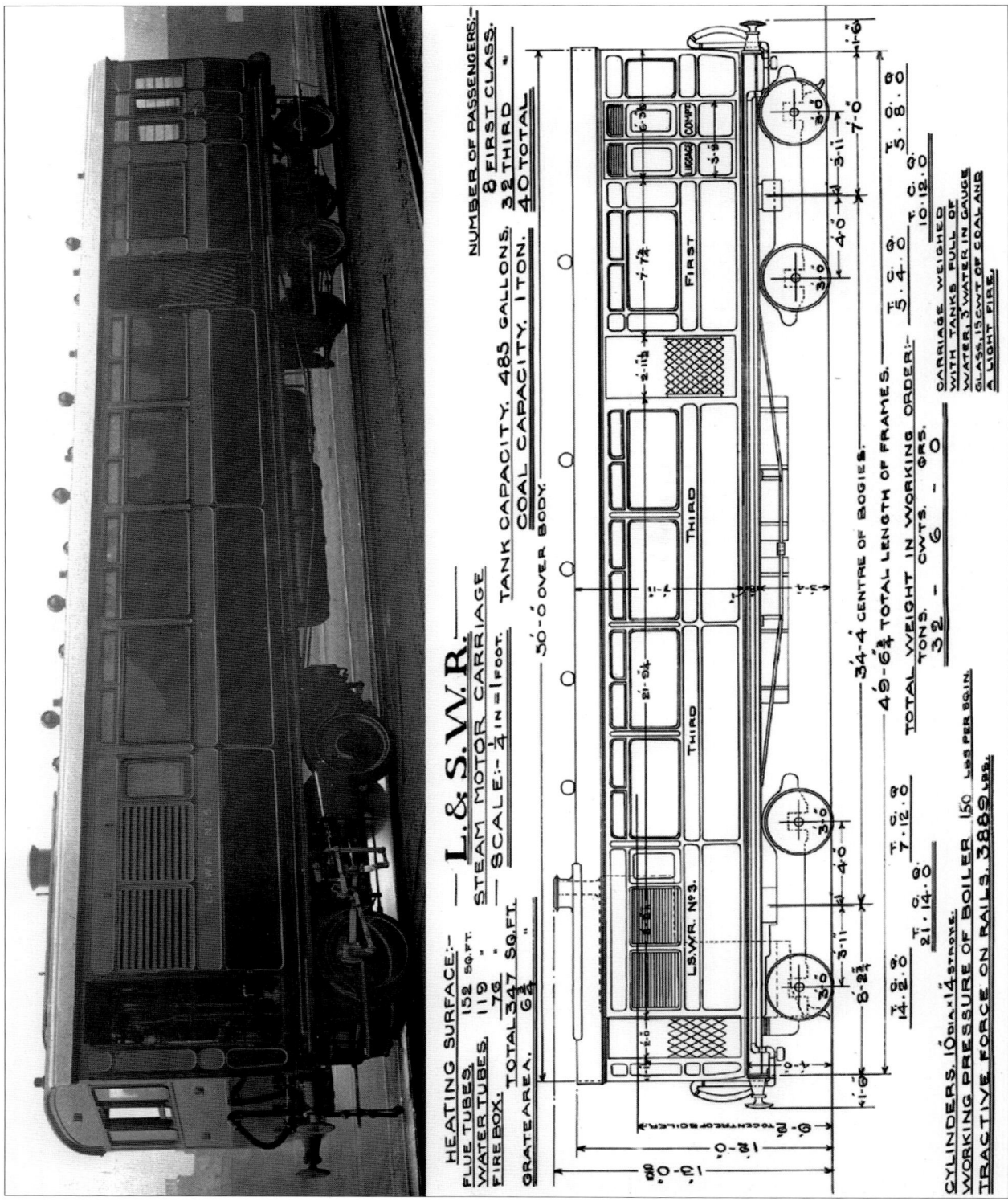

Fig. 414. H13 class railmotor No 5.

Bottom: Fig. 415. Diagram of an H13 class railmotor.

LOCOMOTIVE PROCUREMENT 1895 - 1908

Fig. 416. C14 class locomotive No 736, as original in works grey livery, circa September 1906.

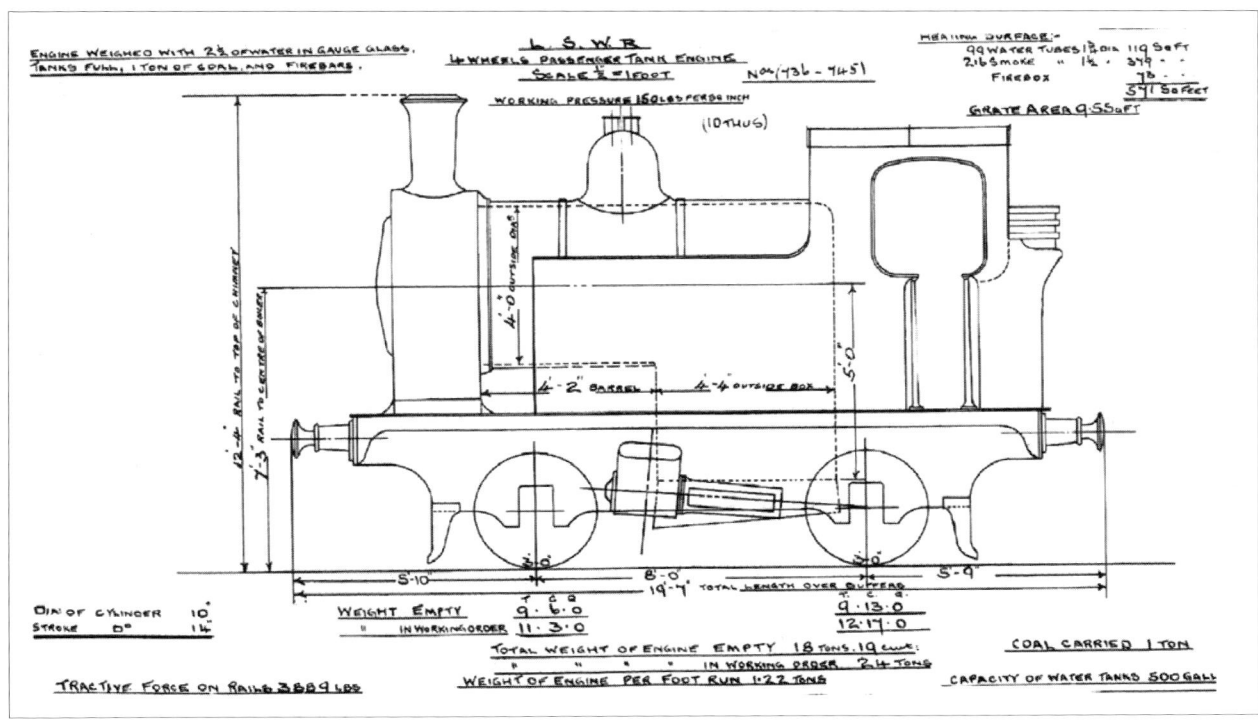

Fig. 417. Diagram of a C14 class locomotive.

Above: Fig. 418. The completed boiler of a C14 class locomotive in Nine Elms Works.

Left: Fig. 419. The boiler mounted on the frames of a C14 class locomotive.

LOCOMOTIVE PROCUREMENT 1895 - 1908

Fig. 420. C14 class locomotive assembled in Nine Elms Works and marked out in chalk ready for lettering.

Fig. 421. C14 class locomotive, originally numbered 744 (built January 1907) now numbered 30589, on a special train which ran from Eastleigh to Botley, then up the Bishops Waltham line and return on the 14th June 1952. It was organised by the Railway Correspondence and Travel Society. *(The late Les Elsey)*

THE LSWR AT NINE ELMS

Fig. 422. C14 class locomotive No 737 with two of the coaches (the maximum permitted load) that were specially designed for service as the Plymouth Motor Train. They are a 48ft Trailer and a 48ft Driving Trailer.

Fig. 423. E14 class locomotive No 335 (the only one of its class) as originally built in works grey livery at Nine Elms, circa November 1907.

LOCOMOTIVE PROCUREMENT 1895 - 1908

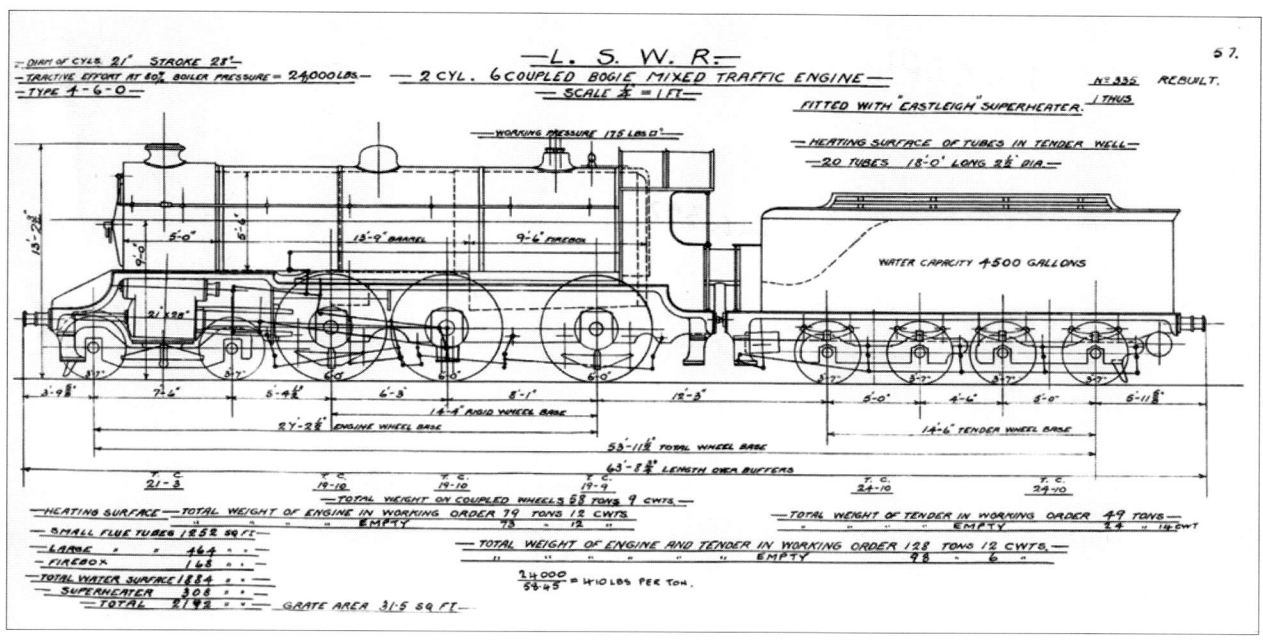

Fig. 424. Diagram of an E14 class locomotive. Urie H15 Class

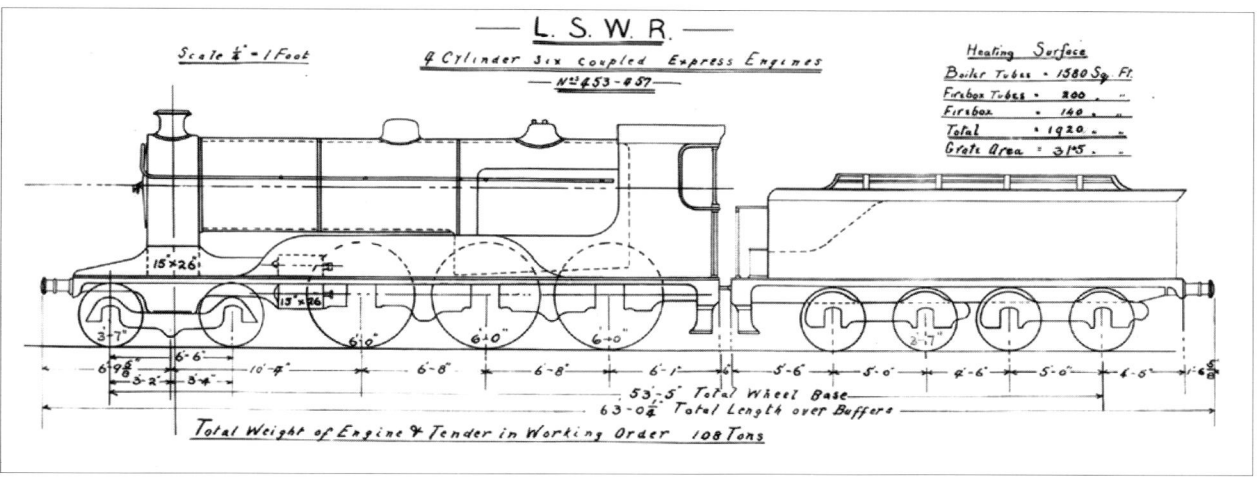

Fig. 425. Diagram of a G14 class locomotive.

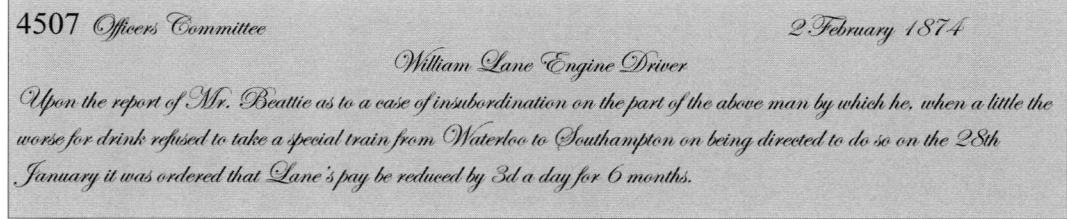

THE LSWR AT NINE ELMS

Top: Fig. 426. G14 class locomotive No 453 as original in works grey livery, circa April 1908.

Right: Fig. 427. K14 class locomotive No 746 named "Dinan" for use in Southampton Docks seen here at Nine Elms, circa April 1908.

LOCOMOTIVE PROCUREMENT 1895 - 1908

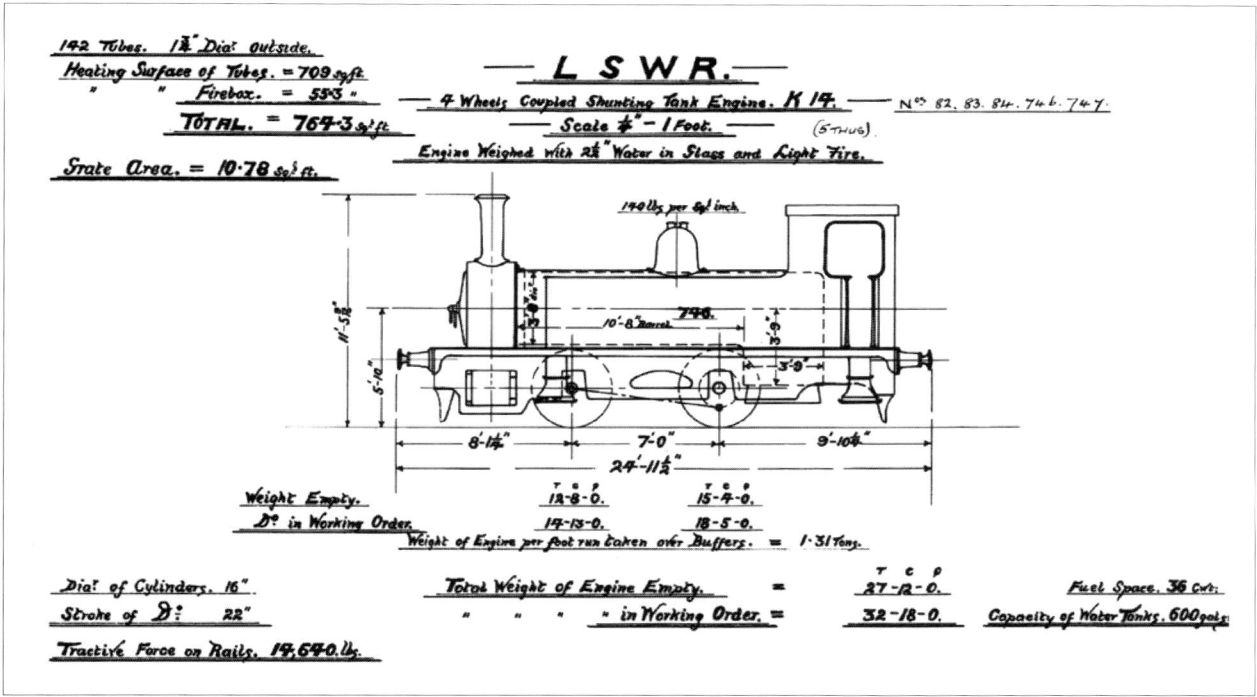

Fig. 428. Diagram of a K14 class locomotive.

Fig. 429. K14 class locomotive No 82 as original at Nine Elms, circa June 1908. This was one of the last three locomotives (all K14 class) to be built at Nine Elms.

THE LSWR AT NINE ELMS

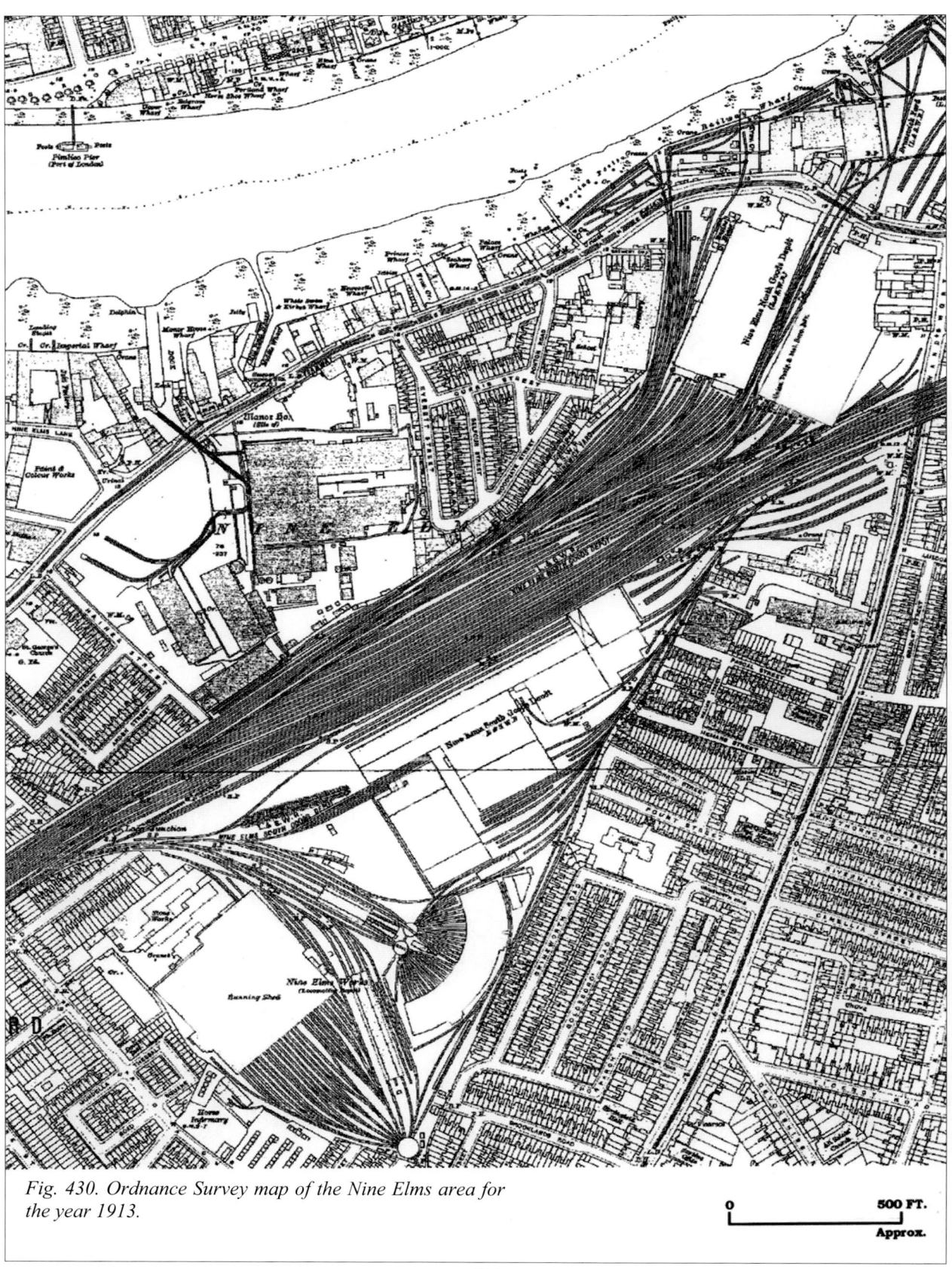

Fig. 430. Ordnance Survey map of the Nine Elms area for the year 1913.

11
CONCLUSIONS

Figure 431 shows the locomotive procurement figures during the Adams and Drummond periods. Separate indications are given for the locomotives produced by Nine Elms (black columns), and sub-contractors (white columns). The total number of locomotives delivered during this period was 911. 547 of them were produced by the Nine Elms Works during the period from 1887 to 1908, which amounts to an average of 27 per year. (This is the same average as was achieved by Drummond alone-see page 262).

The chart includes 26 locomotives ordered by W. G. Beattie but not delivered until 1878/82 during Adams's reign. It does not include the two Terrier class tank engines purchased from the LBSCR in 1903.

In 1909 the locomotive works moved to new premises at Bishopstoke, already occupied by the Company's Carriage and Wagon works, which had moved from Nine Elms in 1890. This site was originally described in official documents as being "a waste area 5 miles north of Southampton". The town of Eastleigh did not exist then, and it was the move of the Railway works to that site that was responsible for its development. The next extract from Peter F. Winding's article in the magazine *Railway World* is relevant:

Although the extension to the erecting shop might suggest otherwise, it was always on the agenda that the Locomotive Department would eventually have to follow the C & W down to Bishopstoke. With stock increasing at the rate of 100 locomotives every 10 years it was only a matter of time before the works reached saturation point ... but a more cogent reason was the location of the works in London at the easternmost end of a system that spread over 200 miles to the west. In this respect it cannot have escaped the notice of the directors that the South Western was the only major British railway company to tolerate such a situation, but in the event it was, a third and very different factor that decided the issue. It stemmed from the acquisition of Southampton Docks by the Company in 1892. Prior to this the Docks Company had not done too well, but under the tremendous enterprise of the South Western management this situation was quickly reversed, and within a decade the port had become one of the busiest in the United Kingdom. This was reflected in a tremendous increase in rail traffic between London and Southampton, and by 1905 Nine Elms was reaching saturation point with freight traffic and would have to be considerably enlarged within the next few years. To do this there was no alternative but to close the locomotive works and make the site available to the

Fig. 431.

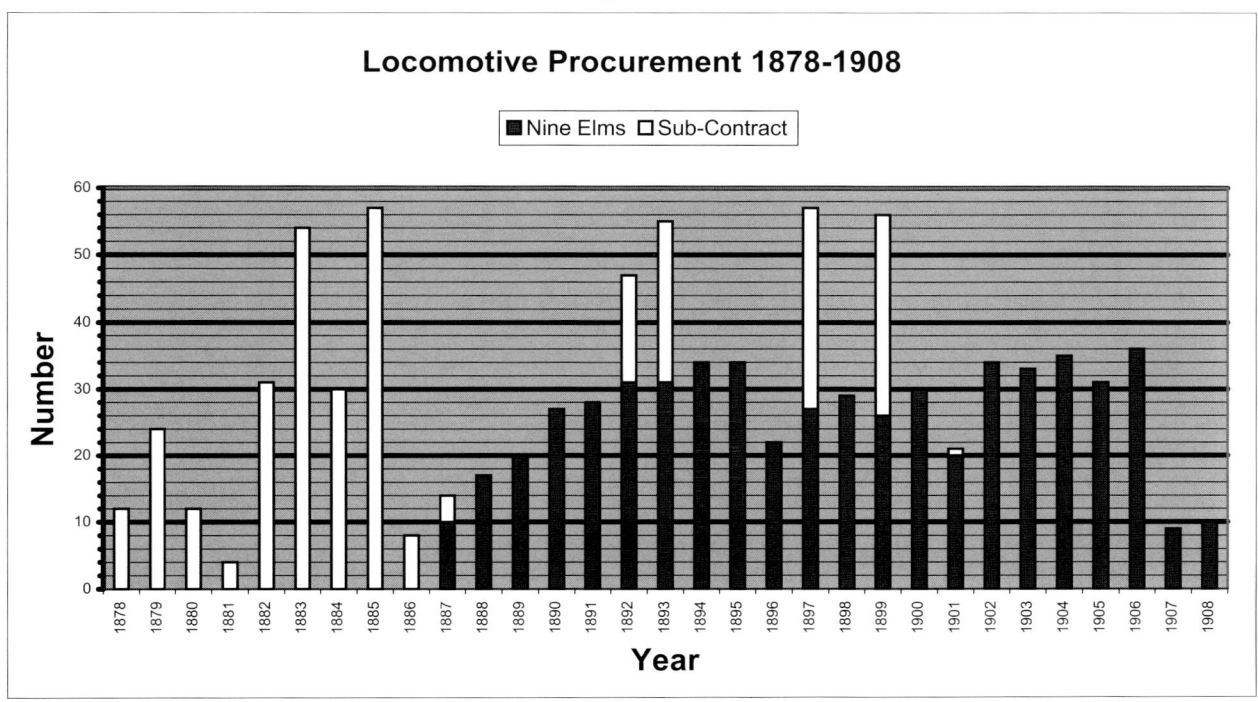

THE LSWR AT NINE ELMS

Goods Department, a proposition to which Drummond heartily agreed, since he had been waiting for just such an opportunity to carry out his own plans for thoroughly modern workshops at Eastleigh.

The Ordnance Survey produced another map of the area in 1913 which is reproduced in Figure 430. It shows the final form of the site with the goods depot having taken over all of the works area and the motive power depot having extended its linear running shed to 25 tracks in width. The motive power depot lasted generally in this form until the late 1960s. Over the years Nine Elms Works was also responsible for obtaining and maintaining locomotives that were employed at various sites away from the works and the main part of the system, such as the Bodmin and Wadebridge railway (even before it was connected to the line in 1895), the Engineer's Department at Wimbledon, Southampton Docks (again, even before the LSWR acquired the Southampton Dock Company in 1892), and a number of Manning Wardle saddle tank locomotives used at various sites around the system. Details of these involvements have not been included due to a lack of available space, but we hope to include them in a second volume, which will continue the story up to 1923, if sufficient interest is shown in this volume. I have attempted in this book to give an account of the service that our forbears gave to our transport system often under difficult conditions and poor wages, but nevertheless with dedication. This book then is dedicated to them.

Fig. 432. South Western excellence, G14 class locomotive No 457 on a Waterloo - Exeter dining car express.

Appendix A

The London and South Western Railway Company, Chief Administrators and Officials

Chairmen

Sir Thomas Baring, Bart, MP .... 1832 to 1833
John Wright ....1834 to 1836
John Eastthorpe ....1837 to 1840
Robert Garnett, MP ....1841 to 1842
W.J. Chaplin ....1843 to 1852
Hon Francis Scott, MP 1853
Sir William Heathcote 1854
W.J. Chaplin ....1854 to 1858
Capt Charles E. Mangles ....1859 to 1872
C. Castleman ....1873 to 1874
Hon Ralph H. Dutton .... 1875 to 1892
Wyndham S. Portal .... 1892 to 1899
Lieut-Col Hon. H.W. Campbell .. 1899 to 1904
Sir Charles Scotter, Bart .... 1904 to 1910
Sir Hugh Drummond, Bart ....1911 to 1922

Secretaries

E.L. Stevens................................... 1832
W. Reed 1835
A. Morgan 1841
P. L. Campbell 1846
W. Harding 1849
C. J. Brydges 1852
A. Bulkley 1853
L. Crombie 1853
F. Clarke 1862
F.J. Macaulay 1880
G. Knight 1898

Locomotive Superintendents

Joseph Woods 1838
John Viret Gooch 1841
Joseph Beattie 1850
W.G. Beattie 1871
W. Adams 1878
D. Drummond 1895
R.W. Urie 1912

General Managers

C. Stovin (Traffic Manager) 1839
A. Scott (Traffic Manager) 1852
        (General Manager) 1870
Sir Charles Scotter 1885
Sir Charles Owens 1898
Sir Herbert Walker 1912

Engineers

Francis Giles 1834
Joseph Locke 1837
Albino Martin 1840
John Bass 1849
John Strapp 1853
W. Jacomb 1870
E. Andrews 1887
J.W. Jacomb-Hood 1901
A.W. Szlumper 1914

Appendix B

Appendix B is on page 334, and lists the more important mechanical details of most of the locomotive classes ordered by Nine Elms. There are a few classes missing because such details were not available, and a few more because they were not sufficiently different from allied classes that have been included. Column headings are given in the list, but in some cases additional details of column content are given below:

Build date — Build date of the first locomotive of the class
Wheel Diameter (in) — Driving wheel diameter
Heating Surface Combustion Chamber (sq ft) — Surface area of the combustion chamber, where fitted
Loco Adhesive Weight (tons) — Total weight on the driving wheels only
Tractive Effort (lb) — Calculated using the formula: $TE = \dfrac{d \times d \times s \times n \times p}{2 \times D}$
where d is the cylinder bore, s the stroke, n the number of cylinders, p the mean effective pressure (= 85% of boiler pressure), D the driving wheel diameter; all dimensions in inches, tractive effort is in pounds
Adhesive Factor: — Locomotive adhesive weight divided by the Tractive Effort

Appendix C

Appendix C is on pages 335 to 360, and comprises a list of all the locomotive numbers issued to Nine Elms engines from 1835 to 1909. Several different engines often used the same number usually, but not always, at different times. Letters used at the head of each column are described below:

A   LSWR number
B   Either the sub-contractor's works number, or the Nine Elms order number
C   Locomotive class and type
D   Locomotive name, where carried
E   Person responsible for ordering the locomotive: WA – William Adams, JB – Joseph Beattie, WB – W.G. Beattie, DD – Dugald Drummond, JG – J.V. Gooch, JL – Joseph Locke, JW – Joseph Woods
F   Manufacturer
G   Date locomotive built
H   Date locomotive withdrawn from LSWR use
I   Further details of the locomotive's history

APPENDIX B

Locomotive Class	Build Date	Wheel Diameter (in)	Cylinder Stroke (in)	Cylinder Bore (in)	No of Cylinders	Heating Surface: Tubes (sq ft)	Heating Surface: Firebox (sq ft)	Heating Surface: Combustion Chamber (sq ft)	Grate area (sq ft)	Pressure (lb/sq in)	Locomotive Weight (tons)	Loco Adhesive Weight (tons)	Tractive Effort (lb)	Adhesive Factor
Sharp Roberts 2-2-2	6/1838	66	18	13	2	476	60		10.5		14.5			
Nasmyth, Gaskell 0-4-0	10/1838	66	18	12	2	495	59			50	12.8	12.8	1669	
Nine Elms Eagle 2-2-2	10/1843	78	21	14.3	2	639	74		9.4	75	17.0		3485	
Nine Elms Bison 0-6-0	12/1845	60	22	15.5	2	998	73		12.8	90	20.3	20.3	6739	6.73
Rothwell 2-2-2	12/1846	78	21	14.3	2					85	30.5		3950	
Nine Elms Mazeppa 2-2-2	3/1847	78	21	14.3	2	998	73		12.8	90	19.8		4182	
Stothert & Slaughter 2-2-2	12/1847	78	22	15	2					90	19.8		4855	
Nine Elms Etna 2-2-2	11/1850	84	20	15	2	998	73		12.8	100	24.5	9.25	4554	4.55
Nine Elms Canute 2-2-2	1/1856	78	21	15	2	725	97	47	16.0	120	26.7	10.6	6179	3.84
Nine Elms Hercules 2-4-0	6/1851	66	22	15	2	708	90		13.5	120	24.0	15.5	7650	4.54
Nine Elms Tartar 2-2-2	5/1852	72	20	14.3	2	708	73		10.5	120	26.4		5753	
Nine Elms Saxon 2-4-0	4/1855	60	24	15	2	967	114	88	15.5	120	29.2	19.4	9180	4.73
Nine Elms Minerva 2-4-0	5/1856	66	20	14.3	2	805	88		13.3	120	28.4		6276	
Nine Elms Tweed 2-4-0	12/1856	72	22	15	2	890	97	67	15.6	120	27.2	16.3	7013	5.19
Nine Elms Clyde 2-4-0	1/1859	84	22	16	2	890	98	67	15.6	120	27.2	16.3	6839	5.32
Nine Elms Undine 2-4-0	7/1859	78	22	15	2	890	99	67	15.6	120	28.6	18.8	6473	6.51
Nine Elms Eagle 2-4-0	7/1862	72	22	15.5	2	903	108		16.9	120	31.3	22.0	7488	6.58
Nine Elms Gem 2-4-0	12/1862	60	22	16	2	967	114	88	15.5	120	31.8	21.2	9574	4.96
Nine Elms Falcon 2-4-0	12/1862	78	22	15	2	903	108		16.9	120	31.7	22.1	6473	7.65
Beyer Peacock 2-4-0WT	2/1863	66	20	15	2	865.5	98.3		14.3	130	30.1	20.5	7534	6.08
Nine Elms Lion 0-6-0	10/1863	60	22	16.5	2	898	138		16.6	130	33.8	33.8	11031	6.85
Beyer Peacock D.F. 0-6-0	2/1866	60	24	17	2	1052	128		17.4	140	35.2	35.2	13756	5.72
Nine Elms 231 class 2-4-0	7/1866	72	22	16.5	2	927.5	120		17.7	130	33.9	23.9	9192	5.81
Nine Elms Volcano 2-4-0	12/1866	72	22	17	2	820	136		17.8	130	34.5	23.4	9758	5.37
Nine Elms Centaur 2-4-0	8/1868	84	22	17	2	1056	120		17.8	130	36.2	24.1	8364	6.45
Nine Elms Vesuvius 2-4-0	12/1869	78	22	17	2	820	136		17.8	130	35.3	23.4	9007	5.81
Beyer Peacock Ilfracombe 0-6-0	3/1873	54	20	16	2	749	69.5		14.0	130	23.8	23.8	10477	5.09
Beyer Peacock S.F. 0-6-0	7/1874	60	22	17	2	893	132		15.5	120	34.1	34.1	10809	7.07
Beyer Peacock Metro 4-4-0T	1/1875	69	24	17	2	896	96		17.4	120	45.8	32.9	10253	7.18
Beyer Peacock 330 class 0-6-0ST	5/1876	50	24	17	2	825	77		14.0	130	34.6	34.6	15329	5.05
Sharp Stewart 348 class 4-4-0	2/1877	79	26	18.5	2	890	106	40	17.9	140	43.5	27.2	13404	4.55
Beyer Peacock 46 class 4-4-0T	6/1879	67	24	18	2	900	83.8		16.0	160	52.8	36.8	15784	5.22
Beyer Peacock 380 class 4-4-0	9/1879	67	24	18	2	1036	90		17.0	160	45.8	29.3	15784	4.16
Beyer Peacock 135 class 4-4-0	11/1880	79	24	18	2	1112	104		17.8	160	46.5	28.7	13387	4.80
Neilson 395 class 0-6-0	11/1881	61	24	17.5	2	1080	97		17.8	140	37.6	37.6	14339	5.87
R. Stephenson 445 class 4-4-0	4/1883	85	24	18	2	1051	111		17.8	160	44.0	27.7	12442	4.98
R. Stephenson 415 class 4-4-2T	10/1883	67	24	17.5	2	949	104		18.3	160	54.9	27.8	14919	4.17
R. Stephenson 460 class 4-4-0	6/1884	79	24	18	2	1051	110		17.8	160	46.7	29.8	13387	4.98
Nine Elms A12 0-4-2	5/1887	73	26	18	2	1131	116		17.0	160	42.4	31.7	15694	4.52
Nine Elms O2 0-4-4T	12/1889	48	24	17	2	898	89		13.8	160	44.6	29.3	19652	3.34
Nine Elms X2 4-4-0	6/1890	85	26	19	2	1245	122		18.0	175	48.2	29.7	16426	4.04
Nine Elms T3 4-4-0	12/1892	79	26	19	2	1194	126		19.8	175	48.6	30.6	17673	3.87
Nine Elms B4 0-4-0T	11/1893	46	22	16	2	766	57		10.8	140	33.8	33.8	14649	5.16
Nine Elms T1 0-4-4T	4/1894	67	26	18	2	1121	110		17.0	160	53.0	35.2	17099	4.60
Nine Elms G6 0-6-0T	6/1894	48	26	17.5	2	898	89		13.8	160	45.2	45.2	22560	4.49
Nine Elms T6 4-4-0	9/1895	85	26	19	2	1194	126		19.8	175	50.1	31.7	16426	4.32
Nine Elms X6 4-4-0	12/1895	79	26	19	2	1194	126		19.8	175	49.7	31.5	17673	3.99
Nine Elms T7 4-2-2-0	8/1897	79	26	15	4	1307	142	215	27.4	175	54.6	37.7	22030	3.83
Nine Elms C8 4-4-0	6/1898	79	26	18.5	2	1067	124		20.4	175	46.8	31.7	16755	4.24
Nine Elms T9 4-4-0	6/1899	79	26	18.5	2	1187	148	138	24.0	175	46.2	32.2	16755	4.30
Nine Elms E10 4-2-2-0	4/1901	79	26	14	4	1344	156	190	27.4	175	49.0	39.9	19191	4.65
Nine Elms K10 4-4-0	11/1901	67	26	18.5	2	1068	124	100	20.4	175	46.7	32.6	19756	3.70
Nine Elms L11 4-4-0	5/1903	67	26	18.5	2	1187	148	165	24.0	175	50.6	35.5	19756	4.02
Nine Elms S11 4-4-0	6/1903	73	26	19	2	1222	163	165	24.0	175	52.0	35.0	19126	4.10
Nine Elms L12 4-4-0	6/1904	79	26	19	2	1222	163	165	24.0	175	54.0	37.1	17673	4.70
Nine Elms F13 4-6-0	9/1905	72	24	16	4	2210	160	357	31.5	175	76.7	56.1	25387	4.95
Nine Elms F14 4-6-0	11/1907	72	24	16	4	2210	161	357	31.5	175	77.9	56.4	25387	4.98
Nine Elms G14 4-6-0	4/1908	72	26	15	4	1580	140	200	31.5	175	71.0	50.7	24172	4.69

APPENDIX C

A	B	C	D	E	F	G	H	I
		0-4-0	Alpha		Thomas Banks & Co	7/1835	6/1839	Ballast engine, to stationary use 6/1839
	78	2-2-2	Deer	JW	C. Tayleur & Co	2/1839	1843	Damaged by Nine Elms fire 16/3/1841
			Defiant	JL	Jones, Turner & Evans			Ballast engine, no other information
	77	2-2-2	Eagle	JW	C. Tayleur & Co	1/1839	8/1842	Sold to William Fairburn & Sons 8/1842
		2-2-0	Falcon	JW	Nasmyth, Gaskell & Co	5/1839	7/1843	
		2-2-0	Hawk	JW	Nasmyth, Gaskell & Co	10/1838	1/1843	
		2-2-0	Lark	JW	Edward Bury	2/1839	3/1841	Destroyed by Nine Elms fire 16/3/1841
			London	JL	Jones, Turner & Evans	5/1837	11/1839	Ballast engine, sold to Thomas Brassey, Contractor
	79	2-2-2	Pegasus	JW	C. Tayleur & Co	4/1839	4/1842	Sold to William Fairburn & Sons 8/1842
		0-4-2	Perseverance	JL	Jones, Turner & Evans			Ballast engine, no other information
			Reed	JL	Jones, Turner & Evans	2/1838	11/1839	Ballast engine, sold to Thomas Brassey, Contractor
	80	2-2-2	Renown	JW	C. Tayleur & Co	6/1839	4/1842	Sold to William Fairburn & Sons 8/1842
			Sam Slick	JL	Jones, Turner & Evans			Ballast engine, no other information
			Shamrock	JL	Jones, Turner & Evans			Ballast engine, no other information
		0-4-2	Southampton	JL	Jones, Turner & Evans	11/1837	1/1839	Ballast engine, sold to Birmingham & Gloucester Railway
		0-4-0	St. George	JL	C. Tayleur & Co	1/1836	12/1837	Ballast engine, sold to David McIntosh, Contractor
	56	2-2-2	Thetis	JW	C. Tayleur & Co	7/1838	8/1842	Sold to William Fairburn & Sons 8/1842
	58	2-2-2	Tiger	JW	C. Tayleur & Co	9/1838	1843	Damaged by Nine Elms fire 16/3/1841
		2-2-0	Tramp	JL	Edward Bury	10/1836	1/1840	Ballast engine, sold to Thomas Brassey, Contractor
		0-4-2	Trio	JL	John Jones	1/1838		Ballast engine, no other information
		0-4-0	Vulture	JL	Murdoch Aitken & Co	3/1836		Ballast engine, no other information
1	55	2-2-2	Sussex	JW	C. Tayleur & Co	6/1838	9/1852	Rebuilt Nine Elms 1/1843
1		Sussex 2-2-2WT	Sussex	JB	Nine Elms	1/1852	9/1872	Duplicated 7/1870
1		Vesuvius 2-4-0	Sussex	JB	Nine Elms	7/1870	5/1898	Duplicated 4/1894
1	F6	T1 0-4-4T		WA	Nine Elms	4/1894	7/1949	
1	K11	K11 Railcar		DD	Nine Elms	4/1903	9/1919	Numbered in separate Joint Committee list, laid aside 8/1914
1	H12	H12 Railcar		DD	Nine Elms	5/1904	11/1916	Numbered in a separate railcar list, laid aside 8/1914
2	57	2-2-2	Tartar	JW	C. Tayleur & Co	8/1838	5/1852	Rebuilt Nine Elms 1/1843
2		Tartar 2-2-2WT	Tartar	JB	Sharp Brothers	5/1852	4/1873	Duplicated 12/1870
2		Vesuvius 2-4-0	Tartar	JB	Nine Elms	12/1870	3/1895	Duplicated 5/1894
2	F6	T1 0-4-4T		WA	Nine Elms	5/1894	2/1949	
2	K11	K11 Railcar		DD	Nine Elms	5/1903	9/1919	Numbered in a separate Joint Committee list, laid aside 8/1914
2	H12	H12 Railcar		DD	Nine Elms	6/1904	11/1916	Numbered in a separate railcar list, laid aside 8/1914
3	59	2-2-2	Transit	JW	C. Tayleur & Co	10/1838	10/1854	Rebuilt as 2-2-2WT 10/1854 No 3
3		2-2-2WT	Transit	JB	Nine Elms	10/1854	10/1872	Rebuild of Tayleur Engine No 3
3		Lion 0-6-0	Transit	JB	Nine Elms	6/1870	4/1897	Duplicated 5/1894
3	F6	T1 0-4-4T		WA	Nine Elms	5/1894	9/1948	
3	H13	H13 Railcar		DD	Nine Elms	10/1905	7/1919	Numbered in a separate railcar list
4	60	2-2-2	Locke	JW	C. Tayleur & Co	11/1838	3/1852	Rebuilt Nine Elms 1/1843
4		Sussex 2-2-2WT	Locke	JB	Nine Elms	2/1852	9/1873	Duplicated 12/1870
4		Vesuvius 2-4-0	Locke	JB	Nine Elms	12/1870	4/1895	Rebuilt Nine Elms 10/1888, duplicated 6/1894
4	F6	T1 0-4-4T		WA	Nine Elms	6/1894	8/1946	
4	H13	H13 Railcar		DD	Nine Elms	11/1905	7/1919	Numbered in a separate railcar list
5	81	2-2-2	Ganymede	JW	C. Tayleur & Co	9/1839	4/1855	Rebuilt Nine Elms 1/1843
5		Hercules 2-4-0	Ganymede	JB	Nine Elms	12/1854	12/1880	Duplicated 3/1873
5		Volcano 2-4-0	Ganymede	JB	Nine Elms	3/1873	5/1897	Duplicated 6/1894
5	F6	T1 0-4-4T		WA	Nine Elms	6/1894	1/1950	
5	H13	H13 Railcar		DD	Nine Elms	12/1905	11/1916	Numbered in a separate railcar list
6	82	2-2-2	Cossack	JW	C. Tayleur & Co	10/1839	10/1852	Rebuilt Nine Elms 1/1843
6		Sussex 2-2-2WT	Cossack	JB	Nine Elms	3/1852	6/1877	Duplicated 1/1871
6		Vesuvius 2-4-0	Cossack	JB	Nine Elms	1/1870	12/1895	Rebuilt Nine Elms 6/1886, duplicated 6/1894
6	F6	T1 0-4-4T		WA	Nine Elms	6/1894	11/1947	
6	H13	H13 Railcar		DD	Nine Elms	12/1905	11/1916	Numbered in a separate railcar list
7	2	2-2-2	Venus	JW	Sharp Roberts	6/1838	7/1871	Rebuilt at Nine Elms 11/1854
7		Lion 0-6-0	Venus	JB	Nine Elms	7/1870	2/1893	
7	F6	T1 0-4-4T		WA	Nine Elms	7/1894	5/1951	
7	H13	H13 Railcar		DD	Nine Elms	1/1906	11/1916	Numbered in a separate railcar list
8	8	2-2-2	Vesta	JW	Sharp Roberts	9/1838	8/1873	Rebuilt at Nine Elms 8/1854
8		Lion 0-6-0	Vesta	JB	Nine Elms	7/1870	3/1898	Duplicated 8/1894
8	F6	T1 0-4-4T		WA	Nine Elms	8/1894	5/1949	
8	H13	H13 Railcar		DD	Nine Elms	1/1906	11/1916	Numbered in a separate railcar list
9	5	2-2-2	Chaplin	JW	Sharp Roberts	7/1838	2/1855	
9		Chaplin 2-2-2WT	Chaplin	JB	Nine Elms	7/1856	8/1877	Duplicated 12/1870
9		Lion 0-6-0	Chaplin	JB	Nine Elms	12/1870	3/1893	
9	F6	T1 0-4-4T		WA	Nine Elms	8/1894	7/1948	
9	H13	H13 Railcar		DD	Nine Elms	2/1906	11/1916	Numbered in a separate railcar list
10	11	2-2-2	Aurora	JW	Sharp Roberts	10/1838	2/1856	
10		Chaplin 2-2-2WT	Aurora	JB	Nine Elms	7/1856	1/1871	
10		Lion 0-6-0	Aurora	JB	Nine Elms	1/1871	4/1897	Duplicated 8/1894
10	F6	T1 0-4-4T		WA	Nine Elms	8/1894	9/1948	
10	H13	H13 Railcar		DD	Nine Elms	3/1906	7/1919	Numbered in a separate railcar list
11	1	2-2-2	Minerva	JW	Sharp Roberts	6/1838	8/1850	Rebuilt as 2-2-2WT No 11 9/1850

APPENDIX C

A	B	C	D	E	F	G	H	I
11		2-2-2WT	Minerva	JB	Nine Elms	9/1850	8/1856	Rebuild of Sharp Roberts engine No 11
11		Minerva 2-4-0WT	Minerva	JB	Nine Elms	5/1856	9/1883	Duplicated 3/1873
11		Volcano 2-4-0	Minerva	JB	Nine Elms	3/1873	4/1889	
11	S6	T1 0-4-4T		WA	Nine Elms	6/1895	7/1944	
11	H13	H13 Railcar		DD	Nine Elms	3/1906	11/1916	Numbered in a separate railcar list
12	18	2-2-2	Jupiter	JW	Sharp Roberts	12/1838	4/1852	
12		Tartar 2-2-2WT	Jupiter	JB	Sharp Brothers	6/1852	2/1872	Duplicated 2/1871
12		Lion 0-6-0	Jupiter	JB	Nine Elms	2/1871	6/1898	Duplicated 6/1895
12	S6	T1 0-4-4T		WA	Nine Elms	6/1895	1/1933	
12	A14	H13 Railcar		DD	Nine Elms	5/1906	11/1916	Numbered in a separate railcar list
13	13	2-2-2	Orion	JW	Sharp Roberts	12/1838	3/1852	
13		Tartar 2-2-2WT	Orion	JB	Sharp Brothers	6/1852	4/1872	Duplicated 7/1871
13		Lion 0-6-0	Orion	JB	Nine Elms	7/1871	7/1899	Duplicated 6/1895
13	S6	T1 0-4-4T		WA	Nine Elms	6/1895	2/1949	
13	A14	H13 Railcar		DD	Nine Elms	5/1906	11/1916	Numbered in a separate railcar list
14	21	2-2-2	Mercury	JW	Sharp Roberts	12/1838	4/1852	
14		Sussex 2-2-2WT	Mercury	JB	Nine Elms	4/1852	10/1871	Duplicated 7/1870
14		Vesuvius 2-4-0	Mercury	JB	Nine Elms	8/1870	6/1898	Rebuilt Nine Elms 1/1895, duplicated 6/1895
14	S6	T1 0-4-4T		WA	Nine Elms	6/1895	7/1933	
14	B14	H13 Railcar		DD	Nine Elms	6/1906	11/1916	Numbered in a separate railcar list
15	16	2-2-2	Mars	JW	Sharp Roberts	12/1838	2/1852	
15		Sussex 2-2-2WT	Mars	JB	Nine Elms	5/1852	11/1873	Duplicated 8/1870
15		Vesuvius 2-4-0	Mars	JB	Nine Elms	8/1870	11/1898	Duplicated 7/1895
15	S6	T1 0-4-4T		WA	Nine Elms	7/1895	7/1944	
15	B14	H13 Railcar		DD	Nine Elms	6/1906	11/1916	Numbered in a separate railcar list
16		Summers 2-2-0	Southampton	JW	Summers, Groves & Day	8/1839	see 176	Rebuilt Fairburn 12/1844, Nine Elms 8/1859, renumbered No 176
16		Minerva 2-4-0WT	Salisbury	JB	Nine Elms	6/1856	8/1877	Duplicated 8/1872
16		Lion 0-6-0	Stonehenge	JB	Nine Elms	6/1872	4/1899	Duplicated 8/1895
16	S6	T1 0-4-4T		WA	Nine Elms	8/1895	1/1946	
17		2-2-2	Queen	JG	William Fairburn & Sons	10/1841	12/1851	
17		Tartar 2-2-2WT	Queen	JB	Sharp Brothers	7/1852	5/1874	Duplicated 12/1871
17		Vesuvius 2-4-0	Queen	JB	Nine Elms	12/1871	1/1898	Duplicated 9/1895
17	S6	T1 0-4-4T		WA	Nine Elms	9/1895	1/1945	
18		2-2-2	Albert	JG	William Fairburn & Sons	11/1841	2/1852	
18		Tartar 2-2-2WT	Albert	JB	Sharp Brothers	7/1852	7/1871	
18		Vesuvius 2-4-0	Albert	JB	Nine Elms	7/1871	12/1893	Rebuilt Nine Elms 10/1886
18	S6	T1 0-4-4T		WA	Nine Elms	9/1895	5/1935	
19		2-2-2	Briton	JG	William Fairburn & Sons	12/1841	6/1852	
19		Sussex 2-2-2WT	Briton	JB	Nine Elms	6/1852	4/1876	Duplicated 7/1871
19		Vesuvius 2-4-0	Briton	JB	Nine Elms	7/1871	7/1899	Duplicated 11/1895
19	S6	T1 0-4-4T		WA	Nine Elms	11/1895	11/1937	
20		2-2-2	Princess	JG	William Fairburn & Sons	1/1842	3/1852	
20		Sussex 2-2-2WT	Princess	JB	Nine Elms	6/1852	12/1871	Duplicated 6/1871
20		Vesuvius 2-4-0	Princess	JB	Nine Elms	7/1871	2/1894	
20	S6	T1 0-4-4T		WA	Nine Elms	11/1895	5/1951	
21		2-2-2	Prince	JG	William Fairburn & Sons	2/1842	12/1852	
21		Hercules 2-4-0	Prince	JB	Nine Elms	4/1853	6/1883	Duplicated 12/1871
21		Vesuvius 2-4-0	Prince	JB	Nine Elms	12/1871	3/1898	Rebuilt Nine Elms 1/1886
21	B12	M7 0-4-4T		DD	Nine Elms	1/1904	3/1964	
22		2-2-2	Giraffe	JW	G. & J. Rennie	6/1838	9/1871	Rebuilt William Fairburn & Sons 4/1842, and Nine Elms 7/1855
22		Lion 0-6-0	Giraffe	JB	Nine Elms	7/1871	12/1891	
22	E9	M7 0-4-4T		DD	Nine Elms	1/1899	5/1958	
23		2-2-2	Antelope	JW	G. & J. Rennie	7/1838	11/1871	Rebuilt William Fairburn & Sons 1842, and Nine Elms 10/1855
23		Lion 0-6-0	Antelope	JB	Nine Elms	11/1871	6/1898	
23	E9	M7 0-4-4T		DD	Nine Elms	1/1899	10/1961	
24		2-2-2	Elk	JW	G. & J. Rennie	9/1838	7/1871	Rebuilt William Fairburn & Sons 10/1841, and Nine Elms 2/1856
24		Lion 0-6-0	Elk	JB	Nine Elms	12/1871	12/1889	
24	E9	M7 0-4-4T		DD	Nine Elms	1/1899	3/1963	
25		2-2-2	Reindeer	JW	G. & J. Rennie	10/1838	1/1872	Rebuilt William Fairburn & Sons 1842, and Nine Elms 11/1856
25		Volcano 2-4-0	Reindeer	JB	Nine Elms	7/1872	12/1892	
25	E9	M7 0-4-4T		DD	Nine Elms	2/1899	5/1964	
26		2-2-2	Gazelle	JW	G. & J. Rennie	11/1838	8/1854	Rebuilt by William Fairburn & Sons 1842
26		Hercules 2-4-0	Gazelle	JB	Nine Elms	6/1854	4/1885	Duplicated 7/1872
26		Volcano 2-4-0	Gazelle	JB	Nine Elms	7/1872	9/1894	
26	E9	M7 0-4-4T		DD	Nine Elms	2/1899	5/1959	
27		Eagle 2-2-2	Eagle	JG	Nine Elms	10/1843	1862	
27		Eagle 2-4-0	Eagle	JB	Nine Elms	7/1862	1/1887	Duplicated 11/1885
27	3453	395 class 0-6-0		WA	Nielson & Co	11/1885	3/1917	Duplicated 1/1904
27	B12	M7 0-4-4T		DD	Nine Elms	1/1904	11/1959	
28		Eagle 2-2-2	Hawk	JG	Nine Elms	3/1844	10/1862	
28		Eagle 2-4-0	Hawk	JB	Nine Elms	9/1862	3/1887	Duplicated 11/1885
28	3454	395 class 0-6-0		WA	Nielson & Co	11/1885	3/1917	Duplicated 1/1904

APPENDIX C

A	B	C	D	E	F	G	H	I
28	B12	M7 0-4-4T		DD	Nine Elms	1/1904	9/1962	
29		Eagle 2-2-2	Falcon	JG	Nine Elms	6/1844	5/1863	
29		Falcon 2-4-0	Falcon	JB	Nine Elms	12/1862	2/1885	Duplicated 11/1885
29	3455	395 class 0-6-0		WA	Nielson & Co	11/1885	4/1958	Duplicated 2/1904
29	B12	M7 0-4-4T		DD	Nine Elms	2/1904	5/1964	
30		Eagle 2-2-2	Vulture	JG	Nine Elms	7/1844	1862	
30		Eagle 2-4-0	Vulture	JB	Nine Elms	11/1862	12/1886	Duplicated 12/1885
30	3456	395 class 0-6-0		WA	Nielson & Co	12/1885	4/1917	Duplicated 2/1904
30	B12	M7 0-4-4T		DD	Nine Elms	3/1904	10/1959	
31		2-2-2	Leeds	JW	Fenton, Murray & Jackson	7/1839	10/1853	
31		Hercules 2-4-0	Leeds	JB	Nine Elms	7/1852	6/1884	Duplicated 3/1873
31		Volcano 2-4-0	Leeds	JB	Nine Elms	3/1873	12/1897	
31	V7	M7 0-4-4T		DD	Nine Elms	3/1898	5/1963	
32		2-2-2	Eclipse	JW	Fenton, Murray & Jackson	7/1839	10/1852	
32		Hercules 2-4-0	Eclipse	JB	Nine Elms	4/1853	3/1880	Duplicated 7/1873
32		Vesuvius 2-4-0	Eclipse	JB	Nine Elms	7/1873	12/1893	
32	V7	M7 0-4-4T		DD	Nine Elms	3/1898	7/1963	
33		2-2-2	Phoenix	JW	Fenton, Murray & Jackson	4/1840	9/1851	
33		Tartar 2-2-2WT	Phoenix	JB	Sharp Brothers	7/1852	3/1873	Duplicated 2/1872
33		Standard 2-4-0WT	Phoenix	JB	Nine Elms	11/1871	10/1890	
33	V7	M7 0-4-4T		DD	Nine Elms	4/1898	12/1962	
34		2-2-2	Crescent	JW	Fenton, Murray & Jackson	8/1840	3/1852	Rebuilt as 2-2-2WT No 34 3/1852
34		2-2-2WT	Crescent	JB	Nine Elms	3/1852	3/1856	Rebuilt from 2-2-2 No 34 3/1852
34		Chaplin 2-2-2WT	Osprey	JB	Nine Elms	8/1856	8/1877	Duplicated 5/1874
34	1411	Standard 2-4-0WT	Osprey	JB	Beyer Peacock & Co	6/1874	11/1895	
34	V7	M7 0-4-4T		DD	Nine Elms	4/1898	2/1963	
35	41	2-2-2	Vivid	JW	Rothwell & Co	7/1839	12/1853	
35		Hercules 2-4-0	Vivid	JB	Nine Elms	8/1854	11/1880	Duplicated 6/1873
35		Vesuvius 2-4-0	Vivid	JB	Nine Elms	6/1873	12/1895	Rebuilt Nine Elms 10/1891
35	V7	M7 0-4-4T		DD	Nine Elms	4/1898	2/1963	
36	42	2-2-2	Comet	JW	Rothwell & Co	7/1839	7/1851	
36		Sussex 2-2-2WT	Comet	JB	Nine Elms	7/1852	6/1872	Duplicated 2/1872, hired to IoW Railway 6/1872 to 7/1875 then sold
36		Standard 2-4-0WT	Comet	JB	Nine Elms	12/1871	12/1894	
36	V7	M7 0-4-4T		DD	Nine Elms	5/1898	1/1964	
37	43	2-2-2	Arab	JW	Rothwell & Co	9/1839	2/1853	
37		Hercules 2-4-0	Arab	JB	Nine Elms	6/1853	6/1880	Duplicated 2/1874
37		Vesuvius 2-4-0	Arab	JB	Nine Elms	2/1874	5/1898	
37	V7	M7 0-4-4T		DD	Nine Elms	5/1898	5/1958	
38	44	2-2-2	Vizier	JW	Rothwell & Co	9/1839	10/1851	Rebuilt as 2-2-2WT No 38 3/1852
38		2-2-2WT	Vizier	JB	Nine Elms	3/1852	9/1871	Rebuilt from 2-2-2 No 38 3/1852
38		Lion 0-6-0	Vizier	JB	Nine Elms	6/1871	7/1899	Duplicated 6/1898
38	V7	M7 0-4-4T		DD	Nine Elms	5/1898	3/1958	
39	45	2-2-2	Wizard	JW	Rothwell & Co	11/1839	4/1855	
39		Minerva 2-2-2WT	Wizard	JB	Nine Elms	7/1856	4/1880	Duplicated 2/1874
39		Vesuvius 2-4-0	Wizard	JB	Nine Elms	2/1874	12/1897	Rebuilt Nine Elms 5/1887
39	V7	M7 0-4-4T		DD	Nine Elms	5/1898	3/1963	
40		2-2-0	Garnett (Fly)	JW	Summers, Groves & Day	6/1839	2/1851	
40		Hercules 2-4-0	Windsor	JB	Nine Elms	7/1852	5/1884	Duplicated 2/1874
40		Vesuvius 2-4-0	Windsor	JB	Nine Elms	12/1873	1/1899	Rebuilt Nine Elms 12/1887, duplicated 6/1898
40	V7	M7 0-4-4T		DD	Nine Elms	6/1898	6/1961	
41		0-4-2	Ajax	JG	Jones, Turner & Evans	11/1841	10/1855	Sold 10/1855 to Horner & Molesworth
41		Hercules 2-4-0	Ajax	JB	Nine Elms	3/1855	7/1883	Duplicated 1/1875
41		Vesuvius 2-4-0	Ajax	JB	Nine Elms	12/1874	4/1897	
41	E9	M7 0-4-4T		DD	Nine Elms	3/1899	8/1957	
42		0-4-2	Atlas	JG	Jones, Turner & Evans	12/1841	9/1852	Sold to Bodmin & Wadebridge Railway 9/1852
42		Hercules 2-4-0	Atlas	JB	Nine Elms	11/1852	6/1883	Duplicated 6/1883
42		Vesuvius 2-4-0	Atlas	JB	Nine Elms	1/1875	4/1897	Duplicated 1/1875
42	E9	M7 0-4-4T		DD	Nine Elms	3/1898	6/1957	
43		0-4-2	Milo	JG	Sharp Roberts	11/1841	12/1850	To store, Northam, scrapped 1851
43		Hercules 2-4-0	Milo	JB	Nine Elms	12/1851	5/1880	Duplicated 1/1875
43		Vesuvius 2-4-0	Milo	JB	Nine Elms	1/1875	7/1898	
43	E9	M7 0-4-4T		DD	Nine Elms	3/1898	6/1961	
44		0-4-2	Pluto	JG	Sharp Roberts	12/1841	12/1854	Sold to Bodmin & Wadebridge Railway 12/1854
44		Hercules 2-4-0	Pluto	JB	Nine Elms	11/1854	2/1884	Duplicated 10/1875
44	1533	Standard 2-4-0WT	(Pluto)	JB	Beyer Peacock & Co	10/1875	11/1898	
44	E9	M7 0-4-4T		DD	Nine Elms	3/1898	9/1961	
45		0-4-2	Titan	JG	Sharp Roberts	2/1842	10/1855	Sold 10/1855 to Horner & Molesworth
45		Tweed 2-4-0	Titan	JB	Nine Elms	12/1856	5/1880	
45	2507	0415 class 4-4-2T			Robert Stephenson & Co	10/1883	12/1924	Duplicated 4/1905
45	X12	M7 0-4-4T		DD	Nine Elms	5/1905	12/1962	
46		0-4-2	Minos	JG	Sharp Roberts	2/1842	12/1850	To store, Northam, scrapped 1851
46		Hercules 2-4-0	Minos	JB	Nine Elms	9/1851	3/1875	

337

APPENDIX C

Fig. 433. Drummond C8 class 4-4-0 No 294 in the camp of the rival at Exeter St. Davids, circa 1904. The driver has clearly ignored the long time exposure necessary as both his legs and the framing of the engine can be seen.

(Roger Carpenter)

APPENDIX C

A	B	C	D	E	F	G	H	I
85	B4	B4 0-4-0T	Alderney	WA	Nine Elms	10/1891	1/1949	To Southampton Docks and named 4/1900
86		Rothwell 2-2-2	Shark	JG	Rothwell & Co	11/1847	3/1865	
86		Falcon 2-4-0	Shark	JB	Nine Elms	7/1867	1/1895	Duplicated 12/1891
86	B4	B4 0-4-0T	Havre	WA	Nine Elms	12/1891	3/1959	To Southampton Docks 2/1896
87		Rothwell 2-2-2	Stentor	JG	Rothwell & Co	11/1847	7/1866	
87		Falcon 2-4-0	Stentor	JB	Nine Elms	8/1867	5/1890	
87	B4	B4 0-4-0T		WA	Nine Elms	12/1891	12/1958	
88		Rothwell 2-2-2	Sirius	JG	Rothwell & Co	12/1847	11/1867	
88		Falcon 2-4-0	Sirius	JB	Nine Elms	10/1867	12/1895	Duplicated 10/1892
88	B4	B4 0-4-0T		WA	Nine Elms	10/1892	7/1959	
89		Rothwell 2-2-2	Saturn	JG	Rothwell & Co	12/1847	6/1865	
89		Volcano 2-4-0	Saturn	JB	Nine Elms	12/1867	10/1894	Duplicated 11/1892
89	B4	B4 0-4-0T	Trouville	WA	Nine Elms	11/1892	3/1963	To Southampton Docks and named 3/1901
90		Rothwell 2-2-2	Sybil	JG	Rothwell & Co	12/1847	4/1866	
90		Volcano 2-4-0	Sybil	JB	Nine Elms	1/1868	12/1892	
90	B4	B4 0-4-0T	Caen	WA	Nine Elms	11/1892	5/1948	To Southampton Docks and named 3/1901
91		Rothwell 2-2-2	Spitfire	JG	Rothwell & Co	1/1848	1/1868	
91		Volcano 2-4-0	Spitfire	JB	Nine Elms	2/1868	5/1886	
91	B4	B4 0-4-0T		WA	Nine Elms	11/1892	8/1948	
92		Rothwell 2-2-2	Charon	JG	Rothwell & Co	1/1848	6/1868	
92		Lion 0-6-0	Charon	JB	Nine Elms	5/1867	6/1906	Duplicated 12/1892
92	B4	B4 0-4-0T		WA	Nine Elms	12/1892	4/1949	
93		Rothwell 2-2-2	Cyclops	JG	Rothwell & Co	5/1848	12/1866	
93		Lion 0-6-0	Cyclops	JB	Nine Elms	5/1867	8/1892	
93	B4	B4 0-4-0T	St. Malo	WA	Nine Elms	12/1892	4/1960	To Southampton Docks and named 4/1896
94		Rothwell 2-2-2	Camilla	JG	Rothwell & Co	5/1848	4/1869	
94		Lion 0-6-0	Camilla	JB	Nine Elms	6/1867	4/1897	Duplicated 12/1892
94	B4	B4 0-4-0T		WA	Nine Elms	12/1892	3/1957	
95		Rothwell 2-2-2	Centaur	JG	Rothwell & Co	5/1848	4/1869	
95		Centaur 2-4-0	Centaur	JB	Nine Elms	8/1868	12/1895	Duplicated 11/1893
95	D6	B4 0-4-0T	Honfleur	WA	Nine Elms	11/1893	4/1949	To Southampton Docks and named 2/1896
96		Rothwell 2-2-2	Castor	JG	Rothwell & Co	5/1848	12/1867	
96		Centaur 2-4-0	Castor	JB	Nine Elms	8/1868	10/1894	Duplicated 11/1893
96	D6	B4 0-4-0T	Normandy	WA	Nine Elms	11/1893	10/1963	To Southampton Docks and named 12/1893
97		Rothwell 2-2-2	Pegasus	JG	Rothwell & Co	8/1848	5/1866	
97		Centaur 2-4-0	Pegasus	JB	Nine Elms	9/1868	6/1898	Duplicated 11/1893
97	D6	B4 0-4-0T	Brittany	WA	Nine Elms	11/1893	2/1949	To Southampton Docks and named 12/1893
98		Rothwell 2-2-2	Plutus	JG	Rothwell & Co	8/1848	10/1867	
98		Centaur 2-4-0	Plutus	JB	Nine Elms	9/1868	5/1898	Duplicated 11/1893
98	D6	B4 0-4-0T	Cherbourg	WA	Nine Elms	11/1893	2/1949	To Southampton Docks and named 5/1900
99		Rothwell 2-2-2	Phlegon	JG	Rothwell & Co	9/1848	4/1869	
99		Centaur 2-4-0	Phlegon	JB	Nine Elms	9/1868	5/1899	Duplicated 12/1893
99	D6	B4 0-4-0T		WA	Nine Elms	12/1893	2/1949	
100		Rothwell 2-2-2	Python	JG	Rothwell & Co	9/1848	7/1868	
100		Centaur 2-4-0	Python	JB	Nine Elms	10/1868	2/1899	Duplicated 12/1893
100	D6	B4 0-4-0T		WA	Nine Elms	12/1893	2/1949	
101		Bison 0-6-0	Lion	JG	Nine Elms	6/1848	1/1864	
101		Lion 0-6-0	Lion	JB	Nine Elms	12/1863	12/1887	
101	3459	395 class 0-6-0		WA	Nielson & Co	12/1885	2/1959	Duplicated 4/1908
101	K14	B4 0-4-0T	Dinan	WA	Nine Elms	4/1908	11/1948	Was No 746 until 2/1922, to Southampton Docks and named 11/1893
102		Bison 0-6-0	Lioness	JG	Nine Elms	7/1848	7/1866	
102		Lion 0-6-0	Lioness	JB	Nine Elms	1/1864	5/1887	
102	D6	B4 0-4-0T	Granville	WA	Nine Elms	12/1893	9/1963	To Southampton Docks and named 4/1896
103		Bison 0-6-0	Tiger	JG	Nine Elms	8/1848	1/1864	
103		Lion 0-6-0	Tiger	JB	Nine Elms	1/1864	7/1887	
103	D6	B4 0-4-0T		WA	Nine Elms	12/1893	5/1949	
104		Bison 0-6-0	Tigress	JG	Nine Elms	9/1848	5/1865	Rebuilt as Lion class No 104 5/1865
104		Lion 0-6-0	Tigress	JB	Nine Elms	5/1865	4/1882	Rebuilt from Bison class No 104 5/1865
104	2905	415 class 4-4-2T		WA	Robert Stephenson & Co	7/1885	11/1921	Duplicated 4/1905
104	X12	M7 0-4-4T		DD	Nine Elms	4/1905	5/1961	
105		Bison 0-6-0	Leopard	JG	Nine Elms	10/1848	10/1863	Rebuilt as Lion class No 105 10/1863
105		Lion 0-6-0	Leopard	JB	Nine Elms	10/1863	9/1886	Rebuilt from Bison class No 105 10/1863
105	3460	395 class 0-6-0		WA	Nielson & Co	12/1885	4/1918	Duplicated 4/1905
105	X12	M7 0-4-4T		DD	Nine Elms	4/1905	6/1963	
106		Bison 0-6-0	Panther	JG	Nine Elms	11/1848	12/1865	Rebuilt as Lion class No 106 12/1865
106		Lion 0-6-0	Panther	JB	Nine Elms	12/1865	6/1885	Rebuilt from Bison class No 106 12/1865
106	2606	415 class 4-4-2T		WA	Robert Stephenson & Co	8/1885	3/1923	Duplicated 3/1905
106	X12	M7 0-4-4T		DD	Nine Elms	4/1905	11/1960	
107		Stothert 2-2-2	Gem	JG	Stothert & Slaughter	12/1847	5/1862	
107		Gem 2-4-0	Gem	JB	Nine Elms	12/1862	11/1885	
107	2607	415 class 4-4-2T		WA	Robert Stephenson & Co	9/1885	11/1921	Duplicated 5/1905
107	X12	M7 0-4-4T		DD	Nine Elms	5/1905	3/1964	

APPENDIX C

A	B	C	D	E	F	G	H	I
108		Stothert 2-2-2	Ruby	JG	Stothert & Slaughter	12/1847	12/1864	
108		Lion 0-6-0	Ruby	JB	Nine Elms	1/1869	10/1894	
108	C12	M7 0-4-4T		DD	Nine Elms	3/1904	5/1964	
109		Christie 2-2-2	Rocklia	JG	Christie, Adams & Hill	10/1848	3/1869	
109		Lion 0-6-0	Rocklia	JB	Nine Elms	2/1869	3/1898	
109	C12	M7 0-4-4T		DD	Nine Elms	3/1904	7/1961	
110		Christie 2-2-2	Avon	JG	Christie, Adams & Hill	12/1848	4/1868	
110		Lion 0-6-0	Avon	JB	Nine Elms	2/1869	4/1897	
110	C12	M7 0-4-4T		DD	Nine Elms	3/1904	5/1963	
111		Christie 2-2-2	Test	JG	Christie, Adams & Hill	2/1849	3/1870	
111		Lion 0-6-0	Test	JB	Nine Elms	1/1869	7/1899	
111	C12	M7 0-4-4T		DD	Nine Elms	4/1904	1/1964	
112		Christie 2-2-2	Trent	JG	Christie, Adams & Hill	3/1849	4/1869	
112		Lion 0-6-0	Trent	JB	Nine Elms	2/1869	5/1900	
112	B10	M7 0-4-4T		DD	Nine Elms	7/1900	2/1963	
113		Christie 2-2-2	Stour	JG	Christie, Adams & Hill	5/1849	11/1866	
113		Lion 0-6-0	Stour	JB	Nine Elms	2/1869	8/1898	
113	G9	T9 4-4-0		DD	Nine Elms	6/1899	5/1951	
114		Christie 2-2-2	Frome	JG	Christie, Adams & Hill	12/1849	7/1868	
114		Volcano 2-4-0	Frome	JB	Nine Elms	7/1869	8/1894	
114	G9	T9 4-4-0		DD	Nine Elms	6/1899	5/1951	
115		Etna 2-2-2	Vulcan	JG	Nine Elms	11/1850	3/1871	Duplicated 1/1869
115		Volcano 2-4-0	Vulcan	JB	Nine Elms	8/1869	9/1894	
115	G9	T9 4-4-0		DD	Nine Elms	7/1899	5/1951	
116		Etna 2-2-2	Stromboli	JG	Nine Elms	5/1851	5/1880	Duplicated 1/1869
116		Volcano 2-4-0	Stromboli	JB	Nine Elms	8/1869	6/1898	
116	G9	T9 4-4-0		DD	Nine Elms	7/1899	4/1951	
117		Etna 2-2-2	Volcano	JG	Nine Elms	8/1851	6/1870	Duplicated 6/1869
117		Volcano 2-4-0	Volcano	JB	Nine Elms	8/1869	2/1895	
117	G9	T9 4-4-0		DD	Nine Elms	7/1899	7/1961	
118		Etna 2-2-2	Etna	JG	Nine Elms	3/1850	3/1880	Duplicated 8/1872
118		Volcano 2-4-0	Etna	JB	Nine Elms	8/1872	6/1892	
118	G9	T9 4-4-0		DD	Nine Elms	7/1899	5/1951	
119		Etna 2-2-2	Vesuvius	JG	Nine Elms	10/1851	4/1870	
119		Vesuvius 2-4-0	Vesuvius	JB	Nine Elms	12/1869	12/1898	
119	G9	T9 4-4-0		DD	Nine Elms	8/1899	12/1952	
120		Etna 2-2-2	Hecla	JG	Nine Elms	5/1852	5/1872	Duplicated 1/1870
120		Lion 0-6-0	Hecla	JB	Nine Elms	1/1870	3/1899	
120	G9	T9 4-4-0		DD	Nine Elms	8/1899	7/1963	
121		Etna 2-2-2	St. George	JG	Nine Elms	1/1853	3/1870	
121		Vesuvius 2-4-0	St. George	JB	Nine Elms	12/1869	2/1898	
121	G9	T9 4-4-0		DD	Nine Elms	9/1899	4/1951	
122		Etna 2-2-2	Britannia	JG	Nine Elms	4/1853	4/1870	
122		Vesuvius 2-4-0	Britannia	JB	Nine Elms	12/1869	12/1895	
122	G9	T9 4-4-0		DD	Nine Elms	9/1899	3/1951	
123		Etna 2-2-2	The Duke	JG	Nine Elms	10/1853	2/1878	
123	1833	46 class 4-4-0T		WA	Beyer Peacock & Co	6/1879	1/1886	Rebuilt as 4-4-2T No 123 1/1886
123	1833	46 class 4-4-2T		WA	Nine Elms	1/1886	11/1921	Rebuilt from 4-4-0T No 123 1/1886, duplicated 2/1903
123	G11	M7 0-4-4T		DD	Nine Elms	2/1903	7/1959	
124		Saxon 2-4-0	Saxon	JB	Nine Elms	4/1855	11/1877	
124	1834	46 class 4-4-0T		WA	Beyer Peacock & Co	6/1879	3/1883	Rebuilt as 4-4-2T No 124 3/1883
124	1834	46 class 4-4-2T		WA	Nine Elms	3/1883	11/1921	Rebuilt from 4-4-0T No 124 3/1883, duplicated 2/1903
124	G11	M7 0-4-4T		DD	Nine Elms	2/1903	5/1961	
125		Saxon 2-4-0	Norman	JB	Nine Elms	4/1855	1/1885	
125	2608	415 class 4-4-2T		WA	Robert Stephenson & Co	9/1885	7/1961	Duplicated 7/1911
125	X14	M7 0-4-4T		DD	Nine Elms	8/1911	12/1962	
126		Saxon 2-4-0	Dane	JB	Nine Elms	5/1855	9/1883	
126	2609	415 class 4-4-2T		WA	Robert Stephenson & Co	9/1885	12/1924	Duplicated 8/1911
126	X14	M7 0-4-4T		DD	Nine Elms	9/1911	5/1937	
127		Saxon 2-4-0	Goliath	JB	Nine Elms	5/1855	4/1881	
127	2125	330 class 0-6-0ST		WB	Beyer Peacock & Co	5/1882	12/1925	Duplicated 9/1911
127	X14	M7 0-4-4T		DD	Nine Elms	9/1911	11/1963	
128		Saxon 2-4-0	Samson	JB	Nine Elms	6/1855	3/1881	
128	2126	330 class 0-6-0ST		WB	Beyer Peacock & Co	5/1882	7/1931	Duplicated 9/1911
128	X14	M7 0-4-4T		DD	Nine Elms	9/1911	1/1961	
129		Saxon 2-4-0	Albion	JB	Nine Elms	6/1855	7/1885	
129	2610	415 class 4-4-2T		WA	Robert Stephenson & Co	10/1885	5/1924	Duplicated 10/1911
129	X14	M7 0-4-4T		DD	Nine Elms	10/1911	11/1963	
130		Canute 2-2-2	Harold	JB	Nine Elms	1/1856	12/1880	
130	1835	46 class 4-4-0T		WA	Beyer Peacock & Co	7/1879	6/1885	Rebuilt as 4-4-2T No 130 6/1885
130	1835	46 class 4-4-2T		WA	Nine Elms	6/1885	5/1924	Rebuilt from 4-4-0T No 130 6/1885, duplicated 2/1903
130	G11	M7 0-4-4T		DD	Nine Elms	2/1903	12/1959	

APPENDIX C

A	B	C	D	E	F	G	H	I
46	1832	46 class 4-4-0T		WA	Beyer Peacock & Co	6/1879	4/1924	Rebuilt as 4-4-2T No 46 4/1886
46	1832	46 class 4-4-2T		WA	Nine Elms	4/1886	4/1924	Rebuilt from 4-4-0T No 46 4/1886, duplicated 4/1905
46	Y12	M7 0-4-4T		DD	Nine Elms	5/1905	2/1959	
47		2-2-0	Raven	JG	Nasmyth, Gaskell & Co	8/1839	6/1844	To stationary use, sold for scrap 10/1852
47		Hercules 2-4-0	Taurus	JB	Nine Elms	10/1851	6/1882	
47	2508	0415 class 4-4-2T		WA	Robert Stephenson & Co	10/1883	11/1921	Duplicated 4/1905
47	Y12	M7 0-4-4T		DD	Nine Elms	5/1905	2/1960	
48		0-4-2	Hercules	JG	Jones, Turner & Evans	9/1840	12/1850	To store, Northam, scrapped 1851
48		Hercules 2-4-0	Hercules	JB	Nine Elms	6/1851	10/1883	
48	2509	0415 class 4-4-2T		WA	Robert Stephenson & Co	10/1883	11/1921	Duplicated 4/1905
48	Y12	M7 0-4-4T		DD	Nine Elms	6/1905	1/1964	
49		Bison 0-6-0	Bison	JG	Nine Elms	12/1845	10/1863	Rebuilt as Lion class No 49 10/1863
49		Lion 0-6-0	Bison	JB	Nine Elms	10/1863	6/1885	Rebuilt from Bison class No 49 10/1863, duplicated 10/1883
49	2510	0415 class 4-4-2T		WA	Robert Stephenson & Co	10/1883	10/1921	Duplicated 4/1905
49	Y12	M7 0-4-4T		DD	Nine Elms	6/1905	6/1962	
50		Bison 0-6-0	Buffalo	JG	Nine Elms	3/1846	8/1871	
50		Lion 0-6-0	Buffalo	JB	Nine Elms	4/1865	1/1886	Duplicated 11/1883
50	2511	0415 class 4-4-2T		WA	Robert Stephenson & Co	11/1883	12/1927	Duplicated 5/1905
50	Y12	M7 0-4-4T		DD	Nine Elms	6/1905	1/1962	
51		Bison 0-6-0	Elephant	JG	Nine Elms	5/1846	12/1863	Rebuilt as Lion class No 51 12/1863
51		Lion 0-6-0	Elephant	JB	Nine Elms	12/1863	1/1886	Rebuilt from Bison class No 51 12/1863, duplicated 11/1883
51	2512	0415 class 4-4-2T		WA	Robert Stephenson & Co	11/1883	11/1921	Duplicated 10/1905
51	B13	M7 0-4-4T		DD	Nine Elms	11/1905	9/1962	
52		Bison 0-6-0	Rhinoceros	JG	Nine Elms	6/1846	4/1870	
52		Lion 0-6-0	Rhinoceros	JB	Nine Elms	6/1865	11/1890	Duplicated 11/1883
52	2513	0415 class 4-4-2T		WA	Robert Stephenson & Co	11/1883	11/1921	Duplicated 11/1905
52	B13	M7 0-4-4T		DD	Nine Elms	12/1905	5/1964	
53		Mazeppa 2-2-2	Mazeppa	JG	Nine Elms	3/1847	9/1865	
53		Lion 0-6-0	Mazeppa	JB	Nine Elms	7/1865	7/1893	Duplicated 11/1883
53	2514	0415 class 4-4-2T		WA	Robert Stephenson & Co	11/1883	11/1921	Duplicated 11/1905
53	B13	M7 0-4-4T		DD	Nine Elms	12/1905	5/1964	
54		Mazeppa 2-2-2	Medea	JG	Nine Elms	5/1847	3/1867	
54		Lion 0-6-0	Medea	JB	Nine Elms	8/1865	4/1893	Duplicated 12/1883
54	2515	0415 class 4-4-2T		WA	Robert Stephenson & Co	12/1883	7/1927	Duplicated 11/1905
54	B13	M7 0-4-4T		DD	Nine Elms	12/1905	1/1959	
55		Mazeppa 2-2-2	Medusa	JG	Nine Elms	3/1847	11/1862	
55		Gem 2-4-0	Medusa	JB	Nine Elms	3/1863	4/1884	Duplicated 12/1883
55	2516	0415 class 4-4-2T		WA	Robert Stephenson & Co	12/1883	9/1924	Duplicated 11/1905
55	B13	M7 0-4-4T		DD	Nine Elms	12/1905	9/1963	
56		Mazeppa 2-2-2	Mentor	JG	Nine Elms	5/1847	7/1862	
56		Gem 2-4-0	Mentor	JB	Nine Elms	4/1863	10/1885	Duplicated 12/1883
56	2517	0415 class 4-4-2T		WA	Robert Stephenson & Co	12/1883	11/1921	Duplicated 12/1905
56	D13	M7 0-4-4T		DD	Nine Elms	1/1906	12/1963	
57		Mazeppa 2-2-2	Meteor	JG	Nine Elms	3/1847	9/1862	
57		Gem 2-4-0	Meteor	JB	Nine Elms	5/1863	11/1885	Duplicated 12/1883
57	2518	0415 class 4-4-2T		WA	Robert Stephenson & Co	12/1883	11/1921	Duplicated 12/1905
57	D13	M7 0-4-4T		DD	Nine Elms	1/1906	6/1963	
58		Mazeppa 2-2-2	Sultan	JG	Nine Elms	7/1847	7/1865	
58		Lion 0-6-0	Sultan	JB	Nine Elms	1/1866	1/1889	
58	2601	0415 class 4-4-2T		WA	Robert Stephenson & Co	6/1885	4/1925	Transferred from No 68 3/1889, duplicated 2/1906
58	D13	M7 0-4-4T		DD	Nine Elms	3/1906	9/1960	
58	F9	F9 4-2-4		DD	Nine Elms	6/1899	8/1940	Mr Drummond's "Bug", was No 733, renumbered 58S 12/1924
59		Mazeppa 2-2-2	Sirocco	JG	Nine Elms	7/1847	4/1864	
59		Lion 0-6-0	Sirocco	JB	Nine Elms	2/1866	12/1897	Duplicated 6/1890
59	2602	0415 class 4-4-2T		WA	Robert Stephenson & Co	7/1885	12/1925	Transferred from No 77 6/1890, duplicated 2/1906
59	D13	M7 0-4-4T		DD	Nine Elms	3/1906	2/1961	
60		Mazeppa 2-2-2	Sappho	JG	Nine Elms	10/1847	3/1865	
60		Lion 0-6-0	Sappho	JB	Nine Elms	2/1866	5/1890	
60	2603	0415 class 4-4-2T		WA	Robert Stephenson & Co	7/1885	11/1921	Transferred from No 78 8/1890, duplicated 2/1906
60	D13	M7 0-4-4T		DD	Nine Elms	3/1906	7/1961	
61		Mazeppa 2-2-2	Snake	JG	Nine Elms	12/1847	3/1870	
61		Volcano 2-4-0	Snake	JB	Nine Elms	7/1869	6/1896	Duplicated 6/1888
61	T1	T1 0-4-4T		WA	Nine Elms	6/1888	12/1932	
62		Mazeppa 2-2-2	Serpent	JG	Nine Elms	12/1847	10/1866	
62		Volcano 2-4-0	Serpent	JB	Nine Elms	7/1869	12/1888	
62	T1	T1 0-4-4T		WA	Nine Elms	12/1888	3/1933	
63		Fairburn 2-2-2	Alecto	JG	William Fairburn & Sons	12/1846	3/1867	
63		Volcano 2-4-0	Alecto	JB	Nine Elms	12/1866	12/1890	Duplicated 12/1888
63	T1	T1 0-4-4T		WA	Nine Elms	12/1888	2/1933	
64		Fairburn 2-2-2	Acheron	JG	William Fairburn & Sons	12/1846	4/1872	
64		Volcano 2-4-0	Acheron	JB	Nine Elms	12/1866	7/1892	Duplicated 12/1888
64	T1	T1 0-4-4T		WA	Nine Elms	12/1888	4/1932	

APPENDIX C

A	B	C	D	E	F	G	H	I
65		Fairburn 2-2-2	Achilles	JG	William Fairburn & Sons	3/1847	12/1871	
65		Lion 0-6-0	Achilles	JB	Nine Elms	1/1870	4/1897	
65	T1	T1 0-4-4T		WA	Nine Elms	12/1888	9/1934	
66		Fairburn 2-2-2	Actaeon	JG	William Fairburn & Sons	1/1848	6/1866	
66		Volcano 2-4-0	Actaeon	JB	Nine Elms	1/1867	3/1894	Duplicated 12/1888
66	T1	T1 0-4-4T		WA	Nine Elms	12/1888	3/1932	
67		Fairburn 2-2-2	Aeolus	JG	William Fairburn & Sons	10/1847	7/1863	
67		Gem 2-4-0	Aeolus	JB	Nine Elms	8/1863	6/1885	
67	T1	T1 0-4-4T		WA	Nine Elms	12/1888	10/1931	
68		Fairburn 2-2-2	Apollo	JG	William Fairburn & Sons	11/1846	2/1864	
68		Falcon 2-4-0	Apollo	JB	Nine Elms	12/1864	6/1887	Duplicated 6/1885
68	2601	415 class 4-4-2T		WA	Robert Stephenson & Co	6/1885	4/1925	Renumbered 58 3/1889
68	T1	T1 0-4-4T		WA	Nine Elms	3/1889	10/1931	
69		Fairburn 2-2-2	Argus	JG	William Fairburn & Sons	4/1847	1/1868	
69		Falcon 2-4-0	Argus	JB	Nine Elms	4/1863	5/1886	Duplicated 11/1885
69	3457	395 class 0-6-0		WA	Nielson & Co	11/1885	2/1953	Renumbered 83 3/1889
69	T1	T1 0-4-4T		WA	Nine Elms	3/1889	10/1931	
70		Fairburn 2-2-2	Ariel	JG	William Fairburn & Sons	9/1847	1/1868	
70		Falcon 2-4-0	Ariel	JB	Nine Elms	9/1864	10/1887	
70	T1	T1 0-4-4T		WA	Nine Elms	4/1889	8/1934	
71		Fairburn 2-2-2	Alaric	JG	William Fairburn & Sons	1/1848	12/1863	
71		Falcon 2-4-0	Alaric	JB	Nine Elms	2/1863	12/1887	Duplicated 11/1885
71	3458	395 class 0-6-0		WA	Nielson & Co	11/1885	10/1916	Renumbered 84 6/1889
71	D2	T1 0-4-4T		WA	Nine Elms	6/1889	1/1936	
72		Fairburn 2-2-2	Arrow	JG	William Fairburn & Sons	11/1847	9/1864	
72		Falcon 2-4-0	Arrow	JB	Nine Elms	11/1864	12/1887	
72	D2	T1 0-4-4T		WA	Nine Elms	6/1889	6/1933	
73		Rothwell 2-2-2	Fireball	JG	Rothwell & Co	12/1846	3/1867	
73		Clyde 2-4-0	Fireball	JB	Nine Elms	5/1864	3/1888	
73	D2	T1 0-4-4T		WA	Nine Elms	10/1889	1/1936	
74		Rothwell 2-2-2	Firebrand	JG	Rothwell & Co	12/1846	1/1867	
74		Clyde 2-4-0	Firebrand	JB	Nine Elms	6/1864	10/1887	
74	D2	T1 0-4-4T		WA	Nine Elms	10/1889	4/1934	
75		Rothwell 2-2-2	Fireking	JG	Rothwell & Co	2/1847	5/1866	
75		Clyde 2-4-0	Fireking	JB	Nine Elms	7/1864	5/1888	
75	D2	T1 0-4-4T		WA	Nine Elms	12/1889	2/1935	
76		Rothwell 2-2-2	Firefly	JG	Rothwell & Co	2/1847	11/1862	Rebuilt 2-2-2WT 11/1862
76		Firefly 2-2-2WT	Firefly	JB	Nine Elms	11/1862	10/1871	
76		Standard 2-4-0WT	Firefly	JB	Nine Elms	12/1871	7/1899	Duplicated 4/1890
76	D2	T1 0-4-4T		WA	Nine Elms	4/1890	8/1933	
77		Rothwell 2-2-2	Hecla	JG	Rothwell & Co	5/1847	3/1865	Re-named "Wildfire" 5/1852
77		Falcon 2-4-0	Wildfire	JB	Nine Elms	7/1865	5/1885	
77	2602	415 class 4-4-2T		WA	Robert Stephenson & Co	7/1885	12/1925	Renumbered 59 6/1890
77	D2	T1 0-4-4T		WA	Nine Elms	6/1890	5/1932	
77	D14	C14 0-4-0T		DD	Nine Elms	2/1907	3/1959	Was No 745, duplicated 12/1918, renumbered 77S 10/1927
78		Rothwell 2-2-2	Hecate	JG	Rothwell & Co	6/1847	10/1862	
78		Gem 2-4-0	Hecate	JB	Nine Elms	5/1863	5/1885	
78	2603	415 class 4-4-2T		WA	Robert Stephenson & Co	7/1885	11/1921	Renumbered 60 8/1890
78	D2	T1 0-4-4T		WA	Nine Elms	8/1890	11/1933	
79		Rothwell 2-2-2	Harpy	JG	Rothwell & Co	7/1847	2/1869	Used as stationary engine at Ringwood 2/1869
79		Falcon 2-4-0	Harpy	JB	Nine Elms	9/1865	11/1888	
79	D2	T1 0-4-4T		WA	Nine Elms	9/1890	12/1933	
80		Rothwell 2-2-2	Hornet	JG	Rothwell & Co	7/1847	4/1864	
80		Falcon 2-4-0	Hornet	JB	Nine Elms	11/1865	1/1892	Duplicated 9/1890
80	D2	T1 0-4-4T		WA	Nine Elms	9/1890	1/1936	
81		Rothwell 2-2-2	Herod	JG	Rothwell & Co	8/1847	1/1867	
81		Falcon 2-4-0	Herod	JB	Nine Elms	12/1865	10/1890	
81	D6	B4 0-4-0T	Jersey	WA	Nine Elms	11/1893	2/1949	To Southampton Docks 11/1893
82		Rothwell 2-2-2	Sultana	JG	Rothwell & Co	8/1847	12/1865	
82		Falcon 2-4-0	Sultana	JB	Nine Elms	1/1866	5/1885	
82	2604	415 class 4-4-2T		WA	Robert Stephenson & Co	7/1885	11/1921	Duplicated 5/1908
82	K14	B4 0-4-0T		DD	Nine Elms	6/1908	6/1957	
83		Rothwell 2-2-2	Siren	JG	Rothwell & Co	9/1847	6/1866	
83		Falcon 2-4-0	Siren	JB	Nine Elms	9/1866	5/1898	Duplicated 3/1887
83	3457	395 class 0-6-0		WA	Nielson & Co	11/1885	2/1953	Was 69 until 3/1889, duplicated 6/1908
83	K14	B4 0-4-0T		DD	Nine Elms	6/1908	11/1959	
84		Rothwell 2-2-2	Styx	JG	Rothwell & Co	9/1847	5/1865	
84		Falcon 2-4-0	Styx	JB	Nine Elms	10/1866	4/1897	Duplicated 6/1889
84	3458	395 class 0-6-0		WA	Nielson & Co	11/1885	10/1916	Was 71 until 6/1889, duplicated 6/1908
84	K14	B4 0-4-0T		DD	Nine Elms	6/1908	8/1959	
85		Rothwell 2-2-2	Saracen	JG	Rothwell & Co	11/1847	4/1868	
85		Falcon 2-4-0	Saracen	JB	Nine Elms	12/1866	10/1888	

APPENDIX C

A	B	C	D	E	F	G	H	I
131		Canute 2-2-2	Rufus	JB	Nine Elms	2/1856	3/1881	
131	2127	330 class 0-6-0ST		WB	Beyer Peacock & Co	5/1882	10/1924	Duplicated 10/1911
131	A15	M7 0-4-4T		DD	Nine Elms	10/1911	12/1962	
132		Canute 2-2-2	Conqueror	JB	Nine Elms	3/1856	12/1875	
132	1836	46 class 4-4-0T		WA	Beyer Peacock & Co	7/1879	11/1885	Rebuilt as 4-4-2T No 132 11/1885
132	1836	46 class 4-4-2T		WA	Nine Elms	11/1885	12/1924	Rebuilt from 4-4-0T No 132 11/1885, duplicated 3/1903
132	G11	M7 0-4-4T		DD	Nine Elms	3/1903	10/1962	
133		Canute 2-2-2	Crescent	JB	Nine Elms	4/1856	2/1878	
133	1837	46 class 4-4-0T		WA	Beyer Peacock & Co	7/1879	1/1885	Rebuilt as 4-4-2T No 133 1/1885
133	1837	46 class 4-4-2T		WA	Nine Elms	1/1885	11/1921	Rebuilt from 4-4-0T No 133 1/1885, duplicated 3/1903
133	G11	M7 0-4-4		DD	Nine Elms	3/1903	3/1964	
134		Canute 2-2-2	Ironsides	JB	Nine Elms	12/1855	7/1856	Rebuilt to 2-4-0 No 134 7/1856
134		Undine 2-4-0	Ironsides	JB	Nine Elms	7/1856	1/1885	Rebuilt from 2-2-2 No 134 7/1856
134	3461	395 class 0-6-0		WA	Nielson & Co	12/1885	8/1916	Duplicated 4/1903
134	D12	L11 4-4-0		DD	Nine Elms	4/1904	2/1951	
135		Canute 2-2-2	Canute	JB	Nine Elms	5/1856	3/1878	
135	1948	135 class 4-4-0		WA	Beyer Peacock & Co	11/1880	11/1921	Duplicated 8/1902, renumbered 0370 4/1914
135	V10	K10 4-4-0		DD	Nine Elms	9/1902	5/1949	
136		Saxon 2-4-0	Goth	JB	Nine Elms	7/1857	1/1885	Duplicated 11/1880
136	1949	135 class 4-4-0		WA	Beyer Peacock & Co	11/1880	12/1913	Duplicated 8/1902
136	V10	K10 4-4-0		DD	Nine Elms	9/1902	1/1947	
137		Saxon 2-4-0	Hun	JB	Nine Elms	8/1857	12/1885	Duplicated 11/1880
137	1950	135 class 4-4-0		WA	Beyer Peacock & Co	12/1880	12/1913	Duplicated 9/1902
137	A11	K10 4-4-0		DD	Nine Elms	9/1902	8/1949	
138		Saxon 2-4-0	Vandal	JB	Nine Elms	9/1857	11/1884	Duplicated 12/1880
138	1951	135 class 4-4-0		WA	Beyer Peacock & Co	12/1880	12/1913	Duplicated 9/1902
138	A11	K10 4-4-0		DD	Nine Elms	10/1902	1/1947	
139		Saxon 2-4-0	Lombard	JB	Nine Elms	9/1857	9/1885	Duplicated 12/1880
139	1952	135 class 4-4-0		WA	Beyer Peacock & Co	12/1880	12/1924	Duplicated 10/1902, renumbered 0307 3/1914
139	A11	K10 4-4-0		DD	Nine Elms	10/1902	10/1948	
140		Saxon 2-4-0	Gaul	JB	Nine Elms	11/1857	11/1880	Duplicated 12/1880
140	1953	135 class 4-4-0		WA	Beyer Peacock & Co	12/1880	12/1924	Duplicated 10/1902, renumbered 0310 5/1914
140	A11	K10 4-4-0		DD	Nine Elms	10/1902	1/1950	
141		Saxon 2-4-0	Celt	JB	Nine Elms	12/1857	8/1878	Duplicated 12/1880
141	1954	135 class 4-4-0		WA	Beyer Peacock & Co	12/1880	12/1913	Duplicated 10/1902
141	A11	K10 4-4-0		DD	Nine Elms	11/1902	10/1949	
142		Canute 2-2-2	Eugenie	JB	Nine Elms	1/1857	10/1878	
142	1955	135 class 4-4-0		WA	Beyer Peacock & Co	12/1880	12/1913	Duplicated 11/1902
142	C11	K10 4-4-0		DD	Nine Elms	11/1902	1/1950	
143		Nelson 2-4-0WT	Nelson	JB	Nine Elms	7/1858	8/1882	Duplicated 12/1880
143	1956	135 class 4-4-0		WA	Beyer Peacock & Co	12/1880	8/1922	Duplicated 11/1902, renumbered 0312 5/1914
143	C11	K10 4-4-0		DD	Nine Elms	11/1902	9/1948	
144		Nelson 2-4-0WT	Howe	JB	Nine Elms	8/1858	11/1884	Duplicated 1/1881
144	1957	135 class 4-4-0		WA	Beyer Peacock & Co	12/1880	11/1921	Duplicated 11/1902, renumbered 0347 4/1914
144	C11	K10 4-4-0		DD	Nine Elms	11/1902	7/1949	
145		Nelson 2-4-0WT	Hood	JB	Nine Elms	8/1858	4/1885	Duplicated 1/1881
145	1958	135 class 4-4-0		WA	Beyer Peacock & Co	1/1881	12/1913	Duplicated 12/1902
145	C11	K10 4-4-0		DD	Nine Elms	12/1902	10/1948	
146		Tweed 2-4-0	Tweed	JB	Nine Elms	7/1858	3/1878	
146	1959	135 class 4-4-0		WA	Beyer Peacock & Co	1/1881	12/1913	Duplicated 12/1902
146	C11	K10 4-4-0		DD	Nine Elms	12/1902	2/1948	
147		Tweed 2-4-0	Isis	JB	Nine Elms	8/1858	7/1881	
147	2561	460 class 4-4-0T		WA	Robert Stephenson & Co	6/1884	1/1927	Duplicated 9/1910
147	K14	B4 0-4-0T	Dinard	WA	Nine Elms	4/1908	2/1949	Was No 747 until 2/1922, to Southampton Docks and named 4/1908
148		Tweed 2-4-0	Colne	JB	Nine Elms	9/1858	11/1878	
148	3462	395 class 0-6-0		WA	Nielson & Co	12/1885	9/1916	Duplicated 6/1904
148	D12	L11 4-4-0		DD	Nine Elms	5/1904	3/1952	
149		Canute 2-2-2	Napoleon	JB	Nine Elms	7/1858	3/1878	
149	2128	330 class 0-6-0ST		WB	Beyer Peacock & Co	5/1882	10/1930	Duplicated 12/1902
149	E11	K10 4-4-0		DD	Nine Elms	12/1902	1/1947	
150		Canute 2-2-2	Havelock	JB	Nine Elms	8/1858	11/1881	
150	2129	330 class 0-6-0ST		WB	Beyer Peacock & Co	5/1882	5/1929	Duplicated 12/1902
150	E11	K10 4-4-0		DD	Nine Elms	12/1902	2/1948	
151		Canute 2-2-2	Montrose	JB	Nine Elms	9/1858	12/1875	
151	1777	Single Frame 0-6-0	Montrose	WB	Beyer Peacock & Co	4/1878	5/1924	Rebuilt Nine Elms 11/1890, duplicated 12/1902
151	E11	K10 4-4-0		DD	Nine Elms	12/1902	2/1950	
152		Canute 2-2-2	Marmion	JB	Nine Elms	10/1858	12/1875	
152	1778	Single Frame 0-6-0	Marmion	WB	Beyer Peacock & Co	4/1878	8/1921	Rebuilt Nine Elms 6/1891, duplicated 12/1902
152	E11	K10 4-4-0		DD	Nine Elms	12/1902	2/1949	
153		Canute 2-2-2	Victoria	JB	Nine Elms	6/1859	9/1884	
153	2939	395 class 0-6-0		WA	Nielson & Co	3/1883	1/1933	Duplicated 12/1902
153	E11	K10 4-4-0		DD	Nine Elms	1/1903	2/1949	

APPENDIX C

Fig. 434. Drivers H. Bullard and B. Bartlett at Bournemouth Central, January 1903. Standing in front of a Dubs& Co T9 No 725.
(C.H. Eden)

APPENDIX C

A	B	C	D	E	F	G	H	I
154		Nile 2-4-0WT	Nile	JB	Nine Elms	4/1859	7/1882	
154	2940	395 class 0-6-0		WA	Nielson & Co	3/1883	9/1959	Duplicated 5/1903
154	L11	L11 4-4-0		DD	Nine Elms	5/1903	3/1951	
155		Nile 2-4-0WT	Cressey	JB	Nine Elms	5/1859	8/1882	
155	2941	395 class 0-6-0		WA	Nielson & Co	3/1883	4/1958	Duplicated 5/1903
155	L11	L11 4-4-0		DD	Nine Elms	5/1903	3/1951	
156		Nile 2-4-0WT	Hogue	JB	Nine Elms	6/1859	9/1882	
156	2942	395 class 0-6-0		WA	Nielson & Co	3/1883	7/1917	Duplicated 6/1903
156	L11	L11 4-4-0		DD	Nine Elms	6/1903	4/1951	
157		Clyde 2-4-0	Clyde	JB	Nine Elms	1/1859	6/1883	
157	2943	395 class 0-6-0		WA	Nielson & Co	3/1883	8//1916	Duplicated 6/1903
157	L11	L11 4-4-0		DD	Nine Elms	6/1903	3/1952	
158		Clyde 2-4-0	Lacy	JB	Nine Elms	2/1859	11/1884	Duplicated 3/1883
158	2944	395 class 0-6-0		WA	Nielson & Co	3/1883	3/1917	Duplicated 6/1903
158	L11	L11 4-4-0		DD	Nine Elms	6/1903	11/1950	
159		Clyde 2-4-0	Castleman	JB	Nine Elms	3/1859	3/1887	Duplicated 3/1883
159	2945	395 class 0-6-0		WA	Nielson & Co	3/1883	10/1916	Duplicated 9/1903
159	O11	L11 4-4-0		DD	Nine Elms	9/1903	3/1951	
160		Tweed 2-4-0	Thames	JB	Nine Elms	3/1859	6/1877	
160	1787	Single Frame 0-6-0	Thames	WB	Beyer Peacock & Co	4/1878	8/1921	Rebuilt 12/1890, duplicated 3/1900
160	M9	G6 0-6-0T		WA	Nine Elms	3/1900	4/1959	
160	1856	380 class 4-4-0		WA	Beyer Peacock & Co	9/1879	7/1923	Was No 382 until 1/1914, then renumbered and duplicated 0160
161		Tweed 2-4-0	Shannon	JB	Nine Elms	5/1859	3/1879	
161	2130	330 class 0-6-0ST		Wb	Beyer Peacock & Co	5/1882	5/1926	Duplicated 9/1903
161	O11	L11 4-4-0		DD	Nine Elms	9/1903	2/1950	
162		Tweed 2-4-0	Severn	JB	Nine Elms	6/1859	3/1878	
162	1788	Single Frame 0-6-0		WB	Beyer Peacock & Co	4/1878	5/1924	Rebuilt Nine Elms 12/1886, duplicated 3/1900
162	M9	G6 0-6-0T		WA	Nine Elms	4/1900	3/1958	
162	1862	380 class 4-4-0		WA	Beyer Peacock & Co	11/1879	12/1925	Was No 388 until 1/1914, then renumbered and duplicated 0162
163		Undine 2-4-0	Undine	JB	Nine Elms	7/1859	11/1884	Duplicated 5/1883
163	2946	395 class 0-6-0		WA	Nielson & Co	5/1883	5/1956	Duplicated 9/1903
163	O11	L11 4-4-0		DD	Nine Elms	10/1903	10/1951	
164		Undine 2-4-0	Psyche	JB	Nine Elms	9/1859	10/1883	Duplicated 5/1883
164	2947	395 class 0-6-0		WA	Nielson & Co	5/1883	9/1916	Duplicated 9/1903
164	O11	L11 4-4-0		DD	Nine Elms	10/1903	9/1951	
165		Undine 2-4-0	Circe	JB	Nine Elms	10/1859	12/1886	Duplicated 5/1883
165	2948	395 class 0-6-0		WA	Nielson & Co	5/1883	4/1918	Duplicated 9/1903
165	O11	L11 4-4-0		DD	Nine Elms	11/1903	4/1951	
166		Undine 2-4-0	Ariadne	JB	Nine Elms	11/1859	10/1884	Duplicated 5/1883
166	2949	395 class 0-6-0		WA	Nielson & Co	5/1883	9/1916	Duplicated 4/1904
166	D12	L11 4-4-0		DD	Nine Elms	4/1904	7/1950	
167		Undine 2-4-0	Atalanta	JB	Nine Elms	12/1859	12/1884	Duplicated 5/1883
167	2950	395 class 0-6-0		WA	Nielson & Co	5/1883	12/1956	Duplicated 5/1904
167	D12	L11 4-4-0		DD	Nine Elms	5/1904	9/1949	
168		Undine 2-4-0	Electra	JB	Nine Elms	1/1860	12/1886	Duplicated 1/1886
168	3463	395 class 0-6-0		WA	Nielson & Co	1/1886	12/1917	Duplicated 5/1904
168	D12	L11 4-4-0		DD	Nine Elms	5/1904	2/1950	
169		Clyde 2-4-0	R. H. Dutton	JB	Nine Elms	1/1859	1/1885	
169	2000	415 class 4-4-2T		WA	Dubs & Co	11/1884	6/1926	Duplicated 8/1904
169	F12	L11 4-4-0		DD	Nine Elms	8/1904	7/1949	
170		Undine 2-4-0	Cupid	JB	Nine Elms	4/1860	3/1885	Duplicated 11/1884
170	2001	415 class 4-4-2T		WA	Dubs & Co	11/1884	11/1921	Duplicated 8/1904
170	F12	L11 4-4-0		DD	Nine Elms	8/1904	6/1952	
171		Undine 2-4-0	Sylph	JB	Nine Elms	5/1860	1/1885	Duplicated 11/1884
171	2002	415 class 4-4-2T		WA	Dubs & Co	11/1884	11/1921	Duplicated 8/1904
171	F12	L11 4-4-0		DD	Nine Elms	9/1904	8/1951	
172		Undine 2-4-0	Zephyr	JB	Nine Elms	5/1860	10/1886	Duplicated 1/1886
172	3464	395 class 0-6-0		WA	Nielson & Co	1/1886	9/1916	Duplicated 8/1904
172	F12	L11 4-4-0		DD	Nine Elms	9/1904	6/1952	
173		Undine 2-4-0	Nymph	JB	Nine Elms	6/1860	1/1885	Duplicated 11/1884
173	2003	415 class 4-4-2T		WA	Dubs & Co	11/1884	11/1921	Duplicated 8/1904
173	F12	L11 4-4-0		DD	Nine Elms	10/1904	4/1951	
174		Undine 2-4-0	Naiad	JB	Nine Elms	6/1860	5/1884	
174	3465	395 class 0-6-0		WA	Nielson & Co	2/1886	7/1917	Duplicated 5/1906
174	K13	L11 4-4-0		DD	Nine Elms	5/1906	7/1951	
175		Undine 2-4-0	Hebe	JB	Nine Elms	6/1860	9/1886	Duplicated 2/1886
175	3466	395 class 0-6-0		WA	Nielson & Co	2/1886	8/1916	Duplicated 5/1906
175	K13	L11 4-4-0		DD	Nine Elms	6/1906	11/1951	
176		ex-Summers 2-2-0	Southampton	JB	Nine Elms	8/1859	10/1869	No 16 rebuilt by Nine Elms 8/1859, and renumbered 176
176		Lion 0-6-0	Dragon	JB	Nine Elms	1/1870	3/1891	
176	D6	B4 0-4-0T	Guernsey	WA	Nine Elms	10/1893	6/1948	To Southampton Docks 11/1893
177	331	Standard 2-4-0WT		JB	Beyer Peacock & Co	2/1863	4/1844	Rebuilt as 2-4-0 No 177 4/1884

345

APPENDIX C

A	B	C	D	E	F	G	H	I
177		Standard 2-4-0		JB	Beyer Peacock/Nine Elms	4/1884	6/1893	Rebuilt from 2-4-0WT No 177 4/1884, duplicated 12/1889
177	O2	O2 0-4-4T		WA	Nine Elms	12/1889	10/1959	
178	332	Standard 2-4-0WT		JB	Beyer Peacock & Co	2/1863	9/1844	Rebuilt as 2-4-0 No 178 9/1884
178		Standard 2-4-0		JB	Beyer Peacock/Nine Elms	9/1884	4/1897	Rebuilt from 2-4-0WT No 178 9/1884, duplicated 12/1889
178	O2	O2 0-4-4T	Fishbourne	WA	Nine Elms	12/1889	12/1966	Renumbered W14, and named from May 1936
179	333	Standard 2-4-0WT		JB	Beyer Peacock & Co	2/1863	4/1884	Rebuilt as 2-4-0 No 179 4/1884
179		Standard 2-4-0		JB	Beyer Peacock/Nine Elms	4/1884	4/1895	Rebuilt from 2-4-0WT No 179 4/1884, duplicated 3/1890
179	O2	O2 0-4-4T		WA	Nine Elms	3/1890	12/1959	
180	334	Standard 2-4-0WT		JB	Beyer Peacock & Co	2/1863	6/1884	Rebuilt as 2-4-0 No 180 6/1884
180		Standard 2-4-0		JB	Beyer Peacock/Nine Elms	6/1884	9/1892	Rebuilt from 2-4-0WT No 180 6/1884, duplicated 4/1890
180	O2	O2 0-4-4T	Chale	WA	Nine Elms	4/1890	3/1967	Renumbered W31, and named from May 1927
181	335	Standard 2-4-0WT		JB	Beyer Peacock & Co	3/1863	8/1884	Rebuilt as 2-4-0 No 181 8/1884
181		Standard 2-4-0		JB	Beyer Peacock/Nine Elms	8/1884	12/1893	Rebuilt from 2-4-0WT No 181 8/1884, duplicated 5/1890
181	O2	O2 0-4-4T	Freshwater	WA	Nine Elms	5/1890	10/1966	Renumbered W35, and named from April 1949
182	336	Standard 2-4-0WT		JB	Beyer Peacock & Co	3/1863	11/1883	Rebuilt as 2-4-0 No 182 11/1883
182		Standard 2-4-0		JB	Beyer Peacock/Nine Elms	11/1883	9/1895	Rebuilt from 2-4-0WT No 182 11/1883, duplicated 5/1890
182	O2	O2 0-4-4T		WA	Nine Elms	5/1890	1/1960	
183	379	Standard 2-4-0WT		JB	Beyer Peacock & Co	10/1863	5/1884	Rebuilt as 2-4-0 No 183 5/1884
183		Standard 2-4-0		JB	Beyer Peacock/Nine Elms	5/1884	12/1893	Rebuilt from 2-4-0WT No 183 5/1884, duplicated 5/1890
183	O2	O2 0-4-4T		WA	Nine Elms	5/1890	9/1961	
184	380	Standard 2-4-0WT		JB	Beyer Peacock & Co	10/1863	8/1885	Rebuilt as 2-4-0 No 184 8/1855
184		Standard 2-4-0		JB	Beyer Peacock/Nine Elms	8/1885	6/1895	Rebuilt from 2-4-0WT No 184 8/1855, duplicated 6/1890
184	O2	O2 0-4-4T	Merstone	WA	Nine Elms	6/1890	12/1966	Renumbered W27, and named from March 1926
185	381	Standard 2-4-0WT		JB	Beyer Peacock & Co	11/1863	1/1886	Rebuilt as 2-4-0 No 185 1/1886
185		Standard 2-4-0		JB	Beyer Peacock/Nine Elms	1/1886	3/1897	Rebuilt from 2-4-0WT No 185 1/1886, duplicated 6/1890
185	O2	O2 0-4-4T		WA	Nine Elms	6/1890	5/1940	
186	382	Standard 2-4-0WT		JB	Beyer Peacock & Co	11/1863	9/1885	Rebuilt as 2-4-0 No 186 9/1885
186		Standard 2-4-0		JB	Beyer Peacock/Nine Elms	9/1885	10/1895	Rebuilt from 2-4-0WT No 186 9/1885, duplicated 7/1890
186	O2	O2 0-4-4T	Ashey	WA	Nine Elms	7/1890	12/1966	Renumbered W28, and named from March 1926
187	383	Standard 2-4-0WT		JB	Beyer Peacock & Co	11/1863	10/1884	Rebuilt as 2-4-0 No 187 10/1884
187		Standard 2-4-0		JB	Beyer Peacock/Nine Elms	10/1884	6/1894	Rebuilt from 2-4-0WT No 187 10/1884, duplicated 10/1890
187	B3	O2 0-4-4T		WA	Nine Elms	10/1890	8/1945	
188	384	Standard 2-4-0WT		JB	Beyer Peacock & Co	11/1863	10/1884	Rebuilt as 2-4-0 No 188 10/1884
188		Standard 2-4-0		JB	Beyer Peacock/Nine Elms	10/1884	11/1895	Rebuilt from 2-4-0WT No 188 10/1884, duplicated 10/1890
188	B3	O2 0-4-4T	Totland	WA	Nine Elms	10/1890	8/1955	Renumbered W23, and named from April 1925
189	390	Standard 2-4-0WT		JB	Beyer Peacock & Co	12/1863	8/1885	Rebuilt as 2-4-0 No 189 8/1885
189		Standard 2-4-0		JB	Beyer Peacock/Nine Elms	8/1885	6/1897	Rebuilt from 2-4-0WT No 189 8/1885, duplicated 10/1890
189	B3	O2 0-4-4T		WA	Nine Elms	10/1890	7/1933	
190	391	Standard 2-4-0WT		JB	Beyer Peacock & Co	12/1863	12/1883	Rebuilt as 2-4-0 No 190 12/1883
190		Standard 2-4-0		JB	Beyer Peacock & Co	12/1883	12/1892	Rebuilt from 2-4-0WT No 190 12/1883, duplicated 11/1890
190	B3	O2 0-4-4T	Godshill	WA	Nine Elms	11/1890	12/1962	Renumbered W25, and named from June 1925
191	392	Standard 2-4-0WT		JB	Beyer Peacock & Co	1/1864	12/1885	Rebuilt as 2-4-0 No 191 12/1885
191		Standard 2-4-0		JB	Beyer Peacock & Co	12/1885	6/1896	Rebuilt from 2-4-0WT No 191 12/1885, duplicated 11/1890
191	B3	O2 0-4-4T		WA	Nine Elms	11/1890	3/1933	
192	393	Standard 2-4-0WT		JB	Beyer Peacock & Co	1/1864	10/1885	Rebuilt as 2-4-0 No 192 10/1885
192		Standard 2-4-0		JB	Beyer Peacock & Co	10/1885	9/1894	Rebuilt from 2-4-0WT No 192 10/1885, duplicated 11/1890
192	B3	O2 0-4-4T		WA	Nine Elms	11/1890	8/1961	
193	394	Standard 2-4-0WT		JB	Beyer Peacock & Co	1/1864	8/1884	Rebuilt as 2-4-0 No 193 8/1884
193		Standard 2-4-0		JB	Beyer Peacock & Co	8/1884	1/1895	Rebuilt from 2-4-0WT No 193 8/1884, duplicated 11/1890
193	B3	O2 0-4-4T		WA	Nine Elms	11/1890	4/1962	
194	395	Standard 2-4-0WT		JB	Beyer Peacock & Co	1/1864	12/1884	Rebuilt as 2-4-0 No 194 12/1884
194		Standard 2-4-0		JB	Beyer Peacock & Co	12/1884	8/1896	Rebuilt from 2-4-0WT No 194 12/1884, duplicated 11/1890
194	B3	O2 0-4-4T		WA	Nine Elms	12/1890	8/1933	
195	493	Standard 2-4-0WT		JB	Beyer Peacock & Co	2/1865	4/1884	Rebuilt as 2-4-0 No 195 4/1844.
195		Standard 2-4-0		JB	Beyer Peacock & Co	4/1884	12/1888	Rebuilt from 2-4-0WT No 195 4/1884
195	B3	O2 0-4-4T	Cowes	WA	Nine Elms	12/1890	5/1956	Renumbered W15, and named from May 1936
196	494	Standard 2-4-0WT		JB	Beyer Peacock & Co	3/1865	12/1884	Rebuilt as 2-4-0 No 196 12/1884
196		Standard 2-4-0		JB	Beyer Peacock & Co	12/1884	6/1896	Rebuilt from 2-4-0WT No 194 12/1884, duplicated 11/1890
196	B3	O2 0-4-4T		WA	Nine Elms	3/1891	11/1937	
197	495	Standard 2-4-0WT		JB	Beyer Peacock & Co	3/1865	6/1888	
197	K3	O2 0-4-4T		WA	Nine Elms	6/1891	2/1953	
198	496	Standard 2-4-0WT		JB	Beyer Peacock & Co	3/1865	6/1896	Duplicated 6/1891
198	K3	O2 0-4-4T	Carisbrooke	WA	Nine Elms	6/1891	6/1964	Renumbered W36, and named from April 1949
199	497	Standard 2-4-0WT		JB	Beyer Peacock & Co	3/1865	12/1888	
199	K3	O2 0-4-4T		WA	Nine Elms	6/1891	12/1962	
200	498	Standard 2-4-0WT		JB	Beyer Peacock & Co	3/1865	2/1885	Rebuilt as 2-4-0 No 200 2/1885
200		Standard 2-4-0		JB	Beyer Peacock & Co	2/1885	10/1892	Rebuilt from 2-4-0WT No 200 2/1885, duplicated 6/1891
200	K3	O2 0-4-4T		WA	Nine Elms	6/1891	8/1962	
201	1409	Standard 2-4-0WT		JB	Beyer Peacock & Co	5/1874	12/1888	
201	K3	O2 0-4-4T	Newport	WA	Nine Elms	7/1891	8/1955	Renumbered W34, and named from April 1947
202	1410	Standard 2-4-0WT		JB	Beyer Peacock & Co	5/1874	7/1898	Duplicated 7/1891
202	K3	O2 0-4-4T	Alverstone	WA	Nine Elms	7/1891	5/1966	Renumbered W29, and named from April 1926

APPENDIX C

A	B	C	D	E	F	G	H	I
203	544	Standard 2-4-0WT		JB	Beyer Peacock & Co	5/1865	12/1888	
203	K3	O2 0-4-4T		WA	Nine Elms	8/1891	12/1955	
204	545	Standard 2-4-0WT		JB	Beyer Peacock & Co	5/1865	5/1886	Rebuilt as 2-4-0 No 204 5/1886
204		Standard 2-4-0		JB	Beyer Peacock & Co	5/1886	6/1891	Rebuilt from 2-4-0WT No 204 5/1886
204	K3	O2 0-4-4T		WA	Nine Elms	8/1891	1/1953	
205	546	Standard 2-4-0WT		JB	Beyer Peacock & Co	5/1865	12/1888	
205	K3	O2 0-4-4T	Sandown	WA	Nine Elms	9/1891	5/1966	Renumbered W21, and named from June 1924
206	547	Standard 2-4-0WT		JB	Beyer Peacock & Co	5/1865	4/1887	Rebuilt as 2-4-0 No 206 4/1887
206		Standard 2-4-0		JB	Beyer Peacock & Co	4/1887	6/1892	Rebuilt from 2-4-0WT No 206 4/1887, duplicated 9/1891
206	K3	O2 0-4-4T	Osborne	WA	Nine Elms	9/1891	11/1955	Renumbered W19, and named May 1923
207	548	Standard 2-4-0WT		JB	Beyer Peacock & Co	6/1865	9/1886	Rebuilt as 2-4-0 No 207 9/1886
207		Standard 2-4-0		JB	Beyer Peacock & Co	9/1886	5/1890	Rebuilt from 2-4-0WT No 207 9/1886
207	D4	O2 0-4-4T		WA	Nine Elms	12/1891	6/1957	
208	549	Standard 2-4-0WT		JB	Beyer Peacock & Co	6/1865	9/1895	Duplicated 12/1891
208	D4	O2 0-4-4T	Seaview	WA	Nine Elms	12/1891	12/1966	Renumbered W17, and named from May 1930
209	638	Standard 2-4-0WT		JB	Beyer Peacock & Co	4/1866	10/1887	Rebuilt as 2-4-0 No 209 10/1887
209		Standard 2-4-0		JB	Beyer Peacock & Co	10/1887	12/1893	Rebuilt from 2-4-0WT No 209 10/1887, duplicated 12/1891
209	D4	O2 0-4-4T	Calbourne	WA	Nine Elms	12/1891	3/1967	Renumbered W24, and named from April 1925
210	639	Standard 2-4-0WT		JB	Beyer Peacock & Co	4/1866	5/1886	Rebuilt as 2-4-0 No 210 5/1886
210		Standard 2-4-0		JB	Beyer Peacock & Co	5/1886	6/1896	Rebuilt from 2-4-0WT No 210 5/1886, duplicated 12/1891
210	D4	O2 0-4-4T	Whitwell	WA	Nine Elms	12/1891	5/1966	Renumbered W26, and named from June 1925
211	640	Standard 2-4-0WT		JB	Beyer Peacock & Co	4/1866	6/1889	
211	D4	O2 0-4-4T	Shanklin	WA	Nine Elms	3/1892	12/1966	Renumbered W20, and named from May 1923
212	641	Standard 2-4-0WT		JB	Beyer Peacock & Co	4/1866	10/1887	Rebuilt as 2-4-0 No 212 10/1887
212		Standard 2-4-0		JB	Beyer Peacock & Co	10/1887	7/1892	Rebuilt from 2-4-0WT No 212 10/1887
212	D4	O2 0-4-4T		WA	Nine Elms	5/1892	12/1959	
213	642	Standard 2-4-0WT		JB	Beyer Peacock & Co	5/1866	2/1887	Rebuilt as 2-4-0 No 213 2/1887
213		Standard 2-4-0		JB	Beyer Peacock & Co	2/1887	5/1896	Rebuilt from 2-4-0WT No 213 2/1887, duplicated 5/1892
213	D4	O2 0-4-4T		WA	Nine Elms	5/1892	2/1953	
214	643	Standard 2-4-0WT		JB	Beyer Peacock & Co	5/1866	12/1886	Rebuilt as 2-4-0 No 214 12/1886
214		Standard 2-4-0		JB	Beyer Peacock & Co	12/1886	6/1896	Rebuilt from 2-4-0WT No 214 12/1886, duplicated 6/1892
214	D4	O2 0-4-4T		WA	Nine Elms	6/1892	7/1940	
215	694	Standard 2-4-0WT		JB	Beyer Peacock & Co	5/1866	10/1886	Rebuilt as 2-4-0 No 215 10/1886
215		Standard 2-4-0		JB	Beyer Peacock & Co	10/1886	4/1897	Rebuilt from 2-4-0WT No 215 10/1886, duplicated 6/1892
215	D4	O2 0-4-4T	Brading	WA	Nine Elms	6/1892	12/1966	Renumbered W22, and named from June 1924
216	695	Standard 2-4-0WT		JB	Beyer Peacock & Co	5/1866	12/1887	
216	D4	O2 0-4-4T		WA	Nine Elms	6/1892	11/1957	
217	696	Standard 2-4-0WT		JB	Beyer Peacock & Co	5/1866	1/1887	Rebuilt as 2-4-0 No 217 1/1887
217		Standard 2-4-0		JB	Beyer Peacock & Co	1/1887	6/1896	Rebuilt from 2-4-0WT No 217 1/1887, duplicated 6/1892
217	D4	O2 0-4-4T	Ventnor	WA	Nine Elms	6/1892	12/1966	Renumbered W16, and named from May 1936
218	697	Standard 2-4-0WT		JB	Beyer Peacock & Co	6/1866	6/1891	
218	D4	O2 0-4-4T	Bembridge	WA	Nine Elms	8/1892	12/1966	Renumbered W33, and named from May 1936
219	698	Standard 2-4-0WT		JB	Beyer Peacock & Co	6/1866	10/1892	
219	D4	O2 0-4-4T	Shorwell	WA	Nine Elms	9/1892	9/1965	Renumbered W30, and named from April 1926
220	699	Standard 2-4-0WT		JB	Beyer Peacock & Co	6/1866	4/1893	Duplicated 8/1892
220	D4	O2 0-4-4T	Ningwood	WA	Nine Elms	9/1892	12/1965	Renumbered W18, and named from May 1930
221	569	Double Frame 0-6-0	Scotia	JB	Beyer Peacock & Co	2/1866	12/1894	Duplicated 9/1892
221	D4	O2 0-4-4T		WA	Nine Elms	9/1892	8/1953	
222	570	Double Frame 0-6-0	Cambria	JB	Beyer Peacock & Co	2/1866	3/1899	Duplicated 9/1892
222	D4	O2 0-4-4T		WA	Nine Elms	9/1892	2/1933	
223	571	Double Frame 0-6-0	Colossus	JB	Beyer Peacock & Co	3/1866	4/1894	Duplicated 10/1892
223	D4	O2 0-4-4T		WA	Nine Elms	10/1892	10/1961	
224	572	Double Frame 0-6-0	Gallia	JB	Beyer Peacock & Co	3/1866	5/1897	Duplicated 10/1892
224	D4	O2 0-4-4T		WA	Nine Elms	10/1892	2/1958	
225	573	Double Frame 0-6-0	Hibernia	JB	Beyer Peacock & Co	3/1866	10/1894	Duplicated 11/1892
225	D4	O2 0-4-4T		WA	Nine Elms	11/1892	12/1962	
226	574	Double Frame 0-6-0	Anglia	JB	Beyer Peacock & Co	3/1866	8/1891	
226	D4	O2 0-4-4T	Bonchurch	WA	Nine Elms	11/1892	10/1964	Renumbered W32, and named from May 1928
227	1698	330 class 0-6-0ST		WB	Beyer Peacock & Co	6/1877	5/1930	Duplicated 11/1894, renumbered 316 12/1899
227	R6	O2 0-4-4T		WA	Nine Elms	11/1894	6/1933	
228	1699	330 class 0-6-0ST		WB	Beyer Peacock & Co	6/1877	4/1929	Duplicated 12/1894, renumbered 328 12/1899
228	R6	O2 0-4-4T		WA	Nine Elms	12/1894	8/1943	
229	1779	Single Frame 0-6-0		WB	Beyer Peacock & Co	4/1878	10/1925	Rebuilt Nine Elms 5/1886, duplicated 12/1894
229	R6	O2 0-4-4T		WA	Nine Elms	12/1894	3/1961	
230	1780	Single Frame 0-6-0		WB	Beyer Peacock & Co	4/1878	12/1889	Rebuilt Nine Elms 10/1888
230	R6	O2 0-4-4T		WA	Nine Elms	12/1894	7/1956	
231	575	231 class 2-4-0		JB	Beyer Peacock & Co	7/1866	6/1895	Duplicated 12/1894
231	R6	O2 0-4-4T		WA	Nine Elms	12/1894	2/1953	
232	576	231 class 2-4-0		JB	Beyer Peacock & Co	7/1866	6/1892	
232	R6	O2 0-4-4T		WA	Nine Elms	1/1895	9/1959	
233	577	231 class 2-4-0		JB	Beyer Peacock & Co	8/1866	7/1895	Duplicated 1/1895
233	R6	O2 0-4-4T		WA	Nine Elms	1/1895	2/1958	

APPENDIX C

A	B	C	D	E	F	G	H	I
234	578	231 class 2-4-0		JB	Beyer Peacock & Co	8/1866	5/1897	Duplicated 2/1895
234	R6	O2 0-4-4T		WA	Nine Elms	2/1895	3/1937	
235	579	231 class 2-4-0		JB	Beyer Peacock & Co	8/1866	4/1897	Duplicated 3/1895
235	R6	O2 0-4-4T		WA	Nine Elms	3/1895	2/1933	
236	580	231 class 2-4-0		JB	Beyer Peacock & Co	8/1866	1/1899	Duplicated 3/1895
236	R6	O2 0-4-4T		WA	Nine Elms	3/1895	1/1960	
237	751	Double Frame 0-6-0		JB	Beyer Peacock & Co	12/1866	10/1894	
237	D9	G6 0-6-0T		WA	Nine Elms	9/1898	2/1949	
238	752	Double Frame 0-6-0		JB	Beyer Peacock & Co	12/1866	7/1891	
238	D9	G6 0-6-0T		WA	Nine Elms	9/1898	12/1962	Transferred to service stock 12/1960 as DS682 (Meldon Quarry)
239	753	Double Frame 0-6-0		JB	Beyer Peacock & Co	12/1866	5/1897	
239	D9	G6 0-6-0T		WA	Nine Elms	9/1898	10/1948	
240	754	Double Frame 0-6-0		JB	Beyer Peacock & Co	1/1867	12/1893	
240	D9	G6 0-6-0T		WA	Nine Elms	10/1898	3/1949	
241	755	Double Frame 0-6-0		JB	Beyer Peacock & Co	1/1867	6/1899	
241	E9	M7 0-4-4T		DD	Nine Elms	5/1899	7/1963	
242	756	Double Frame 0-6-0		JB	Beyer Peacock & Co	1/1867	10/1891	
242	M7	M7 0-4-4T		DD	Nine Elms	2/1897	7/1958	
243	758	Standard 2-4-0WT		JB	Beyer Peacock & Co	1/1867	6/1889	
243	M7	M7 0-4-4T		DD	Nine Elms	3/1897	9/1958	
244	759	Standard 2-4-0WT		JB	Beyer Peacock & Co	1/1867	4/1897	
244	M7	M7 0-4-4T		DD	Nine Elms	3/1897	10/1957	
245	760	Standard 2-4-0WT		JB	Beyer Peacock & Co	2/1867	12/1891	
245	M7	M7 0-4-4T		DD	Nine Elms	4/1897	11/1962	
246	761	Standard 2-4-0WT		JB	Beyer Peacock & Co	2/1867	9/1898	Duplicated 4/1897
246	M7	M7 0-4-4T		DD	Nine Elms	4/1897	10/1961	
247	762	Standard 2-4-0WT		JB	Beyer Peacock & Co	2/1867	6/1896	
247	M7	M7 0-4-4T		DD	Nine Elms	4/1897	10/1961	
248	763	Standard 2-4-0WT		JB	Beyer Peacock & Co	2/1867	11/1898	Duplicated 4/1897
248	M7	M7 0-4-4T		DD	Nine Elms	5/1897	7/1961	
249	764	Standard 2-4-0WT		JB	Beyer Peacock & Co	11/1867	12/1890	
249	M7	M7 0-4-4T		DD	Nine Elms	5/1897	7/1963	
250	765	Standard 2-4-0WT		JB	Beyer Peacock & Co	11/1867	3/1891	
250	M7	M7 0-4-4T		DD	Nine Elms	5/1897	7/1957	
251	766	Standard 2-4-0WT		JB	Beyer Peacock & Co	11/1867	12/1889	
251	M7	M7 0-4-4T		DD	Nine Elms	6/1897	7/1963	
252	767	Standard 2-4-0WT		JB	Beyer Peacock & Co	12/1867	12/1890	
252	M7	M7 0-4-4T		DD	Nine Elms	6/1897	2/1959	
253	768	Standard 2-4-0WT		JB	Beyer Peacock & Co	12/1867	12/1893	
253	M7	M7 0-4-4T		DD	Nine Elms	6/1897	10/1961	
254	769	Standard 2-4-0WT		JB	Beyer Peacock & Co	12/1867	9/1898	Duplicated 7/1897
254	M7	M7 0-4-4T		DD	Nine Elms	8/1897	5/1964	
255	838	Standard 2-4-0WT		JB	Beyer Peacock & Co	10/1868	6/1895	
255	M7	M7 0-4-4T		DD	Nine Elms	8/1897	9/1960	
256	839	Standard 2-4-0WT		JB	Beyer Peacock & Co	10/1868	12/1898	Duplicated 8/1897
256	M7	M7 0-4-4T		DD	Nine Elms	8/1897	5/1959	
257	840	Standard 2-4-0WT		JB	Beyer Peacock & Co	10/1868	6/1896	Duplicated 6/1892
257	G6	G6 0-6-0T		WA	Nine Elms	6/1894	2/1949	
258	841	Standard 2-4-0WT		JB	Beyer Peacock & Co	11/1868	6/1886	
258	G6	G6 0-6-0T		WA	Nine Elms	8/1894	7/1961	
259	842	Standard 2-4-0WT		JB	Beyer Peacock & Co	11/1868	11/1890	
259	G6	G6 0-6-0T		WA	Nine Elms	9/1894	11/1950	
260	843	Standard 2-4-0WT		JB	Beyer Peacock & Co	11/1868	7/1891	
260	G6	G6 0-6-0T		WA	Nine Elms	9/1894	11/1958	
261	844	Standard 2-4-0WT		JB	Beyer Peacock & Co	11/1868	2/1898	Duplicated 9/1894
261	G6	G6 0-6-0T		WA	Nine Elms	9/1894	11/1948	
262	845	Standard 2-4-0WT		JB	Beyer Peacock & Co	11/1868	7/1892	
262	G6	G6 0-6-0T		WA	Nine Elms	9/1894	11/1949	
263	1089	Standard 2-4-0WT		JB	Beyer Peacock & Co	9/1871	10/1898	Duplicated 10/1894
263	G6	G6 0-6-0T		WA	Nine Elms	10/1894	9/1949	
264	1090	Standard 2-4-0WT		JB	Beyer Peacock & Co	9/1871	12/1894	
264	G6	G6 0-6-0T		WA	Nine Elms	10/1894	1/1949	
265	1091	Standard 2-4-0WT		JB	Beyer Peacock & Co	9/1871	4/1897	Duplicated 10/1894
265	G6	G6 0-6-0T		WA	Nine Elms	10/1894	8/1949	
266	1092	Standard 2-4-0WT		JB	Beyer Peacock & Co	10/1871	2/1898	Duplicated 10/1894
266	G6	G6 0-6-0T		WA	Nine Elms	10/1894	7/1960	
267	1093	Standard 2-4-0WT		JB	Beyer Peacock & Co	10/1871	11/1890	
267	C7	G6 0-6-0T		WA	Nine Elms	10/1896	1/1949	
268	1094	Standard 2-4-0WT		JB	Beyer Peacock & Co	10/1871	5/1890	
268	C7	G6 0-6-0T		WA	Nine Elms	10/1896	11/1950	
269	1095	Standard 2-4-0WT		JB	Beyer Peacock & Co	10/1871	6/1889	
269	C7	G6 0-6-0T		WA	Nine Elms	10/1896	10/1949	

APPENDIX C

A	B	C	D	E	F	G	H	I
270	1096	Standard 2-4-0WT		JB	Beyer Peacock & Co	10/1871	12/1893	
270	C7	G6 0-6-0T		WA	Nine Elms	11/1896	1/1959	
271		Lion 0-6-0		JB	Nine Elms	6/1872	4/1897	
271	X7	G6 0-6-0T		WA	Nine Elms	12/1897	9/1948	
272		Lion 0-6-0		JB	Nine Elms	6/1872	12/1891	
272	X7	G6 0-6-0T		WA	Nine Elms	2/1898	8/1960	Transferred to service stock 6/1950 as DS3152 (Meldon Quarry)
273	1163	Double Frame 0-6-0		JB	Beyer Peacock & Co	8/1872	5/1924	Rebuilt 4/1893, duplicated 2/1898, renumbered 273A 9/1917
273	X7	G6 0-6-0T		WA	Nine Elms	2/1898	3/1949	
274	1164	Double Frame 0-6-0		JB	Beyer Peacock & Co	8/1872	4/1923	Rebuilt 7/1893, duplicated 2/1898, renumbered 0229 1/1914
274	X7	G6 0-6-0T		WA	Nine Elms	2/1898	10/1960	
275	1165	Double Frame 0-6-0		JB	Beyer Peacock & Co	8/1872	4/1906	Rebuilt 7/1887, duplicated 2/1898
275	X7	G6 0-6-0T		WA	Nine Elms	3/1898	12/1949	
276	1166	Double Frame 0-6-0		JB	Beyer Peacock & Co	9/1872	4/1906	Rebuilt 3/1887, duplicated 4/1900
276	M9	G6 0-6-0T		WA	Nine Elms	4/1900	10/1949	
277	1167	Double Frame 0-6-0		JB	Beyer Peacock & Co	9/1872	5/1924	Rebuilt 1/1896, duplicated 4/1900, renumbered 277A 10/1917
277	M9	G6 0-6-0T		WA	Nine Elms	4/1900	11/1961	
277	1860	380 class 4-4-0		WA	Beyer Peacock & Co	10/1879	8/1924	Was 386 until 3/1914, then renumbered and duplicated 0277
278	1168	Double Frame 0-6-0		JB	Beyer Peacock & Co	9/1872	4/1924	Rebuilt 9/1886, duplicated 5/1900, renumbered 278A 9/1917
278	M9	G6 0-6-0T		WA	Nine Elms	5/1900	12/1948	
279		Vesuvius 2-4-0		JB	Nine Elms	2/1873	6/1897	Rebuilt Nine Elms 9/1886
279	D9	G6 0-6-0T		WA	Nine Elms	11/1898	12/1949	
280		Vesuvius 2-4-0	Persia	JB	Nine Elms	2/1873	5/1896	Rebuilt Nine Elms 4/1886
280	K9	T9 4-4-0		DD	Nine Elms	10/1899	5/1951	
281		Vesuvius 2-4-0		JB	Nine Elms	2/1873	4/1898	Rebuilt Nine Elms 9/1887
281	K9	T9 4-4-0		DD	Nine Elms	11/1899	10/1951	
282	1208	Ilfracombe 0-6-0		WB	Beyer Peacock & Co	3/1873	5/1909	Rebuilt Nine Elms 6/1889, duplicated 3/1889, renumbered 349 12/1889
282	K9	T9 4-4-0		DD	Nine Elms	11/1899	3/1954	
283	1209	Ilfracombe 0-6-0		WB	Beyer Peacock & Co	3/1873	12/1913	Rebuilt 4/1888, duplicated 11/1899, sold to S&MLR 12/1914
283	K9	T9 4-4-0		DD	Nine Elms	12/1899	12/1957	
284	1210	Ilfracombe 0-6-0		WB	Beyer Peacock & Co	3/1873	12/1913	Rebuilt 3/1888, duplicated 11/1899, sold to K&ESR 6/1914
284	K9	T9 4-4-0		DD	Nine Elms	12/1899	4/1958	
285	1269	Double Frame 0-6-0		JB	Beyer Peacock & Co	4/1873	6/1921	Rebuilt 9/1889, duplicated 1/1900, renumbered 285A 11/1917
285	O9	T9 4-4-0		DD	Nine Elms	1/1900	6/1958	
286	1270	Double Frame 0-6-0		JB	Beyer Peacock & Co	5/1873	3/1924	Rebuilt 11/1886, duplicated 2/1900, renumbered 286A 8/1917
286	O9	T9 4-4-0		DD	Nine Elms	1/1900	4/1951	
287	1271	Double Frame 0-6-0		JB	Beyer Peacock & Co	5/1873	8/1921	Rebuilt 6/1895, duplicated 2/1900, renumbered 287A 11/1917
287	O9	T9 4-4-0		DD	Nine Elms	1/1900	8/1961	
288	1272	Double Frame 0-6-0		JB	Beyer Peacock & Co	5/1873	4/1923	Rebuilt 8/1894, duplicated 2/1900, renumbered 288A 12/1917
288	O9	T9 4-4-0		DD	Nine Elms	2/1900	12/1960	
288	1859	380 class 4-4-0		WA	Beyer Peacock & Co	10/1879	8/1924	Was 385 until 3/1914, then renumbered and duplicated 0288
289	1273	Double Frame 0-6-0		JB	Beyer Peacock & Co	5/1873	8/1921	Rebuilt 10/1886, duplicated 2/1900, renumbered 289A 10/1917
289	O9	T9 4-4-0		DD	Nine Elms	2/1900	11/1959	
290	1274	Double Frame 0-6-0		JB	Beyer Peacock & Co	5/1873	12/1913	Rebuilt 3/1887, duplicated 6/1898, renumbered 351 12/1899
290	C8	C8 4-4-0		DD	Nine Elms	6/1898	10/1933	
291		Lion 0-6-0		JB	Nine Elms	9/1873	12/1887	
291	C8	C8 4-4-0		DD	Nine Elms	6/1898	1/1935	
292		Lion 0-6-0		JB	Nine Elms	9/1873	7/1886	
292	C8	C8 4-4-0		DD	Nine Elms	6/1898	1/1936	
293		Lion 0-6-0		JB	Nine Elms	10/1873	12/1887	
293	C8	C8 4-4-0		DD	Nine Elms	7/1898	2/1935	
294		Vesuvius 2-4-0		JB	Nine Elms	4/1873	1/1899	Rebuilt Nine Elms 6/1895, duplicated 4/1898
294	C8	C8 4-4-0		DD	Nine Elms	8/1898	2/1933	
295		Vesuvius 2-4-0		JB	Nine Elms	1/1874	12/1893	
295	C8	C8 4-4-0		DD	Nine Elms	10/1898	8/1935	
296		Vesuvius 2-4-0		JB	Nine Elms	1/1874	6/1896	
296	C8	C8 4-4-0		DD	Nine Elms	11/1898	11/1935	
297		Vesuvius 2-4-0		JB	Nine Elms	1/1874	9/1894	Rebuilt Nine Elms 2/1888
297	C8	C8 4-4-0		DD	Nine Elms	11/1898	6/1936	
298	1412	Standard 2-4-0WT		JB	Beyer Peacock & Co	6/1874	12/1962	Duplicated 11/1898
298	C8	C8 4-4-0		DD	Nine Elms	11/1898	1/1938	
299	1413	Standard 2-4-0WT		JB	Beyer Peacock & Co	6/1874	12/1889	
299	C8	C8 4-4-0		DD	Nine Elms	11/1898	8/1937	
300	1428	Ilfracombe 0-6-0		WB	Beyer Peacock & Co	6/1874	12/1913	Rebuilt 9/1890, duplicated 12/1900, sold to S&MR 12/1914
300	T9	T9 4-4-0		DD	Nine Elms	12/1900	3/1961	
301	1429	Ilfracombe 0-6-0		WB	Beyer Peacock & Co	6/1874	11/1905	Rebuilt Nine Elms 5/1890, duplicated 12/1900
301	T9	T9 4-4-0		DD	Nine Elms	12/1900	8/1959	
302	1360	Single Frame 0-6-0		WB	Beyer Peacock & Co	7/1874	11/1921	Rebuilt Nine Elms 7/1886, duplicated 12/1900
302	T9	T9 4-4-0		DD	Nine Elms	12/1900	9/1952	
303	1361	Single Frame 0-6-0		WB	Beyer Peacock & Co	7/1874	11/1921	Rebuilt Nine Elms 7/1886, duplicated 12/1900
303	T9	T9 4-4-0		DD	Nine Elms	12/1900	6/1951	
304	1362	Single Frame 0-6-0		WB	Beyer Peacock & Co	7/1874	4/1906	Rebuilt Nine Elms 10/1892, duplicated 1/1901
304	T9	T9 4-4-0		DD	Nine Elms	12/1900	9/1957	

APPENDIX C

A	B	C	D	E	F	G	H	I
305	1363	Single Frame 0-6-0		WB	Beyer Peacock & Co	7/1874	12/1913	Rebuilt Nine Elms 8/1886, duplicated 1/1901
305	X9	T9 4-4-0		DD	Nine Elms	2/1901	4/1951	
306	1364	Single Frame 0-6-0		WB	Beyer Peacock & Co	7/1874	9/1892	Rebuilt Nine Elms 2/1887
306	3525	700 class 0-6-0		DD	Dubs & Co	5/1897	4/1962	Was No 702 until 7/1898
307	1365	Single Frame 0-6-0		WB	Beyer Peacock & Co	7/1874	1/1914	Rebuilt Nine Elms 5/1886, duplicated 2/1901
307	X9	T9 4-4-0		DD	Nine Elms	2/1901	12/1952	
307	1952	135 class 4-4-0		WA	Beyer Peacock & Co	12/1880	12/1924	Was No 139, renumbered and duplicated 0307 3/1914
308	1366	Single Frame 0-6-0		WB	Beyer Peacock & Co	7/1874	9/1892	
308	3526	700 class 0-6-0		DD	Dubs & Co	5/1897	9/1961	Was No 703 until 7/1898
309	1367	Single Frame 0-6-0		WB	Beyer Peacock & Co	7/1874	10/1890	Rebuilt Nine Elms 8/1886
309	3527	700 class 0-6-0		DD	Dubs & Co	5/1897	12/1962	Was No 704 until 7/1898
310	1368	Single Frame 0-6-0		WB	Beyer Peacock & Co	8/1874	1/1914	Rebuilt Nine Elms 7/1893, duplicated 2/1901
310	X9	T9 4-4-0		DD	Nine Elms	4/1901	5/1959	
310	1953	135 class 4-4-0		WA	Beyer Peacock & Co	12/1880	12/1924	Was No 140, renumbered and duplicated 0310 5/1914
311	1369	Single Frame 0-6-0		WB	Beyer Peacock & Co	8/1874	10/1925	Rebuilt Nine Elms 11/1886, duplicated 2/1901
311	X9	T9 4-4-0		DD	Nine Elms	4/1901	7/1952	
312	1370	Single Frame 0-6-0		WB	Beyer Peacock & Co	8/1874	1/1914	Rebuilt Nine Elms 9/1894, duplicated 5/1901
312	X9	T9 4-4-0		DD	Nine Elms	5/1901	1/1952	
312	1956	135 class 4-4-0		WA	Beyer Peacock & Co	12/1880	6/1923	Was No 143, renumbered and duplicated 0312 5/1914
313	1371	Single Frame 0-6-0		WB	Beyer Peacock & Co	8/1874	12/1913	Rebuilt Nine Elms 10/1887, duplicated 5/1901
313	G10	T9 4-4-0		DD	Nine Elms	9/1901	7/1961	
314	1414	Standard 2-4-0WT		JB	Beyer Peacock & Co	6/1874	12/1962	Duplicated 5/1901
314	G10	T9 4-4-0		DD	Nine Elms	9/1901	5/1951	
315		Vesuvius 2-4-0		JB	Nine Elms	2/1875	7/1890	Rebuilt Nine Elms 11/1886
315	3528	700 class 0-6-0		DD	Dubs & Co	5/1897	12/1962	Was No 705 until 7/1898
316		Vesuvius 2-4-0		JB	Nine Elms	2/1875	2/1899	
316		330 class 0-6-0ST		WB	Beyer Peacock & Co	6/1877	5/1930	Was No 227, then 0227 until 12/1899, duplicated 6/1912
316	3539	700 class 0-6-0		DD	Dubs & Co	8/1897	12/1962	Was No 459 until 6/1912
317		Vesuvius 2-4-0		JB	Nine Elms	3/1875	12/1895	
317	3529	700 class 0-6-0		DD	Dubs & Co	5/1897	7/1961	Was No 706 until 7/1898
318	1354	Metropolitan 4-4-0T		WB	Beyer Peacock & Co	1/1875	10/1906	Duplicated 8/1900
318	B10	M7 0-4-4T		DD	Nine Elms	8/1900	12/1959	
319	1355	Metropolitan 4-4-0T		WB	Beyer Peacock & Co	1/1875	1/1909	Duplicated 8/1900
319	B10	M7 0-4-4T		DD	Nine Elms	8/1900	1/1960	
320	1356	Metropolitan 4-4-0T		WB	Beyer Peacock & Co	1/1875	12/1913	Duplicated 9/1900
320	B10	M7 0-4-4T		DD	Nine Elms	9/1900	3/1963	
321	1357	Metropolitan 4-4-0T		WB	Beyer Peacock & Co	1/1875	2/1907	Duplicated 9/1900
321	B10	M7 0-4-4T		DD	Nine Elms	9/1900	9/1962	
322	1358	Metropolitan 4-4-0T		WB	Beyer Peacock & Co	2/1875	1/1908	Duplicated 10/1900
322	C10	M7 0-4-4T		DD	Nine Elms	9/1900	11/1958	
323	1359	Metropolitan 4-4-0T		WB	Beyer Peacock & Co	2/1875	9/1906	Duplicated 10/1900
323	C10	M7 0-4-4T		DD	Nine Elms	10/1900	12/1959	
324	1517	Ilfracombe 0-6-0		WB	Beyer Peacock & Co	3/1875	8/1910	Rebuilt Nine Elms 6/1888, duplicated 10/1890, sold to S&MR 1/1911
324	C10	M7 0-4-4T		DD	Nine Elms	10/1900	9/1959	
325	1534	Standard 2-4-0WT		JB	Beyer Peacock & Co	10/1875	12/1888	
325	3530	700 class 0-6-0		DD	Dubs & Co	6/1897	12/1962	Was No 707 until 7/1898
326	1535	Standard 2-4-0WT		JB	Beyer Peacock & Co	10/1875	2/1897	
326	3531	700 class 0-6-0		DD	Dubs & Co	6/1897	2/1962	Was No 708 until 7/1898
327	1536	Standard 2-4-0WT		JB	Beyer Peacock & Co	11/1875	10/1892	
327	3532	700 class 0-6-0		DD	Dubs & Co	6/1897	5/1961	Was No 709 until 7/351898
328	1537	Standard 2-4-0WT		JB	Beyer Peacock & Co	11/1875	9/1898	
328		330 class 0-6-0ST		WB	Beyer Peacock & Co	6/1877	4/1929	Was No 228, then 0228 until 12/1899, duplicated 11/1911
328	A15	M7 0-4-4T		DD	Nine Elms	11/1911	3/1963	
329	1538	Standard 2-4-0WT		JB	Beyer Peacock & Co	11/1875	12/1962	Duplicated 11/1901
329	K10	K10 4-4-0		DD	Nine Elms	11/1901	4/1950	
330	1591	330 class 0-6-0ST		WB	Beyer Peacock & Co	5/1876	12/1924	Duplicated 9/1905
330	F13	F13 4-6-0		DD	Nine Elms	9/1905	7/1924	
331	1592	330 class 0-6-0ST		WB	Beyer Peacock & Co	5/1876	11/1930	Duplicated 9/1905
331	F13	F13 4-6-0		DD	Nine Elms	9/1905	2/1924	
332	1593	330 class 0-6-0ST		WB	Beyer Peacock & Co	5/1876	5/1932	Duplicated 10/1905
332	F13	F13 4-6-0		DD	Nine Elms	10/1905	8/1924	
333	1594	330 class 0-6-0ST		WB	Beyer Peacock & Co	5/1876	7/1929	Duplicated 10/1905
333	F13	F13 4-6-0		DD	Nine Elms	10/1905	8/1924	
334	1595	330 class 0-6-0ST		WB	Beyer Peacock & Co	5/1876	8/1932	Duplicated 11/1905
334	F13	F13 4-6-0		DD	Nine Elms	12/1905	10/1924	Laid aside as unserviceable 12/1921
335	1596	330 class 0-6-0ST		WB	Beyer Peacock & Co	5/1876	5/1932	Duplicated 11/1907
335	E14	E14 4-6-0		DD	Nine Elms	11/1907	1/1914	
336	1600	Single Frame 0-6-0		WB	Beyer Peacock & Co	7/1876	11/1921	Rebuilt Nine Elms 9/1889, duplicated 9/1901
336	G10	T9 4-4-0		DD	Nine Elms	10/1901	2/1953	
337	1601	Single Frame 0-6-0		WB	Beyer Peacock & Co	7/1876	5/1924	Rebuilt Nine Elms 9/1893, duplicated 9/1901
337	G10	T9 4-4-0		DD	Nine Elms	10/1901	12/1958	
337	1864	380 class 4-4-0		WA	Beyer Peacock & Co	11/1879	12/1924	No 390 until 1/1914, then renumbered and duplicated 0377

APPENDIX C

A	B	C	D	E	F	G	H	I
338	1602	Single Frame 0-6-0		WB	Beyer Peacock & Co	7/1876	12/1924	Rebuilt Nine Elms 9/1892, duplicated 9/1901
338	G10	T9 4-4-0		DD	Nine Elms	10/1901	4/1961	
339	1603	Single Frame 0-6-0		WB	Beyer Peacock & Co	7/1876	8/1891	
339	3533	700 class 0-6-0		DD	Dubs & Co	6/1897	5/1962	Was No 710 until 1898
340	1604	Single Frame 0-6-0		WB	Beyer Peacock & Co	7/1876	7/1903	Rebuilt Nine Elms 11/1889, duplicated 11/1901
340	K10	K10 4-4-0		DD	Nine Elms	11/1901	6/1948	
341	1605	Single Frame 0-6-0		WB	Beyer Peacock & Co	7/1876	12/1924	Rebuilt Nine Elms 1/1893, duplicated 11/1901
341	K10	K10 4-4-0		DD	Nine Elms	12/1901	12/1949	
342	1606	Single Frame 0-6-0		WB	Beyer Peacock & Co	8/1876	12/1924	Rebuilt Nine Elms 6/1894, duplicated 11/1901
342	K10	K10 4-4-0		DD	Nine Elms	12/1901	1/1947	
343	1607	Single Frame 0-6-0		WB	Beyer Peacock & Co	8/1876	5/1921	Rebuilt Nine Elms 9/1891, duplicated 11/1901
343	K10	K10 4-4-0		DD	Nine Elms	12/1901	1/1948	
344	1608	Single Frame 0-6-0		WB	Beyer Peacock & Co	8/1876	12/1916	Rebuilt Nine Elms 6/1891, duplicated 1/1902
344	L10	K10 4-4-0		DD	Nine Elms	1/1902	1/1947	
345	1609	Single Frame 0-6-0		WB	Beyer Peacock & Co	8/1876	12/1925	Rebuilt Nine Elms 7/1891, duplicated 1/1902
345	L10	K10 4-4-0		DD	Nine Elms	2/1902	9/1949	
346	1610	Single Frame 0-6-0		WB	Beyer Peacock & Co	8/1876	12/1883	
346	3534	700 class 0-6-0		DD	Dubs & Co	8/1897	11/1962	Was No 711 until 1898
347	1611	Single Frame 0-6-0		WB	Beyer Peacock & Co	8/1876	9/1925	Rebuilt Nine Elms 7/1893, duplicated 3/1902
347	L10	K10 4-4-0		DD	Nine Elms	3/1902	1/1947	
347	1957	135 class 4-4-0		WA	Beyer Peacock & Co	12/1880	11/1921	Was No 144, renumbered and duplicated 0347 4/1914
348	2657	348 class 4-4-0		WB	Sharp Stewart & Co	2/1877	3/1905	Rebuilt Nine Elms 9/1888, duplicated 6/1900
348	R9	G6 0-6-0T		WA	Nine Elms	6/1900	8/1948	
349	2658	348 class 4-4-0		WB	Sharp Stewart & Co	2/1877	3/1899	Rebuilt Nine Elms 3/1889
349	1208	Ilfracombe 0-6-0		WB	Beyer Peacock & Co	3/1873	5/1909	Was No 282, duplicated 6/1900, sold to K&ESR 4/1910
349	R9	G6 0-6-0T		WA	Nine Elms	6/1900	7/1961	
350	2659	348 class 4-4-0		WB	Sharp Stewart & Co	2/1877	12/1889	
350	3535	700 class 0-6-0		DD	Dubs & Co	8/1897	3/1962	Was No 712 until 1898
351	2660	348 class 4-4-0		WB	Sharp Stewart & Co	3/1877	11/1889	Rebuilt Nine Elms 5/1889
351	1274	Double Frame 0-6-0		JB	Beyer Peacock & Co	5/1873	12/1921	Was No 290, renumbered 351 12/1899, 0351 6/1900, 351A 6/1917
351	R9	G6 0-6-0T		WA	Nine Elms	6/1900	2/1949	
352	2661	348 class 4-4-0		WB	Sharp Stewart & Co	3/1877	12/1889	
352	3536	700 class 0-6-0		DD	Dubs & Co	8/1897	7/1959	Was No 713 until 1898
353	2662	348 class 4-4-0		WB	Sharp Stewart & Co	3/1877	3/1905	Rebuilt Nine Elms 4/1890, duplicated 6/1900
353	R9	G6 0-6-0T		WA	Nine Elms	6/1900	2/1951	
354	2663	348 class 4-4-0		WB	Sharp Stewart & Co	3/1877	3/1905	Rebuilt Nine Elms 8/1889, duplicated 6/1900
354	R9	G6 0-6-0T		WA	Nine Elms	6/1900	11/1949	
355	2664	348 class 4-4-0		WB	Sharp Stewart & Co	3/1877	12/1890	Rebuilt Nine Elms 5/1889
355	3537	700 class 0-6-0		DD	Dubs & Co	8/1897	2/1961	Was No 714 until 1898
356	2665	348 class 4-4-0		WB	Sharp Stewart & Co	4/1877	3/1905	Rebuilt Nine Elms 12/1889, duplicated 10/1900
356	C10	M7 0-4-4T		DD	Nine Elms	10/1900	12/1958	
357	2666	348 class 4-4-0		WB	Sharp Stewart & Co	4/1877	3/1905	Rebuilt Nine Elms 4/1889, duplicated 10/1900
357	C10	M7 0-4-4T		DD	Nine Elms	10/1900	4/1961	
358	2667	348 class 4-4-0		WB	Sharp Stewart & Co	4/1877	12/1893	
358	A7	T1 0-4-4T		WA	Nine Elms	6/1896	7/1944	
359	2668	348 class 4-4-0		WB	Sharp Stewart & Co	5/1877	4/1890	
359	A7	T1 0-4-4T		WA	Nine Elms	6/1896	10/1943	
360	2669	348 class 4-4-0		WB	Sharp Stewart & Co	5/1877	12/1893	
360	A7	T1 0-4-4T		WA	Nine Elms	6/1896	7/1944	
361	2670	348 class 4-4-0		WB	Sharp Stewart & Co	5/1877	3/1894	
361	A7	T1 0-4-4T		WA	Nine Elms	6/1896	2/1949	
362	2671	348 class 4-4-0		WB	Sharp Stewart & Co	5/1877	10/1892	
362	A7	T1 0-4-4T		WA	Nine Elms	7/1896	2/1939	
363	2672	348 class 4-4-0		WB	Sharp Stewart & Co	5/1877	3/1894	
363	A7	T1 0-4-4T		WA	Nine Elms	7/1896	6/1948	
364	2673	348 class 4-4-0		WB	Sharp Stewart & Co	5/1877	11/1894	
364	A7	T1 0-4-4T		WA	Nine Elms	7/1896	10/1944	
365	2674	348 class 4-4-0		WB	Sharp Stewart & Co	5/1877	10/1898	Duplicated 7/1896
365	A7	T1 0-4-4T		WA	Nine Elms	7/1896	3/1938	
366	2675	348 class 4-4-0		WB	Sharp Stewart & Co	5/1877	3/1894	
366	A7	T1 0-4-4T		WA	Nine Elms	7/1896	10/1948	
367	2676	348 class 4-4-0		WB	Sharp Stewart & Co	5/1877	9/1891	
367	A7	T1 0-4-4T		WA	Nine Elms	7/1896	5/1951	
368	1781	Single Frame 0-6-0		WB	Beyer Peacock & Co	4/1878	3/!893	Rebuilt Nine Elms 12/1888
368	3538	700 class 0-6-0		DD	Dubs & Co	8/1897	12/1962	Was No 715 until 1898
369	1782	Single Frame 0-6-0		WB	Beyer Peacock & Co	4/1878	12/!925	Rebuilt Nine Elms 9/1888, duplicated 4/1901
369	E10	E10 4-2-2-0		DD	Nine Elms	4/1901	9/1926	
370	1783	Single Frame 0-6-0		WB	Beyer Peacock & Co	5/1878	7/1924	Rebuilt Nine Elms 5/1890, duplicated 6/1901
370	E10	E10 4-2-2-0		DD	Nine Elms	4/1901	9/1926	
370	1948	135 class 4-4-0		WA	Beyer Peacock & Co	11/1880	11/1921	Was No 135 until renumbered and duplicated 0370 4/1914
371	1784	Single Frame 0-6-0		WB	Beyer Peacock & Co	5/1878	2/1916	Rebuilt Nine Elms 12/1889, duplicated 6/1901
371	E10	E10 4-2-2-0		DD	Nine Elms	6/1901	9/1926	Laid aside 10/1922

APPENDIX C

Fig. 435. Nine Elms built T9 class No 305, recorded on 13th May 1902.

APPENDIX C

A	B	C	D	E	F	G	H	I
372	1785	Single Frame 0-6-0		WB	Beyer Peacock & Co	5/1878	3/1906	Rebuilt Nine Elms 8/1892, duplicated 6/1901
372	E10	E10 4-2-2-0		DD	Nine Elms	6/1901	4/1927	
373	1786	Single Frame 0-6-0		WB	Beyer Peacock & Co	5/1878	11/1902	Duplicated 7/1901
373	E10	E10 4-2-2-0		DD	Nine Elms	7/1901	4/1927	
374	1838	46 class 4-4-0T		WA	Beyer Peacock & Co	7/1879	12/1924	Rebuilt as 4-4-2T No 374 12/1886
374	1838	46 class 4-4-2T		WA	Nine Elms	12/1886	12/1924	Duplicated 4/1903
374	H11	M7 0-4-4T		DD	Nine Elms	4/1903	10/1959	
375	1839	46 class 4-4-0T		WA	Beyer Peacock & Co	7/1879	7/1925	Rebuilt as 4-4-2T No 375 10/1884
375	1839	46 class 4-4-2T		WA	Nine Elms	10/1884	7/1925	Duplicated 5/1903
375	H11	M7 0-4-4T		DD	Nine Elms	5/1903	9/1962	
376	1840	46 class 4-4-0T		WA	Beyer Peacock & Co	8/1879	2/1914	Rebuilt as 4-4-2T No 376 7/1883
376	1840	46 class 4-4-2T		WA	Nine Elms	7/1883	2/1914	Duplicated 5/1903
376	H11	M7 0-4-4T		DD	Nine Elms	5/1903	1/1959	
377	1841	46 class 4-4-0T		WA	Beyer Peacock & Co	8/1879	1/1925	Rebuilt as 4-4-2T No 377 7/1886
377	1841	46 class 4-4-2T		WA	Nine Elms	7/1886	1/1925	Duplicated 5/1903
377	H11	M7 0-4-4T		DD	Nine Elms	5/1903	8/1962	
378	1842	46 class 4-4-0T		WA	Beyer Peacock & Co	8/1879	5/1923	Rebuilt as 4-4-2T No 378 8/1885
378	1842	46 class 4-4-2T		WA	Nine Elms	8/1885	5/1923	Duplicated 5/1903
378	H11	M7 0-4-4T		DD	Nine Elms	6/1903	12/1962	
379	1843	46 class 4-4-0T		WA	Beyer Peacock & Co	8/1879	11/1921	Rebuilt as 4-4-2T No 379 11/1884
379	1843	46 class 4-4-2T		WA	Nine Elms	11/1884	11/1921	Duplicated 6/1904
379	C12	M7 0-4-4T		DD	Nine Elms	5/1904	10/1963	
380	1854	380 class 4-4-0		WA	Beyer Peacock & Co	9/1879	12/1924	Duplicated 4/1902
380	P10	K10 4-4-0		DD	Nine Elms	4/1902	6/1949	
381	1855	380 class 4-4-0		WA	Beyer Peacock & Co	9/1879	12/1924	Duplicated 4/1902
381	P10	K10 4-4-0		DD	Nine Elms	4/1902	6/1947	
382	1856	380 class 4-4-0		WA	Beyer Peacock & Co	9/1879	7/1923	Duplicated 4/1902, renumbered 0160 1/1914
382	P10	K10 4-4-0		DD	Nine Elms	5/1902	8/1950	
383	1857	380 class 4-4-0		WA	Beyer Peacock & Co	9/1879	12/1913	Duplicated 4/1902
383	P10	K10 4-4-0		DD	Nine Elms	5/1902	6/1949	
384	1858	380 class 4-4-0		WA	Beyer Peacock & Co	9/1879	8/1924	Duplicated 4/1902
384	P10	K10 4-4-0		DD	Nine Elms	5/1902	6/1951	
385	1859	380 class 4-4-0		WA	Beyer Peacock & Co	10/1879	8/1924	Duplicated 4/1902, renumbered 0288 3/1914
385	S10	K10 4-4-0		DD	Nine Elms	5/1902	1/1949	
386	1860	380 class 4-4-0		WA	Beyer Peacock & Co	10/1879	8/1924	Duplicated 5/1902, renumbered 0277 3/1914
386	S10	K10 4-4-0		DD	Nine Elms	6/1902	8/1949	
387	1861	380 class 4-4-0		WA	Beyer Peacock & Co	11/1879	12/1913	Duplicated 5/1902
387	S10	K10 4-4-0		DD	Nine Elms	6/1902	3/1947	
388	1862	380 class 4-4-0		WA	Beyer Peacock & Co	11/1879	12/1925	Duplicated 5/1902, renumbered 0162 1/1914
388	S10	K10 4-4-0		DD	Nine Elms	6/1902	4/1947	
389	1863	380 class 4-4-0		WA	Beyer Peacock & Co	11/1879	12/1913	Duplicated 5/1902
389	S10	K10 4-4-0		DD	Nine Elms	6/1902	7/1951	
390	1864	380 class 4-4-0		WA	Beyer Peacock & Co	11/1879	12/1924	Duplicated 6/1902, renumbered 0377 1/1914
390	V10	K10 4-4-0		DD	Nine Elms	6/1902	10/1950	
391	1865	380 class 4-4-0		WA	Beyer Peacock & Co	12/1879	12/1913	Duplicated 7/1902
391	V10	K10 4-4-0		DD	Nine Elms	7/1902	10/1949	
392	V10	K10 4-4-0		DD	Nine Elms	7/1902	10/1948	
393	2041	Ilfracombe 0-6-0		WB	Beyer Peacock & Co	11/1880	1/1905	Duplicated 4/1902, sold to East Kent Railway 8/1918
393	L10	K10 4-4-0		DD	Nine Elms	4/1902	1/1949	
394	2042	Ilfracombe 0-6-0		WB	Beyer Peacock & Co	11/1880	12/1913	Duplicated 4/1902
394	L10	K10 4-4-0		DD	Nine Elms	4/1902	5/1949	
395	2747	395 class 0-6-0		WA	Nielson & Co	11/1881	10/1916	Duplicated 6/1903
395	S11	S11 4-4-0		DD	Nine Elms	6/1903	9/1951	
396	2748	395 class 0-6-0		WA	Nielson & Co	11/1881	3/1917	Duplicated 6/1903
396	S11	S11 4-4-0		DD	Nine Elms	6/1903	10/1951	
397	2749	395 class 0-6-0		WA	Nielson & Co	12/1887	6/1953	Duplicated 7/1903
397	S11	S11 4-4-0		DD	Nine Elms	7/1903	11/1951	
398	2750	395 class 0-6-0		WA	Nielson & Co	12/1887	4/1917	Duplicated 7/1903
398	S11	S11 4-4-0		DD	Nine Elms	8/1903	11/1951	
399	2751	395 class 0-6-0		WA	Nielson & Co	12/1887	9/1916	Duplicated 7/1903
399	S11	S11 4-4-0		DD	Nine Elms	8/1903	11/1951	
400	2752	395 class 0-6-0		WA	Nielson & Co	1/1882	1/1957	Duplicated 11/1903
400	V11	S11 4-4-0		DD	Nine Elms	11/1903	10/1954	
401	2753	395 class 0-6-0		WA	Nielson & Co	2/1882	3/1917	Duplicated 11/1903
401	V11	S11 4-4-0		DD	Nine Elms	11/1903	8/1951	
402	2754	395 class 0-6-0		WA	Nielson & Co	2/1882	9/1917	Duplicated 11/1903
402	V11	S11 4-4-0		DD	Nine Elms	12/1903	2/1951	
403	2755	395 class 0-6-0		WA	Nielson & Co	3/1882	7/1917	Duplicated 11/1903
403	V11	S11 4-4-0		DD	Nine Elms	12/1903	9/1951	
404	2756	395 class 0-6-0		WA	Nielson & Co	3/1882	4/1918	Duplicated 11/1903
404	V11	S11 4-4-0		DD	Nine Elms	12/1903	9/1951	
405	2757	395 class 0-6-0		WA	Nielson & Co	3/1882	10/1916	Duplicated 9/1906

APPENDIX C

A	B	C	D	E	F	G	H	I
405	P13	L11 4-4-0		DD	Nine Elms	9/1906	1/1951	
406	2758	395 class 0-6-0		WA	Nielson & Co	3/1882	4/1918	Duplicated 9/1906
406	P13	L11 4-4-0		DD	Nine Elms	10/1906	5/1951	
407	K13	L11 4-4-0		DD	Nine Elms	5/1906	10/1950	
408	K13	L11 4-4-0		DD	Nine Elms	5/1906	2/1951	
409	2131	330 0-6-0ST		WB	Beyer Peacock & Co	5/1882	9/1924	Duplicated 6/1906
409	K13	L11 4-4-0		DD	Nine Elms	6/1906	6/1951	
410	2132	330 0-6-0ST		WB	Beyer Peacock & Co	5/1882	9/1930	Duplicated 6/1906
410	M13	L11 4-4-0		DD	Nine Elms	6/1906	12/1949	
411	2133	330 0-6-0ST		WB	Beyer Peacock & Co	6/1882	12/1927	Duplicated 6/1906
411	M13	L11 4-4-0		DD	Nine Elms	6/1906	6/1952	
412	2134	330 0-6-0ST		WB	Beyer Peacock & Co	6/1882	4/1925	Duplicated 7/1906
412	M13	L11 4-4-0		DD	Nine Elms	7/1906	11/1950	
413	2135	330 0-6-0ST		WB	Beyer Peacock & Co	6/1882	1/1931	Duplicated 8/1906
413	M13	L11 4-4-0		DD	Nine Elms	8/1906	2/1951	
414	2136	330 0-6-0ST		WB	Beyer Peacock & Co	6/1882	12/1924	Duplicated 8/1906
414	M13	L11 4-4-0		DD	Nine Elms	8/1906	4/1951	
415	2167	415 class 4-4-2T		WA	Beyer Peacock & Co	8/1882	11/1921	Duplicated 5/1904
415	L12	L12 4-4-0		DD	Nine Elms	6/1904	1/1953	
416	2168	415 class 4-4-2T		WA	Beyer Peacock & Co	8/1882	11/1925	Duplicated 5/1904
416	L12	L12 4-4-0		DD	Nine Elms	6/1904	6/1951	
417	2169	415 class 4-4-2T		WA	Beyer Peacock & Co	9/1882	11/1921	Duplicated 6/1904
417	L12	L12 4-4-0		DD	Nine Elms	6/1904	10/1951	
418	2170	415 class 4-4-2T		WA	Beyer Peacock & Co	9/1882	11/1921	Duplicated 6/1904
418	L12	L12 4-4-0		DD	Nine Elms	7/1904	6/1951	
419	2171	415 class 4-4-2T		WA	Beyer Peacock & Co	9/1882	11/1921	Duplicated 6/1904
419	L12	L12 4-4-0		DD	Nine Elms	7/1904	10/1951	
420	2172	415 class 4-4-2T		WA	Beyer Peacock & Co	9/1882	11/1921	Duplicated 10/1904
420	O12	L12 4-4-0		DD	Nine Elms	10/1904	8/1951	
421	2173	415 class 4-4-2T		WA	Beyer Peacock & Co	9/1882	11/1921	Duplicated 101904
421	O12	L12 4-4-0		DD	Nine Elms	10/1904	8/1951	Damaged in Salisbury accident 30/6/1906
422	2174	415 class 4-4-2T		WA	Beyer Peacock & Co	10/1882	11/1925	Duplicated 10/1904
422	O12	L12 4-4-0		DD	Nine Elms	11/1904	8/1951	
423	2175	415 class 4-4-2T		WA	Beyer Peacock & Co	10/1882	11/1921	Duplicated 10/1904
423	O12	L12 4-4-0		DD	Nine Elms	11/1904	7/1951	
424	2176	415 class 4-4-2T		WA	Beyer Peacock & Co	10/1882	6/1916	Duplicated 10/1904
424	O12	L12 4-4-0		DD	Nine Elms	11/1904	7/1951	
425	2177	415 class 4-4-2T		WA	Beyer Peacock & Co	11/1882	11/1921	Duplicated 12/1904
425	R12	L12 4-4-0		DD	Nine Elms	12/1904	8/1951	
426	2178	415 class 4-4-2T		WA	Beyer Peacock & Co	11/1882	6/1924	Duplicated 12/1904
426	R12	L12 4-4-0		DD	Nine Elms	12/1904	10/1951	
427	2501	415 class 4-4-2T		WA	Robert Stephenson & Co	3/1883	11/1921	Duplicated 12/1904
427	R12	L12 4-4-0		DD	Nine Elms	12/1904	10/1951	
428	2502	415 class 4-4-2T		WA	Robert Stephenson & Co	3/1883	7/1925	Duplicated 12/1904
428	R12	L12 4-4-0		DD	Nine Elms	1/1905	4/1951	
429	2503	415 class 4-4-2T		WA	Robert Stephenson & Co	4/1883	11/1925	Duplicated 12/1904
429	R12	L12 4-4-0		DD	Nine Elms	1/1905	9/1951	
430	2504	415 class 4-4-2T		WA	Robert Stephenson & Co	6/1883	11/1921	Duplicated 1/1905
430	T12	L12 4-4-0		DD	Nine Elms	2/1905	2/1951	
431	2505	415 class 4-4-2T		WA	Robert Stephenson & Co	6/1883	12/1925	Duplicated 1/1905
431	T12	L12 4-4-0		DD	Nine Elms	2/1905	9/1951	
432	2506	415 class 4-4-2T		WA	Robert Stephenson & Co	10/1883	11/1921	Duplicated 1/1905
432	T12	L12 4-4-0		DD	Nine Elms	2/1905	9/1951	
433	2956	395 class 0-6-0		WA	Nielson & Co	4/1883	11/1956	Duplicated 2/1905
433	T12	L12 4-4-0		DD	Nine Elms	3/1905	11/1951	
434	2957	395 class 0-6-0		WA	Nielson & Co	4/1883	4/1918	Duplicated 2/1905
434	T12	L12 4-4-0		DD	Nine Elms	3/1905	2/1955	
435	2958	395 class 0-6-0		WA	Nielson & Co	4/1883	8/1916	Duplicated 9/1906
435	P13	L11 4-4-0		DD	Nine Elms	11/1906	11/1949	
436	2959	395 class 0-6-0		WA	Nielson & Co	4/1883	1/1957	Duplicated 11/1906
436	P13	L11 4-4-0		DD	Nine Elms	11/1906	7/1951	
437	2960	395 class 0-6-0		WA	Nielson & Co	4/1883	4/1918	Duplicated 11/1906
437	P13	L11 4-4-0		DD	Nine Elms	11/1906	11/1949	
438	2961	395 class 0-6-0		WA	Nielson & Co	5/1883	12/1917	Duplicated 3/1907
438	P13	L11 4-4-0		DD	Nine Elms	11/1906	7/1951	
439	2962	395 class 0-6-0		WA	Nielson & Co	5/1883	12/1958	Duplicated 3/1907
439	P13	L11 4-4-0		DD	Nine Elms	12/1906	6/1952	
440	2963	395 class 0-6-0		WA	Nielson & Co	5/1883	12/1950	Duplicated 3/1907
440	S13	L11 4-4-0		DD	Nine Elms	3/1907	5/1951	
441	2964	395 class 0-6-0		WA	Nielson & Co	5/1883	2/1956	Duplicated 4/1907
441	S13	L11 4-4-0		DD	Nine Elms	3/1907	5/1949	
442	2965	395 class 0-6-0		WA	Nielson & Co	5/1883	8/1957	Duplicated 4/1907

APPENDIX C

A	B	C	D	E	F	G	H	I
442	S13	L11 4-4-0		DD	Nine Elms	4/1907	5/1949	
443	2966	395 class 0-6-0		WA	Nielson & Co	5/1883	7/1917	Duplicated 3/1911
443	S13	L11 4-4-0		DD	Nine Elms	5/1907	4/1951	
444	2967	395 class 0-6-0		WA	Nielson & Co	6/1883	3/1917	Duplicated 4/1911
444	S13	L11 4-4-0		DD	Nine Elms	6/1907	11/1951	
445	2535	445 class 4-4-0		WA	Robert Stephenson & Co	4/1883	12/1925	Duplicated 6/1911
446	2536	445 class 4-4-0		WA	Robert Stephenson & Co	4/1883	4/1925	Duplicated 7/1911
447	2537	445 class 4-4-0		WA	Robert Stephenson & Co	5/1883	12/1925	Duplicated 7/1911
448	2538	445 class 4-4-0		WA	Robert Stephenson & Co	5/1883	12/1924	Duplicated 12/1910
449	2539	445 class 4-4-0		WA	Robert Stephenson & Co	6/1883	5/1925	Duplicated 12/1910
450	2540	445 class 4-4-0		WA	Robert Stephenson & Co	6/1883	4/1925	Duplicated 1/1911
451	2541	445 class 4-4-0		WA	Robert Stephenson & Co	7/1883	12/1924	Duplicated 2/1911, renumbered 451A 3/1924, duplicated 6/1924
452	2542	445 class 4-4-0		WA	Robert Stephenson & Co	7/1883	12/1925	Duplicated 2/1911
453	2543	445 class 4-4-0		WA	Robert Stephenson & Co	7/1883	12/1924	Duplicated 4/1908
453	G14	G14 4-6-0		DD	Nine Elms	4/1908	1/1925	
454	2544	445 class 4-4-0		WA	Robert Stephenson & Co	8/1883	12/1924	Duplicated 4/1908
454	G14	G14 4-6-0		DD	Nine Elms	4/1908	1/1925	
455	2545	445 class 4-4-0		WA	Robert Stephenson & Co	8/1883	7/1925	Duplicated 5/1908
455	G14	G14 4-6-0		DD	Nine Elms	4/1908	1/1925	
456	2546	445 class 4-4-0		WA	Robert Stephenson & Co	8/1883	5/1923	Duplicated 5/1908
456	G14	G14 4-6-0		DD	Nine Elms	5/1908	1/1925	
457	G14	G14 4-6-0		DD	Nine Elms	5/1908	1/1925	
458								This number was not used during the Nine Elms period
459	3539	700 class 0-6-0		DD	Dubs & Co	8/1897	12/1962	Was No 716 until 1898
460	3190	460 class 4-4-0T		WA	Neilson & Co	9/1884	1/1929	Duplicated 2/1912
461	3191	460 class 4-4-0T		WA	Neilson & Co	9/1884	10/1926	Duplicated 4/1912
462	3192	460 class 4-4-0T		WA	Neilson & Co	9/1884	4/1926	Duplicated 5/1912, renumbered 462A 2/1924
463	3193	460 class 4-4-0T		WA	Neilson & Co	10/1884	6/1926	Duplicated 3/1912
464	3194	460 class 4-4-0T		WA	Neilson & Co	10/1884	11/1927	Duplicated 6/1912, renumbered 464A 2/1924
465	3195	460 class 4-4-0T		WA	Neilson & Co	10/1884	12/1924	Duplicated 7/1912
466	3196	460 class 4-4-0T		WA	Neilson & Co	10/1884	7/1928	Duplicated 7/1912
467	3197	460 class 4-4-0T		WA	Neilson & Co	10/1884	4/1929	Duplicated 8/1912
468	3198	460 class 4-4-0T		WA	Neilson & Co	10/1884	5/1928	Duplicated 9/1912
469	3199	460 class 4-4-0T		WA	Neilson & Co	10/1884	4/1927	Duplicated 10/1912
470	2562	460 class 4-4-0T		WA	Robert Stephenson & Co	6/1884	4/1929	Duplicated 12/1912
471	2563	460 class 4-4-0T		WA	Robert Stephenson & Co	6/1884	3/1928	Duplicated 1/1913
472	2564	460 class 4-4-0T		WA	Robert Stephenson & Co	6/1884	11/1927	Duplicated 2/1913
473	2565	460 class 4-4-0T		WA	Robert Stephenson & Co	6/1884	10/1928	Duplicated 2/1923, renumbered 473A 2/1924
474	2566	460 class 4-4-0T		WA	Robert Stephenson & Co	8/1884	10/1928	Duplicated 2/1923
475	2567	460 class 4-4-0T		WA	Robert Stephenson & Co	8/1884	4/1926	Duplicated 1/1924, renumbered 475A 2/1924
476	2568	460 class 4-4-0T		WA	Robert Stephenson & Co	8/1884	2/1926	Duplicated 1/1924
477	2569	460 class 4-4-0T		WA	Robert Stephenson & Co	8/1884	10/1927	Duplicated 1/1924
478	2570	460 class 4-4-0T		WA	Robert Stephenson & Co	8/1884	11/1928	Duplicated 1/1924
479	3200	415 class 4-4-2T		WA	Neilson & Co	2/1885	3/1918	Duplicated 10/1911
479	A15	M7 0-4-4T		DD	Nine Elms	11/1911	4/1961	
480	3201	415 class 4-4-2T		WA	Neilson & Co	2/1885	11/1925	Duplicated 11/1911
480	A15	M7 0-4-4T		DD	Nine Elms	11/1911	5/1964	
481	3202	415 class 4-4-2T		WA	Neilson & Co	2/1885	12/1924	Duplicated 11/1911
481	A15	M7 0-4-4T		DD	Nine Elms	12/1911	6/1959	
482	3203	415 class 4-4-2T		WA	Neilson & Co	2/1885	11/1921	Duplicated 2/1914
483	3204	415 class 4-4-2T		WA	Neilson & Co	3/1885	11/1925	Duplicated 3/1914
484	3205	415 class 4-4-2T		WA	Neilson & Co	3/1885	11/1921	Duplicated 4/1914
485	3206	415 class 4-4-2T		WA	Neilson & Co	3/1885	6/1924	Duplicated 6/1914
486	3207	415 class 4-4-2T		WA	Neilson & Co	3/1885	1/1928	Duplicated 12/1913
487	3208	415 class 4-4-2T		WA	Neilson & Co	3/1885	9/1924	Duplicated 1/1914
488	3209	415 class 4-4-2T		WA	Neilson & Co	3/1885	7/1961	Duplicated 3/1914, sold 9/1917, repurchased 3/1946
489	3210	415 class 4-4-2T		WA	Neilson & Co	3/1885	3/1918	Duplicated 5/1914
490	2004	415 class 4-4-2T		WA	Dubs & Co	12/1884	8/1926	Duplicated 6/1914
491	2005	415 class 4-4-2T		WA	Dubs & Co	12/1884	11/1921	Duplicated 7/1914
492	2006	415 class 4-4-2T		WA	Dubs & Co	12/1884	11/1921	Duplicated 7/1921
493	2007	415 class 4-4-2T		WA	Dubs & Co	12/1884	11/1921	Duplicated 7/1921
494	2008	415 class 4-4-2T		WA	Dubs & Co	12/1884	11/1921	Duplicated 8/1921
495	2009	415 class 4-4-2T		WA	Dubs & Co	12/1884	11/1921	Duplicated 8/1921
496	3376	395 class 0-6-0		WA	Nielson & Co	10/1885	1/1956	Duplicated 5/1921
497	3377	395 class 0-6-0		WA	Nielson & Co	11/1885	3/1917	
498	3378	395 class 0-6-0		WA	Nielson & Co	11/1885	9/1917	
499	3379	395 class 0-6-0		WA	Nielson & Co	11/1885	3/1917	
500	3380	395 class 0-6-0		WA	Nielson & Co	11/1885	9/1917	
501	3381	395 class 0-6-0		WA	Nielson & Co	11/1885	3/1917	
502	3382	395 class 0-6-0		WA	Nielson & Co	11/1885	3/1917	
503	3383	395 class 0-6-0		WA	Nielson & Co	11/1885	3/1917	
504	3384	395 class 0-6-0		WA	Nielson & Co	11/1885	7/1917	

APPENDIX C

A	B	C	D	E	F	G	H	I
505	3385	395 class 0-6-0		WA	Nielson & Co	11/1885	7/1917	
506	3386	395 class 0-6-0		WA	Nielson & Co	12/1885	4/1957	Duplicated 10/1920
507	3387	395 class 0-6-0		WA	Nielson & Co	12/1885	10/1916	
508	3388	395 class 0-6-0		WA	Nielson & Co	12/1885	3/1917	
509	3389	395 class 0-6-0		WA	Nielson & Co	12/1885	3/1953	Duplicated 12/1920
510	3390	395 class 0-6-0		WA	Nielson & Co	12/1885	9/1916	
511	3391	395 class 0-6-0		WA	Nielson & Co	12/1885	8/1916	
512	3392	395 class 0-6-0		WA	Nielson & Co	1/1886	12/1917	
513	3393	395 class 0-6-0		WA	Nielson & Co	1/1886	9//1916	
514	3394	395 class 0-6-0		WA	Nielson & Co	1/1886	12/1917	
515	3395	395 class 0-6-0		WA	Nielson & Co	1/1886	6/1933	Duplicated 4/1921
516	2105	415 class 4-4-2T		WA	Dubs & Co	11/1885	11/1921	Duplicated 11/1921
517	2106	415 class 4-4-2T		WA	Dubs & Co	11/1885	12/1925	Duplicated 11/1921
518	2107	415 class 4-4-2T		WA	Dubs & Co	11/1885	11/1921	Duplicated 12/1921
519	2108	415 class 4-4-2T		WA	Dubs & Co	12/1885	7/1926	Duplicated 1/1922
520	2109	415 class 4-4-2T		WA	Dubs & Co	12/1885	1/1961	Duplicated 2/1922
521	2110	415 class 4-4-2T		WA	Dubs & Co	12/1885	4/1925	Duplicated 10/1922
522	2111	415 class 4-4-2T		WA	Dubs & Co	12/1885	10/1928	Duplicated 11/1922
523	2112	415 class 4-4-2T		WA	Dubs & Co	12/1885	11/1921	Duplicated 8/1922
524	2113	415 class 4-4-2T		WA	Dubs & Co	12/1885	11/1925	Duplicated 12/1922
525	2114	415 class 4-4-2T		WA	Dubs & Co	12/1885	11/1921	Duplicated 9/1922
526	2650	460 class 4-4-0T		WA	Robert Stephenson & Co	12/1887	8/1928	
527	A12	A12 0-4-2		WA	Nine Elms	5/1887	7/1930	
528	A12	A12 0-4-2		WA	Nine Elms	9/1887	12/1929	
529	A12	A12 0-4-2		WA	Nine Elms	10/1887	11/1928	
530	A12	A12 0-4-2		WA	Nine Elms	12/1887	4/1931	
531	A12	A12 0-4-2		WA	Nine Elms	12/1887	12/1929	
532	A12	A12 0-4-2		WA	Nine Elms	12/1887	12/1929	
533	A12	A12 0-4-2		WA	Nine Elms	12/1887	12/1929	
534	A12	A12 0-4-2		WA	Nine Elms	12/1887	12/1931	
535	A12	A12 0-4-2		WA	Nine Elms	12/1887	4/1928	
536	A12	A12 0-4-2		WA	Nine Elms	12/1887	12/1929	
537	E1	A12 0-4-2		WA	Nine Elms	3/1888	12/1929	
538	E1	A12 0-4-2		WA	Nine Elms	3/1888	1/1931	
539	E1	A12 0-4-2		WA	Nine Elms	4/1888	8/1930	
540	E1	A12 0-4-2		WA	Nine Elms	4/1888	6/1929	
541	E1	A12 0-4-2		WA	Nine Elms	5/1888	1/1931	
542	E1	A12 0-4-2		WA	Nine Elms	6/1888	10/1928	
543	E1	A12 0-4-2		WA	Nine Elms	6/1888	6/1929	
544	E1	A12 0-4-2		WA	Nine Elms	6/1888	12/1929	
545	E1	A12 0-4-2		WA	Nine Elms	6/1888	11/1931	
546	E1	A12 0-4-2		WA	Nine Elms	6/1888	3/1930	
547	M2	A12 0-4-2		WA	Nine Elms	6/1889	5/1929	
548	M2	A12 0-4-2		WA	Nine Elms	6/1889	10/1928	
549	M2	A12 0-4-2		WA	Nine Elms	6/1889	12/1929	
550	M2	A12 0-4-2		WA	Nine Elms	10/1889	12/1929	
551	M2	A12 0-4-2		WA	Nine Elms	10/1889	1/1932	
552	M2	A12 0-4-2		WA	Nine Elms	10/1889	4/1928	
553	M2	A12 0-4-2		WA	Nine Elms	12/1889	10/1928	
554	M2	A12 0-4-2		WA	Nine Elms	12/1889	11/1931	
555	M2	A12 0-4-2		WA	Nine Elms	12/1889	2/1944	
556	M2	A12 0-4-2		WA	Nine Elms	12/1889	5/1929	
557	T3	T3 4-4-0		WA	Nine Elms	12/1892	4/1936	
558	T3	T3 4-4-0		WA	Nine Elms	12/1892	10/1931	
559	T3	T3 4-4-0		WA	Nine Elms	12/1892	5/1931	
560	T3	T3 4-4-0		WA	Nine Elms	2/1893	5/1932	
561	T3	T3 4-4-0		WA	Nine Elms	2/1893	10/1930	
562	T3	T3 4-4-0		WA	Nine Elms	3/1893	4/1931	
563	T3	T3 4-4-0		WA	Nine Elms	3/1893	8/1945	
564	T3	T3 4-4-0		WA	Nine Elms	4/1893	9/1931	
565	T3	T3 4-4-0		WA	Nine Elms	4/1893	5/1933	
566	T3	T3 4-4-0		WA	Nine Elms	5/1893	8/1931	
567	S5	T3 4-4-0		WA	Nine Elms	5/1893	2/1933	
568	S5	T3 4-4-0		WA	Nine Elms	6/1893	5/1932	
569	S5	T3 4-4-0		WA	Nine Elms	6/1893	1/1932	
570	S5	T3 4-4-0		WA	Nine Elms	6/1893	7/1931	
571	S5	T3 4-4-0		WA	Nine Elms	8/1893	2/1943	
572	S5	T3 4-4-0		WA	Nine Elms	9/1893	10/1931	
573	S5	T3 4-4-0		WA	Nine Elms	9/1893	9/1931	
574	S5	T3 4-4-0		WA	Nine Elms	10/1893	7/1933	
575	S5	T3 4-4-0		WA	Nine Elms	10/1893	1/1932	
576	S5	T3 4-4-0		WA	Nine Elms	11/1893	8/1933	

APPENDIX C

A	B	C	D	E	F	G	H	I
577	X2	X2 4-4-0		WA	Nine Elms	6/1890	2/1933	
578	X2	X2 4-4-0		WA	Nine Elms	12/1890	2/1933	
579	X2	X2 4-4-0		WA	Nine Elms	12/1890	5/1932	
580	X2	X2 4-4-0		WA	Nine Elms	12/1890	2/1933	
581	X2	X2 4-4-0		WA	Nine Elms	12/1890	1/1932	
582	X2	X2 4-4-0		WA	Nine Elms	3/1891	3/1931	
583	X2	X2 4-4-0		WA	Nine Elms	4/1891	1/1931	
584	X2	X2 4-4-0		WA	Nine Elms	4/1891	9/1933	
585	X2	X2 4-4-0		WA	Nine Elms	5/1891	9/1931	
586	X2	X2 4-4-0		WA	Nine Elms	5/1891	11/1942	
587	F3	X2 4-4-0		WA	Nine Elms	10/1891	8/1937	
588	F3	X2 4-4-0		WA	Nine Elms	11/1891	3/1932	
589	F3	X2 4-4-0		WA	Nine Elms	11/1891	5/1931	
590	F3	X2 4-4-0		WA	Nine Elms	12/1891	4/1937	
591	F3	X2 4-4-0		WA	Nine Elms	12/1891	5/1931	
592	F3	X2 4-4-0		WA	Nine Elms	3/1892	12/1936	
593	F3	X2 4-4-0		WA	Nine Elms	3/1892	7/1931	
594	F3	X2 4-4-0		WA	Nine Elms	3/1892	5/1931	
595	F3	X2 4-4-0		WA	Nine Elms	4/1892	12/1930	
596	F3	X2 4-4-0		WA	Nine Elms	5/1892	5/1931	
597	O4	A12 0-4-2		WA	Nine Elms	12/1893	5/1947	
598	O4	A12 0-4-2		WA	Nine Elms	12/1893	3/1947	
599	O4	A12 0-4-2		WA	Nine Elms	12/1893	3/1946	
600	O4	A12 0-4-2		WA	Nine Elms	12/1893	8/1946	
601	O4	A12 0-4-2		WA	Nine Elms	2/1894	12/1934	
602	O4	A12 0-4-2		WA	Nine Elms	3/1894	7/1933	
603	O4	A12 0-4-2		WA	Nine Elms	3/1894	8/1935	
604	O4	A12 0-4-2		WA	Nine Elms	3/1894	6/1933	
605	O4	A12 0-4-2		WA	Nine Elms	3/1894	4/1936	
606	O4	A12 0-4-2		WA	Nine Elms	4/1884	3/1946	
607	4506	A12 0-4-2		WA	Nielson & Co	11/1892	5/1932	
608	4507	A12 0-4-2		WA	Nielson & Co	11/1892	5/1932	
609	4508	A12 0-4-2		WA	Nielson & Co	11/1892	4/1947	
610	4509	A12 0-4-2		WA	Nielson & Co	11/1892	3/1932	
611	4510	A12 0-4-2		WA	Nielson & Co	11/1892	11/1937	
612	4511	A12 0-4-2		WA	Nielson & Co	11/1892	6/1946	
613	4512	A12 0-4-2		WA	Nielson & Co	11/1892	8/1946	
614	4513	A12 0-4-2		WA	Nielson & Co	11/1892	1/1947	
615	4514	A12 0-4-2		WA	Nielson & Co	11/1892	6/1946	
616	4515	A12 0-4-2		WA	Nielson & Co	11/1892	5/1936	
617	4516	A12 0-4-2		WA	Nielson & Co	11/1892	9/1938	
618	4517	A12 0-4-2		WA	Nielson & Co	12/1882	1/1948	
619	4518	A12 0-4-2		WA	Nielson & Co	12/1882	5/1937	
620	4519	A12 0-4-2		WA	Nielson & Co	12/1882	11/1946	Withdrawn 1/1939, but re-instated 9/1939
621	4520	A12 0-4-2		WA	Nielson & Co	12/1882	5/1935	
622	4521	A12 0-4-2		WA	Nielson & Co	1/1883	1/1936	
623	4522	A12 0-4-2		WA	Nielson & Co	12/1892	3/1946	
624	4523	A12 0-4-2		WA	Nielson & Co	1/1893	1/1947	Withdrawn 1/1939, but re-instated 10/1939
625	4524	A12 0-4-2		WA	Nielson & Co	1/1893	1/1947	Withdrawn 1/1939, but re-instated 9/1939
626	4525	A12 0-4-2		WA	Nielson & Co	2/1893	6/1933	
627	4526	A12 0-4-2		WA	Nielson & Co	1/1883	12/1948	
628	4527	A12 0-4-2		WA	Nielson & Co	1/1883	10/1938	
629	4528	A12 0-4-2		WA	Nielson & Co	1/1883	12/1948	Withdrawn 1/1939, but re-instated 10/1939
630	4529	A12 0-4-2		WA	Nielson & Co	2/1893	1/1947	
631	4530	A12 0-4-2		WA	Nielson & Co	2/1893	6/1933	
632	4531	A12 0-4-2		WA	Nielson & Co	1/1893	8/1937	
633	4532	A12 0-4-2		WA	Nielson & Co	2/1893	8/1933	
634	4533	A12 0-4-2		WA	Nielson & Co	2/1893	3/1947	
635	4534	A12 0-4-2		WA	Nielson & Co	2/1893	4/1935	
636	4535	A12 0-4-2		WA	Nielson & Co	2/1893	10/1948	
637	4536	A12 0-4-2		WA	Nielson & Co	3/1893	3/1946	
638	4537	A12 0-4-2		WA	Nielson & Co	3/1893	3/1947	
639	4538	A12 0-4-2		WA	Nielson & Co	3/1893	6/1933	
640	4539	A12 0-4-2		WA	Nielson & Co	3/1893	11/1937	
641	4540	A12 0-4-2		WA	Nielson & Co	3/1893	6/1945	
642	4541	A12 0-4-2		WA	Nielson & Co	3/1893	6/1947	Withdrawn 1/1939, but re-instated 9/1939
643	4542	A12 0-4-2		WA	Nielson & Co	3/1893	7/1947	
644	4543	A12 0-4-2		WA	Nielson & Co	3/1893	3/1946	Withdrawn 1/1939, but re-instated 9/1939
645	4544	A12 0-4-2		WA	Nielson & Co	4/1893	9/1933	
646	4545	A12 0-4-2		WA	Nielson & Co	4/1893	5/1939	
647	K6	A12 0-4-2		WA	Nine Elms	11/1894	2/1933	
648	K6	A12 0-4-2		WA	Nine Elms	11/1894	7/1947	

APPENDIX C

A	B	C	D	E	F	G	H	I
649	K6	A12 0-4-2		WA	Nine Elms	11/1894	3/1946	
650	K6	A12 0-4-2		WA	Nine Elms	1/1895	4/1938	
651	K6	A12 0-4-2		WA	Nine Elms	3/1895	2/1933	
652	K6	A12 0-4-2		WA	Nine Elms	4/1895	1/1947	
653	K6	A12 0-4-2		WA	Nine Elms	4/1895	5/1932	
654	K6	A12 0-4-2		WA	Nine Elms	4/1895	5/1947	
655	K6	A12 0-4-2		WA	Nine Elms	5/1895	3/1936	
656	K6	A12 0-4-2		WA	Nine Elms	5/1895	4/1932	
657	X6	X6 4-4-0		WA	Nine Elms	12/1895	9/1940	
658	X6	X6 4-4-0		WA	Nine Elms	12/1895	12/1946	
659	X6	X6 4-4-0		WA	Nine Elms	12/1895	7/1943	
660	X6	X6 4-4-0		WA	Nine Elms	12/1895	10/1936	
661	X6	X6 4-4-0		WA	Nine Elms	12/1895	12/1936	
662	X6	X6 4-4-0		WA	Nine Elms	12/1895	3/1933	
663	X6	X6 4-4-0		WA	Nine Elms	4/1896	10/1936	
664	X6	X6 4-4-0		WA	Nine Elms	5/1896	12/1942	
665	X6	X6 4-4-0		WA	Nine Elms	6/1896	6/1933	
666	X6	X6 4-4-0		WA	Nine Elms	6/1896	4/1943	
667	M7	M7 0-4-4T		DD	Nine Elms	8/1897	5/1964	
668	M7	M7 0-4-4T		DD	Nine Elms	9/1897	9/1961	
669	M7	M7 0-4-4T		DD	Nine Elms	9/1897	7/1961	
670	M7	M7 0-4-4T		DD	Nine Elms	10/1897	3/1963	
671	M7	M7 0-4-4T		DD	Nine Elms	10/1897	7/1959	
672	M7	M7 0-4-4T		DD	Nine Elms	10/1897	5/1948	
673	M7	M7 0-4-4T		DD	Nine Elms	11/1897	8/1960	
674	M7	M7 0-4-4T		DD	Nine Elms	11/1897	8/1961	
675	M7	M7 0-4-4T		DD	Nine Elms	12/1897	3/1958	
676	M7	M7 0-4-4T		DD	Nine Elms	12/1897	7/1961	
677	T6	T6 4-4-0		WA	Nine Elms	9/1895	2/1933	
678	T6	T6 4-4-0		WA	Nine Elms	10/1895	1/1936	
679	T6	T6 4-4-0		WA	Nine Elms	11/1895	4/1937	
680	T6	T6 4-4-0		WA	Nine Elms	12/1895	6/1937	
681	T6	T6 4-4-0		WA	Nine Elms	12/1895	4/1943	
682	T6	T6 4-4-0		WA	Nine Elms	12/1895	6/1936	
683	T6	T6 4-4-0		WA	Nine Elms	3/1896	8/1933	
684	T6	T6 4-4-0		WA	Nine Elms	3/1896	4/1940	
685	T6	T6 4-4-0		WA	Nine Elms	4/1896	2/1936	
686	T6	T6 4-4-0		WA	Nine Elms	5/1896	5/1936	
687	3510	700 class 0-6-0		DD	Dubs & Co	3/1897	10/1960	
688	3511	700 class 0-6-0		DD	Dubs & Co	3/1897	9/1957	
689	3512	700 class 0-6-0		DD	Dubs & Co	3/1897	11/1962	
690	3513	700 class 0-6-0		DD	Dubs & Co	3/1897	12/1962	
691	3514	700 class 0-6-0		DD	Dubs & Co	3/1897	7/1961	
692	3515	700 class 0-6-0		DD	Dubs & Co	3/1897	2/1962	
693	3516	700 class 0-6-0		DD	Dubs & Co	3/1897	7/1961	
694	3517	700 class 0-6-0		DD	Dubs & Co	3/1897	6/1961	
695	3518	700 class 0-6-0		DD	Dubs & Co	3/1897	12/1962	
696	3519	700 class 0-6-0		DD	Dubs & Co	3/1897	8/1961	
697	3520	700 class 0-6-0		DD	Dubs & Co	4/1897	11/1962	
698	3521	700 class 0-6-0		DD	Dubs & Co	4/1897	5/1962	
699	3522	700 class 0-6-0		DD	Dubs & Co	5/1897	7/1961	
700	3523	700 class 0-6-0		DD	Dubs & Co	5/1897	11/1962	
701	3524	700 class 0-6-0		DD	Dubs & Co	5/1897	7/1961	
702	3525	700 class 0-6-0		DD	Dubs & Co	5/1897	4/1962	Renumbered 306 in 1898
702	3746	T9 4-4-0		DD	Dubs & Co	1/1899	10/1959	
703	3526	700 class 0-6-0		DD	Dubs & Co	5/1897	9/1961	Renumbered 308 in 1898
703	3747	T9 4-4-0		DD	Dubs & Co	1/1899	9/1952	
704	3527	700 class 0-6-0		DD	Dubs & Co	5/1897	12/1962	Renumbered 309 in 1898
704	3748	T9 4-4-0		DD	Dubs & Co	1/1899	10/1951	
705	3528	700 class 0-6-0		DD	Dubs & Co	5/1897	12/1962	Renumbered 315 in 1898
705	3749	T9 4-4-0		DD	Dubs & Co	1/1899	1/1958	
706	3529	700 class 0-6-0		DD	Dubs & Co	5/1897	7/1961	Renumbered 317 in 1898
706	3750	T9 4-4-0		DD	Dubs & Co	1/1899	5/1959	
707	3530	700 class 0-6-0		DD	Dubs & Co	6/1897	12/1962	Renumbered 325 in 1898
707	3751	T9 4-4-0		DD	Dubs & Co	6/1899	3/1961	
708	3531	700 class 0-6-0		DD	Dubs & Co	6/1897	2/1962	Renumbered 326 in 1898
708	3752	T9 4-4-0		DD	Dubs & Co	6/1899	12/1957	
709	3532	700 class 0-6-0		DD	Dubs & Co	6/1897	5/1961	Renumbered 327 in 1898
709	3753	T9 4-4-0		DD	Dubs & Co	6/1899	7/1961	
710	3533	700 class 0-6-0		DD	Dubs & Co	6/1897	5/1962	Renumbered 339 in 1898
710	3754	T9 4-4-0		DD	Dubs & Co	6/1899	3/1959	
711	3534	700 class 0-6-0		DD	Dubs & Co	6/1897	11/1962	Renumbered 346 in 1898

APPENDIX C

A	B	C	D	E	F	G	H	I
711	3755	T9 4-4-0		DD	Dubs & Co	6/1899	8/1959	
712	3535	700 class 0-6-0		DD	Dubs & Co	6/1897	3/1962	Renumbered 350 in 1898
712	3756	T9 4-4-0		DD	Dubs & Co	6/1899	11/1958	
713	3536	700 class 0-6-0		DD	Dubs & Co	6/1897	7/1959	Renumbered 352 in 1898
713	3757	T9 4-4-0		DD	Dubs & Co	6/1899	4/1951	
714	3537	700 class 0-6-0		DD	Dubs & Co	6/1897	2/1961	Renumbered 355 in 1898
714	3758	T9 4-4-0		DD	Dubs & Co	6/1899	3/1951	
715	3538	700 class 0-6-0		DD	Dubs & Co	6/1897	12/1962	Renumbered 368 in 1898
715	3759	T9 4-4-0		DD	Dubs & Co	6/1899	7/1961	
716	3539	700 class 0-6-0		DD	Dubs & Co	6/1897	12/1962	Renumbered 349 in 1898, and 316 in 6/1912
716	3760	T9 4-4-0		DD	Dubs & Co	6/1899	10/1951	
717	3761	T9 4-4-0		DD	Dubs & Co	9/1899	7/1961	
718	3762	T9 4-4-0		DD	Dubs & Co	9/1899	3/1961	
719	3763	T9 4-4-0		DD	Dubs & Co	9/1899	3/1961	
720	T7	T7 4-2-2-0		DD	Nine Elms	8/1897	4/1927	
721	3764	T9 4-4-0		DD	Dubs & Co	9/1899	7/1958	
722	3765	T9 4-4-0		DD	Dubs & Co	9/1899	4/1951	
723	3766	T9 4-4-0		DD	Dubs & Co	9/1899	6/1951	
724	3767	T9 4-4-0		DD	Dubs & Co	9/1899	5/1959	
725	3768	T9 4-4-0		DD	Dubs & Co	10/1899	12/1952	
726	3769	T9 4-4-0		DD	Dubs & Co	10/1899	8/1959	
727	3770	T9 4-4-0		DD	Dubs & Co	10/1899	9/1958	
728	3771	T9 4-4-0		DD	Dubs & Co	12/1899	9/1956	
729	3772	T9 4-4-0		DD	Dubs & Co	12/1899	3/1961	
730	3773	T9 4-4-0		DD	Dubs & Co	12/1899	8/1957	
731	3774	T9 4-4-0		DD	Dubs & Co	12/1899	5/1951	
732	3775	T9 4-4-0		DD	Dubs & Co	12/1899	10/1959	
733	4038	T9 4-4-0		DD	Dubs & Co	11/1901	4/1952	Exhibited at Glasgow in 1901, was No 773 until 12/1924
733	F9	F9 4-2-4		DD	Nine Elms	6/1899	8/1940	Mr Drummond's "Bug", renumbered 58S 12/1924
734		A1X 0-6-0T	(Newington)	DD	LB&SCR, Brighton Works	1/1877	11/1963	Nine Elms purchased 3/1903, to IoW Railway 6/1913, purchased by FY&NR 2/1915
735		A1X 0-6-0T	(Clapham)	DD	LB&SCR, Brighton Works	8/1874	12/1936	Nine Elms purchased 3/1903
736	C14	C14 2-2-0T		DD	Nine Elms	9/1906	3/1917	
737	C14	C14 2-2-0T		DD	Nine Elms	10/1906	12/1917	
738	C14	C14 2-2-0T		DD	Nine Elms	10/1906	3/1917	
739	C14	C14 2-2-0T		DD	Nine Elms	10/1906	2/1917	
740	C14	C14 2-2-0T		DD	Nine Elms	11/1906	12/1916	
741	D14	C14 2-2-0T		DD	Nine Elms	12/1906	12/1957	Duplicated 11/1919(?), converted to 0-4-0T 3/1922
742	D14	C14 2-2-0T		DD	Nine Elms	12/1906	12/1917	
743	D14	C14 2-2-0T		DD	Nine Elms	1/1907	11/1917	Converted to 0-4-0T 6/1913
744	D14	C14 2-2-0T		DD	Nine Elms	1/1907	6/1957	Converted to 0-4-0T 10/1923
745	D14	C14 2-2-0T		DD	Nine Elms	2/1907	3/1959	To 0-4-0T 4/1913, duplicated 12/1918, renumbered 77S 10/1927
746	K14	B4 0-4-0T	Dinan	DD	Nine Elms	4/1908	11/1948	To Southampton Docks and named 4/1908, renumbered 101 2/1922
747	K14	B4 0-4-0T	Dinard	DD	Nine Elms	4/1908	2/1949	To Southampton Docks and named 4/1908, renumbered 147 2/1922
773	4038	T9 4-4-0		DD	Dubs & Co	11/1901	4/1952	Exhibited at Glasgow in 1901, renumbered 733 12/1924

APPENDIX C

Fig. 436. T9 class 4-4-0 No 743, the Glasgow Exhibition Engine, in the course of being fitted out at Nine Elms.